Staging Place

Staging Place

The Geography of Modern Drama

Una Chaudhuri

Ann Arbor

THE UNIVERSITY OF MICHIGAN PRESS

1998 1997 1996 1995   4 3 2 1

A CIP catalogue record for this book is available from the British Library.

Library of Congress Cataloging-in-Publication Data

Chaudhuri, Una, 1951–
    Staging place : the geography of modern drama / Una Chaudhuri.
      p.   cm. — (Theater—theory/text/performance)
    Includes bibliographical references and index.
    ISBN 0-472-09589-7 (hardcover : alk. paper)
      1. Drama—19th century—History and criticism. 2. Drama—20th
century—History and criticism. 3. Setting (Literature) 4. Place
(Philosophy) in literature. I. Title. II. Series.
PN1672.9.C53 1995
809.2'922—dc20
                                         95-13373
                                              CIP

A portion of chapter 1 originally appeared in *Theatre Journal,*
October 1993.

To
Jerzy Grotowski
and
Natty Adams

Last night I dreamed of where I comed from. But where I comed from diduhnt look like nowhere like I been.
—Suzan-Lori Parks, *Imperceptible Mutabilities of the Third Kingdom*

Contents

Acknowledgments

I thank the Department of English at New York University for a grant from the Abraham and Rebecca Stein Faculty Publication Fund. I also thank Johns Hopkins University Press for granting me permission to reprint, as a section of chapter 1, my article "Private Parts: Sex, Class and Stage Space in *Miss Julie,*" *Theatre Journal* (October 1993). Parts of chapter 2 and of the eilogue appeared in a modified version in "'There Must be a Lot of Fish in That Lake': Toward an Ecological Theatre," *Theater* (Spring/Summer 1994).

Unlike the bleak journeys that map out the geography of modern drama, this book has been (as we used to say) a trip, made bright and invigorating by the many friends, colleagues, and students who have provided the necessary road maps and signposts for my wandering. For their support and encouragement, for the deep pleasure of their friendships, and for inspiring me with the example of their own work, I thank the following people: Michael Vannoy Adams, Peter Carey, Marvin Carlson, Elena Climent, Gabrielle Cody, Roger Deakins, Linda Dorff, Elinor Fuchs, Ernest Gilman, Michael Goldman, Lynda Hart, David Hoover, Carol Martin, Janet Neipris, Peggy Phelan, June Schlueter, Richard Schechner, Alison Summers, Gauri Viswanathan, and William Worthen. I thank my Indian family—Usha Baljit Singh, Natasha Singh, Baldeep Singh, Uma Mahajan, and Happy and Binny Singh—for contradicting my thesis about the futility of homecomings; and my American family—Mike, Natty, and Sonu—for making the quest for home seem somewhat less than delusional after all. My deepest debt in the writing of this book is to Robert Vorlicky, the most generous intellectual companion a writer could have. For always finding the worthwhile contours and pleasant prospects in the geography of this book, I thank you, Bob.

Preface

The gravedigger in *Hamlet* makes a good joke about the subject of this book. Asked the ground of Hamlet's madness, he famously replies: "Why, here in Denmark." The ground of Denmark is both place and reason, and this conjunction of space and sense is my subject.

This book began as an inquiry into the ways in which—and the extent to which—the theater grounds its meanings in that essential element of all theatrical presentation: space. What I discovered is that an intricate and often contradictory circuitry links the various spaces, places, and representations of place that the theatrical apparatus makes possible. So complex and so fundamental is this network of relationships that I have come to believe its full articulation (of which the present study is merely a starting point) can yield a new methodology for drama and theater studies, a "geography" of theater capable of replacing—or at least significantly supplementing—its familiar "history."

To theorize a geography of theater, moreover, is to bring theater studies into alignment with a considerable body of contemporary cultural theory, in which space is increasingly replacing time as the significant category of analysis. Taking its inspiration from the writings of Henri Lefebvre, Michel Foucault, Fredric Jameson, Ernesto Laclau, and Edward Soja (to name a few), a growing discourse is being elaborated around such terms as *borders, limits, rootlessness, territoriality, nomadism, habitus, home, homelessness,* and *exile,* employing what Michael Keith and Steve Pile call "a whole range of spatial metaphors . . . position, location, situation, mapping; geometrics of domination, center-margin, open-closed, inside-outside, global-local; liminal space, third space, not-space, impossible space; the city" (1).

This is a book about the imagination of place in modern drama, and about some of the figures and tropes that that imagination consistently favors, notably the figure of home. In keeping with the principle of space that inspires it, the book is not primarily a historical narrative. Rather, it is an exploration, taking as its territory the broad thematic of place in drama. My tools of analysis, though derived from semiotics, are generally recovered from the territory itself: the plays I discuss furnish the terms, concepts, and tropes that flesh out the story I want to tell. Indeed my choice of plays itself is determined solely by these two considerations: how fully does a play engage the issue of place, and how useful are its terms for setting forth a comprehensive account of the issue.

What the plays yielded in analysis was a recurrent sense that dramatic structure reflects deeply ingrained convictions about the mutually constructive relations between people and place. Who one is and who one can be are, in the dramatic works I discuss, a function of *where* one is and how one experiences that place. From the experience of place as one-dimensional and fully determining, to the experience of place as multi-dimensional and creative, the stages of modern drama recount an ongoing *experiment* with place (reflected in—though not mechanically parallel to—the ongoing experimentation with stage space) that suggests an alternative account of the development of modern drama, a possible supplement to the familiar story of dramatic movements usually told.

In the chapters that follow, this is the story I want to tell: that modern drama at first employs, as one of its foundational discourses, a vague, culturally determined symbology of home, replete with all those powerful and empowering associations to space as are organized by the notion of belonging. The dramatic discourse of home is articulated through two main principles, which structure the plot as well as the plays' accounts of subjectivity and identity: a *victimage of location* and a *heroism of departure*. The former principle defines place as the protagonist's fundamental problem, leading her or him to a recognition of the need for (if not an actual enactment of) the latter.

The characterization of place as problem—to which I have given the label *geopathology*—is supported by the stage practice of early modern drama, specifically by the spatial arrangements of naturalism, which function according to a logic of *total visibility*. The many departures from and critiques of this logic that make up the history of modern drama—from expressionism and symbolism to absurdism, epic theater, and other experimental movements—are also departures from the discourse of home as originally established.

The drama's gradual abandonment of the logic of total visibility also moves it toward an increasingly precise and unsentimental recognition of home *as* a discourse, replete with ideological antecedents and consequences. Often within the framework of a failed-homecoming plot, this analysis of the discourse of home makes space for other experiences of place, beyond geopathology. In *Waiting for Godot,* to give a famous example, the failure of homecoming is worked out to the point of diagnosis; it is clear from this play why homecoming is doomed: home itself is displaced, vanished. Beckett places the blame for the failure of homecoming (which is also, as we shall see, a failure of the dramaturgy of *recovery*) not on the characters (or on human nature) but, much more logically, on the figure of home itself, on the effort to force a conjuncture between place and personal identity *for its own sake,* without context or purpose: Didi and Gogo are not merely ignorant of Godot's identity, *they do not know what they want from him.* They cannot locate the *ground* of their desired homecoming, and this is why they are doomed to a victimage of location from which no heroism of departure can rescue them. That their location is as indeterminate and "open" as it is—a homelessness so radical that it has regularly seemed to symbolize a universal condition—is the mark of its detachment from the old discourse of home, which equated home with a sense of entrapment within naturalism's famous four walls.

The transformations that the idea of place undergoes in the course of this century affect dramatic structure as well as stage space, but it is primarily with the former that I am concerned here. The changing meaning of place invariably involves a departure from the "solid state" world of naturalism, as well as from its logic of total visibility, but a systematic analysis of these departures (that is, of the stage practice of *postgeopathic* drama) is beyond the scope of this study. Rather, I have been content to follow and describe the destiny of place as it impacts on dramatic structure and characterology, noting only the most salient theatrological dimensions of this destiny.

The plays treated in this study will seem at first glance to constitute a strange, even bizarre, grouping. The majority of plays discussed are American, but certain European and British plays are included as well; the majority of plays are recent and have negligible critical traditions associated with them, but certain are canonized classics carrying huge critical baggage. I have assumed the liabilities of these unorthodox combinations for two reasons: because these are the plays that allow me to elucidate my topic most effectively, and (more importantly) because an alteration in the canonical ordering is one of the desired effects of pursuing this topic. For example, a number of the plays I treat toward the end are generally classified as "ethnic" or "minority" drama, a classification that has the adverse effect of keeping them outside the critical mainstream; my goal in contextualizing them among more established works is to demonstrate their significance to the whole critical picture of modern drama, a picture that is enriched and illuminated by their presence in it.

One major effect of the unconventional grouping I have chosen is that it produces a more critical and, I believe, a more powerful notion of a phenomenon that has gained wide currency of late: multiculturalism. Rather than leaving multiculturalism in its niche as a slightly updated synonym for ethnic, the analysis of place in modern drama proposes an augmented sense of the possibilities and significance of this rubric. The challenge of multiculturalism, as I see it, is not only that of including new voices and faces in drama but also that of effecting an ideological transformation, a transvaluation of the once-impacted relationship between place and personhood.

In the context of the story this book tries to tell—and in that context only—the experience of displacement reflected in a great deal of contemporary drama participates in the renovation of a paradigm that has a long history. From this perspective, not only plays by "minority" playwrights like David Henry Hwang, José Rivera, and George C. Wolfe but also by white playwrights like Tony Kushner and Caryl Churchill exemplify the potentiality of multiculturalism as a dramatic mode and an ideology.

The presence of several British playwrights (Harold Pinter, Caryl Churchill, Stephen Poliakoff, and Jim Cartwright) in a study dominated by American playwrights may seem harder to justify, because the taxonomy it breaches is more logical than the one separating "ethnic" from mainstream drama. Once again, it is their unique contributions to the dramatic discourse of place that brings them into my story. The whole logic of failed homecoming is simply better elucidated in Pinter's play by that title than anywhere else, and the presence of the figure of America in that play makes it invaluable for understanding how and why that discourse unravels at midcentury. Read in tandem with Churchill's America play *Ice Cream,* Pinter's play sets the stage for those transvaluations of place that I designate by my revised notion of multiculturalism. Similarly, the representation of immigration in Poliakoff's *Coming in to Land* starkly manifests the politics of location to which multiculturalism (in my expanded sense) is a response.

As to my critical method, I have avoided the totalizing impulse that would dredge up scores of examples to illustrate every point I try to make. Instead I have opted for extended analysis of a limited number of texts, following my conviction that the issue I am engaging inscribes itself deeply on the rhetoric, structure, imagery, and characterology of modern plays. The only exception to this method is in chapter 2, where I propose the groundwork of a model of geopathology. Since the ubiquity of this model is crucial to my argument, I have tried to furnish a fair number of examples from a variety of different dramatic modes, including realism, absurdism, and expressionism. In the remaining chapters, however, I allow my analysis of a few specific plays to make my argument, which is that the contemporary theater is, above all, a re*mapping* of the possible terrain of subjectivity.

The Politics of Home and the Poetics of Exile

> I think that it is at least empirically arguable that our daily life, our psychic experience, our cultural languages, are today dominated by categories of space rather than categories of time, as in the period of high modernism.
> —Fredric Jameson, *Postmodernism, or The Cultural Logic of Late Capitalism*

The prevalence of space-based studies in the social sciences and in cultural studies is a response to an increasingly complex cultural experience of space and place,[1] one that has decisively displaced the older paradigms of spatial intelligibility not only in the realm of art but also, thanks to the mass media, in that of public culture, and hence in contemporary consciousness. Therefore, the conceptual horizon for considering the theater's use of space and the drama's discourse on place is an ever-changing one, reflecting changes in the cultural, technological, and even the theoretical processing of space.

For example: during the time this book was being written, an inescapable element of the American popular culture scene was an ad campaign for Pepsi-Cola. The original TV commercials featured Ray Charles accompanied by three gorgeous female backup singers (the Raylettes) in short, shiny, skintight dresses. The main lyric asserted that Pepsi-Cola was "the right one, Baby," to which Ray, supported by the Raylettes, added an enthusiastic (and cinematographically punched-in) "Uh-huh." The commercial became (or was made, through the efforts of the ad agency) so popular that T-shirts and other consumer goods appeared bearing the legend "Uh-huh!" A news item in the *Wall Street Journal* reported that executives at the rival company, Coca-Cola, were going around trying to avoid using the expression "uh-huh" in their conversations! As time went on, the original commercial was expanded and extended and varied in a number of highly effective ways. One of these showed other famous people, including Jerry Lewis, Charo, and Tiny Tim, "auditioning" for Ray's role, doing hilariously bad renditions of the by now famous lyric.

One quite extraordinary installment, for which much anticipation was whipped up by the ad company, and which first aired during the half-time period of the Super Bowl, extended the range of jingle singers far beyond the American pop-cultural scene. This lengthy commercial showed huge gatherings of people in foreign lands—China, India, Japan—singing the jingle in their own various stereotypical ways, with a variety of accents and music styles. One of the scenes showed a group of Buddhist monks sitting cross-legged on the ground in formal rows in a monastery, intoning "uh-huh, uh-huh" in deep and solemn tones, as if it were a mantra or prayer.

The technical brilliance of this commercial, as well as its appropriation of the seductive and stereotypical images often used by the airline and tourist industries of the world, was partly responsible for the pleasure it gave. But there was another, less benign, element in its success as well. Under its cheery good humor and its apparently generous sharing of the pleasures of Pepsi with the peoples of the world, the ad was a blatant inscription of American economic imperialism, and it revealed quite precisely what the semiological—that is, the ideological, aesthetic, and psychological—terms of this imperialism are. In this semiotic, which is also the semiotic of Walt Disney World's World Showcase, parts of the world are isolated and double coded as different and yet the same, their difference being a matter of spectacle, while their sameness is a matter of desire. The spectacular Other, whose otherness is contained within—and figured purely as—superficial *style* (of clothes, architecture, music, etc.) is the necessary foundation for a figuration of universal consumerist desire.

How successful this figuration has been in material terms is now depressingly well known. The triumph of American consumerism goes beyond its undeniable monuments—the McDonald's in Moscow, the Disneyland near Paris, the Pizza Hut in Calcutta, and so on—to the realm of representation itself. The full import of the Pepsi commercial as universalizing discourse did not become clear to me until I saw, on a trip to India, the Indian version of the commercial. Gone were Ray and the Raylettes; in their place a number of Indian actors in different situations sang the same jingle, while the aforementioned Buddhist monks (on loan from the American version of the ad?) intoned their solemn "uh-huhs."

The West's construction of otherness takes a dizzying turn when, supported by the power of multinational capital, it dictates the self-construction of non-Western identities. This spiral of misrepresentation and self-misrepresentation—which has its origins in the orientalist discourse of the earliest colonialisms—is now well established. The logic it obeys is similar to the traditional logic of gender difference, according to which the best woman is a man, because (as Song Liling says in *M. Butterfly*) "only a man knows how a woman is supposed to act" (63). Unlike gender, however, national and ethnic identities are often derived from or directed toward a *geography;* there is a *location* of identity based on race, nation, ethnicity, language—in short, all the elements that together or in part designate the notion of a culture—that is often absent from the discourse of gender. To put it bluntly, the construction of cultural otherness is also a *mapping of the world,* a fact that contributes powerfully to the literalization of accounts of ethnic difference.

A book on place and the representation of place such as this one cannot avoid acknowledging the discourse of the Pepsi commercial as one of its horizons; no contemporary inquiry into the nature of place can ignore the placement and displacement wrought by the global mass media operating in support of a global consumer economy. The images of otherness set to the music of Ray Charles are simply the quintessential summarizing of the current state of the category of place, a category this century has seen beset by extraordinary challenges and changes. As Brecht's astonishing prologue to *The Caucasian Chalk Circle* makes clear, the *meaning* (not merely the ownership) of place has given this century its politics; we should not be surprised to find, as this book argues, that it has also given it its theater, and that a complex engagement with the significance, determinations, and potentialities of place courses through the body of modern drama.

Besides the mass media's capture of otherness—within a web of implied sameness disguised as difference—the second major source of the gradual reinscription of place in the late twentieth century is the revolution in electronic communications. In the modern world of computerized data management and instantaneous information dispersal, a person's basic mode of location is altered. Instead of experiencing life from a fixed point in space and time, the subject of the electronic society is, as Mark Poster writes, "multiplied by databases, dispersed by computer messaging and conferencing, decontextualized and reidentified by TV ads, dissolved and materialized continuously in the electronic transmission of symbols" (74). So thoroughgoing and ubiquitous is this dispersal of subjective experience over multiple electronic channels that human beings can be said to be returning to a nomadic form of existence, wandering over vast global distances daily as they change channels, fax letters, leave messages on answering machines, and have the facts of their socioeconomic lives gathered, stored, and analyzed by myriad marketing concerns.

As Mark Poster puts it, the new version of "who am I?" is firmly anchored in a new form of "*where* am I?"

> If I can speak directly to a friend in Paris while sitting in California, if I can witness political and cultural events as they occur across the globe without leaving my home, if a database at a remote location contains my profile and informs government agencies which make the decisions that affect my life without any knowledge on my part of these events, if I can shop in my home using my TV or computer, then where am I and who am I? In these circumstances, I cannot consider myself centered in my rational, autonomous subjectivity or bordered by a defined ego, but I am disrupted, subverted, and dispersed across social space. (74)

The erasure of spatial particularity, one of the hallmarks of postmodernism, is represented in drama (and elsewhere) through the figure of America. As we shall see in a later chapter, the America of the modern theater's imagination is a principle of dispersal, of dissolution. This America, which we shall meet in various guises throughout this book, is a complex and ultimately redemptive figure, for it is the hinge, the turning point in a more than century-long neglect of the very principle that it seems to erase: space. The rise in the nineteenth century of what Edward Soja calls a "destabilizing historicism" had, by the twentieth, deprivileged space to the point of denying it any explanatory or theoretical force whatsoever. Michel Foucault summarized the situation, asking, "Did it start with Bergson or before? Space was treated as the dead, the fixed, the undialectical, the immobile. Time, on the contrary, was richness, fecundity, life" ("Questions on Geography," 70).

The category of space reenters the field of critical and social theory, as Soja has argued, through the works of Foucault, through structural-ism, and through the writings of Henri Lefebvre. The formulation of a "postmodern critical geography" to counter and complement the rigid historicism of twentieth-century thought is a vast and vital project, of which one of the crucial goals is the recovery of *place*. It is in this area that the figure of America functions as a hinge, for it both *reproduces* and *displaces* the dominant theoretical bias against space. Through its alliance with the principles of progress and of homogeneity, the figure of America first signified a kind of ultimate placelessness, a guarantee of the absolute *un*meaning of place as a component of human experience. But the very success of this figuration—what one might call the hyperbole of American utopianism—proved to be its undoing. In the late twentieth century the figure of America has begun to be required, increasingly, to make good its utopian claims, and the principle of placelessness is confronted by the multivoiced demand for new *placements*. The movement known generally as multiculturalism is in fact a call for America to be reimagined: not, this time, as a utopia, but as what Foucault would call a "heterotopia," a place capable of containing within it many different, even incompatible, places.

As Soja explains it, Foucault's move was to navigate beyond several already ongoing efforts to respatialize social theory:

> Foucault outlined his notion of "heterotopias" as the characteristic spaces of the modern world, superseding the hierarchic "ensemble of places" of the Middle Ages and the enveloping "space of emplacement" opened up by Galileo into an early-modern, infinitely folding, "space of extension" and measurement. Moving away from both the "internal space" of Bachelard's brilliant poetics . . . and the intentional regional descriptions of the phenomenologists, Foucault focused our attention on another spatiality of social life, an "external space," the actually lived (and socially produced) space of sites and the relations between them. (17)

This other spatiality is actually (to apply a neologism) a new *platiality,* a recognition of the signifying power and political potential of *specific places.*

In the theater (to return to the place that concerns me here) the encounter between this new platiality and the figure of America occurs most memorably in the drama of immigration and multiculturalism, which is the subject of the latter part of this book. But before this recent drama can replace the old accounts of space, place, and identity, the drama that supported those accounts must be thoroughly understood, which is to say, in terms of theatrical practice: deconstructed. The figure (or idea, or image, or myth) of America, then, is frequently used in contemporary drama as the vehicle for a critique, an engagement with and finally a revisioning of place. The figure of America is able to serve in this way—that is, in the deconstruction of place as traditionally conceived—because the discourse this figure disrupts most decisively is one that has structured—and continues to structure—traditional dramatic paradigms of place and identity most profoundly: the discourse of home.[2]

The privileged setting of modern drama is the family home.[3] The domestic interior contains the history of a process, begun in the nineteenth century and still unconcluded as the twentieth century nears its end, of a locational stage practice, a way of filling the signifying space of theater with an *environment*. This kind of environmentalism, which enters the drama through realism and naturalism (and which is intimately related to the figure of home), relies on and propagates a very special account of space and place. According to (and then thanks to) this environmentalism, placement becomes available to rational understanding and explanation. That is to say, place enters the positivist project as a factor of knowledge and a code of representation.

The first sign of this new coding of place is the ready divisibility of the world into what Philip Fisher calls "a spectrum of environments," a set of discrete economic zones each with "its local features, types, common languages, heroes and catastrophes" (17).[4] The theater responds to this new view of space by developing a stage practice based on the principle of spatial intelligibility, on the idea that *where* an action unfolds goes a long way toward explaining it. The name of this stage practice is, of course, naturalism, but (as Raymond Williams argued in what remains the most sophisticated discussion of theatrical naturalism) it is not only as *stage* practice but also as a dramatic discourse that naturalism engages and revisions the category of space: "In high naturalism," writes Williams, "the lives of the characters have soaked into their environment. . . . Moreover, the environment has soaked into their lives" (217).

Recognizing that this environmentalism determines dramatic discourse at a deep structural level, Williams singles out a plot device that will become central to the evolving discourse of modern drama: escape, or, more generally, creative displacement. For Williams, naturalism marks only the exhaustion or contradiction of this device. "The prenaturalist conventions of providential escape or of resolution through recognition," he writes, "fall away in the face of this sombre assessment of the weight of the world: not a world which is background, nor an illustrative setting; but one which has entwined itself in the deepest layers of the personality" (217). But the figure of escape is not so quickly depleted. From the late nineteenth century on, the image or idea of escape, of creative displacement, develops into a full-blown poetics of exile, from which the drama of the later twentieth century is still seeking to free itself.

The Politics of Home

That there is a politics to simply being at home is no longer an unfamiliar idea: in terms of recent cultural practice, we saw one aspect of that politics in the transformation of the word *housewife* into the word *homemaker,* a substitution that played out a whole reconceptualization of the power relations between women and domesticity. The historical backgrounds of this shift and its far-reaching theoretical implications are being charted by feminist scholars today.[5] In the area that concerns me directly here, that of theatrical representation, a similar political thematic of home has prevailed. Indeed, as far as the stage is concerned, the ideology we recognize as modern humanism was inaugurated by a decision not to remain in a home as artificial and stifling as a doll's house.

However, as both these examples show, there has long been a certain reductive literalness in this conceptualization of home, one that, for all its desire to liberate or liberalize, will inevitably produce only a limited and ultimately reactionary account of identity. One of the cleverest (and earliest) schemas of this mode of self-production, as well as its disastrous consequences, is to be found in Poe's story "The Fall of the House of Usher," which suggests that the figure of home has long involved a denial of difference. The story shows the damage that unchecked literalism can do, as it forces an unwanted equivalence on several distinct entities: two individuals, a family, a family history, and a house. Poe's account of destruction by sheer reductiveness—all the Ushers collapse together into one undifferentiated heap—is also a deconstruction of the grotesque late-Romantic politics of singular identity, identity that feels itself too securely "housed" in a place where it can no longer be at home.

The theatrical version of the literalized home is to be found in realism, which from its inception has staged both the deterministic power as well as the crisis of this concept. One sign of the crisis is the violent ambiguity, in realism, of spatial signs. Ibsen's famous interactive architectural symbols—his climbable towers, slammable doors, and burnable buildings—help to construct domestic space as a problematic: both the *condition for* and the *obstacle to* psychological coherence. Again and again in Ibsen, the crisis of the concept of home appears as the collision therein of two incommensurable desires: the desire for a stable container for identity and the desire to deterritorialize the self.[6]

The figure of home lends itself to one of the basic impulses of realism—the attempt to locate a space of personal experimentation: experimentation with the definition of persons, and with selfhood. This project dovetails nicely with the sense we have, from the nuclear family setups of the twentieth century, that home is a space of obligatory self-fashioning. As James Ellenwood expressed it in 1939, when the bourgeois discourse of home was at its most unreflective and unproblematized:

> Because, and this is basic, we learn by doing, . . . the home is the one ideal place for working things out realistically. It is the laboratory where most experiments are tried. Other agencies lecture and teach us about good living, but here we are up against life itself. . . . In a home one HAS to work out problems and relationships that, elsewhere, are only theorized over. Here you have to make good. (26–27)

But Ellenwood also isolates a few other characteristics of the figure of home that play into the increasingly paradoxical discourse of realism. Home is both a site of *difference* ("It would take no less than a genius to interest all the members of a family in many common programs," says Ellenwood [6]) and a site of *compulsion* ("It is the place where you have to go when there is no other place you can or want to go. . . . Only rarely does one run away or resign. The normal home is a long sentence" [12]). As we shall see in chapter 2, this contradictory conditionality of the figure of home—its status as both shelter and prison, security and as entrapment—is crucial to its dramatic meaning.

The theatrical conventions of the realist drama made their own contribution to the practice of deriving identity from environment. Under realism's rich re-creation of actual environments lay an attempted closure of fictionality, a will to close the gap between the world of the stage and the world of the spectator (the same will that led, later, to the hyperinclusive theatrology of environmental theater; see chap. 1). Several of the practices of the early naturalists sought to erase the difference between the public nature of theater and the private world of experience.[7] André Antoine, founder of the Théâtre-Libre, recalls that "For our second production, we decided to emphasize that this is no public playhouse, but a special private society, by sending out announcements folded in the form of wedding invitations" (quoted by Waxman, 27). Antoine also had Strindberg's preface to *Miss Julie* translated and distributed to his audiences. As Samuel Waxman notes, "It was another step forward toward the twentieth century 'little' theatre that has become almost universal" (180).

Needless to say, the public was not always ready to be drawn into the imagined intimacy dreamed of by the theater practitioners. Nemirovich-Danchenko, writing on the need to regulate late arrivals, exposes this conflict with spectators, reading so trivial a fact as lateness as a deliberate attempt on the spectator's part "to violate my will" (93). He asserts that he "can't allow it," calling one such spectator a "bourgeois of the first water," and when the problem persists after the Russian Revolution, that kind of spectator is an "imbecile" who thinks "that the revolution gave him the right to do as he liked" (93). He concludes by insisting that "our attitude to the public" is not the attitude of a "master," but that the spectator should be happy and grateful for the privilege of entering. The audience should behave like "charming guests," or "we [will] force it to submit to rules essential for the artistic unity of the spectacle" (93).

The realist stage installed a logic of representation to which the spectator was, essentially, an obstacle, a hindrance, an inconvenience. As I will show in my discussion of *Miss Julie* in chapter 1, the paradox of this drama—the paradox of shared (i.e., public) private experience—involved the spectator in an impossible displacement, where s/he was asked to play the role of ultimate hermeneutic authority while being reminded simultaneously of the authorizing but invisible presence of the omnipotent puppet master/playwright, creator of all meaning.

Certainly the most significant intervention that realism made into the developing discourse on space was through its commitment to what we could now call a platiality of the stage, an emphasis on the particularity and materiality of each dramatic environment. How great a revolution this was is memorably expressed by Nemirovich-Danchenko in the following detailed account of what had been the scenic norm before realism:

> every play must have its own setting. . . . At present in every theatre of the Soviet Union this is commonly accepted as the ABC of the business, but then it seemed like a revolution. The old theatre had its "garden," its "wood"—as the officials themselves contended, "of the most approved verdure"; it had a reception room with soft-lined chairs and a tall lamp in the corner with a yellow shade eminently suited for a comfortable love passage; a large reception room with pillars, painted of course; a middle-class room with red mahogany furniture. In the storeroom of decorations there were "Gothic" and "Renaissance" properties for "classical" plays, as all costume-plays were called by the director, even though they were written by contemporary authors. They had, correspondingly, chairs with high backs, a black carved table, and a curule chair, which the director stubbornly persisted in calling the "culture" chair. All these properties were used now in one play, now in its successor. (90–91)

The fully iconic, single-set, middle-class living room of realism produced so closed and so *complete* a stage world that it supported the new and powerful fantasy of the stage not as a place to pretend in or to perform on but a place to *be,* a fully existential arena. We tend to associate this fantasy primarily with acting theory, and specifically with Stanislavsky, but its effects can also be seen in the new structural emphasis, in realist drama, on arrivals and departures. So literally global is the signification of the stage-home of realism, that simply to enter or leave it becomes a decisive—perhaps *the* decisive—dramatic act.

This is precisely what Chekhov ironizes in his drama. In Chekhov's plays as in Ibsen's, arrivals and departures are used as macrostructural devices, but Chekhov's arrivals and departures, unlike Ibsen's, are marked by a certain comic-pathetic arbitrariness. In historical terms, they look forward to the random wanderings of absurdist characters, led famously by Beckett's vagabonds Didi and Gogo. They initiate a figure of motiveless meandering that gains, much later, a political meaning when it is associated with such overpowering external determinants of movement as governments and technologies: thus, in David Rabe's

Streamers, the soldiers waiting in boot camp to be shipped off to Vietnam express the meaninglessness of arrivals and departures:

> BILLY: How long you think we got?
> ROGER: What do you mean?
> BILLY: Till they pack us up, man, ship us out.
> ROGER: To the war, you mean? To Disneyland? Man, I dunno; that up to them IBMs. Them machines is figurin' that. Maybe tomorrow, maybe next week, maybe never.
>
> (20)

The surprising intrusion of Disneyland into this account of a malevolent and absurd exilic condition is not the merely decorative flourish it might appear to be: as we shall see later, the figure of the artificial environment, of which Disneyland is the most powerful and complex exemplar, haunts the imagination of modern drama from *The Wild Duck* onward, marking the sense of an increasingly catastrophic dispossession of nature, which is the end point and inevitable outcome of that crisis of place we are tracking through the discourse of home.[8]

But already in Chekhov, the act of displacement, shorn of its decisiveness, ceases to be a strategy for the formulation of a stable identity and becomes instead a symptom of its loss. In the legendary dispute between Chekhov and Stanislavsky what was being contested, in part, was the whole politics of deriving individual identities from environments, of grounding in a stage-home characters who were essentially homeless. By contrast, the more stylized, less realistic stagings of Chekhov's plays by contemporary directors like Andre Serban and Peter Brook recover the problematic of identity that naturalism tends to bracket out. To the degree that the stage-home is deliteralized, it reveals itself as a complex and contradictory thematic, precisely an *idea* of home—not a place but a discursive field laid out in such a way as to guarantee its inhabitants a certain psychological homelessness.

In Chekhov's drama, the discourse of home is deconstructed to produce the image of a *static* exilic consciousness, experienced by the characters as a feeling of being homesick while at home. Here the sentimental image of home—as an actual place correlated with a strong and desirable emotional experience (the sense of "belonging")—unravels as the logic linking belonging with exile is revealed to be not a logic of opposition but rather one of supplementarity: the emotional structure that is most familiar, most habitual and homelike, to these characters is the feeling of being displaced from somewhere else. They are not exiled *from* where they belong but exiled *to* where they belong.

However, the literalistic and domestic space of naturalism contained Chekhov's deconstruction and stopped it short of any ideological reformulation of the politics of identity. Exilic consciousness, read either as upper-class malaise or as universal tragic alienation, was ultimately something the spectator could be *at home* with. Once situated in terms of an already well coded "milieu and moment," the contradiction embodied by these characters is easily absorbed into a modernist account of psychological fragmentation and alienation, the same account, indeed, that has made exile itself a privileged poetic figure.

The realist discourse of home relies on a long-standing conceptual structure in which two figures are balanced—and constructed—as opposites: the figures of belonging and exile. The home as house (and, behind it, the home as homeland) is the site of a claim to affiliation whose incontestability has been established by a thick web of economic, juridical, and scientific discourses—which also construct the meaning of exile. It is a usefully ambivalent meaning: on the one hand, exile is branded by the negatives of loss and separation; on the other, it is distinguished by distance, detachment, perspective. For the individual (and exile is a decidedly individualistic figure) the poetics of exile offers a mechanism whereby suffering is exchanged for a certain moral authority, personal rupture for aesthetic rapture, as heard, for example, in Nabokov's reflection that "the break in my destiny affords me in retrospect a syncopal kick that I would not have missed for worlds" (250).

The conjunction of naturalism and certain proxemic compulsions—exile, homelessness—inhabits one of the originary moments of the myth of dramatic modernism, the story of the first production of André Antoine's Théâtre-Libre. As well known, one of the plays to be presented on the first evening, March 30, 1887, was *Jacques Damour,* adapted by M. Leon Hennique from a novel by Emile Zola. For his part, Antoine regarded this association with the name of the controversial father of naturalism not only as the aesthetic and ideological cornerstone of his theater-to-be, but also as a badge of artistic relevance, if not revolutionary correctness: "I realized instantly," he claims, "that Zola's name on our program would guarantee us the attention of [the influential critic] Sarcey" (10). The amateur group with whom Antoine performed, however, felt differently: "Zola's name was already causing some misgivings in our society. Certain of the members were disturbed by the notoriety I was gaining. Finally, the club's name and meeting place were both refused me for such a presentation" (10).

In a sense, then, the Théâtre-Libre is created out of an experience of loss, disenfranchisement, *homelessness*. Certainly that is how it seemed to Antoine himself, who frames his narrative with the image of dispossession. The story of the Théâtre-Libre, as its founder tells it, begins with this first exile and ends with another, more literal one:

> Here ends the odyssey of the Théâtre-Libre. Having set out seven years ago from my garret in the Rue de Dunkerque with forty sous in my pocket, to rehearse our first production in the little wine shop in the Rue des Abesses, I at last find myself in Rome, with almost the same sum in my pocket, surrounded by fifteen companions as dejected as myself, with a hundred thousand francs of debts awaiting me in Paris, and with no idea of what we will do tomorrow. (234)

Antoine's memoir reproduces a characteristic association of modern dramatic thought: spatial specificity is combined with figures of exile and displacement, street and city names mark the *loss* of place. Of course, spatial specificity, indeed literalism, is one of the things the Théâtre-Libre is famous for, and Antoine is justly celebrated for his attention to the details of the spaces his stage re-created. At this level too, an originary moment from the Théâtre-Libre legend links the stage with the discourse of home. Three days before the opening of the first production, Antoine writes: "I had a lot of trouble this morning finding the furniture and properties, since I scarcely had the means to rent them. I spoke to my mother about it, and she allowed me to take the furniture from her dining room—chairs and table—for the room behind the shop in *Jacques Damour*" (19). Thus the first production of Antoine's theater involves him in a literal re-creation of home; later on the situation is reversed, and the stage becomes the site of a "creative" homelessness: "I no longer have a cent or a home; for the time being, I will sleep on a small cot which is folded up during the day and passes for a property" (43).

Homelessness is only the most graphic version of the many displacements that constitute the insistent and pervasive challenges to home, transforming this apparently simple figure into a powerful irreality, something on the order of a fantasy, fable, myth, or impossible dream.

Other displacements, all of which will be discussed in the following pages and all of which are complex figures, even whole discourses, are exile, immigration, and refugeehood. Of these exile is certainly the most fully theorized and poeticized concept, having become nothing short of a symbol for modern culture itself. According to George Steiner, the literature of the twentieth century is best understood as an "extraterritorial" art, expressing the universal experience of exile and refugeehood: "It seems proper that those who create art in a civilization of quasi-barbarism, which has made so many homeless, should themselves be poets unhoused and wanderers across language. Eccentric, aloof, nostalgic, deliberately untimely" (quoted by Said, 357). The names of Conrad, Joyce, Kafka, and Nabokov are sufficient to evoke the principle of a potent exilic consciousness as the shaping force of modern literature. The history of drama supplies its own names: Ibsen, Strindberg, Chekhov, Beckett, Brecht—all experienced and were marked by exile or other displacements; all made dislocation one of the central themes of their drama.

But, as Edward Said points out in his essay "Reflections on Exile," the unparalleled scale of contemporary displacements removes the figure of exile from its earlier status as literary and cultural motif, signifying heightened consciousness and privileged perspective:

But the difference between earlier exiles and those of our own times is, it bears stressing, scale: our age with its modern warfare, imperialism and quasi-theological ambitions of totalitarian rulers—is indeed the age of the refugee, the displaced person, mass immigration. . . . On the twentieth-century scale, exile is neither aesthetically nor humanistically comprehensible: at most the literature about exile objectifies an anguish and a predicament most people rarely experience at first hand. . . . Is it not true that the views of exile in literature and, moreover, in religion obscure what is truly horrendous: that exile is irremediably secular and unbearably historical; that it is produced by human beings for other human beings; and that, like death but without death's ultimate mercy, it has torn millions of people from the nourishment of tradition, family and geography? (357–58)

This terrible truth of actual exile makes its way into Western drama quite late, but when it does, it illuminates the terms of a century-long struggle with the problem of place. This struggle, to which I have given the label geopathology, unfolds as an incessant dialogue between belonging and exile, home and homelessness. At midcentury, a new discourse enters the dialogue and changes the established terms of the drama's engagement with place, displacing as well the dramatic structures that had served the geopathic model. The new discourse centers upon the figure of America, explicating it, first, as a *betrayal* of place, and then finding in it a muted celebration of placelessness. Out of this celebration there emerges, finally, a kind of solution—or at least the beginnings of a new formulation that might redirect, if not entirely overcome, that painful politics of place I am calling geopathology. In the emerging drama of multiculturalism, it seems to me, are the outlines of a new *heterotopic* account of the relationship between persons and places. This account begins by creatively confronting the problem of place, regarding it as a challenge and an invitation rather than as a tragic impasse.

A work that exemplifies this evolving new attitude toward place is Laurie Anderson's epic piece, *United States*. As Henry Sayre points out, Anderson uses performance to realize the postmodern experience of what Gilles Deleuze, describing the logic of Nietzsche's texts, has called "nomadism":

The only conceivable key [to these texts], perhaps, would be in the concept of "embarkation." . . . We embark, then, in a kind of raft of "the Medusa"; bombs fall all around the raft as it drifts towards icy subterranean streams—or towards torrid rivers, the Orinoco, the Amazon; the passengers row together. They are not supposed to like one another, they fight with one another, they eat one another. To row together is to share, to share something beyond law, contract or institution. It is a period of drifting, of "deterritorialization." (144)

According to Sayre, Anderson "manages to 'deterritorialize' the United States, to give her audience a sense that they are in some measure *outside*—or wanderers within—the very place they live" (147).

Employing two tropes that have been involved in the figuration of place from the beginning of the modern period—the tropes of dislocation and of the technologies of representation—Anderson in effect completes what has been a halting but nevertheless progressive reinscription of the figure of home, as well as of the general category of place. That process, begun in midcentury (when it was figured as the failure of homecoming), concludes when, in Sayre's words, "we recognize in [Anderson's] wanderings our own homelessness." Her lavish use of technology—technologies for manipulating sound, image, and even voice—is the extreme realization of a century-long rebellion against the naturalistic theater's dream of total visibility (the inner logic of that dream and the theatrical functioning it dictates are discussed in chap. 1). One playful passage in *United States* encapsulates the whole complex relation between *seeing* and *place:*

> Over the river
> And through the woods
> Whose woods these are
> Long time no see
> Long time no see[9]

The multiple experiences of place invoked here—as home and origin (Grandmother's house), as property (whose woods these are), as travel (miles to go before I sleep)—the copresence of high and low culture (Robert Frost and Little Red Riding Hood), as well as, finally, the muted reference to the dispossession of nature (the river and woods no longer seen): all these are part of the gradually evolving postgeopathological drama of the past two decades. Among the many aspects of geopathic drama that are revisioned in the contemporary theater is one that Anderson (like most other avant-garde practitioners of theater) deeply engages, the problematic of visibility. As Sayre articulates it: "Are we meeting someone we have not seen for a long time, or have we been, for a long time, blind?" (147).

The chapters that follow describe a development that is also, at every "stage," a forecast and a memory. The conventionality of dramatic discourse—dictated by both its public nature as well as its material contextualization in an ongoing theater culture—makes the drama powerfully intertextual. This book traces that intertextuality by tracking not only the figures of home, homelessness, exile, and immigration, but also an apparently unconnected collection of recurring figures that insistently accompany the dramatic discourse of place: addiction, photography, performance, and burial.

Chapter 1, "Plays and Place," presents a theoretical model for the relationship of theatrical space and dramatic place by considering the habitual—and, I argue, false—opposition between naturalism and the experimental stage practice known as environmental theater. An exploration of the theoretics of naturalism as refracted through *Miss Julie* and Strindberg's preface to the play leads to a recognition that naturalism rested on a fantasy of total visibility, of the impossible translation of private experience into public expression. This problematic of a public privacy survives long after naturalism, persisting into environmental theater, where its presence is occluded by new spatial arrangements designed to create "shared experiences" (shared, that is, between the audience and the actors). These spatial arrangements, I argue, are deceptive, and the ideology sustaining them is the subject of Jim Cartwright's play *Road*. As I read it, *Road* stages the politics of place that link environmentalism to its supposed opposite, naturalism, and these politics are intimately connected to the dramatic discourse of home.

Chapter 2, "Geopathology," lays out the terms and consequences of a foundational semiology of place based on the idea of ill placement. Several of the themes and motifs that enter the drama through this semiology persist long into the future; among these, the figures of photography and of performance surface with interesting variations even after the discourse of home has been thoroughly revised through what I have called the "multicultural imagination," the topic of my final chapter. In the last play that I examine in that chapter, Ping Chong's *Nuit Blanche,* the figures of photography and performance are fused into the play's basic expressive strategy, its combination of slides and live action. In this play also, one of the most vibrant undercurrents running through the whole history of this thematic, namely, an ecological current, is brought to the surface. The relation between ecology and geopathology, discovered as early as Ibsen's *Wild Duck,* emerges as crucial to the deterritorialized theatrology of postmodernism.

Before the drama of multiculturalism can reconfigure place, the terms of geopathology have to be confronted. Chapter 3, "America and the Limits of Homecoming," traces the effects of the figure of America on the unraveling discourse of home. Focusing on two transatlantic pairs of plays—first Pinter's *The Homecoming* and Shepard's *Buried Child* and then Caryl Churchill's *Ice Cream* and George C. Wolfe's *The Colored Museum*—this chapter presents an encapsulated history of the dramatic discourse of home, its past and future condensed into the figure of failed homecoming and the dramaturgy of the hidden (and now worthless) secret.

From this analysis, an unexpected image, the image of the buried child, emerges as a privileged—even obsessional—device of the modern dramatic imagination. The figure of the buried child occurs again and again in modern drama, tempting one to turn to psychoanalysis for an explanation. I have preferred simply to track the fate of this strange figure in the evolving postgeopathic platial discourse of modern drama and to link it, finally, to a peculiar figure in the discourse of what Harold Bloom calls "the American religion." According to Bloom, America's obsession with the unborn child marks this culture's unacknowledged commitment to an essentially Gnostic belief system, whereby the essential self is as old as God himself and, like God, no part of the creation. George Bush's apparently contradictory concern for fetuses and unconcern for unwanted infants make a kind of sense from this point of view, valuing the uncreated—or precreated—divine being over the unwanted child who "is sadly fallen away from freedom": "One sees why the fetus and the flag are one; the baby is not alone, and will drain the pious taxpayer, but the fetus can wave over the land of the free, whose Fundamentalists will remain solitary and godlike, poised always *before* the Creation" (57).

Bloom's reading of the American obsession with the unborn child helps to explain the painful contradiction this figure registers when brought into line with another powerful American mythology, America's view of itself as a *place* of exceptional potentiality, a land of unimagined progress and plenty. Bloom's reading would suggest that, for George Bush and his unwitting Gnostic constituency, this land—like the unwanted starving infant over whom the innocent fetus takes precedence—is part of the fallen creation and as such of little intrinsic concern to those whose minds and hearts are turned to the Hereafter. For them, as for Joseph Smith, the Mormon prophet, America is merely the ancient burial ground of a truth awaiting revelation. (The Book of Mormon was said to have lain buried for centuries in upstate New York until the Angel Moroni led Joseph Smith to it.) But another imagination of America, one that celebrates the land itself, its majestic landscapes and its vast spaces, contests this religious vision, substituting another, perhaps secular, faith, whose greatest manifestation has been American ecological thinking. The desecration of America, figured time and time again through the imagery of waste and garbage—the all-American figure of *junk*—provokes a reconsideration of the figure of the buried child. In this ongoing reformulation, the buried child is precious not for its links to a divinity that preexists creation but for its figuration of *recovery:* the hope, however hopeless, that what has been lost or destroyed by industrialization, technology, modernism can somehow be reclaimed, "dug up," revived, and acknowledged for the precious gift it always was.

Once again, it is Laurie Anderson's *United States* that seems to summarize the contradictory logic of the figure of the buried child and its relation to America, to the present, and (if our luck as a species holds out) to the future. In a section entitled "Song for Two Jims," Anderson tells of visiting a family in Kentucky, two parents and four children:

> One day Mrs Taylor told me that she used to have another
> kid, but that he had apparently fallen down one of the holes.
> Her description was very abstract. Nobody tried to rescue him.
> He just fell down the hole. She said: "Well one
> day I saw him out there
> and I was watching
> and then I didn't see him out there no more."

The abstraction of the mother's description of this extraordinary event is the key to its meaning. It is not only, as Sayre says, that "the 'meaning' of the narrative lies in the very meaninglessness of the Taylors' lives" (148), but also that their defective access to meaning (and hence to affect, to feeling) takes the form of—precisely—a sudden invisibility. The buried child of modern drama is the unseen and unseeable force of circumstance; and circumstance, as we shall see, has long been understood as place, or rather as ill placement. In Anderson's text, however, a very precise characterization is given to the traditionally abstract discourse of geopathology, and we should not be surprised to find that that characterization consists of the two major unacknowledged or unconscious themes of geopathic drama: technology and ecology. The hole into which the "kid" falls is one of many deep holes drilled in the shale surrounding the Taylor household—by Standard Oil. The buried child is the covictim—with the land, with the earth itself—of unbridled technological progress.

The midcentury drama of failed homecoming is also the drama in which the figure of the buried child, and the related dramaturgy of discovery, begins to unravel and betray its hitherto invisible functioning. The process is completed in Laurie Anderson's piece, where the buried child finally speaks and, speaking, exposes the logic of its invisibility, naming that which is destroying, erasing, "burying" it:

So hold me, Mom, in your long arms,
in your automatic arms,
your electronic arms . . .
your petrochemical arms,
your military arms,
in your electronic arms.

After the failure of homecoming, the drama embarks on a quest for new places, and language is among the privileged sites of this exploration. Chapter 4, "The Places of Language," looks at the idea of language as place in three plays that also extend the dramatic discourse on America. Eric Overmyer's *On the Verge* links language, place, and the future, a connection that is then reengaged in a more material and historical mode by Caryl Churchill's *Mad Forest* and in a more apocalyptic and ecological mode by Maria Irene Fornes's *The Danube*. The newly awakened desire for a new platiality to replace the geopathic idealization of ill placement moves beyond language in the plays of immigration and multiculturalism that are the subjects of chapters 5 and 6, respectively. In the plays discussed in these chapters, the discourse of place begins to shift—more or less decisively—toward a recognition of the power of actual and specific places, although the old figuration of America as the principle of placelessness is never far away, never finally overcome.

The figures of home and exile have developed, in the course of this century, far beyond the scope of the literary figures with which they were first associated. The massive and agonizing dislocations of the modern age have left the poetics of exile far behind. The question I finally ask, in the epilogue of this book but also from the beginning, is this: How is the experience of dislocation making its voice heard in the theatrical language of the West? Two recent plays serve to outline an answer: Tony Kushner's monumental (and hugely successful) *Angels in America* and Suzan-Lori Parks's fragile (and largely unheralded) *The America Play* allow for a tentative formulation of where the journey beyond geopathology has led us. That both plays focus their reflections on the figure of America suggests that the modern drama's discourse of place has now transmuted itself into something quite site-specific. Both plays' meditations on the approaching millennium, their shared irony toward the morbid seductions of closure, their playful refusal of the logic of last words—all this makes them the ideal vehicle for what a book like this one must seek: a non-ending, an "other" place from which the otherness of place can continue to be explored and enjoyed.

Chapter One

Plays and Place

In other forms of architecture there is a relationship between conscious, articulate design and good functioning: a well-designed hospital may be more efficacious than a higgledy-piggledy one; but as for theatre, the problem of design cannot start logically. It is not a matter of saying analytically what are the requirements, how best they can be organized—this will usually bring into existence a tame, conventional, often cold hall. The science of theatre-building must come from studying what it is that brings about the most vivid relationship between people—and is this better served by asymmetry, even by disorder? If so, what can be the rule of this disorder?
—Peter Brook, *The Empty Space*

The difficulty of separating plays from place is even recorded, quite fortuitously, in the near homonymy of the words that designate them. It is not only the obvious fact that every play takes place in a place, but that the *varieties* of platial experience allowed by the medium of theater—and recorded in dramatic texts—far surpass that of any other art form. In spite of Aristotle's much-lamented relegation of spectacle to the bottom of his list, the history of the theater is framed by endless variations on the actual size, shape, and relationships between the several distinct spaces of the theater. In the Western tradition, this history ranges from the majestic outdoor Theater of Dionysus to the poky black boxes of New York's Lower East Side, and sites of theatrical experience cover the range of possibilities for aligning actors and spectators in ever-changing relationships to each other. If a "rule of disorder" could be found to explain the mysterious functioning of the theatrical apparatus, it would surely be a spatial rule, a practice or policy of relating people to place.

The theater of the twentieth century, and especially of the latter half of the twentieth century, has conducted a vigorous search for just such a

rule of disorder. The experimentation that began with dadaism, continued with Artaud's Theatre of Cruelty and Brecht's epic theater, and
eventually exploded into myriad forms known variously as happenings,
environmental theater, performance art, and, finally, site-specific theater, is a history of practical engagements with the problematic of plays
and place.[1] So thoroughly did this history reconfigure traditional notions
of the allocation of theater space that a recent textbook on performance
invites students to

> Explore the possibilities of working in different spaces, spaces you
> or potential audiences might not ordinarily think of as places for
> certain kinds of performance. Depending on where you are work-
> ing, even campus art galleries or music halls might be a start; the
> more conventional and traditional your typical audience, the likelier
> it is that even these artistic spaces might seem unusual. You might
> move from there to either more public or more private spaces.
> Cafeterias, athletic arenas, shopping malls—to perform in such
> places, particularly depending on what is performed, might be brac-
> ing for audiences and encourage them to regard the nature of perfor-
> mance and its specific content in new and fresh ways. Similarly,
> turning to private homes, residence halls, and other places generally
> thought private (for the daring, a restroom might even be consid-
> ered as a liminal spot—available for the public though all behaviors
> in it are carried out as if in utter privacy!) might make audiences
> think about their own position of privilege as audiences for art.
> Some of these performances may take the forms of interventions,
> disrupting societal practices and offering a critique of them. (Stern
> and Henderson, 431)

The final two sentences of this remarkable invitation, as well as some of
the conceptual categories underlying the whole passage (public/private,
conventional/unusual), reveal that a certain amount of naturalization and
conventionality has seeped into what is still being offered as a radical
practice. The notion of audience privilege, as well as that of "subverting
societal practices," is part of a by now well-established dogma in theater
work, every bit as tenacious as the old exemplary-mimetic one (art holds
the mirror up to nature) that it seeks to displace.

Recorded in countless "experimental" productions, this new dogma
is rooted in a phenomenology of space according to which the position

and orientation of bodies in a specially designated or constructed environment add to or mold the meaning of what those bodies say and do. Whether the theatrical event's spatial arrangements subvert or sustain the audience's privilege, the conscious manipulation involved is now well acknowledged and approved. What is perhaps less well understood is the *politics* of such manipulations—and, more importantly, the ideological ramifications of the very notion of a phenomenology of theater space. Among the latter is a dream of defeating what Jacques Derrida has called "the closure of representation," a possibility offered by the theater more than by any other art because of its use of reality as a medium. If the real can be represented by the real itself, then representation does not have to settle for the limits and frames that constrict it in all the other media.

The history of environmental experimentation follows a fantasy of limitless theatrical signification, an infinity of meaning resulting from the infinite possible reconfigurations of theater space.[2] Richard Schechner, the foremost theorist of environmental theater, gives eloquent voice to this dream of "fullness":

> The fullness of space, the endless ways space can be transformed, articulated, animated—that is the basis of environmental theatre design. It is also the source of environmental performer training. If the audience is one medium in which the performance takes place, the living space is another. The living space includes all the space in the theatre, not just what is called the stage. (*Environmental Theatre*, 1–2)

The premise of environmental theater is, then, an assault on the traditional divisions, taxonomies, and codings of theater space, and a commitment to overriding, erasing, or even destroying them. Challenging what he regarded as one of the most enduring of assumptions about theater—namely, that the performance occurs in a special place, marked off and designated as such within every kind of theater—Schechner envisioned a theater practice beyond this "bifurcation of space," beyond, that is, the division of the participants into performers and audience. Vanquishing the spirit of division, the environmental theater champions a holistic ideal: "The first scenic principle of environmental theatre," continues Schechner, "is to create and use *whole spaces*" (2; emphasis added). The astonishing corollary to this holistic project is a vision of altogether Faustian proportions: "There is no dead space, nor any end to space" (2).

Seeking to transform the rigidly divisive model of theater, Schechner turned to other fields of human activity, notably ritual, for alternatives. The model he discovered was one of *exchange*. In the second of his "Six Axioms for Environmental Theatre" (*Public Domain*, 167–91), Schechner declares that "All the space is used for performance; all the space is used for audience" (175) and connects environmental theater with two kinds of interactive spatial practice: that found in ritual and in street life. The exchange of spaces and roles between performers and spectators that Schechner finds in these activities contributes to an effect that is the fundamental goal of this kind of theatrical practice: in Schechner's words: "a sense of *shared experience* can be engendered" (177; emphasis added). This kind of theatrical experience, one that was equally shared by performers and spectators, was commonly understood to be in the service of intensity, the reasoning being (and, interestingly, hearkening back to Romantic theories of theater) that the most powerful effects—and affect—required organic, holistic, and unified structures.

The ideal of an intense, common experience, variously reflected in the names that certain major environmental theater groups gave themselves—the Open Theatre, the Living Theatre—ultimately derived from Antonin Artaud's visionary Theatre of Cruelty, which "abolish[ed] the stage and the auditorium and replace[d] them with a single site" so that the spectator was "placed in the middle of the action, . . . engulfed and physically affected by it" (96). The Artaudian assault on boundaries, which was to underwrite all later environmental staging, demolished that most enduring of all theatrical frontiers, the audience as disembodied gaze, and redefined it as embodied and performing coactor.

However, the spatial and performative resituation of the audience has another effect as well, one whose subtly contradictory relation to the former ideal—of shared experience—is left unremarked by Schechner when he states: "the audience itself becomes a major scenic element" (177). The unnoticed contradiction—between the audience as full and equal participant versus the audience as a semiotic element to be manipulated and inscribed within the play's scenic discourse—underlies much of the anxious debate and response to what Walter Kerr, in one of the most spirited documents of this anxiety, called "participatory theatre." Kerr's ironically titled essay "Togetherness" discusses Schechner's environmental theater along with several others and reveals (without, however, explicitly naming) its political dimensions. Kerr argues that environmental theater's erasure of the traditional barriers between audience and performance results in effects fundamentally opposed to those being sought: "The effort at fusion tends to fragment the audience. The demand that the audience be more active tends to make it more passive" (51).

The possibility that environmentalism's reconceptualization of theatrical space—as undifferentiated and limitless—may have an uncomfortable political dimension is suggested in the following remarks of Fernand Léger, in which the vocabulary of compulsion, even desperation, reveals that the ideological background of the practice includes a need to *justify* theater in the context of modern mass culture and mass representation:

> Overwhelmed by the enormous stage set of life, what can the artist who aspires *to conquer his public* do? He has only one chance left to take: to rise to the plane of beauty by considering everything that surrounds him as raw material; to select the plastic and theatrical values possible from the whirlpool that swirls under his eyes; to interpret them in terms of spectacle; to attain theatrical unity and *dominate it at any price.* (Quoted by Aronson, 153; emphasis added)

The term "raw material" is especially significant here, marking as it does the relationship I propose to argue later in this book between modern theater practice and ecology. The attitude to theater contained in Léger's remarks is precisely analogous to the ecological position known (and critiqued by radical ecologists) as "resourcism," the idea that the natural world is an endless source of—or factory producing—raw materials for the more advanced factories of modern consumer culture. Regarded thus, the realm of nature (and for Léger and his heirs that of culture as well, especially other, "exotic," cultures) becomes an arena toward which conquest and domination are the appropriate responses.

The success that environmental theater has enjoyed is well known. But, as Kerr's remarks (now all but forgotten) suggest, its political implications remain largely unexamined. I want to suggest that these politics can be located within the homology I have just outlined, between the exploitation of nature and the program of environmental theater. Furthermore, I believe that that analogy can help us to articulate the specifically cultural problematic—or crisis—of representation known as interculturalism. The "politics of ecstasy" that inspired much environmental theater (including what was perhaps the quintessential work of the movement, *Dionysus in 69;* see Schechner, *Public Domain,* 238) has now given way to a very different politics of identity, bringing a range of new issues into the theater. At the end of this chapter I shall analyze a relatively recent play, Jim Cartwright's *Road* (1986), that is situated precisely at the point of intersection between these two kinds of theatrical politics. *Road* marks a moment of self-reflexivity in the history of environmentalist experimentation. As I read it, the play stages the politics—an imperialistic politics—of environmental theater's dream of infinite live space and sets forth the ideological ramifications of this view of theater.

But before a deconstruction of environmental theater like the one offered in *Road* can be fully grasped, the history of this stage practice must be addressed and its peculiar self-occluding ideology must be noted. Environmental theater is burdened with an ideology whose primary characteristic is that it obscures itself, denies its presence. One direction from which this ideology might be glimpsed is in the environmental theater's self-characterization as radical and subversive, and particularly in its insistence on being the opposite of naturalism. Arnold Aronson begins what is surely the most exhaustive study of environmental staging practices by noting the presence of a surprisingly similar impulse in both environmental theater and its supposed opposite, naturalism.

Stanislavski, who for many represents the quintessence of the fourth wall, illusionistic style of staging, once said that he wanted the audience at *Three Sisters* to feel as if they were guests at the Prozorov household. If a spectator at the Moscow Art Theatre should truly feel this way, how does this experience differ from that of the spectators at Grotowski's *Doctor Faustus* who sit at the table with Faustus as his guests, or from The Performance Group's production of *The Tooth of Crime* in which the spectators move with the character Hoss from his kitchen to his bedroom in different parts of the theatre? Clearly, these examples represent differing aspects of environmentalism and there is no single answer. (2)

Aronson goes on to offer several criteria for distinguishing and models for classifying the various kinds of environmentalism, but the implication in this passage that naturalism may be a false other to environmentalism is never taken up explicitly.[3] The relationship between naturalism and environmentalism is, in fact, a continuum that has been disguised as a rupture,[4] and the motivations behind the disguise—the unconscious

motivations, to be sure—derive from its occlusive ideology. The principle that links these two supposedly antithetical practices is what I call the
logic of total visibility and whose terms I explicate through a discussion
of *Miss Julie* below.

For my purposes it is also important to note that all three of the
examples Aronson gives involve *an invitation to a home*. The continuity
between naturalism and environmentalism exists, at least in part, at the
level of a hidden discourse of home and belonging that runs through
modern drama from the nineteenth century onward. Belonging and related concepts, such as privacy, inclusion, participation, occupy the ideological heart of modern drama, which is above all else a drama about
place, and, more specifically, about place as understood through, around,
and beyond the figure of *home.*

The spatiality of modern drama involves a complex figuration of its
favorite setting, the domestic interior. The idea of home that emerges
from this figuration establishes a discourse that can be imagined as a
semantic spectrum whose two poles are occupied by the tropes of belonging and exile. The social, psychological, and philosophical explorations that occupy the early modern drama (the explorations alluded to in
the title of Tom Driver's seminal study *Romantic Quest and Modern Query,*
as well as, though less explicitly, in Robert Brustein's equally seminal
The Theatre of Revolt) occur within and in turn help to define this spectrum. In whatever quests, revolts, contests, and ambitions the heroes of
this drama get involved, they invariably encounter and engage the issue
of home, that is, of belonging and exile. The stage on which the encounter occurs is peculiarly receptive to this discourse, which it mirrors with
its own insistent opposition between the visible and the invisible.

The Theater of Total Visibility

The plot of *Miss Julie* turns on an unusual conjunction of sexual and
spatial determinism, an association from which the issue of class is also
not absent. The aristocratic Julie and her valet Jean are literally and
figuratively trapped into intercourse when, to avoid being seen together
alone, they are forced into hiding in Jean's room. This fateful conceal-
ment, which Strindberg is at pains to characterize also as a fated development, renders the disruption of class roles as sexuality, and sexuality
(that is, transgressive, forbidden, fatal sexuality) as the inevitable outcome of a momentary and enforced *privacy*. In acting according to the

taboos and dictates of a rigid class society, it would seem, the characters are doomed to transgress in two of the orders in which that society inscribes itself, the orders of sexuality and territoriality.

The actual class situation prevailing in Sweden at the time the play was written was, of course, a good deal more complex than such generic terms as "aristocratic" and "valet" can capture. Miss Julie, for instance, belongs to the nobility and can thus claim the title *Fröken,* but it is clear that her family is not without its economic and social vulnerabilities and that the upper-class privilege they enjoy is in the process of unraveling. However, in developing the action that puts Julie into Jean's room, Strindberg generally erases the historical specificities that in reality would have qualified the class opposition between the protagonists. It is not only that both Julie and Jean seem to have a psychological stake in maintaining an extremist account of class difference: the play itself has a similar stake, which is, however, not psychological but ideological and theatrological.

Julie agrees to take refuge in Jean's room when he persuades her that the servants and farmworkers who are headed into the kitchen for re-freshment are mocking her in their song. Jean insists that they do not love her, as she thinks; her sentimental trust in them is misplaced, he says, made impossible by the divisive forces of class difference: "They take the food you give them, but they spit on it as soon as your back is turned" (237). Having made his point, Jean then dictates the course of action with reference to this typically extremist estimation of class rela-tions: "That's what the mob always is—cowards! You can't fight them; you can only run away" (89). Julie's answer then enunciates the play's linking of class difference to spatial determinism: "Run away? Where? There's no way out of here" (239).

The knotting together of the separate systems of sex, class, and space in a dense relation of inevitability is not only the plot of *Miss Julie;* it is also the plot—the ideological project—of naturalism. Both turn on the attempt to renegotiate *and to fix in place* the relationship between individual, private experience and its public meaning. The supposedly private parts of the house in which Miss Julie's personal destiny is played out are in fact as public, as fully determined by social definitions, as are the private parts or roles played by the characters of this play and the actors of naturalist theater.

The notion of private selves, subjective identities—upon which, since Stanislavsky, the theatrology of realism rests—is as much in crisis (already) in *Miss Julie* as is the general concept of privacy, of spaces and experiences to which one has exclusive claims. Within the play (but clearly deriving from its sociohistorical context) an unresolvable contradiction emerges between the idealization of the principle of privacy and its simultaneous qualification. Precisely this contradiction is also the source of a certain discordance within the theoretics of naturalism and can be found structured into its paradigmatic stage space.

The naturalist stage adumbrates a specific relationship between the performance and the spectator, connecting them to each other with an ambitious new contract of total visibility, total knowledge. The promise of the well-stocked stage of naturalism is a promise of omniscience, indeed of a transfer of omniscience from dramatist to spectator. Having been impregnated with "reality," in the form of all those little touches of "innocent verisimilitude" that Bert States memorably describes as "the causal masquerading as the casual" (*Great Reckonings*, 67), the stage space of naturalism seems ready to deliver the whole truth, to dispel the enigmas of past and future from a firmly drawn present. The theater's self-insertion into the naturalistic project sets it "marching," as Zola announced, "from the known to the unknown." The action of *Miss Julie*—the action that puts Julie in Jean's room—is arranged in such a way as to affirm this intrepid new account of theatrical signification and of spectatorship. Yet, even as it highlights and foregrounds its multi-faceted assault on the unknown, the play also demonstrates that the unknown (be it the psychological unknown of character and motivation or the sociopolitical unknown of class history) returns, like the repressed, in disguise. The mask it wears is hard to recognize as a mask, because of its history as Truth: the mask is tragedy. However, the tragic lineaments of this play outline a pseudotragedy only, marking an ideological crisis that reveals itself as a profound ambivalence about, precisely, the age-old gifts of tragedy: truth, knowledge, certainty. It is this ideological crisis, inscribed in the play's unusual stage space as well as in its final moments, that makes *Miss Julie* exemplary of naturalism.

Naturalism as ideological crisis rather than as aesthetic project is enacted at every level of Strindberg's play, not least at the level of its theoretical status, which is derived from its extraordinary relationship to the monumental preface. Strindberg's forceful theorization of his experiment has produced a sort of permanent transgressive structure around the play,[5] a confusion of outside and inside that characterizes many other features of the play as well, including its physical space and its theoretics.

The preface is wrapped around and folded into the play it introduces to a degree unusual even for the heavily prefaced documents of a self-conscious dramatic modernity. It was written after the play but has accompanied the published version from the start, thus determining an interpretive future that is probably radically discontinuous with the play's compositional past.[6]

The ongoing historical relationship between the play and the preface constitutes the conceptual or theoretical space of *Miss Julie* and has, like a physical space, an inside and an outside. In this space as in the literal spaces of the play, inside and outside, as well as visible and invisible, are linked by a hidden logic, a logic of *partial*—not total—visibility. The rhetorical process of the play (and, I am arguing, of naturalism itself) is one that takes these literal spatial oppositions (along with other more figurative ones, especially private and public, known and unknown) and rewrites them so that they are not mutually exclusive opposites but rather versions of each other. In the staging and meaning of the play, just as in the logic of naturalism, inside is not merely contiguous and continuous with outside but thoroughly penetrated by it; similarly, the private is not a realm withdrawn and protected from the public but fully determined by it. In the fiction as much as in the staging of this play, what is performed is the problematic lodged in Strindberg's oxymoronic appellation, the Intimate Theatre.

The inside of the conceptual space of *Miss Julie* is occupied, of course, by the proclaimed ideals of naturalism. Naturalism is "located" in this work (that is, the preface plus the play) as in few others.[7] Indeed by this time in the historiography of dramatic modernism the coincidence between this work and the program of naturalism seems so overdetermined as to be, almost, a relation of caricature. Certainly the heart of the preface is an encapsulated encyclopedia of the dramaturgical and theatrical devices that have come to be identified with the school of Zola: psychosocial complexity and "real door-knobs on the doors."

But Strindberg's rhetorical choices in the preface—notably his wavering between claims of radical innovation and expressions of humility, even despair—position naturalism as a paradoxical, self-contradictory, and transgressive discourse. Strindberg's preface utterly disproves the assumption that a prefatory essay is inherently more univocal and less ambiguous than a literary work.[8] In this text, naturalism appears not as a closed and coherent system but precisely as an *opening,* a gap between two historical systems, one exhausted and moribund, the other still to emerge. In a quite urgent way, Strindberg's preface represents itself as the aperture from which one can begin to glimpse "the repertory that one day shall come" (217). Here and elsewhere, naturalism situates itself on the emergent horizon of theater history, awaiting what Antoine called "the hoped-for generation of new playwrights." What distinguishes this and other manifestos of modernism is the presence here of an overriding futurology, a movement of projection and compulsive displacement into the unknown. Strindberg's preface—but not, significantly, his play—is soaked with future reference, even down to its last lines, which read: "Here is my attempt! If I have failed, there is still time to try again" (217).

The terms I have just used to describe this futurology (projection, displacement, compulsion) indicate how easily this impulse can be, and has been, thematized, contributing some of modern drama's most fertile tropes: the inadequacy of home, the exhilaration of exile, the new victimage of location, the new heroism of departure. All these motifs haunt this play as well, most explicitly in Jean's lengthy fantasy, temporarily shared by Julie, of a future life as a hotelier (that is, not as master of a home but as manager of a space of transience). But the desired displacements, so crucial to writers like Ibsen and Chekhov, have an insubstantial hold on Strindberg's dramaturgy, in which a claustrophobic entrapment prevails. I would suggest that this reflects the much more complicated relationship that Strindberg had with the unknown, and his uneasiness with its new, positivist definition.

As the new frontier of scientific and secular humanism, the unknown presents a deceptively tamer aspect than it had in the past. Once contextualized outside of religious ideology, the unknown appears not as mystery but as enigma, conundrum, and puzzle, a region not merely hospitable to but positively begging for colonization by powerful explanatory systems. Such systems (in *Miss Julie* they are sex and class) are the true protagonists of the drama of naturalism, which, having set as its goal the observation, exposition, and explication of life as it is, must at every moment engage and overcome the unknown. This project involves both the stage and the audience, connecting them to each other in a new—and impossible—contract of total visibility.

One feature of this contract is the necessary reduction of the characters to the status of signs within the plays' philosophical discourse. Unlike their classical predecessors, the inhabitants of naturalistic drama do not participate in the philosophical inquiries embodied by their fates; rather, they are merely the raw material, the data, of the audience's discoveries. The agonized question asked by Miss Julie (both the person and the play)—"Who's to blame for what has happened?" (265)—is really only asked of the spectator. Miss Julie herself quickly dismisses the question, recognizing that it is rendered irrelevant by the determinism of her position: since "I'm still the one who has to bear the guilt, suffer the consequences" (265). However, this is certainly not the attitude that is urged on the spectator or the reader, either by the play or the preface, both of which valorize and encourage a search for systematic understanding. In this way, the naturalist agenda transfers the function of recognition from the protagonists to the spectator; here discovery and revelation are of a purely hermeneutic order, within the theater but outside the drama.

Miss Julie is clearly marked as a hermeneutic construct; its events are accompanied by a persuasive interpretive map, presented mainly in the two dreams that the protagonists recount to each other.[9] Yet these dreams do nothing to *explain* the reversal of positions between Julie and Jean; rather, they *allegorize* it, and they do so in the starkest possible way. As such, they are part of the hermeneutic determinism of the play, that structure that puts the spectator in the position once held by the tragic hero. The crude symbolism of these dreams, their imagery of high and low, up and down, climbing and falling, offers a convenient and schematic key to interpreting the plot, inviting us to read the sexual encounter as a moment of class reversal. That reading is reinforced toward the end of the play with references to a Christian schema whereby "the last shall be first" (264) and "the first shall be the last" (267). Thus the play's answer to Julie's question—"Who's to blame for what has happened?" (265)—is an abstract, structural answer, which reads change in terms of stark oppositions and which emphasizes the extreme points of these oppositions: high and low, first and last. The spaces of the play, however, diagnose the situation quite differently. They bespeak a problem not of hierarchical displacements but of *lateral* movement, a problem of the unavoidable violation of contiguous, mutually exclusive yet mutually dependent spaces.

But before one can read the stage space of *Miss Julie* it is necessary to describe what I have called its conceptual space, characterized by a similarly transgressive structure. The inside of this conceptual space is occupied, as I have said, by the emergent ideal of naturalism. The futurology that frames this ideal, keeping it hazy and indistinct while asserting its necessity, is one way in which its "outside" leaks in. The main substance of this outside, the irrationalism that is programmatically excluded from the positivistic domain of naturalism, is, of course, not alien to modernism in general (and certainly not to Strindberg, who in the years to come was to plumb its depths).[10] My purpose here is to show the extent to which this irrationalism shores up the self-representation of naturalism, making *Miss Julie* a cryptic enactment of both the naturalistic theater and its "double."[11]

This double (or, as I have called it, this outside) is invoked in the very first lines of the preface, in terms that immediately reveal its dismal features—ignorance and religious superstition: "Like the arts in general, the theatre has for a long time seemed to me a *Biblia pauperum,* a picture Bible for those who cannot read" (204). Thus illiteracy, which openly adheres to the irrationalist outside of naturalism, is covertly linked to a central feature of the naturalistic construct, iconicity. The relation of a retrograde illiteracy to a productive, enlightening literalism is established through and across a category with which Strindberg regularly did battle, that of Woman. The link between women and illiteracy, as well as the further connection of both to an illusionistic dramaturgy, is spelled out without delay: "That explains why the theatre has always been an elementary school for youngsters and the half-educated, and for women, who still retain a primitive capacity for letting themselves be deceived" (204). While appearing to herald a departure from the kind of crudely illusionistic—or "deceiving"—drama of a "primitive" past, a drama that had been geared to the "rudimentary and undeveloped mental processes" (204), the preface nevertheless projects a future whose terms remain close to certain categories that it has begun by associating with ignorance and with femaleness, especially the capacity "for succumbing to illusions" (204). For example—and it is an example that will finally bring on stage the equivocal figure whom I read as a deconstruction of naturalism—a little later in the preface, Strindberg explains his innovative abolition of act divisions and intermissions as follows: "I was afraid that the spectator's declining susceptibility to illusion [a development he has previously characterized as an evolution "to the level of reflection, research and experimentation" (204)] might not carry him through the intermission, when he would have time to think about what he has seen and to escape the suggestive influence of the author-hypnotist" (213).

The author-hypnotist is the site of a turbulent ambivalence in Strindberg's theorizing, the point of conflict between two incommensurate views of theater: one as an enlightening and demystifying display of

meaningful causalities, and the other as a symptom of certain inexorable
and mysterious historical forces that exert their influence on both the
form and the content of dramatic art.[12] This vacillation disturbs the
entire conceptual space of *Miss Julie,* of both the play and its accompanying theoretics, in spite of Strindberg's attempt to stabilize his play by
calling it "an exception . . . but an important exception of the kind
which proves the rule" (206). A vivid example of this ambivalence is in
the preface's much-cited passage on modernist characterology, in which
the choice of imagery (and its ostentatious proliferation) suggests an
overleaping of Zola's earnest positivism into something much like
Brechtian irony: "I have noticed that what interests people most nowa-
days is the psychological action. Our inveterately curious souls are no
longer content to see something happen; we want to see how it happens.
We want to see the strings, look at the machinery, examine the double-
bottomed drawer, put on the magic ring to find the hidden seam, look in
the deck for the marked cards" (212). While claiming to further the cause
of a new theater of total visibility and total knowledge, this catalog of
stage tricks keeps dramatic representation firmly lodged in a juvenile and
slightly sleazy prehistory of sideshows and mindless entertainments.

This ironic and alien presence within the conceptual space of *Miss
Julie* comes unexpectedly to dominate the final moments of the play
itself, which are explicitly framed in terms of a certain kind of popular
performance. Just before going off to perform her own "ending" offstage, Julie asks Jean, "Have you ever been to the theater and seen a
hypnotist?" (266). In fact, the preface's figure of hypnosis is woven into
the fabric of Strindberg's play,[13] and, as John Greenway has shown,
contemporaneous theories, debates, and terms about the subject are used
to structure the dialogue between Jean and Julie even prior to the explicit
reference just mentioned.[14]

More importantly, hypnotism is used in *Miss Julie* to correlate the
categories of class and sex in a way that is crucial to the formulation of
naturalist ideology. Here sex and class are first established as powerful
explanatory systems, a power that is then subtly redefined when both
kinds of relations, the relations between the sexes and the relations between the classes, are represented as being in some way analogous to the
enigmatic relationship between hypnotist and hypnotic subject. The
analogy is not merely poetic, and Strindberg's well-known interest in
what he sometimes called "the battle of the brains" is only superficially as
idiosyncratic as it seems. Hypnosis is, in fact, the perfect figure with

which to represent the modernist construction of power along the mutually contradictory axes of freedom and determinism. Here, by being likened to hypnosis, the power systems of sex and class appropriate a certain uncanniness, which will later be used to spawn the play's eventual pseudotragedy. That particular generic outcome will, of course, give naturalism the stamp of aesthetic truth.

However, the protocols of hypnosis inform naturalistic stage space even before Strindberg thematizes them. The kitchen set of *Miss Julie* is, in the first instance, an example of the deterministic single set of realism,[15] whose functioning Strindberg himself characterized with the phrase "the impact of the *recurring* milieu" ("On Modern Drama," 61). According to Bert States, the role of the single set is "the imprisonment of the eye [such that] . . . one of the two senses through which theatre comes to us is locked into a hypnotic sameness" (*Great Reckonings,* 69). In this play, the spell cast by the hypnotic single set is as strong as ever, but another and crucial effect is present as well, a *reflexivity* about the single set, produced by the way this particular one *stages its limits.* Invoking the impressionist painters and their "idea of asymmetrical and open composition" (214), Strindberg breaches the naturalistic contract of total visibility in its own name, substituting a partial visibility offered as an invitation to the spectator's cooperative imagination: "Because the audience cannot see the whole room and all the furniture, they will have to surmise what's missing; that is, their imagination will be stimulated to fill in the rest of the picture" (214). In a movement that is also typical at the level of the play's meaning, the spectator's attention is distracted from its hypnotic fixity, drawn toward the limits and margins of the stage. Upon these margins are inscribed the ideological limitations of naturalism.

The famous partial room of *Miss Julie* is the deliberately deficient space of several hypnotic enthrallments, which function in a way that echoes the unusual stage space: they engage a logic of *partial* visibility, of an attenuated pictorialism by which so much is exposed to view and so much occluded, so many perspectives made available and so many denied, that the persisting enigma of the play seems to record a failure.[16] This is one of the liabilities that *Miss Julie* shares with naturalism, and its traces mark the preface as much as the play. In the former, the stubborn persistence of enigma reveals itself just when Strindberg's positivism is cranked up to its highest pitch: in the famous passage on motivation and causality in naturalism. Just before introducing his own catalog of "circumstances" motivating "the tragic fate of Miss Julie" (206), Strindberg makes the claim, which he calls "a fairly new discovery," that "an event in life . . . is the result of a whole series of more or less deep-rooted causes." The example that follows, however, is not one of multiple causation but rather of multiple *interpretation*, specifically of the determinism of interpretation ("Consider a case of suicide. 'Business failure,' says the merchant. 'Unhappy love,' say the women"—and so on). The conclusion that Strindberg reaches represents a significant slippage from the positivism from which he began and to which he is headed: "But it may be that the reason lay in all of these or in none of them, and that the dead man hid his real reason behind a completely different one that would reflect greater glory on his memory" (206). The sibylline dead man is, I would suggest, the exemplary figure of Strindberg's imagination, and his characteristic space is the partially visible.

Of those instances of hypnotic influence that are incorporated into the plot, the most important is obviously the mutual seduction of Julie and Jean—an influence asserted with reference to several items that were, in Strindberg's time, widely regarded as being conducive to the hypnotic state, including alcohol, somnolence,[17] ocular fixation, and menstruation (Greenway, 31). The final seduction occurs, of course, in Jean's room, offstage and invisible. However, the privacy required by and signified by this consummation does not belong inherently to that space. In fact, the sexual union of Jean and Julie is also the occasion for Jean to *assert* his rights to a private space, however contested these may be: "I'll bolt the door. If they try to break it down, I'll shoot!" (239).

Until this moment of fierce assertion, Jean has been pointedly associated not with places of his own but rather with spatial *transgression* and with various incursions of privacy. The most scandalous of these is the story he himself tells of how, as a boy, he once sneaked into the "Turkish pavilion"—the "Count's private privy" (234)—in the garden of the great house. The humiliating outcome of that adventure not only teaches Jean the lesson that Julie is yet to learn—that the only privacy in the play, that *all* privacy in the play belongs to the count—it also prefigures (in significantly scatological terms) Julie's escape into Jean's room: "And just then I heard someone coming! There was only one way out—for the upper class people. But for me there was one more—a lower one. And I had no other choice but to take it" (234).

Certain actions explicitly called for in the text suggest that Jean's painful lack of privacy as a child ("I lived with seven brothers and sisters and a pig" [233]) has not been overcome but continues in a more subtle form. Twice the text calls for Jean to perform an action while partly visible in the wings. In the first instance, the action deals explicitly with the issue of privacy. Simultaneously, and through the same action, a muted metatheatrical point is made about visual access to stage space, with Julie standing as the fulcrum between Jean's claim to privacy and his vulnerability to (the audience's) view. It is a perfect demonstration of the problematic of total visibility.

> MISS JULIE: You're not embarrassed because I'm here, are you? Just to change? Go in your room and come right back again. Or else stay here and I'll turn my back.
> JEAN: If you'll excuse me, Miss Julie. *(He goes off to the right. His arm can be seen as he changes his jacket.)*
>
> (226)

(Although the stage directions do not specify what Julie's reaction to Jean's choice is, I would think that this would be an important moment of choice for the actress playing the role. Does she allow Jean a measure of privacy, or does she insist on sharing the audience's transgressive view? The choice is sure to have far-reaching effects on the developing relationship: the issue of a personal space is not a light subject for Jean, a man whose self-construction—or at least self-presentation, to Julie—is largely a matter of spaces that he has been denied access to or spaces that he has occupied illicitly. As for Julie, her apparent power over the space of the play turns out to be illusory when it is revealed that she owns nothing. Privacy here is a luxury contingent on *private property,* and the only owner in the play is the absent count.)

The second instance of Jean's partial visibility occurs late in the play, when Jean, who has "slip[ped] out to the right, . . . can be seen in the wings at the right, sharpening his straight razor on a strop held between his teeth and his left hand." From this partially visible position, he "listens to [the conversation between Christine and] Miss Julie with a satisfied expression on his face, now and then nodding approvingly" (261). It is hard to overlook the contrast between this use of the same marginal space, as a site for overhearing, from the first one, as a site for hiding. The difference is also, of course, a difference in Jean, a sign that he has changed, as it were, dramatically: over the course of the play he has performed as a protagonist is supposed to, making of a series of actions a destiny. The event that has wrought this apparent transformation is the sexual encounter, before which his status was such as to give him hardly any control even over his own tiny space. The most obvious explanation for the reversal rests on a profoundly misogynistic logic: Jean becomes Julie's superior when she falls, through sex, to the condition of a mere woman; in identifying herself sexually, she forfeits the immunity her class had given her from the usual debasement associated with being of the wrong sex. Needless to say, this is precisely the interpretation most commonly proffered by critics; it is the one prepared and positioned by the play's "vertical" hermeneutic apparatus. It is, moreover, bluntly stated by Strindberg in the preface: "Apart from the fact that Jean is coming up in the world, he is also superior to Miss Julie in that he is a man" (211).

However, the way in which the play deploys its figure of hypnosis— and the way Jean is positioned and is behaving in this moment of power— suggests a somewhat different and less heroic plot. In a novel entitled *Short Cuts* that he wrote in 1887 (the year before *Miss Julie*), Strindberg says: "The hypnotist says sleep and the person sleeps, or at least behaves like someone asleep. The hypnotist puts a broom in his hand and the broom sways about. *But this is no more remarkable than when a recruit presents arms at a corporal's order!*" (quoted by Lamm, 202; emphasis added). If (as Strindberg seems to be implying here) the orders given to social inferiors are a form of hypnotic suggestion, then Julie has quite simply been hypnotizing Jean during the whole first half of the play. Several times during that section, the giving and obeying of orders are discussed and enacted, with Jean being, of course, on the receiving end. Thus when, after the sexual encounter, the power positions are reversed, Jean's new power is actually the result of an *exchange* of power, a transfer of control from one hypnotist to another. After sex with Miss Julie, Jean seems to have acquired the position of hypnotist (which, let us not forget, the preface has identified as belonging to the author). Indeed, the talk that he is overhearing from his partly visible position in the wings is a kind of posthypnotic suggestion, for Julie is repeating to Christine what Jean had said to her moments before. The repetition signals Jean's influence and power, and—by association—the power of that partly visible, marginal space that Jean mistakenly thinks is his. To learn who really controls the logic of partial visibility, and how, one must return to the role of transgression—the confusion of inside and outside, public and private, absent and present—in the play's structure as well as (and this requires a brief detour) in its history.

Problematic spatial relations and decisions have marked *Miss Julie* from the first. As soon as it was offered for performance, the play engaged the issue of what can be presented to the public and what must remain restricted, private. Karl Otto Bonnier judged it "too risky" even to publish and ventured the opinion that "you will find difficulty in getting it produced" (quoted by Meyer, Introduction, 84). Bonnier was right: Strindberg's play was exiled from its native Sweden for sixteen years. Its first performance occurred in Denmark, but even there it was displaced by court order from the theater where it was scheduled, and it finally found a home, for one night only, at the Copenhagen University Students' Union. Thus *Miss Julie* was first brought to the public as a private performance.

This initial transgression was the first of many produced by *Miss Julie*. Notorious among these is the transgression of autobiography, whereby the empiricist, representative stage of naturalism is suddenly required to display the personal scandals and private demons of a man as peculiar as Strindberg. Not only is there so much biography in *Miss Julie* as to make *both* the protagonists easy to read as representatives of the author,[18] but the play itself produced further transgressive effects: Strindberg was convinced that his wife, who played Julie in the first performance, was having an affair with the man who played Jean. According to a reporter who attended both the first performance and the party following it, Strindberg "stood half-hidden behind a door, his face pale and twisted with jealousy" (quoted by Meyer, Introduction, 87). It is hard to resist assimilating this image of the half-hidden author to the play's logic of partial visibility, especially when we further read, in the same account of the first performance, that "we search in vain for August Strindberg, though it has been announced that he is to attend the performance" (quoted by Meyer, Introduction, 86).

In literal fact as in the discursive logic of naturalism, the author-hypnotist, who (as implied in the preface) must prevent reflection and encourage projection,[19] presents himself as an absence. His power is inscribed as a series of "suggestions" that elicit the spectator's cooperation, even her intellectual assent, and that lead to an inevitable conclusion, *legitimized precisely by the author's absence.* In *Miss Julie*, the ideological meaning of this authorial absence is *staged,* through the figure of the count and his relationship to the fictional space of the play.

Among the most obvious markings of this space are class signs: the stage represents the kitchen of a Swedish manor house. It is the domain of servants, although their dominion is ironic indeed, as we see early in the play when Jean enjoys the "little bit of kidney [that Christine] cut from the veal roast," along with a stolen bottle of the count's wine (221). While the kitchen is the space of the servants' domesticity and privacy, it is not a home to them, not a place they have chosen and arranged for themselves.[20] The privacy that it affords is seriously circumscribed, as is demonstrated so dramatically when the kitchen is invaded by a crowd of merrymaking peasants, forcing Miss Julie and Jean into their fateful hiding. It is worth noting that the kitchen does not offer itself as a refuge to Miss Julie either, although she may seem to be, like her mother, "most at home in the kitchen and the cowsheds" (78). Like its partial representation, the kitchen connotes an inviting openness; like its representation, its accessibility is limited and determined by the interests of the person in ultimate control. In terms of the stage space, that person is the "author-hypnotist"; in terms of the kitchen, it is the count.

The most impressive and permanent signs of the actual power structure governing this space are those that evoke the absent count: the notorious boots—placed from the start "where they are clearly visible to the audience" (220)—and the bell and speaking tube, both silent until the last moments of the play, then horrifyingly alive. These latter two elements of the set relate directly to the position and signification of the play's space, especially to the fact that the kitchen has very limited access to the rest of the house. It seems to be linked to the house only through the courtyard that is partly visible through the large glass door in the back wall. This door is the only way to the rest of the house.[21]

Thus the kitchen is a kind of relegated space, an architectural cul-de-sac held at a physical and psychological distance from the rest of the house. According to Lawrence Stone, this kind of arrangement, made possible by technological inventions like the bell wire and the speaking tube, was part of a process of physical distancing between servants and owners that occurred in the course of the nineteenth century. The owners' desire to guard their privacy against the intrusions of their servants, without at the same time sacrificing the convenience of having ready access to the servants, was reflected in this new configuration of physical distance and technological proximity.

This arrangement was in itself the reflection of a changing class relation, whereby the feudal system of generations of servants was being replaced by a more capitalistic system of servants as workers, often itinerant (like Jean) and temporary. The old kind of servant, familiar to

us from Chekhov, the loyal, trustworthy, and self-sacrificing family
retainer, is nowhere to be found in *Miss Julie;* he has been replaced by
people who feel no devotion to their masters, no sense of obligation.[22] In
fact the relation between masters and servants is staged here as one
fraught with suspicion, contempt, and mutual fear, an alienated relation
entirely dependent on formal bonds and regulations. Jean's professions of
dutiful obedience sound as phony as his pretensions to culture; in fact the
latter directly contradict the former. For all his lectures to Julie about the
importance of knowing her place, Jean's own identification with his
place has clearly been irreversibly disrupted.[23]

As a servant, Jean is in an asymmetrical relation to his position, out
of step with its traditional meaning. A great deal of the dialogue between
Jean and Julie is the articulation of this asymmetry, for Julie constructs
class along certain quaint and sentimental lines that Jean treats with some
irony:

> JEAN: And there I caught sight of a pink dress and a pair of white
> stockings. You! I crawled under . . . thistles that pricked me and
> wet dirt that stank to high heaven. And all the while I could see you
> walking among the roses. I said to myself, "If it's true that a thief
> can enter heaven and be with the angels, isn't it strange that a poor
> man's child here on God's green earth can't enter the count's park
> and play with the count's daughter."
> MISS JULIE: *(sentimentally)* Do you think all poor children have felt
> that way?
> JEAN: *(hesitatingly at first, then with mounting conviction)* If all poor
> ch—? Yes—yes, naturally. Of course!
> MISS JULIE: It must be terrible to be poor.
> JEAN: *(with exaggerated intensity)* Oh, Miss Julie! You don't know!
> A dog can lie on the sofa with its mistress; a horse can have its nose
> stroked by the hand of a countess; but a servant—!
>
>   (235)

Jean is both hyperconscious of class difference (and the behavior
proper to each class) and yet free of essential class identity. Strindberg's
own explanation of what he calls Jean's "unformed and divided" character (210) emphasizes his class-transgressive nature: he is said to despise
his peers yet fear them "because they know his secrets," and "he is
familiar with the ins and outs of good society" (210). A great deal of the

action of the play, especially everything that leads up to the sexual encounter, seems to be a demonstration of Jean's notion that class differences are superficial, and that "maybe at bottom there isn't such a big
difference as we think, between people and people" (236).

But what, then, is the meaning of the play's conclusion, when Jean's
class transgression is so decisively quelled? Significantly, this rout of
Jean's (and indeed all modernity's) attempt to de-essentialize class is
played out as yet another transfer of hypnotic power, this time from Jean
to the now present (but still diegetic) count. The count's peculiar contribution to the play's completion is unmistakably linked to the figure of
hypnosis, a relation that had been explicitly anticipated earlier, in Jean's
confession that "I only have to look at his boots standing there so stiff
and proud and I feel my spine bending" (241). In the play's final moments, Jean has what amounts to a hypnotic epiphany, a recognition of
the "truth" of the trance (*but from within the trance,* making it more demonstration than recognition): "What?! I thought I saw the bell move . . . .
Afraid of a bell! But it isn't just a bell. There's somebody behind it. A
hand that makes it move. And there's something that makes the hand
move" (267). While the overall effect of this passage is to enact, one last
time, Jean's inbred servility, its oddly theoretical content—its assertion
of a signal truth—draws attention to the figure of the count, and specifically to his functioning in a way that reminds us of the preface's "author-
hypnotist."

Strindberg's partly (metonymically) visible count controls the
partly visible space of the play, exerting his influence from the wings.
While his stage signs—the bell and speaking tube—link his power to
sound and aurality, his silence keeps that power diffused, pervasive. The
private parts of the house sought out by the protagonists in their bid for
self-definition are no more secure from this power than the private parts
or roles they try to script for themselves (for example, in the very obviously stereotypical fantasy of a future happy life in a hotel). It is not
simply that the count orchestrates the protagonists' failure to make connections with levels similar to their own (although the failed alliance of
Julie and Jean does mark the triumph of a hegemonic patriarchy over
women and workers); what is much more devastating is the ultimate
removal of responsibility from characters who have largely been formed
around the question of responsibility, of personal agency ("Who's to
blame for what has happened?").

The protagonists' common enemy, the author-hypnotist/count,

manipulates them by rendering them abstract, by returning them to the schematic, even archetypal, categories (high and low, etc.) from which a truer class identification (a self-identification in economic terms, for example) could have rescued them. That is to say, abstraction, typicality, and representativeness, all of which are (dis)embodied in the count himself, are gradually transferred to the two protagonists, dissolving their ostentatiously constructed social and sexual identities into a hypnotic tautology:

> JULIE: What would you do if you were in my place?
> JEAN: In your place? Let me think. . . . An aristocrat, a woman, and fallen. . . . I don't know.—Or maybe I do.
> JULIE: *(picks up the razor and makes a gesture with it)* Like this?
> JEAN: Yes. But I wouldn't do it, you understand. That's the difference between us.
> JULIE: Because you're a man and I'm a woman? What difference does that make?
> JEAN: Just the usual difference—between a man and a woman.
> (265)

The "usual difference"—this one as well as the other supposedly usual difference, between master and servant—is reinstalled here as the closure (in both senses: the denouement and the failure) of a drama of attempted displacement. Here, as Jean formulates it and as Julie embraces it, truth is simply—even trivially—the power of *place*. Now, all that idle talk early in the play about "knowing one's place" is offered as a quasi-supernatural law. In the new tragic universe envisioned by naturalism, place, it would seem, is fate; the power of place (in both its senses, as location and as position) seems to be offering itself as the great truth spawned by the theater of total visibility.

The flicker of revolt recorded in the brief union of Jean and Julie is quickly rewritten as tragedy. But with a qualification. Occluded authority cannot fully disguise itself as occult power. Once he has been glimpsed, the absent puppet master cannot disappear, cannot restore the illusion of total visibility that depends on his absence. Razor in hand, Miss Julie can only mimic, not emulate, the tragic heroines of antiquity, who pay with their lives for knowledge bestowed upon them from another world. The rewriting of fate as place is revealed as merely the final illusion of the author-hypnotist. His control of the play's space of partial visibility is felt one final time, not only in the sound of two sharp rings of the count's bell—which remind us that the other world of tragedy is here only another room—but in the blatantly metatheatrical curtain line: "It's horrible, but there's no other way for it to end.—Go!" (267).

The author-hypnotist exerts his influence by making place within his representational domain for the signs of various bids for self-determination. The logic is the very same as that which (in the preface) justifies the improvised monologue, as giving "the actor a chance to work on his own for once and *for a moment* not to be obliged to follow the author's directions" (213; emphasis added). In structuring the conceptual space of *Miss Julie* around a similar logic of momentary freedom, Strindberg staged the transgressive desires—sexual, social, and mimetic desires—of modernity. In this play, naturalism proposed a world of total visibility—and then performed its limits.

The logic of total visibility that appears, self-canceled, in naturalistic plays like *Miss Julie* finds its fantasies fulfilled in the movement known as environmental theater, whose logic is similar to that of a more familiar, more popular technology, which is its historical contemporary, namely, cinematic wide-screen technology. The desire coded in wide-screen technology—"for a world commodified to conform to the shape of a field of vision determined by human anatomy so as to define 'reality' as 'larger than life' and as extending 'as far as the eye can see' (Nadel, 415)— is similar to the desire of environmental stage practice, for a field of experience organized *around* human anatomy and laid out in such a way as to define reality as readily available to human subjects.

The environmentalist impulse to create holistic and "full" spaces anticipates—and, through its inherent impossibility, makes necessary— some of the spatial practices of postmodernism. In his analysis of the Frank Gehry House in Santa Monica, Fredric Jameson identifies the explicitly ambivalent spatial experience coded in what he calls the "postmodern space proper," a space so mixed in nature and signification that "our bodies inhabit [it] in malaise or delight, trying to shed the older habits of inside/outside categories and perceptions, still longing for the bourgeois privacy of solid walls (enclosures like the old centered bourgeois ego), yet grateful for the novelty of incorporation of yucca plants and what Barthes would have called Californianity into our newly reconstructed environment" (115).

This reframing of spatial experience in such a way as to recall and rename prior experiences[24]—and its implications for theater practice—is the chief burden of Jim Cartwright's 1986 play, *Road*. The play engages and displays the entire range of the problematics that began with environmentalism and have now exploded onto the scene of public culture as hyperspace. Chief among these is the problem, so crucially involved in theater, of representing—*and watching*—"others." As *Road* recognizes, this problem is articulated *by* the discourse of belonging; that is to say (and as we shall see again and again in this study), otherness inhabits the discourse of home.

"Make Yourselves at Home."

In a gesture made familiar by decades of experimental theater practice, *Road* begins before it begins. The play proper is preceded by a preshow, which in turn is preceded by a brief event that is so slight and fragile that I would call it a performance trace. So elusive is this event that many spectators may miss it altogether, not only because it takes place "in the street in front of the theatre" but also because the actions it involves are unremarkable in the extreme. A girl of sixteen named Chantal (who later appears in the play) is "hanging around" outside the theater. She is joined by Linda, a girl of twelve (who, unlike Chantal, does not appear again in the play). The two "sit on the theatre steps and play chalk games, sometimes obscene. As the time for the performance approaches, the House Manager of the theatre should come out and tell them to clear off" (1).

The point of the scene seems to be little more than theoretical, or structural: it marks a transgression of the first boundary of many involved in theatrical spatiality: that between the theater (building) and the outside world. The fact that its content is so attenuated emphasizes its structural meaning—this is transgression qua transgression, a sign that the enclosure of theater is not airtight, that theatrical boundaries are permeable. This notion is, of course, the centerpiece of environmental theater: the "leakage" of meaning between various zones of the theatrical superstructure produces the preferred effects of subversion and disorientation (and, on occasion, of hyperinclusion)[25] that this practice seeks. Here, however, this unassuming transgression—which is underlined by the asymmetrical use of performers (one a character from the play, one not)—enacts a kind of pure or empty leakage, leaving dramatic meaning unmarked, unaffected. It is a sign of what might be called the *pantheatrical impulse* of avant-garde performance, a sign (rather than an instance, being so empty of content) of the theater's desire to get outside itself and code the real as theatrical.

The next event of the play, called the "pre-show" in the published text, begins to reveal the complicated nature of the trace performance, showing it to be less empty than had at first appeared. Like the trace, the preshow is used to transgress a traditional boundary of theater, that between the performance itself and all the activities surrounding it (activities that, according to Erving Goffman, the spectators-to-be participate in in their role as "play-goers"). The preshow takes place in the space marked out specially for the cultivation of that role: the theater lobby. Conventionally, this space serves to prepare the spectators to enter the auditorium and assume their roles as "onlookers." Thus it is a classic liminal space, marking out a spatial and temporal threshold between the outside world and the inside world of theater. As such, it has been one of the most heavily used of spaces in environmental theater, where its usual preparatory functions (such as providing pictures of and billboard-size reviews of the production) have been replaced by more active and interactive links to the production, including the presence of actors in costume, and design elements. The purpose of these activities is to smoothly induct the spectators into the fictional world, and thus, once again, to erase the boundary between the world on stage and the world inhabited by the spectators. The lobby is, then, a particularly useful site for the creation of what Arnold Aronson calls "unified space," a form of staging in which stage and auditorium become integrated (5). Use of the lobby for dramatic purposes can be a step toward creating the ultimate in environmental staging, "surrounding space," the ideal of totally shared space: "As the distinction between spectator and performance space becomes less definable—as there is greater sharing of space—it becomes increasingly difficult to establish frontal relationships, and the performance, therefore, can be considered more environmental (7–8).

The content and affect of Cartwright's preshow, however, are radically different from this ideal. Like the events of the opening performance trace, those of the preshow are not particularly interesting or dramatic; but, unlike those, these include a quality that will characterize the events of the play as a whole: an unpleasant voyeurism. This voyeurism is not erotic; rather, it is, as it were, *sociological,* the product of a systematic double construction of characters and spectators as mutually other. In his first words in the play, the "guide" Scullery drives home the distinction, using a hint of sarcasm that will gradually infect all his communications to the audience. Addressing the audience directly, Scullery says: "Wid' your night yous chose to come and see us. Wid' our night as usual we's all gettin' ready and turning out for a drink. THIS IS OUR ROAD! But tonight it's your road an' all. Don't feel awkward wi' us, make yourselves as home" (5). The irony of this invitation is underlined by Scullery's very next line, slyly incorporating a phrase that only these privileged, well-off "outsiders" could use: "You'll meet 'all sorts' down here."

The world of *Road* is presented—explicitly and from the outset—as the photographic negative of the world from which the spectators come. In the course of the play the effects and meaning of this encounter are laid bare; indeed what seems an encounter is transformed into a confrontation. The implied sense of radical difference between the worlds of the characters and the spectators is first suggested through the presence of a guide figure, who has the effect immediately of evoking certain intertexts for the play, notably, of course, Wilder's *Our Town*. But *Road* exceeds the logic of intertextuality, an excess hinted at unwittingly by Benedict Nightingale's review, calling the play "*Coronation Street* with vomit, excrement and used contraceptives cluttering the gutters, *Under Milk Wood* packed with blunt, despairing curse-words, *Our Town* in terminal disarray" (quoted by Cohn, 45). Instead of employing a logic of intertextuality, producing meaning laterally and associatively, *Road* makes it into an ironic strategy: the parodic relationship between the bitter Scullery and Wilder's godlike Stage Manager is hinted at from the start, when Scullery describes the tour of Road that he is proposing. Far from an invitation to visit an idealized realm of normality, this is to be a grotesque fun-fair ride, a rapid and safely distanced view of a freakish world: "An' owt can happen tonight. He might get a bird. She might ha' a fight, she might. Let's shove off down t'Road and find out! We'll go down house by house. Hold tight! Here we go! Come on! Watch the kerb missis! Road's coming round us! *(He starts laughing, laughing uproariously!)*" (5).

The status of Scullery's invitation—and his tour—is further clarified in the episodes involving the "Professor," an explicit challenge to the anthropological pretensions of the dramatic tradition that began with naturalism and culminated in experimentalism.[26] Plays that re-create "the lower depths" of society for the contemplation and edification of their middle-class audiences are likened, here, to the prostituted academic project of the down-at-the-heels professor, who, "when I got made redundant" embarked on "an anthropological study of 'Road.'" He thought he'd go down in history, but instead "all I did was go down. I lost me wife, me family, half me stomach. Now all I got left is this tape, and this box full of me records, all I could write down really. Long ago I gived up the idea of making a book, and instead, now I just give em out to people for the price of a pint or chips" (19).

The professor's decline from serious field-working anthropologist to street entertainer contains the range of the play's challenge to environmentalism, and especially to its hidden ideology. The few examples that the professor provides of his questionable "art" (equally questionable as scholarship?) suggest both how preposterous a project it is (and would be, whatever the circumstances) and its resemblance to the activity that the spectators of this play are engaged in. The first example the professor gives is of a completed "script," a text he reads out from a card in his shoe box collection:

> "Social Life in Road: Wood Street Drinking Club. An episode that occurred in winter of our Lord nineteen eighty-two. A woman was crapping behind the piano. Two men were fighting over a pie. A row of old prostitutes wer sitting there, still made up as in war years. Price tags on the soles of their shoes when they kick up at you as you walk by. I chose the three pounds thirty-two one and bent her over the billiard table in the back room. Nobody saw. I could tell she didn't like it so I spoke to her afterwards. She said she had to do it to keep her four kids decent. I told her three pounds thirty-two wasn't much, she said she wasn't much and come to that neither was I. That's where we left it." See how easy you can slip when yous a scientist in the slums. (19)

Whereas this example of the professor's documentation grotesquely explodes the myth of the objective observer, the next example, one of textual construction, of information gathering, underscores the absurd incongruity between the lives being led in places like Road and the discourse (of academic sociology, of dramatic naturalism) that seeks to comprehend these lives. A young female inhabitant of Road offers the professor an item for his collection. As she begins to speak, he pulls out his tape recorder and—before turning it over to her—intones: "Memories of Wood Street." The memories the young woman supplies have none of the genial hometown flavor this title suggests; instead they are grim and dismal, like everything in Road:

> Piano, you got splinters if you put your hand on it. Walls, spit yellow. Tables, soaked in beer. The club. The people. There was Slack-mouth, Wriggle. . . . P. H. Pye. Face like a throat. . . . Nelly. Sixty-eight years old and still on the game. But she had that senile habit of wanting sex on the cobbles. Well, when a man walked in wi' no knees you knew he'd been up Nelly. (19–20)

Against the view of difference as something available to various appropriate and useful encodings, *Road* presents another account of difference, one that takes the critique of environmentalism to the extreme and shows it to be a fantasy of inclusion and plenitude that merely inscribes the dominant ideology onto various representations of difference and otherness.

The critique offered by *Road* uses a particular trope of place, one that will become increasingly important to this study: that of the house as home. As we shall see later in this chapter and then throughout this book, the idea of home is deeply structured into the drama of this century, where (since at least *A Doll's House*) it exists in uneasy contention with the figure of the *house*. The painful noncongruence between the literal dwelling and the feeling of being at home provides early modern drama with its fundamental motivations. As the century wears on, this noncongruence is recast in a less tragic mode, yielding the drama of failed homecoming, in which the nostalgia for and the disappointment in various models of belonging (from the psychological to the political to the metaphysical—from *The Visit* to *Mother Courage* to *Waiting for Godot*) are gradually exorcised, and the ground is cleared for seeking subjective coherence outside the narrow discourse of home.

Road is situated on the far side of the poetic and nostalgic discourse of home. The place to which its characters belong, the ominously generic (not to mention slyly and ironically archetypal) name this place bears,[27] "Road" both evokes and undermines notions of belonging. Mocking the naturalist ideal of the universal-particular, Road is a space of all-too-specific, all-too-well-known social realities.[28] Throughout the play, the experience of the inhabitants of Road is presented as a form of imprisonment, but one whose economic and social causes are too vividly apparent to allow for the traditional poetic transformation of entrapment into a heroism of departure. Although the trope of departure or escape is very much present in the play, it exists in emphatic contradiction to the traditional codings of that trope, namely, as lucid and individualistic self-realization. The images of escape in *Road* are pointedly of *shared* escapes, and their mechanisms have little to do with rationality.

The two main images of escape in the play occur at the ends of the two acts, respectively. The first of these, easily the most searing scene in the play, shows the death by starvation of two young people on a hunger strike. The strike, of whom only the two are really aware, is deeply political, the one gesture of true revolt against the grim reality of Road. In the increasingly hallucinatory speeches of the dying boy, the horrific condition of these up-to-date lower depths is transformed into a postmodern morality play, flooded with the miraculous visions and allegorical figures that naturalism had banished from the stage:

> I feel like England's forcing the brain out of me head. I'm sick of it. Sick of it all. People reading newspapers: "EUROVISION LOVERS," "OUR QUEEN MUM," "MAGGIE'S TEARS," being fooled again and again. What the fuck-fuck is it? Bin lying here two weeks now. On and on through the strain. I wear pain like a hat. Everyone's insane. The world really is a bucket of devil sick. . . . Bitterness has swelled like a mighty black rose inside me. Its petals are creaking against my chest. I want it out! . . . IIIIIIIIIIII bring up small white birds covered in bile and fat blood, they was my hopes. I bring up a small hard pig that was my destiny. . . . I blame you BUSINESS and you RELIGION its favorite friend, hand in hand, YOU HAVE MURDERED THE CHILD IN MAN! (38–39)

The ultimate death of Joey and Clare, just before the scripted "Interval" (in which the play's harsh critique of environmental staging escalates), is a moment of great power and lucidity, but the vision Joey voices with his dying breath has no trace of heroism, no offer of redemption, no pretence of moral truth. Moreover, its audience—the audience of the play—is explicitly recognized as being willfully separate from destinies like Joey's, Clare's, and those of the other inhabitants of *Road*: "Look at me. I am pain. I am now from tip to toe. Look at me I am the solution. There is no solution. How about that then. That's the smart-arsest simplest answer going. The last answer to the first question. There is no solution.

(He stops and stares.) But you're all adding a maybe aren't you. *(He winks then dies.)"* (42).

That Joey escapes without the lie of a heroic departure is further ensured by the fact that his extraordinary death does not conclude the play, which still has a long series of pathetic and disturbing scenes to go through before its conclusion. By the time the play arrives at its final scene, the audience is nearly as oblivious of Joey and Clare as the characters have been all along. The play leaves the audience not with Joey's appalling and operatic diatribe but with something very different, a scene of almost accidental liberation brought about through the mysterious mechanism of sheer endurance.

The last scene involves four characters, two men and the two women whom they have picked up in a bar and brought home. After an initial period of giggling, groping, bickering, and general frustration, the women admit, to the bewildered men, that they wanted "somethin' else to happen for a change" (74). Surprisingly, the men take up the challenge and decide to show the women "something different . . . . something that we always do when outside gets to you." The something turns out to be a self-invented ritual of catharsis, in which amazing oracular diatribes are brought on by drinking heavily and then listening to an Otis Redding album. As absurd as this procedure sounds, the theatrical force of the ritual is stunning, astonishing to all concerned: "I never spoke such speech in my life and I'm glad I have," says Louise, concluding: "If I keep shouting somehow a somehow I might escape." Her words are taken up by the others and turned into a chant, repeated over and over again: "Somehow a somehow—might escape," faster and faster, louder and louder, "All pressed together, arms and legs round each other," until finally they become "loud and massive," and there is a blackout and silence.

What can we make of this hyperritualistic ending to a play that, as I am reading it, critiques the theatrical movement that was most closely inspired by ritual—environmentalism—and that incurred all the ideological liabilities of a naive embrace of the so-called primitive world? *Road,* I want to suggest, delineates a counterprinciple to the confident primitivism of (say) *Dionysus in 69.* It is not, as is usual in the formulation of this opposition, a Brechtian counterprinciple, of intellectual self-consciousness or the like. The ideological and affective structure developed in *Road* is markedly distinct from both the inclusive and the critical ideals exemplified by environmentalism and epic theater, respectively.

The play's use of nontraditional theatrical spaces to "wrap" around the play proper does not produce either an entranced or an engaged spectator: the spectator of *Road,* who must move through the unexpectedly filled spaces outside the play proper, is subject to a discourse of difference—of *his or her own* difference, which has the final effect of putting his or her "seeing" of the play deeply in question. When Scullery concludes the play with another one of his ironic invitations—"If you're ever in the area call again. Call again" (81)—the disjunction between his world and "ours" is unmistakable and irrefutable. What Road has to offer is of no use or interest to any of the spectators evoked by the play: the naturalist spectator (in search of insights into the human condition), the environmentalist spectator (in search of an experience of emotional and spiritual plenitude),[29] the epic theater's spectator (in search of historical and political understanding).

The spectator of *Road*—and the logic of the play as a whole—is best rendered by a scene from within the play itself. Scullery points to a window and says "See this derelict house here? I've been meaning to give it a ransacking, see if there's any coppers to be made. You never know" (23). He then clambers up to the window and crawls into the house, out of sight. He returns periodically to report on his spoils, which include, significantly, an old doll, causing Scullery to ruminate: "How is it when, tell me this, when you goes in an old empty house, there's always an old doll, burnt paper and a Christmas card?" (24). Although it is surely only someone writing a book like this one who would connect these remarks with Ibsen's house-prisons, Scullery's continuing and lengthy ransacking of the house is a remarkably apt emblem of the naturalistic project: the discarded household junk he goes through, piece by piece, harks back to all the junk-strewn stages of modern drama, which I shall discuss in a later chapter as marking the exhaustion of naturalism. But even more revealing is the sudden action that ends the scene: just as Scullery emerges from the house with his sackful of plunder, an old man appears at the window and angrily demands to know what is going on. Scullery, amazed, confesses that he "thought there was no one living there," to which the man replies, "Well there bloody well is!" In fact it transpires that there is a *couple* living there, for the old man bickers with an irate offstage wife.

An empty house turns out to be inhabited. Its contents, which had seemed to be junk, turn out to be the possessions of actual people. But these people remain mostly unseen, and thoroughly unknown. This, or something like it, is the logic of *Road,* and it encodes a theatrical experience that challenges the modern drama's deepest assumptions about plays and place. The theater's investment in presence, visibility, and display is revealed in *Road* to be an illusion, a fantasy of anthropological dimensions that seeks to vanquish otherness without the pain of being othered oneself.

In the following chapters, I explore the manifold ways in which, in the thematics of modern drama, the figure of home and ideal of belonging are shot through with otherness. The initial mode of this paradoxical coexistence, which I locate in classical realism, is conspicuous enough to warrant its own label, which I provide, coining the term geopathology to refer to the double-edged problem of place and place as problem that distinguishes early modern drama. This geopathology then unravels—is exposed, ironized, deconstructed—in the drama after midcentury, which responds to the pressures of a world increasingly defined by the actual dislocations of immigration and refugeehood. The story that emerges is one of both rupture and continuity, difference and sameness, for the master trope of modern drama is that image of transformation which nevertheless inscribes the power of the old: the journey.

Chapter Two

Geopathology: The Painful Politics of Location

I didn't understand it at all. But I enjoyed watching. You acted so genuinely. And the scenery was beautiful. *(Pause.)* There must be a lot of fish in that lake.

—Trigorin, in *The Seagull*

The breaks and non sequiturs in Trigorin's response to Treplev's playlet—the disjunctions it recognizes between drama and meaning, acting and sincerity, performance and place, and (most unexpectedly and comically) between art and nature—encapsulate the topic of this chapter. While I shall focus my discussion primarily on the figures of home, exile, and dispossession in early modern drama, the fact I wish to bring out is that these figures are activated and molded by an underlying principle, for which I wish to coin the term *geopathology*. The problem of place—and place *as problem*—informs realist drama deeply, appearing as a series of ruptures and displacements in various orders of location, from the micro- to the macrospatial, from home to nature, with intermediary space concepts such as neighborhood, hometown, community, and country ranged in between.

The most fundamental dislocation is the one that intrudes here so comically, that between humankind and nature, which in terms of the drama (but not only in those terms) makes of nature a mere setting—"scenery." This rupture between human beings and their natural environment is a perceptible subtext in a great deal of post-Romantic drama of the late nineteenth century, especially in the works of Ibsen and Chekhov.[1] However, to grasp the significance of this "ecological" material (it is the least discussed and least understood aspect of modern drama,

55

the whole subject of nature having hitherto been confined within the debate about realism and romanticism), we need first to identify its position in a larger system of thinking and imagining the relationship between places and people.

As I hope to show in this chapter, a painful politics of location informs the realist drama; according to its logic, the rupture with nature is a *dispossession,* which may be radical but is nevertheless a perfectly coherent, even *necessary,* item in a series of not altogether undesirable dislocations. These dislocations are given their meaning from the geopathic paradigm underlying realist drama, which also supports a certain construction of identity: identity as a negotiation with—and on occasion a heroic overcoming of—the power of place.[2]

Acting Home

It is a revealing irony of modern drama that one of its most static, most claustrophobic classics has the word *journey* in its title. O'Neill's *Long Day's Journey into Night* (1940) exemplifies an enduring and deep-seated conflict in modern drama between a kind of "poetry of progress"—or of movement, of development, of *change*—and the magnetic power of place.[3] The tension between these two forces, which Linda Ben-Zvi calls "an espoused escape or freedom and a desired return or fixity" ("Home Sweet Home," 222), serves in effect to idealize the figure of exile by contrasting it, not to its logical opposite, belonging, but to prison.[4] At its most virulent (as, for example, in *Miss Julie,* as we saw in the preceding chapter) this conflict between prison and exile pitches the humanist project of refashioning the self and the world against a reified notion of place as fate. At such times, metaphorized place—in various guises, including such macroconstructs as nation and even nature, as well as more mundane ones such as home and hometown—exerts so powerful and paralyzing an influence upon the protagonists that simple *departure* becomes their overriding mission and desire.

This, precisely, is the conflictual structure of O'Neill's harrowing play, resulting in what I would call a geopathic dramaturgy,[5] in which every character and every relationship is defined by a problem with place. The most conspicuous geopathic symptoms are, of course, Mary Tyrone's addiction and Edmund Tyrone's consumption. The latter functions as a guarantee of a geopathic future, promising to keep Edmund imprisoned in a sanatorium, severed from his one source of freedom and

fulfillment, the sea. The former, Mary's addiction, is explicitly and repeatedly linked by Mary herself to what she regards as her greatest
affliction: effective homelessness. Mary has suffered deeply from the
necessity of living a life on the road with her actor-husband, bearing and
raising her children in an endless series of featureless, anonymous,
shabby hotels. According to her son Edmund, not only her addiction to
morphine but also her hopelessness and incurability are a direct result of
her lifetime of enforced displacement: "You've dragged her around on
the road, season after season, on one night stands, with no one she could
talk to, waiting night after night in dirty hotel rooms for you to come
back with a bun on after the bars closed! Christ, is it any wonder she
didn't want to be cured!" (141).

Now, during a brief summer respite from their bleak travels, Mary
is at a point, if you will, of geopathic crisis. Instead of enjoying a sense of
finally being at home, she finds herself more trapped than ever, in yet
another shabby and lonely place that she haunts, in her drugged state,
"like a mad ghost." To her husband's remark that "This isn't a prison,"
she answers: "No. I know you can't help thinking it's a home." Her fog-
shrouded beach house is a hollow mockery of the peace and comfort of
home, a mere facsimile of the real and longed-for reality: "Oh, I'm so
sick and tired of pretending this is a home!" she says, adding that her
husband doesn't "know how to act in a home!" (67).

The unintended irony of this accusation (directed as it is to a professional actor, and one who is very proud of his talent) is part of a curious
network of images in the play, whereby the figure of home is linked to
two other and apparently unrelated items: addiction and the theater. As a
matter of fact, this three-way link is not unique to this play: dramatic
realism often employs a logic in which these three general ideas—home,
addiction, and performance—are the major categories of a transactional
system that is used to structure the play. In this system, addiction (obsession, compulsion)[6] appears as reaction or even resistance to the vicissitudes of home (the sense of entrapment, of radical inadequacy); at the
same time, it appears as an even more destructive trap than home itself,
threatening to erase the questing self along with his or her originary
space.

The response to this double bind, both on the part of the characters
but more importantly on the part of the drama itself, is performance. For
the characters, acting (lies, dissimulation, self-deception) provides a way
to *occupy* spaces without *inhabiting* them (a solution to the problem of

home). This is the point of the ubiquitous pipe dreams and "vital lies" with which the oppressive here and now of realist drama is regularly negotiated.[7] Performance succeeds, where addiction fails, in easing the symptoms of what I am calling geopathic disorders, the suffering caused by one's location.

But the more complex role of the trope of performance is in mediating the realist play's own anxiety about the power and politics of location. It is not only the characters of realist drama but also its structure that suffers from geopathic disorders. A muted metatheatricality runs like a fault line through the plays of Ibsen, Chekhov, Shaw, O'Neill, Miller,[8] and so on, sending tremors up and down the otherwise solidly mimetic edifice of realism. In *Long Day's Journey into Night,* theatricality—or performance—stands as a constant caveat against the oppressive insistence of place. Between James Tyrone's failure to act as if this were a home and Mary's self-confessed weariness about "pretending that this is a home," the place represented onstage loses some of that sharp delineation as a domestic interior that is the hallmark of realist drama.[9] In its place there emerges a sense of this place as a realm of pretense and masquerade in which the members of the family perform as a kind of ensemble company to simulate the appearance of an ideal home.[10] (The two servants in the house are pointedly not party to this group performance; instead they are a kind of bewildered audience to the family's shaky self-performance, unable to suspend their disbelief: "It's unreasonable to expect Bridget and Cathleen to act as if this was a home," says Mary. "They know it isn't as well as we know it. It never has been and it never will be" [72].)

The driving force of the character's elaborate "act" is addiction, which is figured here as both the symptom and the cause of their failure to realize the various individual and joint ideals of their lives. But addiction—be it to drugs, to alcohol, or to the ambiguous "fog" of self-erasure—is also a kind of counterprinciple to the (idealized and traditional) principle of home and family that haunts the imaginations of all the Tyrones. Moreover, addiction functions as a mechanism for displacing that ideal into a performative sphere, creating a sort of stage within the realist frame; on this addiction-produced stage, the grim conditionality of realism's worldview is suspended, and a liberating kind of homelessness is temporarily achieved.[11] The hypersemiotic quality of this stage is revealed in the effect it has on the characters, turning them into spectators who are always watching each other for the telltale signs of the "poison."

Among the most dramatically productive signs of the poison is narrative. As the characters sink deeper into the fog of the morphine or the alcohol, they begin to reveal the structure of the life stories they have constructed for themselves. So detailed and ample are these stories—and so convincingly interlinked, so mutually supportive—that they begin to establish themselves as the underlying truth of the play. To a degree that is surprising even when we know that this is a highly autobiographical work, the characters of this play take over the hermeneutic project normally reserved for the spectator, reader, and critic, offering lengthy and complex interpretations of their conditions.[12]

However, the "psychoanalysis" performed by the characters remains embedded within what is for the audience a "geoanalysis," a comprehensive evocation and exposure of the meaning, in human terms, of place. The place—the Tyrones' sadly deficient home—exists in relation to a number of other places evoked in the course of the characters' self-narrations: Mary's childhood home, the convent she almost joined, the "decent, presentable homes" she is barred from, the sanatorium to which Edmund must soon go, and the endless succession of sleazy hotels, bars, and brothels where the men in the family have sought comfort. The longed-for home thus appears as a self-displacing place, a place erased by the meeting in it of the incommensurate urges to hide and to escape. Here perhaps more clearly than anywhere else we see the crisis regularly staged by the psychological middle-class realist drama: the conflict between the humanist yearning for a stable container for identity—a home for the self, a room of one's own—and the desire to deterritorialize the self.

The forces that displace the Tyrone home and render it useless as a home are not only the subjective fantasies of the individual family members. Nature conspires with psychological suffering to complete the geopathic picture. The house also exists in relation to the surrounding fog, whose mournful voice, the foghorn, penetrates deep into the family's nightmare. This fog is not only a rather cumbersome symbol wielded by the playwright in his efforts to unify this account of his own biographical past but also a convenient and appropriate metaphor used by the characters themselves to deal with their geopathic conditions. Like the narratives with which the characters displace the present reality of their situation, the fog writes over the sad geography of this failed home and its feeble resistance to the reality of all the other places it is not. The fog promises an ultimate conquest of place, an end to the torturous geopathology that reveals life to be a matter of discrepancy between persons and places.

As a force that can successfully contest the compulsions and limitations of place, the fog (like addiction) appears as a counterprinciple to the fundamental problematic of the play, which is formed by the association of the figures of home and of acting (pretense, deception). The play turns on that early modernist anxiety (fully formulated for the theater by Pirandello) that the self may be a performative construct. In the course of the play the image of the fog comes to be associated with a particular kind of experience, a pointedly antitheatrical experience of self-loss through self-erasure (invisibility).

As a solution to geopathic crisis, the fog recalls various dangerous natural and spatial phenomena in Ibsen, such as Brand's avalanche, the Ekdal's indoor wilderness, the millrace at Rosmersholm, and Solness's tower. The catastrophic role played by these things in the fate of Ibsen's characters has led some critics (notably Errol Durbach) to conclude that Ibsen viewed the natural and human orders as utterly disjunct. In Ibsen's plays, writes Durbach, "nature is no longer instinct with sympathetic Paradisal affinities. It is a world without value, a desolate reality" (160). Durbach is even willing to link this analysis to a model of identity he ascribes to Ibsen: "The self, moreover, in Ibsen's world, has no essential ground of value which finds its counterpart in nature" (16).

What Durbach sees as Ibsen's "fallen world" of nature is actually, I would suggest, an absent world or, perhaps more precisely, a world *of absence*. Absence, or invisibility—that is, *their own* absence and invisibility—is projected onto certain natural phenomena by characters who have got themselves into a state of geopathic crisis. Thus the function fulfilled by the fog in O'Neill's play—the promise of self-erasure—is projected by Nora onto the "freezing black water" (*Four Major Plays*, 105) in which she briefly thinks of drowning herself as a way out of her problem.

But Nora's dream of escape, unlike Edmund's or Mary's, is contrasted to her unprecedented *actual* escape, and *A Doll's House* holds a unique place in the history of the formulation of the geopathic paradigm. As a matter of fact, it is possible to argue that the dramaturgy that links psychological ills to errors of location is both introduced and surpassed in Nora's play, and that Nora herself stands as both the exemplar of and the challenge to the power of place. Around the figure of Nora is constellated not only a new (and well-recognized) social potentiality for women, but also a new application of the politics of place.

Among the many continuities and developments that link the realist drama of Ibsen, Strindberg, and Chekhov to its immediate predecessors, the bourgeois drama and melodrama, one of the most ideologically revealing is the figure of the fallen woman. In the drama of Scribe, Sardou, Dumas, Pinero, and so on, the fallen woman is, as her adjective implies, an *already* fallen woman, a fact that becomes significant in relation to the very different version of the figure to be found in the later drama. Whereas the earlier drama had been content to treat women's "debasement" reactively and retrospectively, characterizing it as something that occurred in the past (the fallen woman was synonymous with the "woman with a past"), the new drama focused itself (and here *Miss Julie* is exemplary) on the moment of the downfall itself and made the process of decline and degradation its subject. In finally surpassing the reactive or historical mode vis-à-vis this sensational figure of offense, the modern drama took a decisive step toward its future as a celebration—even a ritual—of transgression. At the same time, and through the same interest in the processes of decline—of collapse, of loss—this drama discovered its true subject: the problematic of home.[13]

Ibsen's Nora is an exceptionally clear transitional figure in this as in other regards, one whose fortunes reveal that another definition of the woman with the past has always been, as William Worthen notes, "a woman without a *place*" (36). Nora is, in some sense, a woman with a past, although her transgression has been, significantly, in the realm of money rather than sex. But, while the plot of the play relies heavily on devices of the kind found in traditional well-made fallen-woman plays, the interest, novelty, and future importance of the play derives from a very different kind of transformation in Nora. Nora's is a social falling, actually a dropping out, and it differs from the fallings of women like Dumas's Camille or Pinero's Paula Tanqueray in being *(a)* the result of a conscious choice and *(b)* an act oriented toward the future. This latter characteristic also distinguishes Nora's fall from the emergent norm of degeneration or degradation exemplified by characters like Miss Julie, Hedda Gabler, and Mme. Ranevsky. The future orientation of Nora's fall in effect transforms the fall into something else, something that can be understood partly under the figure of revolt (as Robert Brustein showed) but more fully as a function of a new politics of location. Nora's career both during and after the play sketches out a potential reevaluation of the experience of displacement, a potential that is realized in her heroic departure at the end of the play.

However, it is important to note that the heroism of departure enters the thematics of the realist drama only as an impossible ideal, not a practicable plot convention. Even Nora, one of the few characters who succeeded—and so resoundingly[14]—in actually embodying the ideal, is greeted with a chorus of disapproval and dismay that bespeaks profound resistance. Though we may agree with Shaw's portentous remark that "Nora's revolt is the end of a chapter in human history" (quoted by Fjelde, xxv), the actual form of her revolt—literal departure—was not to become the norm for realism. All the skepticism expressed about the conclusion of *A Doll's House,* all the discussions and all the fantasies about its aftermath,[15] made it a one-time-only outcome, a kind of limit text for all future protagonists who share Nora's aspirations.

After Nora, the heroic departure becomes an impossible ideal for "falling" characters like Miss Julie, Hedda Gabler, Rosmer and Rebecca, and Master Builder Solness, who will be forced to resolve the problem of location through the mechanism of pseudotragedy, suicide.[16] Or its triumphant tone will be contrasted ironically to the indecisive departures of Chekhov's characters. To find another dramatic ending that *celebrates* departure as vividly as *A Doll's House* we would have to leave the field of realism altogether and look as far into poetic drama as Synge's comedy, *The Playboy of the Western World.* Not until Synge's Christy Mahon throws off his sense of obligation to a community of fickle listeners and promises to spend the rest of his life "romping" through the world (110) do we get a final exit as ideologically meaningful as Nora's.

Christy's radically transgressive solution to the problem of finding a home can help to illuminate Nora's departure from *her* home. Its dramatic significance lies in its coupling of radical displacement with something other than death—with a *future.* This aspect of the play's dramaturgy has not received the attention it deserves, partly because so much attention has been focused on Ibsen's masterful exposition and exploitation of the past. Yet the figure of prophecy is central to Ibsen's drama, and, as Rolf Fjelde notes, "What is true of *A Doll's House* also applies in kind to all the subsequent plays; all the dead and wounded on this many-sectored battleground of values lie stretched in one direction, like shattered signposts pointing toward *the world to be*" (xxiii; emphasis added).

What distinguishes Nora from all of Ibsen's later "dead and wounded," I would argue, is precisely that her projection into the future is alive and actual, not merely prophesied and virtual. This actualization of the future is responsible for the effect of unstoppable discussion and debate the play unleashed and continues to generate. That is to say, the play's anticlosural conclusion affords a perspective of unusual affective and critical openness, distinctly different from the usual emotional catharsis that accompanies the resolution of a conflict. This perspective in turn makes for a different kind of critical response from that elicited by plays of traditional closure: a response more weighted on the side of politics than aesthetics. As Michael Meyer notes: "No play had ever contributed so momentously to the social debate, or been so widely and furiously discussed among people who were not normally interested in theatrical or even artistic matters" (*Ibsen*, 454). Another important difference between criticism of *A Doll's House* and other plays is that much of it simply *rejects* the conclusion: "more than one commentator has ventured to suggest that the reconciliation has simply been delayed, and that Nora is likely to reopen, in the near future, the door she so precipitately closes behind her" (Quigley, 96).[17]

The fact is that the openness signified by the conclusion, as well as the critical license it implies, is dangerously at odds with the surrounding dramatic context, the realist geopathic dramaturgy that is partly being formulated by this very play. There is much in this new dramaturgy that militates against the unexpected embodiment of a future at the end of the play. So much at odds with realist dramaturgy (which trades principally on its expository mastery) is the play's future-oriented conclusion that *A Doll's House* can be seen not as the beginning of something (as it usually is) but as the end of a short-lived experiment in a transgressive, *prospective* dramaturgy, which was first sketched out in Ibsen's poetic dramas, which would be more fully and ironically theorized by Chekhov, but which would not be taken up and developed until much later.

The radical displacement we associate with Nora infuses the drama that follows *A Doll's House* and gives it its distinctive logic. Through this logic the heroism of departure becomes elaborated as a *victimage of location*. Once Nora leaves, leaving and staying become central and defining moral issues for later characters. They are part of an overall problematizing of location, actually a rendering of location *as* a problematic. That is to say: what happens in drama after Nora's departure is that, thenceforth, location—physical context—appears as both essential and contingent, both determining and changeable. The previously "given" factualness of "where one is" is subtly transformed into a matter of "where one finds oneself," which in turn institutes such questions as where one should go and where one belongs.

The dramatic mode that most fully plays out the logic of geopathology is expressionism, in which the paradoxically static journey of realism is transformed into a basic element of dramatic structure. The "station-drama" structure favored by expressionism thus literalizes realism's heroism of departure but does so, in play after play, in a way that ultimately only reinscribes, with renewed force, its victimage of location. In Georg Kaiser's *From Morn to Midnight*, to take an early and influential example, the geopathic basis of expressionism is thematized from the outset, when the protagonist misreads a situation by imposing realist norms on it. Believing that "Geography can tell us everything" (66), he jeopardizes his job as bank cashier and his livelihood to pursue a lady who turns out to be a married woman with no interest in him. The first stage in his journey brings him to a home that is a caricature of geopathology:

> Grandmother nodding in an armchair. Daughters: one busy with embroidery, the other playing the piano. Wife at the cooking range. Build four walls around this scene, and you have family life.— Comfortable, cosy, contented. Mother—son—grandchildren under one roof. The magic of familiar things—the household spell. Let it work . . . Hearth—home fires burning. Kitchen, daily bread. Chops for dinner. Bedroom, four-poster—in—out. The magic of familiar things. Then one day—on your back, stiff and white. The table pushed back against the wall—cake and wine. In the middle a slanting yellow coffin—screw like, adjustable stand. (67)

This deathly home inaugurates the journey of many an expressionistic hero, but his quest remains inscribed within the geopathic model, culminating in a death (or, in some cases, a death-in-life) that recuperates geopathology's sense of place as fate. Expressionist heroes like Hasenclever's Son *(The Son)*, Ernst Toller's Friedrich *(The Transfiguration)*, O'Neill's Brutus Jones *(The Emperor Jones)* and Yank *(The Hairy Ape)*, Williams's Val *(Orpheus Descending)* and his Quixote and Kilroy *(Camino Real)*—to name only some of the best known—each explore a series of places that hold out the promise of new modes of being, but that ultimately betray an unshakable complicity with the structure of the prison-home of geopathology. The failure of the expressionistic quest for personal liberation is preordained, for the expressionist hero is accompanied by a geopathic relation to place: he holds the impossible conviction that home is a place and that no place can be a home.

U-topian Dramaturgy

We should not be surprised to find the trope of exile grounding Ibsen's philosophical and psychological concerns (including the overarching humanistic one of the self in search of fulfillment and authenticity); exile was the personal condition out of which Ibsen created most of his work.[18] From as early on as *Brand*, the Ibsen protagonist derives the terms of his or her quest for self-realization primarily, if not invariably, from *place*. The identity formation to which he is committed is sharply at odds with the given space of his existence, which must somehow be surpassed.[19] The quintessential Ibsen hero experiences himself geopathically; when he is where he should feel at home, when he is where he supposedly belongs, then does he sense himself most deeply out of place: "Standing here on home-like ground / Stranger to myself I seem" (*Brand, 32*).

Impelled by this sense of ill-location, the humanist quest inscribes itself as a geography, and it is a geography of exile, of a fatal displacement engendered by a fateful quest. The Ibsen hero demands, above all, a space of self-realization: "Cannot room on earth's whole round / Just to be one's self, be found?" (55). In *Brand*—that is, before Ibsen discovered the realist dramaturgy that would be his hallmark—the answer to this question is framed not only idealistically but (quite literally, given the etymology of the word) in *utopian* terms. *Brand* is the working out, in anticipation, of a heroic response to the politics of location that were just around the corner—poised on the threshold, as it were, of Nora's famous door.

Brand is an excellent place to recognize Ibsen's geographical imagination, for its towering protagonist takes so deep an impression from his physical surroundings as to seem to become, by play's end, one of those same icy peaks to which he is so insistently drawn.[20] Brand's rejection of the "earth-bound God" of the valley people requires him to develop a whole new vocabulary to speak of the God he will serve, and the poetics he develops is conspicuously spatial and geographical. So prone is Brand to describe his mission in geographical terms that he seems to be the prophet of a kind of ecological spirituality, one in which such things as commanding heights, wide vistas, and dazzling sunlight seem to be more than merely metaphorical representations of the divine.

Brand begins with a literal version of the trope that, as I have already suggested, contests the claustrophobic and static structure of much realist drama: the trope of the journey. Here, in the next-to-last of Ibsen's pre-realist works, it is a literal journey, which is, moreover, subjected to a further, symbolic displacement, across time. The dangerous crossing that Brand wants to undertake is compared to another, mythic one, in a way that immediately sets up the play's basic question as a geopathic one; namely, is Brand's idealistic religion *out of place* in the modern world?

One of the peasants who is with Brand warns him about the "ice-tarns hereabout, / And once in those, you don't get out!" Brand is unruffled: "We'll cross them," is all he says. The cautious peasant then invokes a mythical ancestry for Brand's proposed act: "On the water walk? / Your doing won't make good your talk." Brand is quick to accept the identification: "Yet one has shown, with faith in God, / A man may pass across dry-shod." The peasant's response is antiheroic in the extreme, anticipating a much later ironic-absurdist valuation of the contemporary application of mythic material: "In *those* days!—Now, he wouldn't stop / Till he touched bottom, neck and crop" (11).[21] With this remark, Ibsen positions his Brand on the other side of a great abyss dividing him from the world of ordinary people (the very world in which Ibsen would soon locate all his drama).

Undeterred by the skepticism of his fellow human beings, Brand makes the now miraculous crossing unharmed. However, between this heroic first journey and the disastrous one with which the play ends, Brand's life sketches out a geoanalysis that will confront all of Ibsen's succeeding protagonists. Again and again in Ibsen's drama, the image of the journey and the idea of departure articulate a powerful poetics of exile, in which an ideal of placelessness—a utopianism, literally—appears as a precondition for self-realization.

In *Brand* the spatialization of metaphysical and moral categories is opposed to a dawning sense, in the protagonist, that only subjective experience is morally meaningful. Thus, early in the play moral differ-ence is expressed in geographical terms, when Brand warns Gerd away from the snowy mountain peaks of idealistic aspiration—"Avoid that place! There's danger there!"—to which Gerd answers, "pointing down-wards" at the village in the valley, "Avoid *that* place, for it is mean" (35). Later on, however, Brand angrily rejects any literal application of the geographical metaphor, seeing in it a kind of cowardly determinism. To the pragmatic sheriff who claims that "A man who to great deeds aspires / Must first look to what his land requires," Brand replies with con-tempt: "O, you! what barriers you erect / Twixt mountain and low-lying land! (89). He then proclaims the only true geography to be subjective: "Within! Within! That is my call! / That is the way I must venture! That is my path! / One's own inmost heart—*that* is the world."

In a way that anticipates—indeed, necessitates—the revolutionary portrayal of Nora's situation in *A Doll's House,* Brand's utopian ideal derives from a set of deficiencies and disappointments clustered around the figure of home. Home here represents a relation of deadly obligation and entrapment, something that prevents people from following the path to Brand's true God. Twice in the first two acts Brand is confronted by someone who expects him to endanger himself for their sake but refuses to risk anything to help, using the excuse of family and home obligations. To the second such person, a woman who wants Brand to cross a raging lake to reach her dying husband and who meets his pleas for help with "Nay, but I've little ones at home," Brand delivers the terrible judgment: "Your house is built upon the sand!" (45).

In a way that reminds us of the autobiographical aspect of this play (for Ibsen too derived his sense of his mission from his relation to a particular kind of place),[22] Brand's initial sense of his mission in life is almost entirely expressed in terms of its distance from and its opposition to the place he must call home. This place, which is to him an "airless hole," "close / As a mine is, or a grave!"(32), stands in challenging and fatal opposition to his soul's home, the mountain peak of thunderous waterfalls and icy paths from which his companions try to keep him, in the play's first scene. For Brand, "home," his own home as well as others', is marked as a place of crippling spiritual alienation: "They stumble home," he says of those who reject his message. Home here is a dehumanizing trap, where those beset by cowardice and selfishness herd together, like cattle: "Come then dullard souls who roam, / This my narrow valley home!" (68).

The homecoming that occurs early in the play is a classic of disappointment, returning Brand to a hometown that appears dull and diminished even beyond his unhappy memory of it:

Now I know my ground: can tell
Every farm and boathouse well,
Every estuary birch . . .
All comes back, like childhood's dream
Only that that I think today
All looks smaller, and more grey.

(31; emphasis added)

The figure of home as a diminished, reductive replica of a real human habitation is actualized, of course, in *A Doll's House*. Michael Meyer reminds us that "fifty years ago Gunnar Heiberg (a director of Ibsen's plays) pointed out how important it is when staging *A Doll's House* that the audience should have the feeling that *a home is being broken up*" (*Ibsen*, 426; emphasis added). Within the play, however, the association between Nora's departure and the idea of a broken home or of a home breaking belongs to Torvald, not to Nora. It is Torvald who, several times during their last conversation, speaks of abandonment and desertion, suggesting a clandestine, even unholy escape: "Abandon your home, your husband, your children! . . . So you'll run out like this on your most sacred vows?" (*Four Major Plays*, 110).[23] Nora, for her part, far from feeling that she is breaking up a home, says she is *returning* to one: "Tomorrow I'm going home—I mean, home where I came from" (110).

Nora's instinctive qualification of the idea of home—"I mean home where I came from"—contains the full range of the meaning of this loaded word in the new politics of location. The immediate cause of the qualification, the very need to qualify and clarify *home*, is Nora's recognition that she has never been an autonomous being, neither in her husband's house nor in her father's. Both these places, she now realizes, were pseudohomes, scaled-down replicas of human habitations: "But our home's been nothing but a playpen. I've been your doll-wife here, just as at home I was Papa's doll-child" (109). Thus Nora's instinctive need to explain what she means by home is a demonstration of her position between tradition and innovation, habit and unfamiliarity. To her, home may still bear the old connotation of originary space, but she has already been displaced enough from that construction of home to sense that it is no longer self-explanatory.

Nora experiences herself, then, as leaving one pseudohome to return to a somewhat more—if only slightly more—authentic version of the same ideal space. Her qualification, however, as well as the global nature of her rejection of her home with Torvald, suggests that she is in fact being launched into another kind of ideal space altogether, not a home at all. It is as if, in the play's final moments, Nora acquires a literary identification different from the fallen-woman one she has been saddled with so far. This momentary new identification (which is what puts her outside the realm of realist drama and is the reason she is not a model for later heroines) is with the picaro, the protagonist of the novel of social and personal discovery.

Nora's description of what she intends to do once she leaves Torvald's house—"begin to learn for myself" and "discover who's right, the
world or I" (111)—recalls the pedagogical model underlying the picaro's
journey. The picaresque hero leaves his home and embarks on a journey
structured as a series of adventures, designed to return him ultimately to
his place of origin, but with a transformed attitude toward it. In the
novel, this attitude is often one of "mature" acceptance. Thus the picaresque novel is usually a profoundly conservative ideological machine,
which uses the figures of travel and the road to *contain* rebellion against
the claustrophobic and restrictive aspects of home. The random adventures of the picaro's journey do not instruct him in any new or alternative
way of living; they serve only as undesirable opposites of the established
life to be had back home.

Of course Nora's picaresque journey, which never develops beyond
the first decisive act of home-leaving, is neither conservative nor otherwise. Rather, the picaresque journey of social evaluation and self-
discovery is gathered up as a potentiality and folded into the final moments of the play, lending them an almost mythological resonance. As I
have already suggested, the ideological meaning of the act of departure
will not emerge until much later. Meanwhile, however, Nora's accom-
plishment will acquire something of the quality of a feat, something
breathtakingly acrobatic, if not downright magical. Among the conventions it will challenge (though *not overthrow*) will be that which links
place to personhood in a relation of essentialism. Specifically, once the
bourgeois-home-as–doll's-house is deemed unsuitable for the important
project of self-actualization, the question of *what kind of place will best
nurture and support selfhood* is increasingly featured in the drama. Thus the
problem of locating and *constituting* a place as a home is a major preoccupation of characters like Hedda, Solness, and Rebecca West.

But the Ibsen character who comes closest to Nora, sharing her
idealism as well as her future orientation, is Gregers Werle from *The Wild
Duck*. Gregers does in act 1 what Nora does at the end of her play: he
leaves home. Having only just returned home after a long absence, an
absence that in itself signals a disturbance in the sentimentalist discourse
of home, he quickly judges his home to be morally uninhabitable; he
quits it with a flourish, making of his departure (temporarily) both a
heroic act and a moral victory.

It is highly revealing of the realist drama's politics of location that
the place Gregers goes to when he makes his ostentatious break with

home and family is not the open road nor the wild world of nature (which is, however, diegetically and symbolically very present in the play) but another home,[24] and one that is at least as problematic as the one he has just left. Gregers has walked out on his father because he believes that old Werle wants him to participate in constructing a hypocritical facsimile of a happy home: "So that's it! That's why I—damn it all!—had to make my personal appearance in town. On account of Mrs. Sorby, family life is in order in this house. Tableau of father and son! . . . When has there ever been family life here? Never, as long as I remember" (135). Ironically, the home to which he goes, that of his friend Hjalmar, is equally false, a home that is, in Gregers's own words, "built on a lie" (135).

The play's analysis of deception and self-deception is located, then, within a problematics of home. It is really *this* play, more than *A Doll's House,* that warrants Gunnar Heiberg's reminder that "the audience should have the feeling that a *home* is being broken up." Moreover, Gregers is shown (by his act of insufficient displacement) to be as mired in the problematics of home as he believes Hjalmar to be: Gregers's newly found "purpose" in life is hollow and ridiculous, as he himself senses ("You'd only laugh if you heard it" [135]), and the process of the play is a systematic demonstration of why this is so.

The result of Gregers's insufficient home-leaving is another home-leaving, Hjalmar's. Unlike Gregers's brusque departure, Hjalmar's is long, drawn out, and slow, taking up a large part of act 5. However, unlike Nora's equally lengthy leave-taking, this one is neither expository nor pedagogical, and certainly not intellectually absorbing. Rather, it is parodic and pathetic, affording yet another opportunity to take the full measure of Hjalmar's triviality and selfishness. It is a scene, in short, in which the heroism of departure is ruthlessly caricatured, its vigor and vibrancy reduced to the terms of laughable cliché: "Oh no, I've got to go out in sleet and snow—tramp from house to house and seek shelter for Father and me," wails Hjalmar, to which Gina responds, with refreshing literalness, "But you haven't any hat, Hjalmar! You've lost your hat" (208).

Gina's resolute resistance to her foolish husband's melodramatic posturing ("she has no feeling at all for the ideal phase of these complications," complains the poor thwarted man!) is crucial to the balance of the scene and to the perspective it is developing on the heroism of departure.

Gina's commonsensical approach to her home, marriage, family, and even to her past—she simply rejects the role of fallen woman in which Hjalmar tries to cast her—functions as a kind of bottom-line construction of home: home as a social fact, subject to the laws of necessity and survival. When Hjalmar proclaims that his earlier belief that "this home was a good place to be" was a "pipe dream" and demands to know if Gina doesn't "every day, every hour, regret this spider web of deception you've spun around me?" she says simply, "Hjalmar dear, I've got so much to think about just with the housework and the day's routine—" and then, recalling his condition when they married, adds generously: "And I shouldn't say nothing about it, either, because *you turned out such a good-hearted husband as soon as you got a house and home*—and now we've made it so snug and cozy here, and pretty soon both Hedvig and I could begin spending a little on food and clothes" (184; emphasis added).

Gina's assumption that happy homes are *made* by people, not given by life, is mirrored in the down-to-earth alliance of Mrs. Sorby and old Werle (which is reminiscent, in turn, of the union of Krogstad and Mrs. Linde). Together these ways of undertaking relationships outline a pragmatic discourse of home, which is placed in thematic contrast to the two extremes represented by Greger's idealism (according to which a happy home can only be built on total honesty) and Dr. Relling's cynicism (according to which all happiness is derived from the careful cultivation of "vital lies"). However, the play's thematic does not develop as a simple conflict between these various constructions of home, these differing points of view on the ingredients and characteristics of a place of happiness. *The Wild Duck* is not a Shavian drama of ideas. The entire philosophical debate in this play is framed within and penetrated by a circumstance that appears to have nothing whatsoever to do with the ideas of the play (except, perhaps, as a form of symbolic restatement): the indoor wilderness.

A great deal has been written about the symbolism of the Ekdal loft and its most important inhabitant, the wild duck. Of the latter, Rolf Fjelde writes memorably that it is "one of those Ibsen symbols that has a way of detaching itself from the text and flying around like ectoplasm. Who is the wild duck? Hjalmar? Old Ekdal? Both? Hedvig? The entire Ekdal family? All the characters? Modern civilized man?" (xxvii). One solution to this problem of floating symbolism is globalization: the decision to treat the entire play and everything in it as subject to an overarching symbolic idea/image. This is, more or less, Fjelde's solution, and his eloquent discussion of the defining power of the play's setting is worth quoting at length:

> Right from the start . . . in that most contemplative room in Werle's house where Hjalmar and Gregers reencounter each other, the keynote is struck, as Northam observes, in the fact that the prevailing light cast by the lampshades is green, the green of nature, the green of the cut forests that take revenge, the green of the depths of the sea. . . . All the characters that reside in the divided setting of the last four acts, with its practical foreground for eating, arguing, doing business, suggestive of the conscious mind, and the more remote, cavernous inner room full of diminished remnants of the natural world, like the unconscious mind—all have gone down, like the wounded wild duck, into the undertow of life. *The Wild Duck* is a drowned world; once we grasp *this basic metaphor of the play* and enter into it imaginatively, we can freely explore the channels of the deep, where the lost voyagers rest suspended, nearly weightless, beyond salvage, in their timeless dream. (xxviii–xxix; emphasis added)

As persuasive as this symbolic interpretation is, I think we should resist it. The play itself contains warning against symbolic readings, associating them primarily with the destructive Gregers, about whom Hedvig says, "I'll tell you something, Mother—it seemed to me . . . as if he meant something else from what he said, all the time" (155). More specifically, the symbolic status of the loft is something almost entirely articulated, within the play, by Gregers, although Hedvig does admit that she sometimes thinks that "the whole room and everything in it is called 'the depths of the sea'" (164). When Hedvig hastens to characterize this fancy as "so stupid," Gregers seizes upon it:

GREGERS: Don't you dare say that.
HEDVIG: Oh yes, because it's only an attic.
GREGERS: Are you so sure of that?
HEDVIG: *(astonished)* That it's an attic!
GREGERS: Yes. Do you know that for certain?
(Hedvig, speechless, stares at him open-mouthed)

(164)

This is the first lesson in symbolic thinking that Hedvig receives at Gregers's hands, and its object is, significantly, the loft. A later lesson, as we know, has fatal consequences, for she takes his symbolic reading of the wild duck (as "the dearest thing you own") one step further and sacrifices her most precious possession, her life. Would it be too much to say, then, that Hedvig's sad death is a case of death by symbolism? And if it is, does it make sense for us to enclose the puzzling attic-wilderness within a symbolic interpretation that would make it stand for the unconscious, for civilization, for defeat, or for something else, in any case for something other than what it is, a replica of nature, an indoor wilderness?

What is the role of the wilderness—both this reduced wilderness and the other one, "up there" in Hoidal—in the play's thematics of home, of deception and self-deception? Gregers and Relling are quick to appropriate this question or problematic for their own theories, and each gives us a "short answer" to the question. Gregers sees the loft as emblematic of old Ekdal's degradation, Relling of his psychic survival:

> Well, what do you think of this bear hunter going into a dark loft to stalk rabbits? There isn't a happier sportsman in the world than the old man when he's prowling around in that junkyard. Those four or five dried-out Christmas trees he's got—to him they're like all the green forests of Hoidal; the hens and the rooster—they're the game bird up in the fir tops; and the rabbits hopping across the floor— they're the bears that call up his youth again, out in the mountain air. (203)

However, another way of reading this curious space is offered in the play, organized around what old Ekdal himself says and does in relation to it. For old Ekdal, the loft is the answer to a question that Gregers puts to him and that he takes very, very seriously: "How can a man like you—such an outdoorsman—live in the middle of a stuffy city, cooped up in these four walls?" (150). The loft is clearly old Ekdal's way of negotiating his enforced alienation from—his *dispossession* of—"all those other things, the very roots of your soul—that cool, sweeping breeze, that free life of the moors and forests, among the animals and birds" (150). What is simply a "waste and wilderness" (167) to his son Hjalmar is to old Ekdal a place of beauty, mastery, fulfillment. His point of view is one that reminds us that the natural world is not merely a source of symbols for the human condition: it has an autonomous power that makes us its creatures and subjects. This is the point made by Ekdal himself, when, in response to the news that the Hoidal woods are being cut into, he says ("as if in fear"): "It's a dangerous business, that. It catches up with you. The woods take revenge" (150). We remember, too, his words at young Hedvig's needless death: "The woods take revenge," he says again, in "hushed" tones (214).

The woods take revenge? Could there possibly be any kind of sense in this strange interpretation of the play's climactic event, or is it nothing but the ravings of a senile old man? I would like to suggest that in fact Ekdal's words are meaningful, and that they are meaningful precisely in a way that escapes the two dominant modes of thinking that are exemplified and contrasted in the play through the other characters: symbolism and literalism.[25] Instead, they employ that mode of discourse in which the symbolic and the literal are most readily fused: the spiritual or religious mode.

Old Ekdal's relationship to the woods can be described as worshipful, and worshipful in a sense that does justice to the "paradoxes and enigmas" of what Robert Pogue Harrison has called "the role of forests in the cultural imagination of the West" (ix). According to Harrison, Western civilization has defined itself through a complex and often contradictory relationship to forests, two instances of which we will see exemplified in plays as seemingly disparate as *The Wild Duck* and (in a later chapter) Caryl Churchill's *Mad Forest:*

> If forests appear in our religions as places of profanity, they also appear as sacred. If they have typically been considered places of lawlessness, they have also provided havens for those who took up the cause of justice and fought the law's corruption. If they evoke associations of danger and abandon in our minds, they also evoke scenes of enchantment. In other words, in the religions, mythologies and literatures of the West, the forest appears as a place where the logic of distinction goes astray. Or where our subjective categories are confounded. (x)

The traumatic relation between humankind and nature is staged, says Harrison, in and *on* the forests. Citing Vico's account of the origin of civilization, Harrison locates the disastrous link, in the West's cultural imagination, between forests and human institutions, especially two that figure prominently in the discourse of geopathology: home and burial. For Vico, the clearing of the forests "was the first decisive act, religiously motivated, which would lead to the founding of cities, nations and empire" (6). This first version of home, like its late parodic variant in the Ekdal household, is predicated on the destruction of the woods. It brings with it both stability and loss, the latter represented in ways that anticipate the buried-child drama of failed homecoming (see chap. 3). Hedvig's death produces the conditions for staging the last and most significant in the list of human institutions derived from the rupture of nature: human burial. The genealogical tree that replaces the real trees must be rooted in the space they had once occupied; thus does humankind *mark* the space it has appropriated from nature: "Through burial of the dead the family defined the boundary of its space of belonging, rooting itself quite literally in the soil, or *humus,* where ancestral fathers lived underground. Humanity is bound to these funeral rites. The *humus* grounds the human. Burial preserves in the soil the essence of humanity" (Harrison, 7). The dissolution of the family in Ibsen's play, and Gregers's ill-conceived attempts to reconstruct the family on a new basis, is a battle of trees: the magical woods of Hoidal are to be replaced by Gregers's "Call to the Ideal," his version of the biblical Tree of Knowledge. It is a battle of two religions, pitting the Christian faith (however secularized) in an abstract and ideal Other World against old Ekdal's pantheistic worship of forests.

Old Ekdal understands and accepts the power of the woods and has lived his life within that understanding. Evidently this way of life has produced a strong identification between the man and the woods, as is evident from the way Gregers greets him and thinks of him. The terrible rift in his life seems to have been felt by him primarily as a loss of this way of life, and his loft wilderness seems to represent the only way he has had available to keep alive his relationship to his woods. Thus his "hunting" there is something like a ritual, regularly performed in order to propitiate the "dangerous" power of the woods.

From the beginning of the play, old Ekdal is represented as one who is out of place. His very first appearance marks him as a geopathic figure, intruding on a place in which he is not only not welcome but positively embarrassing. His incongruity is emphasized both at the start and the end of act 1, when he has to knock to be let out of the office into which he has inadvertently been locked. His later appearances are incongruous as well, as he roams the shabby apartment dressed in his uniform and hunting gear.[26] His cowardly son's denial of him in act 1, while it may not be resonant enough to make old Ekdal a Christ figure,[27] certainly arouses enough sympathy on his behalf to make him—and his relationship to the loft—something more than just comical or pathetic. It makes him, in fact, the exemplar of the most radical geopathic experience, one beside which those of Gregers, Hjalmar, and even Nora, in her play, seem pale and trivial. The displacement old Ekdal suffers from is neither temporary nor curable; it is the loss of nature itself. This loss lies beyond ritual recovery, but not beyond consequence. As we know all too well by now, the woods *do* take revenge.

Theater and Ecology

I propose, then, to reliteralize the Ekdal loft, and to read it as a representation only—and precisely—of the wilderness itself. That is to say, the loft is a reproduction, a copy, and this identity is reinforced by the fact that it is located directly behind a photography studio. The figure of photography, that quintessential representational medium of modern times, frames the loft as well as what the loft in turn frames: namely, the wilderness. Perhaps the question that is raised by Ibsen's strange space is not "What does the indoor wilderness stand for?" but rather, what does representation—the fact itself of mimesis, of mediation—do to the meaning of nature? It is the other side of the question articulated by Walter Benjamin: "Earlier much futile thought had been devoted to the question of whether photography is an art. The primary question— whether the very invention of photography had not transformed the entire nature of art—was not raised" (227). The Ekdal loft is not a symbolic but a *symptomatic* space, in which, as in the modern world itself, the categories of nature and artifice collide and distort each other.

The exemplary product of this collision is a structure that has become rather familiar to us by now, a hundred years after Ibsen's play: the artificial environment. Perhaps our experience of this phenomenon may shed some retrospective light on Ibsen's prescient model of the paradox of a man-made nature. The main feature of this paradox is that advances in mimetic technology (of which photography was only the beginning) produce fake worlds of irreducible *strangeness*. The simulated worlds of contemporary mass entertainment—the theme parks, world showcases, safari parks, tropical shopping plazas, and so on—become ever more uncanny as they become more perfect. As the technologies of representation approximate ever more closely to techniques of reproduction, the world that is being re-created so precisely recedes ever more quickly from our grasp.

The prototype for the Ekdal loft was, no doubt, that peculiar nineteenth-century building, the glass house. As Georg Kohlmaier and Barna von Sartory write in their study of this phenomenon, glass houses, built at great expense and to enormous public delight, constituted a kind of "theatre of nature," where "the scientific control of natural processes—the basis of the new industry—was realized with the use of glass, iron and steam in the cultivation of plants" (1). Partly expressions of the collective European anxiety about the colonial exploitation of the world, partly recognitions of industrialization's transformation of nature into a commodity, these "museums" displayed the "masterpieces of nature" to a delighted and increasingly class-diverse audience, masking the "dismantling of nature [that] took place behind the scenes, [while] the longed-for paradise retreated to even greater distances" (1). Ancestors of the great world fairs to come (the first of which took place in Joseph Paxton's Crystal Palace in 1851), as well as of the huge organized amusements of later mass entertainment, the glass houses figured forth a new relation of the human and natural worlds, making the latter a privileged sign of the superiority of the former.[28]

Preserving and tending nature in this spectacular way, Western man staged himself as lord of the imperiled green world. But the glass house, as space, did not fail to register the contradictions of this hypocritical fantasy; as Kohlmaier and von Sartory say, the "greenhouse was a place of retreat from the real world, but at the same time it was full of the politics of the day" (7). The economic tensions and class conflicts of a rapidly changing society played a role in the projects for "people's palaces" and "strategic greenery" to offset the ever-worsening plight of the working class:

> Man was, according to belief, a work force yet more than merely a work force; he was a thinking, feeling, physical creature who in the stony expanse of the city had become almost entirely hired labor and who had cut himself off from his true nature. The purpose of this utopia [the glass house] was to give this nature back to him. The way to that should not be a return to nature but a step towards a humanized industrialization in which agriculture, nature and society were to be provided for. (14)

The harsh reality of an aggressive capitalism underlies the sentimentalism of the Ekdal loft as much as it did that of the charming winter palaces of the time. In both, capitalist exploitation—be it of forests or people—requires that nature be artificially reproduced, preserved, and displayed. The end product of this process is something with far-reaching consequences in modern experience, especially in the modern theater: it is the naturalization of the artificial. Just how thoroughgoing that process has been is perhaps best shown in the drama of that most sensitive victim of modernization, Tennessee Williams. As David Savran has recently argued in his reassessment of the gender politics and dramatic form in Williams's drama, surrealism provided the terms for Williams's radical project of "desubjectification." The surrealists' effort to "foment ontological, erotic and political revolution" (94) included an assault on the traditional artistic myths of individual vision and expression and a reordering—or disordering—of artistic form. The counterartistic "signature" of the surrealists was, as C. W. E. Bigsby writes, "the ascription of uncommon properties to common objects, the confrontation of apparently unrelated objects, ideas, or words and the wilful dislocation of object and context" (56).

The dislocation that characterizes Williams's drama (and that David Savran has investigated so thoroughly in the area of gender) also extends to place and clarifies the terms of what might be called a negative ecology of drama, originating in *The Wild Duck*. Williams's *Orpheus Descending* (1957) contains the final form of the Ekdal loft: it is the confectionery, which is described as an almost invisible contrast to the drab and grim dry goods store in which the play is set, especially to the "sinister looking artificial palm tree in a greenish-brown jardiniere" on the landing. The confectionery, no less artificial, nevertheless bespeaks another relation to nature, just as the Ekdal loft did in contrast to the prosaic photography studio before it: "But the confectionery, which is seen partly through a wide arched door, is shadowy and poetic like some inner dimension of the play" (*Orpheus Descending*, 11). The confectionery is, of course, a space of memory and desire. It represents the lost sense of belonging that Lady Torrance seeks to recover; like old Ekdal's lost woods in Hoidal, the confectionery is the orchard turned wine garden that had provided the childhood idyll for Lady and her father. Her present "father"—her aged and tyrannical husband Jabe—recognizes and voices the true logic of this space, the disastrous consequences of an artificial nature. In answer to Lady's pleas for appreciation of its artistic quality, Jabe Torrance declares: "Yeh. Artistic as hell" (109).

Another staging of nature occurs in Williams's *Suddenly Last Summer* (1958), a play that is, one might say, set *within* such spaces as the Ekdal loft and Lady's confectionery. It is a space in which the boundaries between the natural and artificial—and with them other boundaries, of time, of biology—are completely blurred. Though set in a house,

> the interior is blended with a fantastic garden which is more like a tropical jungle, or forest, in the prehistoric age of giant fern forests when living creatures had flippers turning to limbs and scales to skin. The colors of this jungle-garden are violent, especially since it is steaming with heat after rain. There are massive tree-flowers that suggest organs of a body, torn out, still glistening with undried blood; there are harsh cries and sibilant hissings and thrashing sounds in the garden as if it were inhabited by beasts, serpents and birds, all of savage nature. (9)

The "savageness" of this nature is, however, immediately qualified. In the play's first line, Mrs. Venable reveals that this space, which had belonged to her dead son Sebastian, is in fact a plant museum like those that had flourished in the glass houses of the nineteenth century, with the "Latin names of the plants printed on tags attached to them" (10). The garden (which, as the doctor observes, is "like a well-groomed jungle") reflects not only what it does for Mrs. Venable, namely her son's methodical nature, but also the modern dream of taxonomic and epistemological control over nature. In the transgressive, category-confusing space of Sebastian's "jungle-garden," "Nothing was accidental, everything was planned and designed" (11).[29]

In *The Wild Duck,* the dispossession of nature—and its consequences for the theater—are analyzed through the conjunction of photography and the two customary figures that I mentioned in discussing *Long Day's Journey into Night* above, addiction and performance. In *The Wild Duck,* addiction of the most common type, addiction to alcohol, affects two characters, one of whom is old Ekdal. But old Ekdal is addicted to the loft as well, as is made perfectly clear in the second act, where he uses it as he does alcohol, to escape the deficiencies of the home. Yet the loft, being a performance, a mimetic space, is no match for reality. It is, quite pointedly, a simulacrum of the real, located in a photography studio. A desperate attempt to counter a desperate geopathology, it stands self-defeated, marking the very thing it was meant to mask: the loss of nature. What the photography-framed loft reveals is the anxiety of realism vis-à-vis the world of nature. This is the same anxiety coded into Tolstoy's reported insult to Chekhov: "Tolstoy is reported to have said that Chekhov was a photographer, a very talented photographer it is true, but still only a photographer" (Baring, 78).

The realistic stage is not merely the context or background or environment of the dramatic action: it is part of the dramatic logic. That is to say that realism actually lives out, though surreptitiously, the kind of magical thinking that makes a *place*—say, Prospero's island, or the Forest of Arden—the cause of the drama's events and transformations. The characters of realism, written to be taken more seriously as "real people" than any characters ever before, perform a very specific version of the real, in which location is not contingent but profoundly determining. In classical drama the influencing of inner by outer space (of subjectivity by environment) was either a poetic conceit or, when literal, a remarkable exception (for example, when Horatio warns Hamlet away from a part of the battlements because "The very place puts toys of desperation / . . . into every brain / That looks so many fadoms to the sea / and hears it roar beneath [1.4.75–78]). In general the function of the objective world was to furnish poetic material and to stand, symbolically, for subjective states. As Bert States has argued, the objective world was in a sense as unreal as Macbeth's hallucinated dagger, an index only of human intentionalities, nothing more (*Great Reckonings,* 58).

Much more, on the other hand, is signified by the profusion of objects that clutter the realist stage. Such items as (to name only the best known) Nora's Christmas tree, General Gabler's pistols, Laura's glass menagerie, Willy's suitcases are, for want of a better word, *characters* in the play. Their significance is not confined to the short circuitry of symbolism; rather they exercise a direct, unmetaphorical power in the formulation of the dramatic action.

Moreover, the profusion of these objects is significant in itself, though this significance does not become clear until much later, until we get to the junk-strewn stages of Pinter, Mamet, Shepard. These extreme renditions of the naturalist principle of a full re-creation of reality (what William Worthen memorably terms "the mastering integration of the mise-en-scène" [55]) are richly and ironically metaphorical, conveying an image of the modern world as junkyard and trash heap. Through this image, naturalism reveals an apprehension it has long concealed, regarding the growing rupture between the human and the natural. In asserting the deterministic force of environment, naturalism concealed the partialness of its definition of environment. In defining human existence as a seamless social web, naturalism enacted (though it did not acknowledge) the terrible rupture with nature that Brecht was to stage in *Baal*. Though its thematics kept in touch with nature through images of polluted baths, cherry orchards, and wild ducks, the ideological discourse of realism thrust the inanimate world into the shadows, from which it emerged in the ghostlike form of discrete objects.

The junkyards of Pinter and Mamet, as well as the denuded stages and ash cans of Beckett, participate in a negative theater ecology that pervades the theater of this century. From the polluted streams of Stockmann's town to Beckett's ash cans and beyond, the significance of the ecological thematic of modern drama emerges when we understand it within the system of relating places to people that I have been describing. In the logic of geopathology, the break with nature is a coherent, even *necessary*, item in a series of not altogether undesirable dislocations. The construction of identity as a negotiation with the power of place, and the forging of heroism out of the device of departure, makes nature one of its casualities.

Ecotheater

The heroism of departure organizes more than a particular kind of plot. It participates directly in the formulation of a certain kind of fixed individualistic identity, one that creates itself by removing itself from places judged to be unsatisfactory. The discourse of home out of which this account of individualist subjectivity arises is a profoundly ambiguous discourse, naming home as both the goal and the cause of self-actualizing departure. To this discourse is linked a tensely contradictory—utopian— theatrology, in which literalism and symbolism act equally to construct place as both all-determining and ultimately irrelevant.

These productive paradoxes of realism's thematics as well as of its theatrical functioning have proved to be remarkably tenacious, surviving several waves of innovation and experimentation. Expressionism, epic theater, absurdist theater: all these movements have tinkered with but not essentially altered either realism's geopathology or its logic of total visibility. The dramatic texts they have produced depict characters in what I would call ecological transit, utterly and irremediably at odds with their environments. While a variety of attitudes have been developed toward this condition, from Beckett's dark pessimism to Brecht's buoyant optimism, its terms remain those of a politics of home and a poetics of exile.

Geopathology remains in force until it is recognized for what it is and directly confronted. In the following chapters I shall discuss a number of different attempts, more and less successful, to do just that. The first assault on geopathology comes in the characteristic drama of the midcentury, the drama of homecoming. Through this structure, the discourse of home begins to unravel, and an elaborate symptomology develops to indicate that the cultural source of homecoming's failure is the figure of America. The precise terms of America's fatal intervention into the discourse of home is the subject of the next chapter. Here, however, I would like to race ahead, as it were, beyond the failure of homecoming and examine one possible solution to the stranglehold of geopathology, achieved precisely by a recognition, an exposure, and a systematic spurning of its terms.

The theater of Spalding Gray will be my paradigm for a new eco-theater that defeats the logic of total visibility as well as the poetics of exile by establishing a new relationship between itself and its world (the latter including, crucially, the author and the audience). As it happens, Gray has done one piece, entitled *Terrors of Pleasure: The House,* in which the problems—cultural as well as psychological—of geopathology are fully thematized and theorized. The ideas and the theater practice that emerge outline a theater ecology in which identity is in process and visibility is in quotation marks.

In *Terrors of Pleasure* the figure of home is put under pressure from its two habitual and contradictory usages (which together constitute the ambiguous discourse of home)—as literal place (a longed-for stable container for identity) and as metaphoric principle of entrapment (the desire to deterritorialize the self). Both these versions of home collide comically here, and the logic that has held them together for so long falls apart.

At one point in the play Gray holds up a copy of Jeremy Rifkin's *Entropy.* This book, Gray tells us, appeared providentially in his life at the very moment that he was about to admit defeat in his battle against the miserable Catskills house that he had been foolish enough to buy.

Rifkin's pop-science explanation of universal decay and degradation was comically comforting to the beleaguered homeowner: "Somehow it explained why the house was the way it was," he confides. The conjunction of the idea of private property with that of an inevitable and universal homelessness gives Gray's piece its fundamental theme, that of desire as coded in contemporary American culture: materialistic, self-centered, and doomed to frustration.

The Gray persona in this and other pieces is a mechanism by which the theater regains its function as a certain kind of home, a specific place to be inhabited for a specific time and in a special way: not exclusively, not through ownership, but for the direct sharing of experience. Thus Gray's practice stands against postmodernism's entropic dissemination of ideas and images; it is a theater of *gathering together,* and its modes are those of an ecological imperative: narrative (continuity), memory (recycling), and austerity (conservation).

He walks in—not "on"—and sits down. He places a small stack of books neatly on the little desk. Then he looks at the people. A long look—a measuring up, not apprehensive, not coy, just deliberate. The kind of look that passes between two people just before they lift a particularly heavy, or unwieldy, or fragile, object. The important thing is that it is a look, not a gaze; it inaugurates a time of active watching-listening, not a process of passive inscription in some one or other established structure of dramatic meaningfulness.

Spalding Gray's simple appraising look at the audience is the first of many formal transgressions that characterize his practice. His form is a departure, of course, from such traditional dramatic conventions as the soliloquy and the aside and direct address (which it resembles), but it is also not quite an uncomplicated arrival at alternate forms like stand-up comedy and storytelling (which it also resembles). The position it occupies conceptually is not so much a liminal one between the global fiction of drama and the insistent self-presence of performance art, but rather a *transgressive* one, not a position at all, in fact, but an effect, a demonstration, as in a lecture hall or a laboratory, of certain of the elemental possibilities of theater.

However, Gray's practice is not experimental in the sense of the models I have just evoked by mentioning lecture halls and laboratories, Brecht and Grotowski, respectively; and his findings do not merely duplicate theirs. The particular transformation of theater space that Gray achieves calls for another model, and his monologue *Terrors of Pleasure* suggests one: the paradigm developed and explored in this as in other of Gray's pieces is that of a new kind of home. The idea of the theater as a home, or as a refuge from a certain metaphorical homelessness, involves a double revisioning, both of the theater and of home. It redirects performance toward a confrontation with certain urgent paradoxes of an emerging future, an encounter that *Terrors of Pleasure* figures at several levels: personal, political, and dramaturgical.

In the preface to the collection of monologues entitled *Sex and Death to the Age 14,* Gray relates the genesis, in paradox, of his practice:

> *Because my work had stopped I had a feeling that the world was also coming to an end.* I told her I thought we had come to the end of the white middle-class world as we knew it. She took me at my word and said, "Well, Spalding during the collapse of Rome, the last artists were the chroniclers." And all the bells went off inside me. Of course, I thought. I'll chronicle my life, but I'll do it orally, because to write it down would be in bad faith, it would mean I believed in a future. . . . Each performance was to be a personal epitaph. Each night my personal history would disappear on a breath. (xii; emphasis added)

This strategy for keeping faith when all faith is gone is Gray's response to finding himself, like so many contemporary writers and performers, in that familiar postmodern, preapocalyptic zone with which (thanks to writers like Jameson, Baudrillard, Lyotard, Hassan) we are now so familiar. To his self-effacing artistic method Gray adds another idea, the first glimpse of a consciousness that eventually suffuses not only *Terrors of Pleasure* but also, I would argue, his entire practice. Explaining why he chooses performance rather than text as the medium for his chronicle of a dying civilization, he says: "it would be just another product cluttering up the world, not to mention destroying all the trees needed to make paper for the books." It is from this simple, perhaps even simplistic, recognition of the necessary relation between our claims to a self-expressive life *in* the world and our actual modes of belonging *to* this world that I derive the special orientation of Gray's performance work toward what I would call an ecological consciousness.

Ecology and its cosmic shadow, entropy, are the subjects of *Terrors of Pleasure,* the final referents for the extravagant (and superficially contradictory) affects mentioned in the title, in which Aristotle and Horace also lurk, strangely at odds with each other. The conjunction of these two orders of incommensurability—the one psychological, the other theatrological—provides the parameters for an imaginal ecology of and in the theater, a revisioning of the mutual responsibilities of representation and environment. Having done his stint with environmental theater, Spalding Gray points toward an ecotheater in which the exhausted dichotomy between self and role revives and is revived as a transgressive selfhood that insists on situating itself, however temporarily, in the "real" (the material, the natural, the historical) world.

The figure of entropy connects Gray to a by now extensive tradition of American writing. As Tony Tanner notes, "Among the writers who use the actual word [entropy] in their work are Norman Mailer, Saul Bellow, John Updike, John Barth, Walker Percy, Stanley Elkin, Donald Barthelme" (14). Two others, whom both he and Colin Greenland discuss in detail, are, of course, William Burroughs and Thomas Pynchon, the latter of whom has written what is probably the ultimate glass house story, going far beyond the Ekdal's loft and Sebastian's jungle garden to envision life in a "hothouse"—an ecological closed system (reminiscent of the ill-fated project known as Biosphere) in which a man waits for the "heat-death" of the universe, which may have already occurred. According to Colin Greenland, the literary appropriation of the second law of thermodynamics may have been encouraged by Norbert Wiener's suggestive (and for my argument, and Gray's play, crucial) linking of entropy with the figure of home. In *The Human Use of Human Beings,* Wiener writes: "But while the universe as a whole, if indeed there is a whole universe, tends to run down, *there are local enclaves whose direction seems opposed to that of the universe at large* and in which there is a limited and temporary tendency for organization to increase. Life finds its *home* in some of these enclaves" (12; emphasis added). For Spalding Gray, the opposed pulls of entropy and home making provide the occasion for trying out an alternative way of living, one that cannot be named but can perhaps be *embodied* theatrically, in the creation of a new mode of theatrical experience and address that notes and exceeds the exhausted forms of traditional theater. In this sense his practice exemplifies the sense of renewal implied in John Barth's definition of *exhaustion:* "By 'exhaustion' I do not mean anything so tired as the subject of physical, moral or intellectual decadence, only the used-upness of certain forms or exhaustion of certain possibilities—by no means necessarily a great cause for despair" (70). As Barth suggests, the movement beyond exhaustion is possible; what Greenland calls the "felt ultimacies of verbal and cultural catastrophe" (194) call out for new representational strategies. In the realm of theater, Gray's ecotheater outlines one such strategy.

The literal environment of Gray's performance is furnished phatically, to signify nothing but its appropriateness for presenting Gray's kind of monologue. As a transgressive gesture, this baring of the stage has impeccable avant-garde credentials, but never before has the choice of poverty been so systematically elucidated by the text it (un)stages. And never before has the blank stage been more directly required to yield up its stored powers of communication, its potential for community.

A good example of how the text glosses the minimalist staging choices involves the glass of water from which, before he begins to speak, Gray takes a careful sip. At this point the gesturality involved is, again, purely phatic, signifying the undisguised nature of the performer. He drinks his water the way some musicians tune their instruments before they start to play. It is not until much later, when we are deep in the narrative of Gray's mock-heroic struggles against entropy and pollution, that the glass of water sitting so innocently on the desk suddenly fills up with so much meaning as to reduce to fluff the legendary dramatic burden once imposed by Scribe on the same innocuous object.

Gray takes his final sip of water when he tells us of the crowning disappointment in a long series of disasters befalling the miserable country house he has been foolish enough to buy. The series brings him to a point where almost the only thing he has left to feel good about is the wonderful well water he will have as soon as a broken pipe is fixed. "Just then the plumber called out, 'Mr. Spalding, go try the water now.' I rushed back into the house, turned on the tap and the water burst forth, smelling of death. The whole room filled up with the smell of a dead animal, but I was in such a hurry that I drank half a glass before I realized it" (237). It is at this point in the performance that Gray takes his sip, provoking a ripple of laughter that is immediately followed by a shocked recognition of the meaning of clean water. The link forged at that moment between the stage present and the earlier narrated experience—a link that flows through the glass(es) of water—is crucial to and constitutive of Gray's theater practice.

The play ends with a distraught Gray calling the board of health, afraid he has contracted rabies from his well, only to be told, reassuringly, that rabies is hydrophobia, the fear of water, "and what would an animal with a fear of water be doing jumping into a well?" (237). The idea of creatures going against nature extends to the two key concepts upon which one can map the terms of Gray's ecotheater: home and the self. The identification of the first with private property, and of the second with the first (i.e., the equation: home = house = self) inaugurates the terrorism of material pleasure: "I was thinking that we should buy a house because renting wasn't enough for me; I wanted to have the sense of *ownership*. I thought it'd be kind of like growing up, like having a child, if you *owned* your own house" (202). In stark contrast to this deeply valorized fantasy (according to which home is synonymous not only with family and self-respect but also with *house,* that is, with private property) stands the experience of ordinary "unaccommodated" man in his contemporary guise: urban, helpless, entirely at the mercy of rapacious "entrepreneurs" (as it says on one man's business card) who charge him exorbitantly to come out to his house to pronounce on the worthlessness of his furnace, his refrigerator, his porch, his foundations.

The sense of authenticity and legitimacy he had hoped for remains as elusive as ever. Far from belonging to a community, Gray finds himself reduced to the condition of a lonely squatter: "I was spending a lot of time now just drinking out on the porch, taking it 'one day at a time,' as Alcoholics Anonymous says, just sitting outside and cooking on my hibachi" (215). Finally, the cold-hearted specialists deliver their verdict, and a moment of comic recognition occurs:

> the house was built on clay. That's why everything including the chimney (and the old family barbecue in the yard, which was now at a very disturbing angle) was that way. Essentially, this lovely hill-and-dale affair was a big mound of wet clay moving towards the trout stream on the other side of the road. Nature was taking its course. The thought of the house in perpetual motion was too much. *I wanted a house that would stand still for years.* (216; emphasis added)

The idea of flux, of "perpetual motion," is explored in various ways, including through the ironic anecdote about Rifkin's book *Entropy.* Gray quotes several passages from Rifkin; the book is one of those he has in the little pile on his desk. And quotation, along with less explicit forms of intertextuality, furnishes Gray with a crucial technique for redefining the kind of selfhood and the kind of presence by which his ecotheater moves beyond the supposed ideological impasse of postmodernism.

Unlike the disseminative intertextuality associated with postmodernism (intertextuality as pastiche, in Jameson's famous formulation), the intertextual mechanisms in Gray's pieces belong to a system of memory, of *recuperation* and *conservation*. While his chosen performance form bespeaks perpetual change, irretrievable loss (his monologue is never the same from night to night, and the various recorded versions also differ) its presentation to any given audience is carefully coded as a *recovery,* a premeditated, well-prepared *gathering together* of nuggets of significance. The self-directed irony of the presentation does not dilute the meaning being offered; if anything, as William Demastes has argued, it enhances it by dismissing the liability of the artist's authority.

An example of this construction of a transgressive and undisguisedly historical performance self across the many boundaries of living and representation (that is, across mimesis) comes in the visit Gray receives, on his first morning in his new house, from some Jehovah's Witnesses. Seeing them approach, Gray fondly imagines that they are friendly neighbors come to welcome him to his new community. But, he soon observes, "they're not bearing cakes or pies" (213). Instead, they give him the Good News—that they are going to live forever. He, however, is in grave danger of extending his present homelessness into the hereafter. All his praying, they assure him, will be useless unless he joins them. They drive the point home with what is, in the circumstances, a rather cruel simile: "It will be like putting paint on a house that is falling down" (214). Impressed by their perspicuity, he buys their book, entitled *Let Your Kingdom Come.* It is, sure enough, one of the books now on the desk, and a picture from it has awed Gray so much that he has actually had it blown up to poster size. He holds it up for the audience to see as he describes its ridiculous representation of utopia, a welter of iconographical clichés among which he discovers the cliché that has victimized him:

There's a leopard in a tree, smiling, content, not ready to jump. There's a little black girl holding a baby leopard in her arms. There's a white boy standing between two loving parents, the mother carrying a Thanksgiving-style fruit basket and the father holding a garden hoe and a rake. Then there are some blacks with fruit baskets on their heads behind him, and *there are houses with perfect foundations under them all around.* (214; emphasis added)

Like other (non)props used in the performance—such as his girl-friend's polaroids of the house, the tape recording of a message left on Gray's answering machine by the man who sold him the house, and the pack of cards with which Gray demonstrates the principle of entropy—the enlarged picture is an ironized instance of how the otherwise trivial paraphernalia of memory finds its home and destination before an audi-ence for and with whom that transgressive phenomenon known as Spalding Gray signifies itself. Like a Lazarus come not from the dead but from living he has come to tell us all that he will tell us all (and show us some). His presence, and that of the few books and objects he has with him, guarantees the minimal historical continuity out of which a future may be imagined. As he says in the play's last line (after deciding that life is too short to start worrying about rabies): "Where do I go from here?" (237).

Against the image of a poor ecotheater, in which a very idiosyn-cratic and *localized* knowledge might be directly shared, stands the story, also told in *Terrors of Pleasure,* of an altogether different kind of perfor-mance, in which the raw material of selfhood is not transgressively en-acted but trans*formed*, repackaged and recoded for a voracious representa-tion industry:

> Renee said, "Enough of this depending on other people. We've got to put together our own package." And she comes up with the idea of trying to sell my life story to Warner Brothers for a feature film. And by God, they're interested. We condense my stories . . . It will be about this character, Sterling Gray, a Huck Finn–Candide-type who gets into all these weird situations. (228)

However, the deal falls through, because Spalding and Renee can't decide how their story ends. Interestingly enough, the point on which they are stuck is the question (put to them by the studio representative) of how their personal relationship turns out: do they get married, or do they separate? No other option seems available. Apparently marriage and domesticity are still Hollywood's imperatives (so long after Nora's de-parture) as much as home ownership had been Gray's. When Gray pleads that he can hardly commit himself to a fictional relationship more than he has been able to to a real one, the film executive is unequivocal: "We have to have it completely clear."

Thus the mimetic machine that demands superficial narrative clarity practices a terrorism—of pleasure, of closure—on the contingent, historical self, who must then seek refuge and hospitality back in the theater of perpetual motion. This is the model (as well as the theorization) for an ecotheater, in which that rupture with nature so long, so anxiously (and often so surreptitiously) registered by the drama of this century is brought into the dramatic spotlight, and its consequences are allowed to indicate directions for future formulations of character, identity, and selfhood.

Chapter Three

America and the Limits
of Homecoming

The bourgeois theatre set most of its scenes in small domestic rooms, with an occasional picnic or a visit to the law courts. It thought it understood the world and believed that nothing in it needed to be changed very much. Things merely needed to be adjusted from time to time with the right word of advice, the right letter or the right sympathy.
—Edward Bond, "Us, Our Drama and the National Theatre"

America did stand for, at one time, when England was, it did stand, my people came, it must have stood for, a long time ago of course. No they are both . . .
—Vera, in *Ice Cream,* by Caryl Churchill

The incoherence of cultural difference in the late twentieth century rewrites the discourses of home, homeland, family, and history. As we have seen, the figure of home had, like other figures, a certain clear definition within the homogeneity of Western bourgeois culture: it was a problem, but an *intramural* problem, as it were, a problem whose solution was assumed to lie in close proximity to the figure of home itself, if not actually within it. That is to say, the problem of home was understood as a problem of *location,* with solutions that grouped themselves around certain mechanisms of literal placement. In the theater, environmental realism was a precise reflection of this figuration of home, producing a stage furnished on the principle of immediate spatial intelligibility and a drama organized around the actions of arriving, staying, leaving, returning, and so on.

The dissolution of that homogeneous idea of culture redefines the problem of home as a problematic: something that does not simply pose personal problems for individuals and groups but something that conflicts conceptually with their overall cultural outlook and expectations. To express this change as briefly as possible: we begin with the sense of home as a place that exists in some definite relation to the group of people whose home it is; certainly, it is a place in need of adjustments (as Edward Bond notes) and improvements that would better serve the psychological needs of its inhabitants, but it is a fully recognizable place, known and given. We then move to a deepening uncertainty about the reality of home, both as place and as idea.

An emblem of this difference is the shift of focus in drama from actions of *leaving home* to *homecomings*. Although the act of returning home is an archetypally regressive act—"going home is always going *back* home," writes James Hillman (200)—it is used in the later modern drama not to recuperate identity but rather to stage the difficulties, even impossibility, of such recuperation. However, this refusal of the sentimental possibilities of homecoming does not exhaust the usefulness of the figure itself. Beyond sentimental fixing and grounding of agitated and alienated selves, the figure of homecoming survives and allows playwrights to dramatize a postnostalgic condition, enforced by those re-theorizations of social and psychological experience that have finally abandoned the deterministic and originary explanations of nineteenth-century humanism.

In the realm of theater practice, this new discourse of home as homecoming helps to articulate new principles of representation and of the functioning of stage space, and these have, in turn, affected critical practice. A preeminent example of the conjunction between a new spatiality of theater, a new vision of the production of dramatic meaning, and a new critical paradigm is to be found in the works of Harold Pinter, who has also, of course, written what is perhaps the greatest homecoming play of this century. Pinter's account of the vicissitudes of returning to the place marked as home constitutes one definitive formulation of the new discourse of home; another one, more tentative but no less revealing of the processes that have called forth this new discourse, is Sam Shepard's *Buried Child,* perhaps the American equivalent in importance to Pinter's *The Homecoming.* Both plays trace the patterns and perils of actual homecomings, but in doing so they engage themes and issues that go beyond dramas of literal homecoming. Another and more recent transatlantic pair of plays, Caryl Churchill's *Ice Cream* and George C. Wolfe's *The Colored Museum,* will help us to pursue these other themes and issues, most of which can be apprehended under the figure of displacement.

Displacement, then—personal, historical, and cultural displacement—is unexpectedly the true subject of this chapter on homecoming. In the plays I shall discuss, the link between homecoming and displacement involves several other links, such as the surprising one between a new dramaturgy—an antisecretive, nonrevelatory dramaturgy—and the figure of America. Certain *un*linkings are involved as well, notably of that previously impacted connection between home and place. This is the problem that Pinter's drama above all others struggles with, for Pinter is seduced by place, trapped into its figures even when he is trying hardest to escape its boundaries: "I do not sit in a cozy corner in one room, speaking through a loudspeaker. My preoccupation is not a cozy corner. It is the house."

Provincialism

Perhaps more than any other playwright, Pinter's practice has been understood and characterized in spatial terms.[1] One reason for this is Pinter's own famous account, given early in his career, of the composition of his first few plays: "I went into a room and saw one person standing up and one person sitting down, and a few days later I wrote *The Room*. I went into another room and saw two people sitting down, and a few years later I wrote *The Birthday Party*. I looked through a door into a third room, and saw two people standing up and wrote *The Caretaker*" ("Writing for Myself," 174).

This authoritative marshaling of dramatic actions into certain acute configurations has had a decisive impact on Pinter criticism, offering itself as a powerful *critical* model (not to mention a promise of some solid ground beneath the plays' characteristic opacity). Thus the Pinter room has helped to organize many an account of Pinter's typical moves and meanings, most notably of his equivocal evocations of primal pleasures and primal fears. The structure of the room as a boundaried space, capable of keeping out as well as keeping in, allows it to function as a referent for such thematics as danger versus safety, infantile sexuality versus oedipal threat, political passivity versus active resistance. Among the earliest critical uses of the image of the room was as a way to ground existentialist readings of Pinter's plays. These made of the room a compensatory device, a refuge from a certain Heideggerian "ontological insecurity" that has "man clinging to the room that offers identity and safety in a world commanded by strange and unkind gods" (Gordon, 1).

But it is, at the very least, problematic to treat the room as an inverse symbol of man's radical homelessness, his lack of real context in the world of meaning (the condition directly staged, for example, by Beckett in the featureless landscape of *Godot*). The fact is that the rooms surrounding Pinter's characters are as equivocal as the characters themselves. The mode of their contribution to the plays' meanings is not symbolic but performative, demonstrating, as Bert States says, that "rooms, like all [theater] images, must eventually justify their presence; they must inhabit the people who inhabit them" (*Great Reckonings*, 46).

One approach to the room that places it in a historical development of wide importance is suggested in an early essay by John Lahr, on what he calls "the bond of naturalism" between Pinter and Chekhov. Lahr finds Pinter's world utterly lacking in those "blessings of nature [that] are omnipresent" in Chekhov's world. According to Lahr, "Chekhov is writing . . . at the brink of a significant shift in man's attitude towards nature; his characters are both victims of its indifference and witnesses of its glory" ("Pinter and Chekhov," 64). The shift seems complete by the time we get to Pinter, whose world appears "hermetically sealed off from nature" ("Pinter and Chekhov," 62). Lahr argues the historical contrast with reference to an exchange, in *The Caretaker*, which occurs as two characters stand at a window and look out at what lies just outside their room:

DAVIES: Looks a bit thick.
ASTON: Overgrown.
DAVIES: What's that? A pond?
ASTON: Yes.
DAVIES: What you got, fish?
ASTON: No. There isn't anything in there. *(Pause.)*

A report by someone looking out of a window, especially a report as grim as this one, can hardly escape an intertextual linkage with that moment in Beckett's *Endgame* when Clov looks out of his high window, on Hamm's behalf (and ours, certainly), and sees "Nothing." Clov's account of life outside his hugely symbolic room evokes, in turn, that definitive formulation of modern drama ecology, Gogo's "You and your landscapes! Tell me about the worms." Pinter's vision is widely assumed to be close to Beckett's, whom he once praised for leaving "no stone unturned and no maggot lonely" (quoted by Lahr, "Pinter and Chekhov," 61). But the resemblance between them does not go much beyond their ecological dystopianism. For Pinter, the world outside the room is inaccessible to meaning, or accessible only via an obdurately unsignifying paranoia of the sort embodied in The Birthday Party's Goldberg and McCann.[2] When the outside world intrudes, it is negatively and subjectively, and we glimpse it only as the characters' fear.[3] This is emphatically not the case for Beckett, whose creations of acute self-consciousness depend upon the continuing presence and signification of an objective world of nature, impinging mightily on the characters yet separate from and independent of them (see Chaudhuri, "Who Is Godot?").

Methodologically, Lahr's approach suggests that we relinquish the idea that a play's spatial structure is a masterful choice—deliberately excluding other options—and regard it instead as one aspect of a larger system of meaning at work in the play as a whole. From this perspective, Pinter's practice, as far as the room is concerned, is not purely a matter of authorial control over meaning: it is also the sign of a certain historically determined limitation on the possibilities of dramatic meaning. This is indicated (though unwittingly) in one of the earliest and most eloquent of the readings of the room, by Arthur Ganz (1972): "The room becomes for Pinter a way of blocking out the diffuse claims of the external world and concentrating on the central facts of existence as he conceives them" (12–13). That is to say, the closed structure of Pinter's favorite dramatic space is also the closure of a certain representation, a representation, significantly, of the world that lies outside of private or domestic experience: the public world.[4] By situating his characters in these markedly bounded spaces, Pinter seems to be saying (to paraphrase one of his most problematic characters) that certain questions do not fall within his province.

The carefully self-limiting character I have just alluded to is, of course, Teddy, the mock-prodigal son of The Homecoming, whose lack of response to the shocking behavior of his family and his wife is the central puzzle of the play. To say that Teddy is a professor of philosophy would be merely accurate; the remarkable thing is that Pinter has made Teddy's link to philosophy as specifically significant as the other characters' less cerebral professions, so specific in fact that one could say that his whole characterization is pointed toward the moment when he makes his famous distinction between "operat[ing] on things and not in things" (61), a philosophy of dedicated superficiality. Teddy's profession gives him the means to articulate his limitations; his identity is wholly contained within his measured refusal to take the bait offered by his brother Lenny,[5] and to engage in a philosophical discussion:

> LENNY: Eh, Teddy, you haven't told us much about your Doctor-ship of Philosophy. What do you teach?
>
> TEDDY: Philosophy.
>
> LENNY: Well, I want to ask you something. Do you detect a certain logical incoherence in the central affirmations of Christian theism?
>
> TEDDY: *That question doesn't fall within my province.*
>
> LENNY: Well, look at it this way . . . you don't mind my asking you some questions, do you?
>
> TEDDY: *If they're within my province.*
>
> (51–52; emphasis added)

The question of what lies within Teddy's—or any one else's "province"—which is also a question of relevance, and thence a question of belonging and of home, is centrally important to Pinter. Here, it produces a specific thematic that organizes both the dramatic action (what the play's characters say and do) and the dramatic logic (what the play's spectators see and think). That thematic is announced in the play's title, although this self-nomination marks a deceptive simplicity, indeed a mystification. That the act of coming home is overdetermined by the culture is evident from the very existence of the composite word that Pinter has appropriated for his title; but his play, as it proceeds, rejects the many inscriptions—psychological, sociological, and literary—upon the apparently simple act of returning home. Teddy's homecoming is neither a "proper" homecoming, nor is it Teddy's (since it is taken over, so shockingly, by Ruth).

At the level of dramatic action, the failure of homecoming occurs because, as Austin Quigley puts it, "the word 'home' is construed in different ways by different characters and the nature of the different constructions becomes manifest in the kinds of social structure that each of the characters seeks to impose on the others" (174). At the level of dramatic logic, homecoming is frustrated (creatively and memorably frustrated) because it is framed here within a larger problematic, one that is of special interest to a politically committed playwright like Pinter, and which can be stated as follows: what is the present home of (dramatic) representation? What lies within the modern playwright's province?

Another kind of relation to the outside world, and one that stands in significant contradistinction both to Pinter's rejection and Beckett's acceptance, is that found in the plays of Sam Shepard. In *Buried Child* the dramatic action in many ways parallels that of *The Homecoming,* but the dramatic logic is completely different: while Pinter's deadpan method warns spectators to survey his enigmas from the safety of *their* own "province," Shepard's method encourages, invites, even forces spectators to traverse the conceptual space of his play, to recognize its intertextual furnishings, to "come home." As we shall see, the many threads of cultural allusions that Shepard weaves into the fabric of his play connect its characters willy-nilly to the "outside," that is to the actual sociocultural world of the audience watching it. Whether that connection eventually amounts to an ideological analysis is a matter of much controversy and importance. That is to say, while the "provinciality" of a Pinter is certainly transgressed in Shepard's work, the extent of that transgression—specifically its extension into the political sphere—is uncertain. Still, there is no doubt that the road to locating a politics of home and homecoming in contemporary drama leads through (if not *to*) Shepard.

Buried Child and *The Homecoming* bear a striking resemblance at the level of plot; both dramatize decidedly bizarre homecomings by sons who have been away for some time (in each case, it so happens, for six years). In both cases, the returning son is accompanied by a woman who is not known to the rest of the family. In both cases, too, the homecoming triggers a series of more or less explosive revelations, culminating in the unearthing (in Shepard, literally) of something that had been festering, hidden, for many years.

But it is not these plot similarities that I shall focus on, except to indulge a paradox and note that these similarities are both too superficial and not superficial enough. Though spread over the surface of the plays for all to see, they do not supersede or cancel out the implied depths of their respective plays. This is what I mean by saying that they are not superficial *enough:* all these similarities—the grotesque families, the monstrous fathers, the traumatized sons, the alien women, the act of homecoming itself—all these motifs belong to surfaces that seem to exist in relation to certain depths (of meaning, of course, but also of mystery). These surfaces are an instance of superficiality *in the service of depth*—depth-creating surfaces.

The opposition between surface and depth undergoes substantial analysis in the new discourse of home; at the thematic level of this discourse, the old conjunction between place and personal identity is shown to have established itself partly through the figure of roots, roots reaching deep into the heart and past of a particular location. The unraveling of that figuration of identity, as something deeply rooted in place, preoccupies the drama of the second half of this century, so much of which can be read as an agonized response to the challenge thrown out by Brecht in the prologue to *The Caucasian Chalk Circle*. The idea of natural affiliation to a particular place (be it the place of individual birth, the place of collective origin, or the place of historical habitation) has given the twentieth century its politics; it should not surprise us that it pervades our drama, making depth and rootedness one of its most habitual tropes.

At the level of dramatic composition, the opposition between surface and depth is more firmly in place, much slower to unravel. Indeed, the surface-depth opposition has long been the norm for dramatic structure, certainly as envisioned by the practice of criticism, for which this opposition is an enabling assumption.[6] Whether the surface is regarded as concealing (the position of hermeneutics) or as revealing (semiotics), the presence of a more or less hidden depth has long been regarded as the hallmark of a work of art. But minimalism, of which Pinter is considered to be, with Beckett, a preeminent practitioner, produces a new inflection on the surface-depth metaphor for artistic structure.

Undeep Knowledge

It is often said that Pinter's minimalism, his careful selection of the bare essentials of person, place, and utterance, is the source of his hermeneutic and affective power. Pinter's practice, for all its spatial metaphoricity, displaces the well-stocked stage of realism and its claims to what I have called environmental intelligibility. To put it another way, if Teddy is an incarnation of philosophy as refusal, Pinter himself cultivates a certain passionate resistance to naturalism's philosophy of omniscience, a refusal sensed and expressed in Ganz's remark, quoted above, about Pinter's rooms "blocking out the diffuse claims of the external world."

In Pinter's own many self-characterizations, this refusal is interpreted as a rejection of a self-confident and moralistic dramaturgy, a resolute opposition to all "philosophies, tracts, dogmas, creeds, ways out, truths, answers" (quoted by Lahr, "Pinter and Chekhov," 61). Pinter is part of—indeed, the prime representative of—the modern theater's antihermeneutic bias. Like Beckett, like Ionesco, like Albee, like dozens of makers of modern plays, Pinter refuses both to assign single meanings to his plays himself and to valorize efforts in that direction by others.[7]

The resistance to stated and stat*able* meaning has several sources, including a deep distrust of dogma, of anything that might suggest propaganda for a cause. But of course it has dogmatic qualities of its own, such as its insistence on the mysteriousness of ordinary life, on the lack of coherence and predictability in human experience. All these themes (staged so memorably in *Godot*) find their echo in Pinter, clothed in characteristically spatial imagery:

> The world is full of surprises. A door can open at any moment and someone will come in. We'd love to know who it is, we'd love to know exactly what he has on his mind and why he comes in, but how often do we know what someone has on his mind or who this someone is, and what goes to make him and make him what he is, and what his relationship is to others? (Quoted by Esslin, 31)

The themes of surprise and mystery run through Pinter's many pronouncements about his dramaturgy, which repeatedly plead the playwright's lack of special knowledge, especially in the area of character. If we recall that passage in Strindberg's preface to *Miss Julie* which has been read as the definitive statement of naturalist characterology, and which declares his characters to be richly revelatory "conglomerations of past and present stages of civilization"(65), Pinter's characterology seems the opposite: "My characters tell me so much and no more, with reference to their experience, their aspirations, their motives, their history. Between my lack of biographical data about them and the ambiguity of what they say there lies a territory which is not only worthy of exploration but which it is compulsory to explore" (quoted by Lahr, Introduction, xi). In what is, in effect, the postnaturalistic version of the logic of total visibility, Pinter "offer[s] a vision of life in its *ambiguous* entirety" (Lahr, "Pinter and Chekhov," 61; emphasis added).

The move that interests me is the one (documented by Susan Merritt

as "Changing Views of Pinter's 'Ambiguity,'" 68–78) whereby this strongly urged epistemological *deficiency* gets transformed into an aspect of dramaturgical mastery. How does the mystified spectator of life's "surprises" become the meticulous visionary about whose dramatic world people can say that "every gesture and word counts for something" (Lahr, Introduction, xiii)? We can glimpse one moment of that transformation in one of the founding texts of what I would call "the Pinter myth," that famous letter in which Pinter responded with such witty reflexivity to the hermeneutic inquiry of some anonymous (and predictably female) spectator (see Esslin, 30).

Demanding information on identities and relationships, the woman took her place in the slot assigned by the myth to those hermeneutically naive ones whose search for even rather ordinary certainties is the mark of an abiding and anachronistic faith in certitudes. Critics have been quick to enjoy the joke at the expense of such lowbrows, using it, perhaps, as a means of personal liberation from the narrow confines of their own earlier hermeneutic practices, which always referred meaning to the intentions of the writer and which assumed these intentions to be both richly complex as well as *masterful,* that is, textually controlling.[8] In its revisionary form, as developed in Pinter criticism, this enabling assumption is replaced by another, where textual mastery is separated from thematic *intention* and transferred to structural or phenomenological *practice.* And one of the structures most often urged in the explication of a Pinter text is, as I have already said, the spatial structure, particularly the room.

In the case of *The Homecoming,* the meaningfulness of space has never been contested. In fact, it has been valorized from a number of different perspectives, including that of the play's first director, Peter Hall, for whom "all of Harold's work relates to a confined space where people confront each other in often very ugly terms" (12), and whose interpretation of the play rested on a reading of its world as a particular kind of place, a jungle. Space also functions as a metaphor for some of the characters' major concerns, as in Teddy's concern that his room be there, unchanged, just as it always was, or Max's threats to Sam that he will throw him out of the house as soon as he stops bringing in money.

The climax of the play captures this privileging of space in a way that shows how bizarre and menacing space can be: the shocking proposal that Ruth become a prostitute operating out of a flat that the family would provide for her is met with Ruth's cold-blooded—and spatially

literalistic—query: "How many rooms would this flat have?" According to one of the members of the original cast, John Normington, the actor who created the role of Sam, this was "the most shattering moment" (140) of the play.

The concern with space and place has been the basis for several of the best-known readings of the play, most notably that by Irving Wardle, which states unequivocally that "The play . . . has to be understood in territorial terms or not at all" (40). Finally, most of the psychological interpretations of the play ground themselves explicitly or otherwise in the glaring[9] spatial fact alluded to by Teddy in the following famous speech: "What do you think of the room? Big, isn't it? It's a big house. I mean, it's a fine room, don't you think? Actually, there was a wall, across there . . . with a door. We knocked it down . . . years ago . . . to make an open living area. The structure wasn't affected, you see. My mother was dead" (21).

This speech sanctions a structural approach not only to the space of the play[10] (with its attendant thematics, extended from other plays, of inside versus outside) but also to the family and its dynamic.[11] That is to say, Teddy's speech suggests that we regard the family of the play not primarily as a number of individuals but rather as a unit, a system, a *structure*. This then allows a reading of the plot that can easily accommodate the shocking and—yes—mysterious behavior of the characters, translating it into the sheerest logic: "the lady does it" (Walker) because she must: the structure of the situation requires it.

The characterization of the family as a definite structural unit, with determining rules and inflexible codes,[12] bestows upon it a kind of conceptual power; in fact, it elevates the family to the status of a myth. This view of the family underlies a great many readings of the play, most of which proceed according to a distinct logic that has both dramaturgical and ideological components. A passage from R. F. Storch's essay "Pinter's Happy Families" expresses that logic so well that it is, I think, worth quoting at length, with certain emphases added:

Pinter's plays affect us because they are about the middle-class family, both as sheltering home longed for and dreamed of, and as many-tentacled monster strangling its victim. . . . The London stage since 1945 (to look no further) has been very much occupied with the family as trap-door to the underworld. . . . Pinter, however, is by far the most radical in breaking with the naturalistic conventions of *drame bourgeois*. If he is obsessed with the peculiar horrors of the middle-classes, this is not within the larger view of social class, but simply because they epitomize everything that is horrifying in every family situation today. *He makes us see that class distinctions are curiously out of date* [emphasis added] for today's theatre, and that a kitchen sink is no more enlightening than a coffee table. (Storch 136–37)

To dehistoricize and de-class-ify the family is, in this formulation, to make it more real (later in his essay, Storch speaks of "the very heart of reality, the bourgeois family" [146]). This move, of course, follows quite seamlessly from certain other modern intellectual assumptions, many of which, as Bert States points out, spring to mind as soon as one confronts the play: "we explain the play as a study in psychic ambiguity: under the banal surface, a massive Oedipal syndrome (like the part of the iceberg you don't see) bumps its way to grisly fulfillment. Or, beneath Freud lurks Jung and the archetypal: the father-son 'contest,' the 'fertility rite' on the sofa, the Earth Mother 'sacrifice,' the tribal sharing of her body (a Sparagmos for sure), the cyclic 'return,' and so on" ("Pinter's *Homecoming*," 149).

States's rapid-fire listing of psychological motifs makes his point: these supposedly "hidden" meanings are so common, so instinctive in our culture, that their ready identification in acts of interpretation is suspect, unsatisfactory. To States, they exist in the play only as by-products of something else: an irreducible strangeness deliberately cultivated by the playwright. Part of that strangeness, I would add, is derived from a certain specific displacement—of the myth of the family (which has first been carefully installed as a structural ground for the play) by another myth, that of America.

The displacement I have in mind, which makes the family not its theme but rather its site or stage, is organized around the figure of Teddy. He is, of course, the departed (displaced) son, whose act of separation is put into high relief by the continued residence in the family house of the other sons, all grown men. But Teddy's displacement is rendered decisive not by his mere absence from the family (which, as Lenny contemptuously intimates, is easily remedied by having an empty chair at every gathering) but rather by the presence of another family, elsewhere. The structural meaning of this other family is first brought into play in the following loaded exchange between Teddy and Ruth:

RUTH: Don't you like your family?
TEDDY: Which family?
RUTH: Your family here.
TEDDY: Of course I like them. What are you talking about?
(54)

The structural meaning produced by the other family is equivocal, because that other family is a mirror image of this one (it also has three sons and an absent mother). This doubleness creates a hermeneutic choice, since repetition always incarnates both sameness and difference. Mirror images can be read as they have been by the mimetic tradition in drama (long before Hamlet's explicit injunction to the players), that is, as clarifying and confirming the nature of the original. Or they can be regarded as instances of radical alterity, along the lines suggested by Baudrillard when he writes that "Counterfeit and reproduction imply always an anguish, a disquieting foreignness. . . . Reproduction is dia-bolical in its very essence; it makes something fundamental vacillate" (*Selected Writings,* 182). Thus on the one hand, at an abstract, thematic level, the American "mirror" family of *The Homecoming* reinforces the mythic status, in the play, of the family, lending it the resonance of a magical family from legend or fairy tale. On the other hand, at the level of the action and of the characters—and as Teddy's reaction shows—the doubling of the family disturbs the implied implacability of *this* particular family and portrays it not as mythic structure but as an experiential matrix, characterized by alternatives, options, and confusion.

The double family of *The Homecoming* presents us with a choice. Do we take the doubleness as an iteration of the deterministic family of Freudian and other legend, universal and timeless? Or are we to read it (or rather, them) as the traces left by the unraveling of the mythic family? Such a choice in fact articulates a basic problematic of modern experience, born of the thoroughgoing theorization of that experience. As they circu-late through the many explanatory frames and systems offered by modern thought (some of which were so neatly evoked by States's laundry list, above), ideas like family and home become alienated and ironized. The problematic is even clearer in *Buried Child,* where the choice between myth and not-myth is not just present but presented and theorized, by being put in relation to other kinds of codes. *Buried Child* furnishes a kind of stereoscopic perspective on the family, not merely treating it as a mythic structure but staging the *processes* of its coding as myth.

Chief among these processes is repetition, which in Shepard's hands tilts entirely toward one of the two meanings, sameness and difference, that we have identified with it. All the repetition in *Buried Child* is repetition as sameness, the process of mythmaking. Perhaps the most conspicuous instance is realized in proxemic terms: the occupancy of the battered living room couch. When the play opens, the enfeebled patriarch, Dodge, still possesses it, though with so tenuous a hold as to make him seem its prisoner. The power bestowed by the couch is so fragile that Dodge is even afraid to fall asleep lest, like a parodic Henry IV, he lose all he has to his greedily impatient son. "I don't wanna lay down for a while! Every time I lay down something happens! (whips off his cap, points at his head) Look what happens! (pulls his cap back on) You go lie down and see what happens to you! See how you like it! They'll steal your bottle! They'll cut your hair! They'll murder your children!" (93–94).

Nevertheless, the couch is a symbol of power, as becomes clear when the brutal Bradley occupies it at the end of the second act, only to relinquish it to Vince in the final act. The final act is in fact a rather deliberate demonstration of the logic of the transfer of power from Dodge and Bradley to Vince. It is a mythic logic, just as it is in Shakespeare's *Henry the Fourth,* engaging the two subsidiary themes of the symbolic birth of the hero and the continuity of past and future. Though Vince is clearly no Prince Hal, he is much closer to Hal than to that other prodigal, Pinter's Teddy, for Vince is a willing vehicle for the assertion of family as myth, disposed to define himself in its terms:

I could see myself in the windshield. My face. My eyes. I studied my face. Studied everything about it. As though it was another man. As though I could see his whole race behind him. . . . His face became his father's face. Same bones. Same eyes. Same nose. Same breath. And his father's face changed to his Grandfather's face. And it went on like that. Changing. Clear on back to faces I'd never seen before but still recognized. Still recognized the bones underneath. . . . I followed my family clear back to Iowa. Every last one. Straight into the corn belt and further. (130)

It is not only the imagery here that mythologizes the family, associating it with race and tribe; within the structure of the play this speech repeats the terms (though not the sentiments) of another, earlier speech, delivered by Dodge:

DODGE: His name doesn't mean a hoot in hell to me. Not a tinkle in the well. You know how many kids I've spawned? Not to mention Grand kids and Great Grand kids and Great Great Grand kids after them?

SHELLY: And you don't remember any of them?

DODGE: What's to remember? Halie's the one with the family album. She's the one you should talk to. She'll set you straight on the family heritage if that's what you're interested in. She's traced it all the way back to the grave.

SHELLY: What do you mean?

DODGE: What do you think I mean? How far back can you go? A long line of corpses! . . . Who gives a damn about bones in the ground?

(112)

Though Dodge and Vince assign different values to the family, they both experience it mythologically, and the play reinforces this meaning through the proxemic repetition associated with the couch. A further emphasis is provided by the blanket, which acquires symbolic meaning as it circulates between the three men who are engaged in the power struggle.

Also overdetermining the mythic meaning of this power struggle is the famous corn, which associates this family's transfer of power with a specific mythology.[13] And it is certainly no accident that (as Thomas Nash has argued) the particular myth invoked by the corn, the myth of the Corn Spirit or Corn King, is a kind of myth par excellence, having been regarded by early anthropologists as an ur-myth, underlying many other myths, religions, and drama itself. This myth is so literally invoked in this play that Halie's blunt question, "What's the meaning of this corn, Tilden?" is actually a moment of *mise-en-abîme,* a moment where the text reveals its basic functioning. What Halie's question stages is the fact that *Buried Child,* as a whole, asks how mythic meaning can or cannot be bestowed on human experience. By articulating the idea that the corn has (or doesn't have) meaning—that is, by raising the possibility that dramatic symbolism can (or cannot) occur—the play briefly disengages itself from—precisely—the symbolic project, and in doing so also from the logic of meaningful depths under opaque surfaces. The *mise-en-abîme* is a moment of reflexive irony, which in this case hints punningly that symbolic constructions may be rather corny.

Of course it is not only this moment of *mise-en-abîme* that destabilizes the mythic structure of *Buried Child*. In fact, Halie's question about the corn only works as *mise-en-abîme* because an entirely different way of reading events and people is exemplified all over the play. The techniques used to articulate this countermythic or antisymbolic mode within the play are literalization and intertextuality, both, as we shall see, techniques of surface. An early example of how intertextuality works to render experience trivial and parodic occurs when Vince and Shelly first enter. Their opening conversation makes it clear that the family in the play is going to be put in relation to another American family, no longer mythic but rather stereotypic—the American family as feeble cultural joke:

> SHELLY: This is the house?
> VINCE: This is the house.
> SHELLY: I don't believe it!
> VINCE: How come?
> SHELLY: It's like a Norman Rockwell cover or something.
> VINCE: What's a'matter with that? It's American.
> SHELLY: Where's the milkman and the little dog? What's the little dog's name? Spot. Spot and Jane. Dick and Jane and Spot.
>
> (83)

The idea of the Norman Rockwell family, or rather, the possibility that that stereotypical image could somehow exist in reality triggers a response in Shelly that borders on the hysterical. Significantly, Shelly is the closest thing in this play to a spectator surrogate; her hysteria creates an open, ironic response-space into which the play's mythic subversions constantly invite the spectator.

As a character too, Shelly is most disruptive of the mythic impulse, because her mode is the obstinately literalistic. Of the mysterious vegetables that Tilden keeps bringing in from the backyard, it is not the mythic corn but the commonplace carrots that she is associated with. These carrots are resolutely *a*metaphorical—if they refer to anything at all it is only, intertextually, to that carrot in *Godot* of which the best that could be said was, "It's a carrot!" Unlike the corn (which could have "deep" meaning or be merely corny) the carrots are objects of praxis and performance, to be used by the spectator, as Shelly prompts, "to keep busy," to get through whatever must be gotten through: "I'll stay and I'll cut carrots. And I'll cook the carrots. And I'll do whatever I have to do to survive. Just to make it through this" (94). For Shelly, there is no question of finding meaning in these carrots; they exist onstage as adjuncts to a pragmatic necessity, survival.

What is mainly evoked by Shelly's carrots, then, is the irony that this archetypal American home is something to be survived. In its transformation from safe haven to dangerous lair the institution of the home follows the decay of that other institution, the family. As staged in *Buried Child,* the historicity of the institution of the family generates the following paradox: the struggle to survive as a family member, to ensure familial identification, is shown to have arisen out of the *decline* of the family—from immemorial myth to stereotype steeped in oblivion:

DODGE: Who are you to expect anything? Who are you supposed to be?

VINCE: I'm Vince! Your Grandson!

DODGE: Vince. My Grandson. . . .

VINCE: You haven't seen me for a long time.

DODGE: When was the last time?

VINCE: I don't remember.

DODGE: You don't remember?

VINCE: No.

DODGE: You don't remember? How am I supposed to remember if you don't remember?

(89)

The transformation of the family from a living receptacle of the individual's memory to the site of his being forgotten is linked in both *Buried Child* and *The Homecoming* with a specific mode of representation. That mode—namely, photography—has often been associated with realism; the relationship is in fact very superficial, a resemblance of surfaces. Beyond their shared appearance of actuality, theatrical realism and photography are opposites, for while the former is formulated by means of a heavy reliance on the specificity of place, the latter has the effect of reducing location to a temporary contingency. Photography was recognized from the first as a conquest over place and time, for through it "The momentary glance, the ineffable memory, the detailed and textured surface, could . . . be lifted from its particular time and place, separated from the powerful grasp of the material environment, yet still remain real, visible and permanent" (Stuart Ewen, 24).

This "mirror with a memory," as Oliver Wendell Holmes called it (53), gives both Pinter and Shepard the ideal figure for their account of the unraveling of the old discourse of home and family. Without disturbing the naturalistic surface of the drama—indeed while actually enhancing that surface by means of their reputation for accurately reflecting the real, what John Tagg calls their (false) "phenomenological guarantee" (3)—photographs enter both plays as carriers of an undeniable dissemination, of which the first casualty is the mythic family of tradition.

The relationship between the figure of photography and the myth of family is hinted at briefly toward the end of Pinter's play, when Max pulls out a snapshot of himself from his wallet and gives it to Teddy to take back to America with him, to show his sons. As Max phrases it, the photos serve as source or at least mechanism of ongoing family connections: "Do your boys know about me? Eh? Would they like to see a photo, do you think, of their grandfather?" (79). Teddy accepts, and the ensuing transfer of the image is, in itself, as natural and normal as could be. What makes it absolutely terrifying and abnormal is, of course, the context, which has the effect of "rewriting" the photograph: as a bribe (it is taken out of a wallet) or worse, as a payment (it is being sent to the boys in place of their mother).

The dramatic context also comments upon the photograph, placing it in the aftermath of what is, as I shall argue below, the pseudoclimax of the play, Sam's irrelevant revelation. That anticlimactic climax concludes the play's "debt" to naturalist dramaturgy, the dramaturgy of bringing what is hidden to light. What remains once Uncle Sam has said his piece and (not) died is the superficial mystery of images, of which there can be no better emblem than the photograph.

But again the full significance of the figure of photography to that of the family is staged in *Buried Child*. The reported upstairs room "with all the pictures" makes us, like Shelly, scrutinize photographic images for answers to the mysterious degradation of this family. The passage in which Shelly tells Dodge that "Your whole life's up there hanging on the wall" is one of the most allegorical passages in the play, inviting us to join Shelly in her quest for the truth of this family and its past. We can't help noticing, then, that the walls of the reported gallery are also covered with "crosses," suggesting—what? The problem with the allegorical mode as introduced into this play is that we are never allowed to forget its arbitrariness. The crosses could sanctify the photographic record of this family's past with myth and mystery, or they could defile it with irony. Similarly, Shelly's description of a family picture in which "All the kids are standing out in the corn" could authenticate Tilden's claims during the play of a rebirth of the farm, but it could equally well signal Tilden's unhinged regression into the past. Finally, there is the following metatheatrically loaded exchange between Shelly and Dodge, in which the issue is precisely the signifying potential of the photographs they and we have been scrutinizing:

> DODGE: That isn't me! That was never me! This is me! Right here. This is it. The whole shootin' match, sittin' right in front of you.
> SHELLY: So the past never happened as far as you're concerned?
> DODGE: The past? Jesus Christ. The past. What do you know about the past?
> SHELLY: Not much. I know there was a farm.
>
> (111)

It is tempting to read this farm as the allegorical representation of the old America, the onetime heartland, now crumbling through neglect by the new mythologies being generated from what Dodge insists is the "stupid country" of Los Angeles (90). Or we can, like Dodge, reject outright the meaningfulness of those images, deny their claim to the status of historical "evidence." Their role in the play has less to do with guiding interpretation than with staging its problematic, heaping up signs that cumulatively textualize this family.

It is not only the mythological heartland farmhouse, or even the stereotypical suburban household of "turkey dinners and apple pie" (91), that haunts this house. We are also aware here of other families, famous families from other classic American plays. Together, they work to locate this house and its occupants within a textual and cultural geography that makes America something quite other than a place: a text.

One family that stands behind all the troubled families of American drama are the Tyrones of *Long Day's Journey into Night*. They survive in *Buried Child* not only as a clamor of disappointment, resentment, and betrayal but also in one specific image: the estranged mother hovering in an upstairs space, lost in her own reality. Shepard's mother, Halie, is the robust opposite of the wraithlike Mary Tyrone, but she is, like her predecessor, irreparably severed from her spouse and sons, and she, too, vainly seeks solace in religion. In another way, she is a slightly grotesque parody of Linda Loman, uselessly offering her husband "pills" for a condition that clearly goes beyond physical remedies. *Death of a Salesman* is intertextually present here in other ways as well: the dream of vegetation (in one's own backyard), the nostalgia for a lost rural America, the generations of failed aspirations and blasted hopes, the alternative (tried unsuccessfully by Biff and Tilden) of nomadic freedom.

The terrible troubles between fathers and sons link *Buried Child* not only to *Salesman* but also, even more literally, to another O'Neill play, *Desire under the Elms,* which inscribes itself both on the play's space (the opening stage direction mentions "the shapes of dark elm trees" [63]) and on its sensationalist thematics of "buried treasure" (105) and, of course, of incest. But perhaps the most insistently present other family here is the nonfamily of *Who's Afraid of Virginia Woolf?* The "buried child" of the title is Shepard's version, or rather his *staging,* his putting into high relief, as it were, of the driving mechanism of much American drama, a mechanism best exemplified in Albee's classic. The unseen child—dead, buried, denied, or unborn—is American drama's version of the "hidden secret" of realist dramaturgy.[14] Shepard's use of it shows both *how* it has worked in the past *and also why it cannot work in that way anymore.*

The imaginary child created by Albee's George and Martha resembles Shepard's buried child in being an anchor for certain characteristic preoccupations of American drama: the animosity between the generations, powerlessness as impotence, family as pathology. Like George (and also like Willy Loman), Dodge represents the failed American male, exhausted and consumed by an impossibly demanding ideal of success. Like George, Dodge is in retreat from life, cut off from love, his marriage a tedious battleground. Finally, and again like George, Dodge "kills" the invisible/impossible child of love. In all these actions, Dodge enacts the fundamental logic of the dramatic tradition to which he belongs: according to this logic, the ruinous end to a life of disappointment and violence is "redeemed" by the anagnorisis that there was a *cause,* a reason—hidden somewhere *deep,* in the past, or even deep in the structure of the present—for all the suffering. Unlike his predecessors, however, Dodge inhabits a dramatic world where this entire thematic is no longer symbolized or (to redirect our attention to the surface-depth metaphor) "subtextualized."

The literalism of *Buried Child,* which gives the play its extraordinary ending, marks its break with that symbolic dramaturgy of American realism to which it is intertextually linked. When, at the end of the play, Tilden enters carrying in his arms the muddy remains of the buried child, the image suddenly jolts into sharp focus the symbolic device on which so much previous drama had depended for its meaning. The actual bundle of bones is in defiant *excess* of all those previously produced meanings, no matter how rich and complex and "deep" they may have been. Moreover, this unearthed body is the sign that retroactively engages the literalist, superficial code of the play, devalorizing such mythemes as the corn (= fertility), the haircut (= castration), the lost leg (= impotence). Brought to the surface, the body exemplifies a discourse of surface, whereby meanings are produced by the lateral associations of intertextuality rather than the deep resonances of myth.

Cloaking an archetypal plot with a web of allusion, *Buried Child* stages the contemporary conflict of interpretation,[15] the problem of assigning meaning in the absence of collective faith and in the context of terrible interpersonal dislocations, beyond mere obliviousness: "You think just because people propagate they have to love their offspring?" (112). The interplay between the main action, which as we have seen is rather obviously and laboriously coded as myth, and the intertextual field surrounding it produces an explosion of effects that cumulatively suggest that something beneath the surface needs to be dug up. But "Digging Up *Buried Child*" (as one of the critical articles on the play is entitled) is not the process of hermeneutic clarification one would expect. The tiny corpse that appears at the end of the play places its materiality against all the attempted symbology of the play, especially against the overdetermined mythemes of home and family.

The fact that digging up the buried child does not unearth meaning is staged in the extraordinary scene of hermeneutic struggle that concludes the play. Halie, speaking from her invisible upstairs space, rapidly enacts the mythic reading that the play has offered as an option throughout. She authenticates Tilden's account of the outside, adding a powerful mytheme of her own: "Tilden was right about the corn you know. I've never seen such corn. . . . Tall as a man already. This early in the year. Carrots too. Potatoes. Peas. *It's like a paradise out there,* Dodge" (132; emphasis added). She then goes on to explain this inexplicable, indeed magical, development, using terms that reintroduce those very explanatory frames of mythology and psychology (now cranked up to an allegorical pitch) that the literalism of the corn and the corpse has challenged:

Maybe it was the rain. . . . Good hard rain. Takes everything
straight down deep to the roots. The rest takes care of itself. You
can't force a thing to grow. You can't interfere with it. It's all
hidden. It's all unseen. You just gotta wait till it pops out of the
ground. Tiny little shoot. Tiny little white shoot. All hairy and
fragile. Strong though. Strong enough to break the earth even. It's a
miracle, Dodge. I've never seen a crop like this in my whole life.
Maybe it's the sun. Maybe that's it. Maybe it's the sun. (132)

It is not only the climactically placed pun on "sun" (which, by the way,
links this play with that epitome of dramatic overdetermination, *Hamlet*)
but also the more explicit instability of the thrice-repeated "Maybe" that
makes this conclusion at least as antimythic as mythic, as intertextual as
archetypal, as affirmative of surface associations as of deep truths.

In *Buried Child,* the figures of home and family become the site for
an exceptional homecoming—that of the dramatist. While Pinter carefully rules certain things out of his province, ignoring the world outside
his characters' narrowly circumscribed interpersonal spaces, and while
Beckett humbly stages the world of nature, however attenuated and
estranged from the human, Shepard's dramaturgy embraces both what's
"out there" and all the ways of making sense of it, including those, like
mythology and intertextuality, that contradict each other.[16] Shepard's
dramaturgy renews the defunct project of what I have (earlier in this
book) called environmentalism but in a very different philosophical register, far removed from its positivistic origin. This version presents the
real world as neither independent of nor prior to representation, but fully
interpenetrated by it.

Shepard's dramaturgy assumes an overcoded world, a reality always
in the process of moving into and out of frames of meaning created by
previous cultural practice.[17] In this world the figure of home, for example, is not only a sentimental idea of belonging (although it is that as
well), it is also an image distilled from—or rather traced out by—the
myriad mass-produced representations of a commercial culture. Thus a
new magazine ad version of home usurps the affect as well as the mythological charge of the old heartland-farmhouse version, replacing the old
paradise of abundance and fertility (conjured up by Halie's last speech)
with one of manufactured plenty. In *True West,* a character describes this
new moment in the discourse of home, conveying not only its appearance but also the dangerous economy of desire it organizes: "Like a

paradise. Kinda' place that sort of kills you inside. Warm yellow lights. Mexican tile all around. Copper pots hangin' over the stove. Ya' know like they got in the magazines. Blonde people movin' in and outa' the rooms, talking to each other. *(Pause)* Kinda' place you wish you sort of grew up in, ya' know" (12).

Shepard's plays situate themselves on the representational borders of the different images of home and family, in the interstices between the various cultural codes—from the mythological to the medialogical—that generate these images. They are dramas of cultural imagery (we could call them *museum plays,* taking the suggestion in the title of George Wolfe's *The Colored Musem,* which I discuss below). They take their place in the discourse of mass-produced, mediated images identified by writers like Baudrillard, Eco, and Jameson as the discourse of post-modernity. These writers also locate for us the region par excellence of mass-produced and mass-consumed images; it is the same region that haunts these plays of homecoming and perverts their mythic impulses.

America

The America of Pinter's *The Homecoming* is an abstraction, almost a nonplace. The associations that the characters supply for it conform largely to the stereotype that has existed in Britain since midcentury of America as a technologically advanced but culturally sterile zone of material comfort. Teddy is the main agent of this characterization, and the resistance he meets from his wife exposes the psychological dimension of his "America." Not only is his America woefully insipid, but Ruth's insistence on situating America in opposition to "here" suggests that Teddy's adopted home is not to him a real place at all but merely a refuge from—or refusal of—his actual home, "here."

> TEDDY: . . . The boys are at the pool . . . now . . . swimming. Think of it. Morning over there. Sun. We'll go anyway, mmnn? It's so clean there.
> RUTH: Clean.
> TEDDY: Yes.
> RUTH: Is it dirty here?
> TEDDY: No, of course not. But it's cleaner there.
> RUTH: You find it dirty here?
> TEDDY: I didn't say I found it dirty here. *(Pause.)* I didn't say

that. *(Pause.)* . . . You can help me with my lectures when we get
back. I'd love that. I'd be so grateful for it, really. We can bathe till
October. You know that. Here, there's nowhere to bathe, except
the swimming bath down the road. You know what it's like? It's
like a urinal. A filthy urinal.

(55)

Ruth's psychological acuity is dazzling. The ease and rapidity with which
she maneuvers Teddy into the oppositional logic she has introduced lead
us to dismiss America along the same psychological lines, that is, as
merely Teddy's place of escape from a reality he cannot face.

But perhaps there is something other than individual psychology in
the play's image of America. After all, that image had, for Pinter's audience, very powerful associations; as Dick Hebdige puts it, by the late
1950s in Britain, "the associations which had begun to congregate
around the term 'Americanisation' are organised to the point where they
are about to be translated into full-fledged connotational codes" (57).
Chief among these connotations is the one reflected in Teddy's bland
evocation of life in America: of a homogenized cultural wasteland. As
Hebdige points out, this image had a particularly chilling force for
Britons, who regarded it as the image of their unavoidable future. The
massive contemporaneous dissatisfactions with and critiques of British
culture (such as those voiced by Osborne's Jimmy Porter and distantly
echoed in Teddy's "filthy urinal") were not only responses to a perceived
decline; they were given an additional grim twist by the prevailing conviction that the decline would be reversed in a monstrous direction,
exemplified by America. For all its conspicuous difference from Britain,
America, with its seductive materialistic triumphs, was regarded as the
inevitable shape of things to come, "a paradigm for the future threatening every advanced industrial democracy in the western world" (52–53).

In *The Homecoming* this idea is directly signaled by the fact that the
family's double—its younger version, or next generational incarnation,
as it were—is situated in America. Teddy's position, from this perspective, is that of a kind of unwilling but necessary cultural transmitter,
moving from the "filth" of a disastrous past into the blank slate of a
"clean" future. The locating of that future in America, along with certain
subtle alignments to that location, marks a significant development in the
dramatic discourse of home.

The figure of America as it briefly appears in *The Homecoming* evokes a peculiar kind of space: space that has not evolved—or cannot evolve—to the condition of place, that is of local identity. The America of the play includes no city or state names; it is a vast undifferentiated space that can only be described in naturalistic terms, not cultural ones. It is the perfect rendition of what Howard Kunstler has called "The Geography of Nowhere," where the whole "culture of place-making [has been] thrown away in [the] eagerness to become a drive-in civilization" (273). To Teddy's image of long sunny summers around swimming pools Ruth adds another image, less attractive but equally elemental, characterizing America as an alien world lacking all human habitation: "It's all rock. And sand. It stretches . . . so far . . . everywhere you look. And there's lots of insects there. *(Pause.)* And there's lots of insects there" (53). America appears as an alien land capable of providing a restricted set of pleasures—chiefly physical ones—but essentially inhospitable to human life at any level deeper than the physical. America, that is, is portrayed as a land of land, a space of surfaces. Upon these surfaces are inscribed the ready formulas of mass-cultural existence, a discourse of vapid clichés. Teddy's description of life in America bristles with unmarked quotation marks: "She's a great help to me over there. She's a wonderful wife and mother. She's a very popular woman. She's got a lot of friends. It's a great life, at the University . . . you know . . . it's a very good life. We've got all . . . We've got everything we want. It's a very stimulating environment" (50).

The last ready-made phrase, "stimulating environment," clinches the rigid structure of banalities in which Teddy has sought to house an alternative life. But the dramatic and verbal context of this stilted affirmation of a "new" life fully exposes its futility as a new paradigm of home. For Teddy's speech is both preceded and followed by references to time and continuity, the second reference subtly but decisively denying the first. The first is one of Max's typically preposterous formulations: "Listen, live in the present, what are you worrying about? I mean, don't forget the earth's about five thousand million year's old, at least. Who can afford to live in the past?" (50). Something about this nonsense is disturbing enough to Teddy to bring on his cliché-ridden outpouring of his life in America, which staggers to a conclusion with the bland statement that "We have three boys, you know." But Max's response shows that this is no innocuous statement of fact; rather it is the sign that he has actually won a complicated round in his battle of wits with his son on the subject of where home is: "All boys? Isn't that funny? You've got three, I've got three. You've got three nephews, Joey. . . . You could teach them how to box" (50). He has maneuvered Teddy into tacitly admitting that what he has in America is a pale and bloodless copy of a real home, a merely simulated environment that is no match for the (violent) forces of family.

The America of *The Homecoming* is described, treated, and used in a way that suggests another meaning for homelessness, along the associational lines of the German word *unheimlich* (literally "unhomelike")—uncanny. The strangeness of this insect-blown expanse of rock and sand, with its oases of comfort and conformity, makes it the antithesis of home as constituted previously, with its twin literalizations in place (house) and people (family). This America is not only unhomelike: it is the very principle of homelessness in contemporary experience. It is not only the place that can never support true dwelling, but also the reason that all homecomings are become impossible.

This then is the function of Pinter's brief America: it is the cultural reference point for a wholesale unraveling of the old discourse of home, whose manifestations are staged in what we could call (and what many critics have treated as) "the spatiosexual politics" of the play—the action of filling a "hole," by whatever shocking means, in a given structure. The "ubiquitous spectre of Americanization" (Hebdige, 52) intervenes definitively into the fantasy of home as originary space,[18] offering the image of a ready-made "very good life" as an alternative to the brutalities of a decaying tradition based on blood ties. And the rate of exchange is not bad: trade in a bitter past for "all that,"—"I mean with the sun and all that, the open spaces . . . all the social whirl, all the stimulation of it all, all your kids and all that, . . . the Greyhound buses and all that, tons of iced water, all the comfort of those Bermuda shorts and all that" (64).

Precisely because it is the abstraction of "all that," the figure of America redirects realist dramaturgy, turning it away from its old environmentalist convictions. America appears (here and elsewhere, as we shall see) as self-displacing place, *a place in which the association of space with place has been ruptured*. It is a place that denies the deep importance of place and celebrates instead the expansiveness and potentiality of surfaces. It is associated (again, here and elsewhere) with limitlessness (in Lenny's sarcastic terms, which reduce the lack of limits to merely boring excess: "no time of the day or night you can't get a cup of coffee or a Dutch gin" [64]). It outlines a style of life and a way of meaning quite other than that based on location. As a figure used to organize a dramatic action, it reverses the old privileging of depths over surfaces, and of deeply rooted, buried truths over superficial appearances. America offers, in short, an invitation to "operate on things and not in things" (61).

Uncle Sam's Secret

The principle of a self-displacing place affects dramatic meaning (especially the thematics of home) as well as dramatic structure. One of the elements most seriously affected is plot organization. The figure of America brings into play a new way of ordering dramatic actions, by which such organizational principles as mystery, revelation, and secret causality are not abandoned but are reframed and accorded a very different emotional charge. The hidden secret of much modern and premodern dramaturgy produced a strong and satisfying dramatic closure based on catharsis, or at least on the achievement of balance. The new dramaturgy displaces the secret enough to show us why its revelation cannot be appropriated for the purposes of thematic resolution.

An excellent illustration of this change is the anticlimactic revelation that concludes *The Homecoming*. The secret that Max's brother Sam had kept bottled up inside him is blurted out when the shocking deal with Ruth has been struck: "MacGregor had Jessie in the back of my cab as I drove them along *(He croaks and collapses)*" (78). The evident failure of this revelation to achieve any of the results traditionally associated with ultimate disclosures—such as retrospective understanding, anticipated harmony, thematic clarity—is underlined by the mock-tragic fate of this pathetic "truth-teller":

MAX: What's he gone and done? Dropped dead?
LENNY: Yes.
MAX: A corpse? A corpse on my floor? Get him out of here? Clear him out of here!
(Joey bends over Sam.)
JOEY: He's not dead.
LENNY: He probably was dead, for about thirty seconds.
MAX: He's not even dead.

(78)

To fully understand the plot meaning of Sam's secret we need, I think, to look at it semiotically rather than hermeneutically. That is to say, instead of using it to dig up other hidden meanings with which to then explain the bizarre central action of the play, we can recognize it as *a failed attempt to accomplish a certain familiar dramatic code*. Regarded in this way, it belongs to a modern tradition of metatheater going back at least as far as Pirandello: the staging of moments at which traditional dramatic expectations are subverted. The particular kind of subversion involved here is akin to the one that was fully theorized in Genet's metaplay *The Blacks*. Late in that play, the onstage audience discovers that what it thought was a dead body on stage was not a body at all and that in fact what it thought was the coffin was just a sheet stretched over two chairs. The unidiomatic outrage expressed by one of the "spectators" conveys the cost of violating the theatrical contract and its "grammar" of rules: "No packing case either! They kill us without killing us and then they lock us up in no packing cases either! (98).[19]

Genet's example is particularly apt here in light of the critical consensus that Pinter's plays signify structurally, that is, primarily in terms of their patterns rather than their characters, dialogue, action. One kind of inflection on this idea would suggest that Pinter's plays are ritualistic, dedicated to "the audience's innate desire to observe pattern worked out to a logical limit or at least a fullness" (Rabillard, 44). From this perspective, Uncle Sam's secret would mark the simultaneous observation and destruction of a crucial pattern: the heroic "discovery" of truth. In terms made clear by both Genet and Artaud, this self-canceling code-accomplishment is that most powerful realization of a ritual: its perversion.

The worthless secret that diverts drama from the traditional course of theatrical meaningfulness also perverts its relationship to its old sponsor, mimesis. The transformation is of a kind I have evoked already in discussing intertextuality in *Buried Child*: the profound meanings associated with mythic stories, images, and patterns are not able to accrue to the play's characters and action because they have been rewritten as stereotypes, that is, as contingent cultural artifacts. If the characters resonate to these images, this does not deepen them to a ground of stable meaning; it dissipates them, unraveling their unique meaning by inserting it into cultural circulation, seen as ongoing and nonoriginary. Similarly, the worthless secret enacts the new banality of depths, rewriting the occult as merely the occluded. Uncle Sam's secret does not explain any more about the mystery of this family to us than it does to them: it is only the mark of a promise of a new inexplicability.

It is also the mark of that aggressive "provinciality" on the part of the playwright that I have identified with Pinter but that he surely shares with much inwardly focused modern art (and whose inevitability Chekhov had foreseen and lamented a century ago). If Pinter moves (as indeed he does) "beyond naturalism," it is in the way he qualifies naturalism's project of "meld[ing] man inextricably to his environment" (Lahr, "Pinter and Chekhov," 60). As John Lahr states, Pinter "uses the conventions of naturalism to go beyond them and chart mankind's evolving sense of its own *boundaries*" (61; emphasis added).

By contrast, Shepard's "America" outlines a new dramaturgy to replace the naturalistic dramaturgy that temporarily expired—"He probably was dead, for about thirty seconds" (78)—toward the end of *The Homecoming*. The stereoscopic focus of Shepard's play, in this case, its equal attention to both myth and the *cultural life* of myth, gives his stage a hypermimetic quality. This dramaturgy is not given over to that "meld[ing of] man . . . to his environment" which renders that environment as something unitary and coherent. Shepard's dramaturgy acknowledges the extent to which the modern environment is an ideological and semiotic construct, combining at least as much man-made imagery as natural material. The last words of the play, "Maybe it's the sun," can serve as an emblem for the multiple references of Shepard's stage, combining as they do the natural, the sociopsychological ("son") and the literary *(Ghosts, Hamlet)* worlds.

The essentials of this new dramaturgy can be glimpsed in the transformation it entails for the thematic of homecoming. Like the one mentioned in Pinter's title, the new homecomings are burdened with ironic quotation marks and skeptical question marks. Where once the gesture of departure was a near guarantee of heroic personal identity, today the attempted act of homecoming stands as emblem of the multiple, complex, and possibly incommensurable identifications given by contemporary culture. From the perspective afforded by these identifications, a perspective often figured by the image of America, home appears as an approachable but ultimately inaccessible space, not a lost paradise appropriate to nostalgia but the preserve of shaky myths and regressive fantasies.[20]

In both *The Homecoming* and *Buried Child* the figure of America disrupts the possibility of homecoming. To see what—if anything—lies beyond the drama of failed homecomings, I turn to another transatlantic pair of plays, in which the figure of America is staged and even spoken more fully. Caryl Churchill's *Ice Cream* and George C. Wolfe's *The Colored Museum* situate themselves in view of political issues in a way that contrasts sharply not only with what I have called the "provincial" self-limiting of Pinter but also with Shepard's undiscriminating play on representational surfaces. They can therefore help to frame the important question of what the politics of postmodernism are.

Ice Cream and *The Colored Museum* engage the themes we have been following in Pinter and Shepard: the problem of coming home, the status of the family as mythic reality or defunct cultural code, the rupture of space and place, the reign of prefabricated images. They also utilize a dramatic structure that takes a measured distance from the dramaturgy of the secret (of mystery, of hidden truths awaiting heroic discovery). In its place we find a dramaturgy of afterthought, a kind of theatrical *musing* on those long-term cultural investments that have taken the place once held in society by myth.

Museumology

The link between George Wolfe's play and the subject of this book is clear and powerful: the play asks us to consider what kind of home anyone can make in a museum. The museum in question is, of course, America, with which it shares the logic of displacement. Only those things are put in museums that have no "organic" place within a society, because they either belong to a different time or to a different place. The museum contains and stages difference and, in so doing, produces an artificial homogeneity in the surrounding culture.

But what happens when the culture itself is organized upon the principle of the museum, when it is a synthetic culture that is constantly staging itself *for* itself? What happens, moreover, when this cultural staging has such a long and successful history that it determines the self-construction even of those subjects whom it most thoroughly oppresses and disenfranchises, when, as Pratibha Parmar writes, "the deeply ideological nature of imagery determines not only how other people think about us but how we think about ourselves" (quoted by hooks, 5)? That is how Wolfe's play characterizes the predicament of African-Americans, faced with levels of oppression far beyond the social and economic. Wolfe's play shows, with great precision, why the kind of solution to this problem that was offered in Genet's play *The Blacks* is inadequate. The existentialist response to oppression, even when performed collectively as theater ritual, is only of limited political value (see Chaudhuri, *No Man's Stage*), especially in the context of an entire culture of images and stereotypes. Genet's Blacks chose to fight the oppressive stereotyping they endure by appropriating and defiantly embodying the available stereotypes. Wolfe's characters—being Americans—are located very far from the possibility of such elective defiance; they exist only to the extent permitted by the stereotypes. Their only gesture of freedom (if that is not an oxymoron) is the practice of parody, with all the limitations inherent in that form.

The parody with which *The Colored Museum* begins is a good example of the play's staging of America as a kind of semiotic machine that generates new forms for old experiences but leaves their core intact, or (to put it in terms more germane to this play's concerns) that provides new "skins" for old wounds but does nothing to ease their pain. In the opening scene, entitled "Git on Board," a "pert and cute" stewardess addresses the familiar fake-friendly patter of airline functionaries to an invisible group of passengers. The prosaic formulas that we all now associate with air travel—the instructions about seat belts, the information about itineraries and weather conditions—are given a grotesque twist by being linked with a very different travel history: "Welcome aboard the Celebrity Slaveship, departing the Gold Coast and making short stops at Bahia, Port-au-Prince and Havana, before our final destination of Savannah. . . . We will be crossing the Atlantic at an altitude that's pretty high, so you must wear your shackles at all times" (2).

The structure of the play develops the idea of tourism as a grotesque traveling museum: it is structured as a journey through Black history, a history of managed stereotypes that has effectively erased the possibility of truthful representations of Black experience. Even the most earnest self-representations of Blacks, especially those (like Lorraine Hansberry's *A Raisin in the Sun*) that are most widely acknowledged as being great and "universal" art, are exposed as literary stereotypes (in that case the stereotype of the "Mama-on-the-Couch Play"). Significantly, Wolfe has indicated that he conceptualizes the canonized African-American dramatic tradition in terms of place, specifically of the house as (geopathic) home: "People kept asking for a 'black' play. I kept asking, 'What's a "black" play. Four walls, a couch and a mama?' I can't live within those old definitions" (quoted in Elam, 291).

Wolfe's solution to the problem of surpassing the geopathic model bears an interesting relationship to Adrienne Kennedy's masterpiece *Fun-*

nyhouse of a Negro, one of the prior texts that, as Harry Elam Jr. has argued, Wolfe is building on.[21] Both plays refer, in their titles, to a decidedly unhomelike construction of America, as a realm of images distorted by ideology (museum) or technology (funnyhouse). Both plays also call for an ample and obvious use of white in their staging, though Wolfe's white stage contrasts with the "color" of his black characters (and thereby alludes to another contemporary classic of Black theater, Ntozake Shange's *For Colored Girls Who Have Considered Suicide When the Rainbow Is Enuf*), whereas Kennedy's white stage participates in a recognition that the discourse of racism depends on a deadly binarism of black and white, whereby the image of a spectrum of color is a deluded fantasy.

That the ubiquity of stereotypes is a threat not only to Black American *representation* but also to the actual identities of Black people is graphically and memorably asserted in a scene entitled "Symbiosis," in which "a Black man in corporate dress" throws objects from his past identifications with Black culture and Black politics into a trash bin, to the great distress of his alter ego, the Kid:

> My first pair of Converse All-Stars. Gone. My first Afro Comb. Gone. My first Dashiki. Gone. My autograph pictures of Stokely Carmichael, Jomo Kenyatta and Donna Summer. Gone. . . . My first jar of Murray's pomade. My first Can of Afro-sheen. My first box of curl relaxer. Gone! Gone! Gone! Elridge Cleaver's *Soul on Ice.* (Wolfe, 7)

The last "object" to be trashed is the Kid himself, whom the man strangles to death when he refuses to let him throw away *The Temptations Greatest Hits.* As the Kid hangs limply in his arms, the man laughs: "Man kills his own rage. Film at eleven." He throws the body in the bin, closes the lid, and explains: "I have no history, I have no past, I can't. It's too much. It's much too much. . . . Being black is too emotionally taxing therefore I will be black only on weekends and holidays" (7).

The trashed kid is, we might say, the buried child of *The Colored Museum,* and, like Shepard's tiny corpse, he carries the play's political outlook. His fate—which includes resurrection, for the scene ends with the kid's arm reaching out to grab the man's arm in a "death grip" (7)— associates him closely with the realist dramatic tradition, much closer to it than is Shepard's exhumed (and hence unquestionably dead) child. The

Kid stands for a politics of recovery, for a reclaiming of submerged identity. Significantly (in that it suggests a trend) Wolfe's position is echoed in the reported statement of Robert Alexander that his recent production of a new version of *Uncle Tom's Cabin* was "an opportunity to 'retrieve Uncle Tom,' that much-maligned figure, from *the cultural dustbin*" (Berson, "Cabin Fever," 22; emphasis added).

More practically, the play dramatizes the coding of even the most trivial and superficial of cultural material. A scene entitled "Hairpiece" has two wigs arguing their respective merits; the afro wig claims to be "a head of hair that's coming from a fo' real place," to which the long, flowing wig retorts: "Don't you dare talk about nothing coming from a 'fo' real place,' Miss Made-in-Taiwan. . . . I am quality. She is kink. I am exotic. She is common. I am class and she is trash. That's right. T-R-A-S-H" (Wolfe, 5–6).

What is trash is seen as a matter of cultural and ideological coding, thus as an area available for potential political intervention. The play ends with a party in which Topsy Washington, "a hurricane of energy," leads the cast in a vision of all Black Americans "dancing to the rhythm of their own definition" (10). The song's refrain "There's madness in me / And that madness sets me free" builds to a crescendo until the ringing allegory of the final line: Miss Pat the Stewardess saying, "Before exiting, check the overhead as *any baggage you don't claim, we trash*" (10; emphasis added).

However, the cultural problematic staged in *The Colored Museum* cannot be resolved by the call to a retrospective madness, no matter how collective, unified, and patterned it may be. The museum principle of America has been so fully exposed in the course of the play, its coercive workings so thoroughly displayed, that the concluding call to salvage certain parts of its holdings—which is in fact a humanist call to establish a history in order to derive an identity—is incoherent and sentimental.[22] To suddenly privilege a part of cultural material and treat it as exempt from the dominant culture's ideological coding is to turn one's back on the logic of intertextuality that one has uncovered and to assert an essential, acultural source for identity: "And here all this time I been thinking we gave up our drums. But now, we still got 'em. I got mine. They're here, in my speech, my walk, my hair, My God, my style, my smile and my eyes" (10). It is a measure of the conclusion's sentimentalist forgetting of intertextuality that drums are used as a metonym for Black culture; Wolfe is treading close to the unwitting racism of O'Neill's *The*

Emperor Jones, where the background drumming has been seen as organizing an offensive chain of associations linking Blacks to primitivism.
   The idea of cultural garbage gradually develops into the hinge for
the fragile political vision of the play. On the one hand, cultural garbage
is the mass-produced stereotypes that oppress Blacks; on the other hand,
what the dominant white culture calls trash can be the lifeblood of Black
identity. This latter potentiality is immensely powerful: "I, too," writes
bell hooks, "am in search of the debris of history" (166), adding (in terms
that clarify both Wolfe's project and his failure to realize it): "Theorizing
black experience, we seek to *uncover, restore, as well as to deconstruct,* so
that *new paths, different journeys* are possible" (172; emphasis added).
Wolfe's play, with its opening invocation of the figure of the journey,
suggests a similar deconstructive project, one that is, however, over-
powered and defeated by his totalized representation of America as a
museum. The reason for this failure, as I shall argue below, is that Wolfe
has failed to recognize and critique the extent to which figure of the
journey *itself* participates in dominant American mythologies.
   The "different journeys" needed to counter the stasis of the museum
tour are all but absent from *The Colored Museum.* What the play conveys
most vividly is *not* the final assertion of hope but rather an analysis of
America as a manufacturer of cultural garbage. Rather than the question
of what if anything can or should be retrieved from the cultural dustbin,
the play focuses on the museum tour itself, presenting a whole series of
stereotypes that "freeze" into sculptures at the end of the play. These
ossified models of Black identity stand in a significant relation to the
museum tour structure of the play, which begins in scene 1 as a journey
through time:

> On your right you will see the American Revolution, which will
> give the U.S. of A. exclusive rights to your life. And on your left,
> the Civil War, which means you will vote Republican until F.D.R.
> comes along. And now we're passing over the Great Depression,
> which means everybody gets to live the way you've been living.
>   *(There is a blinding flash of light. She screams)* Ahhhhhhhhhhh! That
> was World War I, which is not to be confused with World War II
> . . . *(There is a larger flash of light)* . . . Ahhhhh! Which is not to be
> confused with the Korean War or the Vietnam War, all of which
> you play a major role in. (2)

This use of the journey constructs the Colored Museum as one of those Disneyland rides that move visitors comfortably through the many versions of a single ideological narrative. As such, it is the opposite of those "new paths, different journeys" that bell hooks calls for, the ones that can somehow transform the figure of travel itself:

> There is then only the fantasy of escape, or the promise that what is lost will be found, rediscovered and returned. For black folks, reconstructing an archaeology of memory makes return possible, the journey to a place we can never call home even as we reinhabit it to make sense of present locations. Such journeying cannot be fully encompassed by conventional notions of travel. (172–73)

The other "journeying" that hooks envisages is evoked in Wolfe's play only by its opposite, for the parodic slave ship in which his contemporary African-Americans are so cheerily trapped is exclusively furnished with the alienating imagery of stereotypes, that is, with uncanny accounts of uninhabitable subjectivity. As hooks argues, the hegemony of one experience of travel can make it impossible to articulate another experience of it.

Traveling Theater

Edward Said's now famous essay "Traveling Theory" used the figure of travel to focus on a growing concern in cultural theory with the act and effects of cultural displacement.[23] The idea of travel has, however, a much older connection to the image of America, as expressed by J. Wreford Watson: "Movement is part and parcel of the American scene. It does not stop with the holiday season: it is continual. The love of wandering is what led many men to the U.S.A. This love continued with the American people. 'There is something exciting,' cried Homer Zigler in Clyde Davis's *The Great American Novel,* 'about moving, moving, always travelling'" (74).

The American construction of travel as a powerful movement of adventure is recorded in its many novels of pioneering or exploratory adventure. Just a few names—Huck Finn, Captain Ahab, Natty Bumppo—are sufficient to remind us of the literary archetype of the American hero as a man in motion. As one critic puts it, "We are tempted to say that in its fiction as in its life America is distinguished by the mobility of its individuals" (Male, 6).

In American drama, perhaps this archetype is best evoked by the absent father in *The Glass Menagerie,* who used to work for the phone company and "fell in love with long distances" (30). The spirit of this great deserter has haunted not only the drama of his children's blighted lives but many others as well, infecting the static stage of American realism with a great malaise, a painful sense of physical limitation: "The way they boxed us in here," complains Willy Loman, "Bricks and windows, windows and bricks" (17). Willy's tragedy easily boils down to an alienation from the expansive American dream of ceaseless motion, vigorously exemplified in his brother Ben, and in a sad state of crisis in his son Biff. In Miller's version of it, America's romance with perpetual motion is betrayed or contaminated by its other ideal, of material and social success, leaving a born traveler like Biff confused and unhappy.

Shepard's version is slightly different: for him, the pleasure of the road is irreducible, but its meaning is pure myth, out of the reach of cultural praxis or political analysis.[24] As Tilden explains, driving in America is something primitive, infantile, presocial:

> I had a car once! I had a white car! I drove. I went everywhere. I went to the mountains. I drove in the snow. . . . I drove all day long sometimes. Across the desert. Way out across the desert. I drove past town. Anywhere. Past palm trees. Lightning. Anything. I would drive through it and I would stop and I would look around and I would drive on. I would get back in and drive! I loved to drive. There was nothing I loved more. Nothing I dreamed of was better than driving. . . . I don't drive now . . . I'm grown up now. (103)

True to his project of transposing myth into complex and dynamic intertext, Shepard presents the American ideal of travel as a powerful text, but one that, unlike, say, the family, is incapable of undergoing revision, incapable of being captured within the formulas of middle-class realism.[25] As such, travel—driving across America—takes its place among the many losses chronicled by Shepard's drama, losses that cumulatively redefine the vibrant American Dream as an ironic jumble of fantasies. The Shepard character is one whose driving adventure has run aground. Since he lacks the luxury of a hidden secret that will set him free again, he is arrested, trapped, and doomed to repeat or freeze into patterns of deadliness. In Shepard's hands, the traveling theater of America becomes entropic.

A similar entropy—which is, politically speaking, an impasse—greets us at the end of Wolfe's museum tour. Here, however, the born-again Kid from the cultural dustbin does offer a way beyond the impasse, albeit a sentimental way, resuscitating the old depth dramaturgy of hidden meanings and identities rooted deep in the past. Wolfe's solution to the problem of American cultural entropy is as politically ineffectual as another solution to the same problem, offered in another recent American play, Tina Howe's *Approaching Zanzibar*. This is also a travel play, perhaps one of the most literal travel plays of recent times, since every one of its scenes occurs in a different place along the route of a family's journey across America.

The purpose of the journey is a visit to a dying relative, an old woman who is also an earth artist, covering huge tracts of land with her art. As the family drives along, they play the game of geography, stringing together place names in an emblematic quest for connection and completeness (alluded to in the play's A-to-Z title). The game is brought to a successful conclusion when the family's youngest member plays it with her dying aunt, while bouncing higher and higher on the deathbed. The word she repeats at the end of the game is still a place name, but of a very different sort altogether from all the others littered across the play: it is "paradise." This final verbal apotheosis (an apotheosis already so thoroughly ironized—using the same word—in the last speech of *Buried Child*), is linked to a visual one, which fortuitously anticipates the one play that (as I argue in the epilogue) most fully engages the figure of America as travel. As the family gathers around the bed, chanting the word over and over again, the child jumps higher and higher: "Hair flying and nightie billowing, she looks like a reckless angel challenging the limits of heaven. The curtain slowly falls" (102).

The spiritual meaning that Howe ascribes to travel is one way out of the impasse of that American entropy that was diagnosed by Shepard's drama.[26] Tony Kushner's *Angels in America* and Suzan-Lori Parks's *The America Play* (see epilogue) outline another, political possibility. Prefiguring these is Caryl Churchill's *Ice Cream,* which maps out a new semantic and political direction for the idea of displacement.

Travel is the organizing metaphor of Churchill's play, whose two halves are set in England and America, respectively, and whose main characters are two pairs of tourists. That tourism domesticates the figures of travel and of America is dramatized in a scene in which the English visitors to America are showered with "must sees" ("you want to see the Indians. You want to go to the caves . . . you want to see Yosemite National Park" [31–32]). All the while, the visitors try to explain what coming to America has meant to them, evoking the old American myth-meaning of travel, the one expressed by Tilden: "we thought we'd hire a car and just set off and drive . . . right across out west and then . . . down south" (32). However, when, later in the play, the English woman Jaq does take to the road, she seems (even to herself) to be fulfilling a Shepardesque vision of America as a road movie, traversing a landscape of violence, rape, death, and apocalyptic imaginings. The dream of travel as freedom, as adventure into an unknown future world, has been displaced by the American museum.

Moreover, Churchill makes it clear that the museum principle of mass-produced images may be generated by America but is no longer exclusively located there. It enshrouds England as well, covering up the realities of social and economic dislocation with guidebook inanities: "It's twelfth century up the end and thirteenth on top" (2). However, it is clear that the source of this leveling of cultural meaning is America, whose ubiquitous images and values transform other cultures into mere foils to or excrescences on its hegemonic reality.

That this hegemony, powerful though it is, has the texture of banal stupidity is conveyed by its representatives in the play, the American couple whose characteristic mode of thinking is to classify things as either "positive" or "negative." Lance and Vera are visiting England in search of a family history as well as a cultural heritage. In their pathetic quest for "ancestors" they exemplify the principle we have seen adumbrated in Pinter and more fully in Shepard, the principle of the antipathy between the mythic family and the figure of America. The pluralism (not to mention the monetarism) that characterizes their life interferes with Lance and Vera's sentimental venture in family building:

> VERA: Everyone has ancestors.
> LANCE: Yes indeed and this is where they came from. So to that extent this is our history.
> VERA: Your history.
> LANCE: If it's mine it's yours. Like a joint bank account. They would be our children's ancestors.
> VERA: My history's in Russia and Germany and god knows where.

LANCE: Not in America anyhow because America's too damn recent. . . . What nobody knows isn't history.

VERA: Just because someone doesn't know who their grandparents are doesn't make them not exist. Everyone comes from something.

LANCE: That's evolution. I'm talking about history.

(3)

The distinction made here between history and evolution encourages us to see the play's characters almost as a different species from ourselves, and indeed by the end of the play we shall see how they belong to a kind of posthomecoming world that we may or may not want to recognize as our own. In any case, the contrasting of history and evolution and the distancing of the former process from the figure of America suggest that the American experience is an experience of radical displacement, affecting the very basis of history, which is the possibility of access to specific, differentiated facts: "When I think of my European ancestors," confesses the Jewish American Vera, "I see this long row of women picking cabbages. . . . It's a cliche, I guess I think in cliches all the time" (13).

Among the clichés they live by is the notion of England as America's opposite, endowed with a tangible past ("Eight hundred years . . . I've been touching the walls to try and believe it" [2]) and a well-proportioned history ("We think the nineteenth century is history. We had wilderness and aboriginal people. For the British the nineteenth century is just now, they hardly notice it's gone" [2]). Ironically, when the American characters do eventually manage to locate some vestiges of the mythical family they have been looking for, they are confronted with a very different perspective on the relationship between England and America. Phil, an English third cousin they have found, articulates the new relationship—a reverse imperialism—between America and England, in terms that recall and also reverse the terrible judgment voiced by Pinter's Teddy when he characterized England as a "filthy urinal." Phil identifies the source of the pollution; it is none other than America:

Hamburgers are disgusting, we have them here thank you very much, so much American filth here, I completely loathe the United States of America. . . . Turn on the TV and it's American cops blowing each other through walls, this is happening all over the world. People have their own walls, they have their own policemen,

they have their own guns, they have their own deaths, thank you
very much. No wonder America is paranoid, you export all this
filth you think someone's going to throw it back at you. (9–10)

As Phil articulates it, the epidemic of American mass culture in the
world threatens to erase history itself ("Did you know the Contras think
the Americans won in Vietnam because of Rambo?" [10]), and this is a
process that overwhelms critical thought. Thus the same person—Phil
himself—who so eloquently decried the saturation of world media by
America also confesses that "The idea of Oregon, the word Oregon, just
the word Oregon really thrills me" (9). The myth of America seduces
even those whose memory, history, and culture it is erasing: this is the
perspective that refutes Wolfe's project, in *The Colored Museum*, of reclaiming the "trash" of American mass culture for the construction of a
new Black history. By contrast, *Ice Cream* suggests that the entropy of
the museum world—the world of mass-produced images and historical
clichés—may be too final to admit of recovery and recycling. A posthomecoming politics that wants to move beyond the impasse of the
figure of America must proceed otherwise.

The America of Discovery

While the figure of America makes a mockery of the sentimental family
ties of old, it underwrites the formation of new, ad hoc families, "found
families" as it were, new containers for the forces of feeling, loyalty,
love: "We would do anything for you," Vera tells Phil. "I would die. Do
I speak in cliches? I *would* die" (15). As it happens, the course of the play
provides an unexpected opportunity to test Vera's claim, an opportunity
that is also, less obviously, a chance to see what kind of dramaturgy
might represent such a world of ad hoc families.

The fact is that *Ice Cream* starts where traditional plays often end:
with an act of recognition, a family reunion. The American couple meet
their English cousins, Phil and his sister Jaq, as early as the fourth of the
play's twenty scenes, in a scene that is a broad parody of the ideas of both
family and reunion. Family is mocked as the four characters try to sort
through a hopelessly tangled skein of relationships: "So great aunt Dora
was my great /—was your greatgrandfather's—grandmother's brother's
daughter—mother's great / grandmother's" (5) and so on, for over two
pages of the script. Reunion is caricatured in the scene's anticlimactic

conclusion, when the family ties established through such hard work are summarized once again in clichés:

VERA: Do you not like family?
PHIL: I quite fancy Americans.
LANCE: Well I'm certainly very glad we found you. It's a great thrill for us.
PHIL: Shall we go for a curry? *(Blackout)*

(7)

No sooner is recognition accomplished than a second late element of traditional realist drama is introduced: the secret. *Ice Cream* gives us another literal burial, but it is not, significantly, the burial of anything thematically significant or personal like a child of incest. Instead, the four characters bury the body of a man whom Phil has killed, supposedly in self-defense. We never find out who the man was, or how he was related to Phil (Phil himself dies, accidentally, later in the play: who *he* was and whom he killed prove—amazingly—to be a matter of no dramatic consequence whatsoever). This is, one might say, burial for burial's sake, a purely formal evocation of the drama of the hidden secret. As Vera later describes it to her analyst back in America: "I joined in, I helped bury him in a wood at night, we put the dead leaves over, we ran all round in the dead leaves so they'd all be churned up so nobody—. And nobody ever did find him" (26).

The analyst's interpretation of the story (which, despite Vera's protestations, he seems to take to be a dream) reads like a checklist of all the traditional uses of the dramatic device of the hidden or buried secret: "The man in the woods is your dead ancestors, your unborn children and the part of yourself that you fear to have discovered. . . . The man in the woods is also me" (27). The final remark is suggestive in a way that of course the speaker does not intend: this burial that inaugurates a new kind of family drama, one that attempts to go beyond the failure of homecoming, marks the closure of a certain order of interpretation. The man in the woods is, in a sense, the hermeneutic principle, which has responded so well to a retrospective, causalist dramaturgy but which offers little to an open-ended, prospective, posthomecoming drama. For the fact is that "nobody ever *did* find him." The crime does not, as we might expect, provide the play with its structure. While it does draw this strange family closer together (even ironically suggests that this is the

true meaning of family ties—bonds of shared guilt and fear), this close-
ness does not become the subject of the play. Instead, the crime has the
effect of putting the play into motion, in a sense. The second half of *Ice
Cream*, set in the United States, has Phil and Jaq arrive in America and
begin a grotesque parody of tourism, in the course of which two other
deaths occur, including Phil's.

The mode of the play in this American half makes of death an
incidental occurrence, even a joke. For example, during the party given
by Lance and Vera to welcome their cousins to America, everyone gets
drunk and laughs uproariously about Phil's crime: "We buried him in a
forest—You what?—Yes, we buried—We buried him in a forest.—We
dug a hole.—Isn't this great?—And is this a secret?—Not any more"
(34). The scene ends with a guest marveling at the story of the crime, in
terms that prepare us for the remaining socioanalysis of the play, an
analysis that manages, in a very brief span of time, to present the associational chain that links America to displacement, via the figures of crime,
adventure, lawlessness, and a peculiarly amoral religiosity: "You got
away with murder. My god. Some adventure. Wow. Is this true? Jee-
zus."*(They are all laughing and shouting. Blackout)* (35).

The displacement that *Ice Cream* attributes to America (its displacement not only of other cultures, as Phil charges, but also its self-
displacement) furnishes the play with its main ideological critique.[27] But
it does more. It also serves as the play's *alternative* to the retrospective
dramaturgy of hidden truths brought to light, of depths of meaning
waiting to be unearthed. By adopting a dramatic logic of surface meaning, which is to say an acausal logic in which things happen without
preparation and planning, Churchill chooses displacement as her own
guiding principle, a choice that is not fully illuminated until the play's
very last—and extraordinarily luminous—moment.

The transformation of displacement from a thematic element to a
structural principle is an extremely difficult and risky venture. Since
displacement, or dislocation, is identified within the play's political analysis as being one of the most egregious symptoms of modernity's crisis,
it is tempting (for us and perhaps also for Churchill) to insert it into a
nostalgic Manichaean allegory, in which displacement becomes the la-
mentable opposite of a lost coherence, a mode of being that balances self
with an unbroken history and a stable geography.

The conclusion of *Ice Cream* easily lends itself to this kind of oppositional reading, for it seems to supply a whole slew of well-coded, familiar contrasts: first world/third world, modern/traditional, urban/rural, and so on. In the play's last scene, Jaq is in an airport, waiting to catch a plane back to England. In the previous scene, she has informed Vera and Lance of yet another death, this one of a history professor who tried to rape her and whom she pushed over a cliff into a lake. This sensational tabloid-style killing ("the view was really spectacular, and I gave him a push" [46]) has gone undetected as well, though Churchill reminds us, through the fearful Lance, of the prehistory of such acts, in the fiction and drama of our tradition: "even if he's totally decomposed there will be documents . . . even if he's a skeleton even if it's when we're old they'll raise him up out of the lake" (48). By this time in the play, the dramatic logic is securely enough established to assure us that Lance is fretting unnecessarily.

However, the death of the rapist-historian (here as in other minimalisms, allegory encrusts the play's surfaces) has had an important consequence. It has made Jaq decide to abandon her tour of America: "So I'd better go home" (47). This is why, in the play's last scene, she is at the airport. Significantly, Vera and Lance (who have reluctantly paid for her ticket home) are not at the airport to see her off; actually they have judged Jaq's act of self-defense too vile to allow her to be the "family" they spent their vacation hunting for: "You are some kind of monster, I opened my heart. Are you my family? your brother, you're both, I was so happy to find—You're nothing to do with me, I won't be involved in—You sicken, inhuman . . ." (49).

So Jaq is at the airport alone, allowing Churchill to do the unthinkable (in terms of traditional dramaturgy)—introduce a new major character in the last few minutes of the play. Thus even at the level of dramatic structure the South American woman passenger embodies displacement. Taking the place (in the situation, the departure scene) of the family that Jaq has gradually lost, she emphasizes her relation to the figure of family by what she says, describing her grandfather's death. She seems to stand for tradition, for family ties, for an old world of community and continuity. But to read her in this way—or only in this way—is to miss the extent to which she is a transgressive figure, a carrier of magical, even marvelous new meanings.

The transgressive element is, first, literal: though she speaks in terms that evoke tradition, she is a sort of revenant messenger, one who has traveled from and is now traveling back to her remote village in South America to report on her grandfather's death in some foreign place (presumably, America):

> The flight is the shortest part. I arrive at night and sleep at the airport and at half past six I get on a bus. Twelve hours on the bus and I stay with some friends who have a bar. In the morning I get on the boat and it arrives in the afternoon. Everyone will come in the evening to hear how my grandfather died. We could afford only one person to come and see him. (49)

Her appearance is transgressive as well, since nothing she says makes her geographical identity clear, except in the almost archetypal association with remoteness—a distant land, reached by journeying through air, land, and water. Most transgressive of all is her behavior, which breaches all the codes of rational social intercourse: the woman—in every respect "a perfect stranger"—asks Jaq to go with her: "Change your flight," she says. And when Jaq explains, "I'm not going to the same place. I'm going—" she says: "Change your destination" (50).

Change your destination. This is the transmutation of displacement from a symptom of cultural crisis to a strategy within a visionary political agenda. In spite of her magical appearance, the woman is not a deus ex machina, nor is she altogether a figment of fantasy. She herself corrects that potential interpretation, positioning herself within a new epistemology that would displace the present patronizing valuation of magic and fantasy, displace it all the way outside anything rationalism can manage:

> WOMAN: My grandfather breathed and stopped, breathed and stopped. Then I saw there was a butterfly in the room. When it went out of the window my grandfather breathed and stopped and didn't breathe again. What do you think?
>
> JAQ: I think it was a coincidence.
>
> WOMAN: I know how to think it was a coincidence. I went to university in Chicago. But I know how else to think of it.
>
> (50)

The last exchange of the play is perhaps the fullest realization of the revised principle of displacement, for it explicitly rewrites the figure of home as a movable place, a place of discovery, a place to be discovered. Here again there is the danger of a nostalgic reading, which would situate Jaq and the woman at opposite sides of a great divide; but the woman's choice of the word "go" (instead of "come") suggests that there is cooperation here rather than conflict, a joint venture (whatever it may be, *to* wherever it may be) rather than a tug-of-war:

> JAQ: I want to be at home and have a cup of tea.
> WOMAN: Go and find out. I love you already. Go and find out.
>
> (51)

Here, the incoherence of cultural difference is replaced by a crystal-clear project that makes displacement *its practice rather than its problem.* The question she asks (and, at least as I read the play, answers) takes displacement as a given; it is, in fact, framed as a choice between two familiar modes of displacement: "Are you a tourist or a traveller?" (33).

Caryl Churchill uses the mutual encounter of America and England not only to criticize the crisis of values that has brought the world to the verge of extinction, but also to think *through* this crisis to something beyond. Like Jaq, the play resists the certainty that "the world's about to end" (40). Out of its mock-apocalyptic confrontation with global extinction, it engages the possibility of a postnostalgic, posthomecoming sociality and identity, an identity that constructs place instead of being constructed by it.

The politics that *Ice Cream* inaugurates, then, is a politics of possibility. In the following two chapters, I shall discuss a number of plays that explore and elaborate that politics in terms of two specific registers: language and travel. The first of these, language, has long been recognized as a privileged site of postrealist dramatic experimentation: the innovations of expressionism and absurdism particularly having been largely charted as a new *poetics*. Into that poetics I propose to import the figure of travel, thereby remapping verbal experimentation as a response to the dislocations following upon what I have called the limits (or failure) of homecoming.

Chapter Four

The Places of Language

The intersection of a politics of location and a poetics of displacement
marks a postmodern moment in which mapping and story-telling vie as
technologies of identity formation.

—Caren Kaplan

The plays I shall be treating in this chapter were all created during the last
decade. Their contemporaneity dictates the shared feature that shall concern me here: their exploration of the place of language and narrative in
the dramatizing of displacement. The three plays I shall focus on—Eric
Overmyer's *On the Verge,* Caryl Churchill's *Mad Forest,* and Maria Irene
Fornes's *The Danube*—all undertake an effort to re-create dramatic language as a possible solution to the problems of place as originally defined
by the geopathological dramatic tradition.

This revisioning of dramatic place (and not only of dramatic place
but of place itself, of the very concept of spatial location) is in fact a
return to one of the fundamental figurations of place that I have focused
on in earlier chapters: the discourse of home. The experimentation undertaken in the plays at hand reminds us that home always was, among
other things, a place of distinctive and (for the inhabitants) memorable
language use. A family was, and is, among other things, a community of
speakers. Even more to the point for us, these speakers were often story-
tellers, participants in the creation and repetition of narratives that then
came to constitute the unofficial family history.

The telling of stories serves as the basic unit of a new system of self-
location envisioned by the plays in this chapter. Each of these plays has
narrative as one of its subjects, and each of them, with very different
effects, frames narrative within a problematic of language. The most
common among these problematics is censorship, but translation—the

problem of interlinguistic communication in a world desperately in need
of connection—is also a major concern.

The *topographic* theater represented by these plays is a response, if
not a solution, to geopathology. It posits a new kind of placement, not in
any one circumscribed and clearly defined place but in the crossroads,
pathways, and junctions between places. At the extreme it advocates a
new kind of placelessness that departs decisively from Ibsen's utopianism, suggesting instead the possibility of a *polytopianism:* placelessness
not as the absence or erasure of place but as the combination and layering, one on top of another, of many different places, many distinct
orders of spatiality.

What's It Got to Do with Burma?

Of the three plays I shall deal with here, the most explicitly and self-
consciously topographical is Eric Overmyer's *On the Verge,* whose subtitle, *The Geography of Yearning,* indicates the metaphorical direction of
its inquiry into the nature of place. Like a number of recent theater
works, including Robert Wilson's *The Forest* (1989) and Meredith
Monk's *Atlantis* (1992), *On the Verge* uses the figure of travel to explore
cultural and personal issues. But whereas for Wilson the journey is a
metaphor for history and for Monk it is a metaphor for spiritual quest,
for Overmyer travel is a celebration of the imagination. As one of his
characters photographs "an imaginary native," she conjures with words
to reveal the premise of the play: "Image. Native. Image-Native. Imaginative" (27). Travel here is a hunt for images, verbal images mostly but
also a few striking visual ones, especially one that can shed light on the
play's unusual relationship to the realist dramatic tradition from which it
otherwise departs so thoroughly. The image, which I shall discuss later,
marks the play as being in part a commentary on the role of the stage in
dealing with the object-drenched world of the present.

On the Verge* is the comic saga of three American "lady travellers"
who, in 1888, set off to explore terra incognita. Their adventures evoke
some of the archetypal associations of travel, especially that of the vital—
and vitalizing—encounter with the Other. At the same time, their journey entails a revisioning of the terms of that encounter in such a way as to
redefine otherness itself. The Other is defined in this play as an effect of
language, a matter of new words. However, since the main lexicon from
which these new words are drawn is, in the ladies' temporal terms, the

"future," which is, of course, our present and past, the encounter with the Other is in fact an encounter with the self, the cultural self of twentieth-century America.

This appropriation of the trope of travel for cultural self-analysis resembles in some ways the move of geopathology, in which problems of self are figured as and through problems of place and placement. However, Overmyer's strategy avoids the geopathic trap by choosing a linguistic rather than a psychological register for its characterology. The play's three protagonists experience the future (our present and past) as a region of objective and material existence, not as a subjective state. Their approach to it is scientific, anthropological; although each of them has enough personalized biographical background to flesh out a traditional realist character, their theatrical life is given to cultural experience, especially to linguistic and poetic discovery, rather than to self-searching. The experience they afford us, therefore, is quite different from that afforded by geopathic drama, which codes the world subjectively and binarily: here versus there, outside versus inside, belonging versus not belonging. This play codes the world as cultural space, a highly differentiated and infinitely signifying arena awaiting a special strategy of (re)discovery.

The play opens on a bare stage, where "the ladies are in a hot, white light." Their opening remarks, after one of them announces that it is "Day One. Landfall," immediately evoke the play's characteristic and paradoxical use of verbal detail to conjure spatial uncertainty: "Beach.—Island or continent?—Isthmus or archipelago?—Beach. Narrow ribbon. Cliff face. Sheer. Beyond—?—Up and over—?—Unbearable anticipation. Mysterious interior" (1).

The naming of the unknown is the central problematic of *On the Verge*, and its conviction seems to be that the unknown names itself. The elaborate strategies of discovery devised by human beings to record and decode the unknown are therefore rather redundant, even somewhat ludicrous. We learn in scene 2 that among the items the travelers are carrying with them is "a gross of hand-tinted picture postcards." Fanny admits to having had them fabricated since "I anticipate they will not be readily available en route." They are representations in all senses of that problematic word, both mimetic and projective: "preconceptions" of the unknown, "generic scenes of general interest. Generic fauna. Generic jungle. Generic bush" (3).

Over against the fantasied imagery of otherness represented by the postcards is set a mode of representation long associated with theatrical realism: photography. The placement and role of the photograph in this play illuminate its problematic (which as we have seen stretches all the way back to *The Wild Duck*[1] and made its contribution to the ironic realism of the failed-homecoming plays of Pinter and Shepard). In this play, the figure of photography is introduced in close proximity to the image of the body as coded object. While making the inventory of their baggage, Mary unpacks a rhinestone tiara and a blond wig, which she explains as follows: "Whenever I must palaver with pasha or poobah, I don this tonsorial getup. And lay out a formal tea. It never fails to impress." Then she concludes: "It stands to reason. Savages are naked. For the most part" (4). The cartoonish scene evoked by these lines is the immediate context for the figure of photography. Continuing the inventory, Alex announces, to the amazement of her companions, that she has "a Kodak!" They examine the camera as if it were some magical object, while Alex explains that "the film, it's called, captures the image. . . . Like honey. Insects in amber. Silver nitrate" (4). As the scene progresses, other perspectives are added to this poetic one, providing what is in fact a quite sophisticated, if playful, reflection on the nature of photography.

Photography's capture of the image, it is hinted, is reductive, even deathly. Like "insects in amber," the human bodies it seizes are frozen and lifeless. No wonder, then, that "the natives say they steal your spirit," and Mary, who believes that "physical specimens are what count. . . . something [one] can lay one's hands on," finds photography "misleading." Against these two very different objections, one supernaturalistic, one materialistic, Alex argues the value of photography, stressing its unique temporalization: "An unseen moment that would have vanished without a trace is brought to light. The spirit is not stolen. It is illuminated" (5).

The fixing, even the *redeeming* of time from oblivion and irrelevance is one of photography's gifts; another, far less obvious but perhaps much more valuable, is the peculiar lesson that its specific technology teaches: the lesson of a certain kind of patient imagination, which Alex calls "trust." The lady travelers' situation heightens this condition of photography, for the time between the inception and the completion of the photograph is drawn out much further than usual:

> FANNY: You won't see what you've Kodaked?
> ALEX: Not until we return home.

FANNY: How do you know that it works?

ALEX: You just trust. "You click." You store. You protect. You wait.

FANNY: You hope and pray.

ALEX: You trust. Transport. Guard with your very life. Years of deserts, mountains, pagan tribesmen, and inclement weather. Back in civilization, you hand over your nascent images. Have they survived the travails of the trek? Breathless, you await the results of the chemical revelation. With a little luck—voila! Kodaks! Lovely mementos. And, best of all, incontrovertible proof for posterity. Documentation.

(4-5)

This innocent association between the figures of travel and of photography, according to which the photograph completes the journey—brings it all home, as it were—is thoroughly contested in the play, which playfully undermines all systematic attempts to record and document the experience of travel.

Among the discourses that turn travel into misrepresentation are the "lurid tabloids" that are often mentioned because one of the women, Fanny, happens to be a correspondent for one of them, *True Trek*. It is the kind of publication that prefers to refer to a crocodile as "The Mighty Silurian," and that regularly includes in its fare scandalous accounts of the behavior of rival correspondents: "Some years back," recalls Fanny, "my arch nemesis on *The Globetroteress* reported I had got myself up in male haberdashery" (10). The genre of travel writing featured in these journals saturates the play in the form of brief "journal entries" with which each scene concludes. These statements, which are delivered directly to the audience by one or other of the three women and which, according to the author's prefatory note, should be spoken as *text* ("they are not being written in the moment, but have been composed previously, and are now being shared") encapsulate the play's metaphorization of travel. In these texts, the entire world-cultural matrix is transformed into an elaborate spectacle of which even the most bizarre details are supportive rather than disruptive of the alien onlooker's pleasure:

In Kuala Lumpur, the seraglio of the Sultan was—a honeycomb. It was as many chambered as the heart of a tribe. I recall the cavernous steam rooms on cold evenings, full of echoing voices and escarp-

ments of mist. The inlaid geometric gold-leaf calligraphy. The rat-
tan sofas. The acres of tile the color of the sky. And a sponge
conjured from the exoskeleton of an indigenous fruit. The loofah.
Loofah—. (17)

To call this speech orientalist or Eurocentric is obviously an understate-
ment. Its disregard for any but the most spectacular attributes of other
cultures (with its implicit indifference to the deeper level of cultural
difference) is so outrageous as to remove it altogether from the realm of
any kind of intercultural discourse, however regressive. Rather, it is a
purely verbal discourse, a *poetics of travel* that apprehends the world
primarily as a source for exotic *words*.

That meaning is not, of course, apolitical; its politics, difficult
though they are to discern, are of a kind often identified with postmodernism, and they involve a certain view of history and of difference as
absence, as erasure. One direction from which these politics can be
glimpsed is the play's treatment of gender. The issue of gender is introduced early in the play, when Mary, the anthropologist among them
(who later dismisses photography because she wants "Physical evidence.
Not impressions. Not imagery. Not emotion. Objectivity. Not poetry"
[5]), gives us her first journal entry:

> Before I began my travels in the uncharted reaches of the world, an
> avuncular colleague took me aside. "I have heard your peregrina-
> tions are impelled, in part, by scientific curiosity," he said. "Allow
> me to offer you some sage counsel. Always take measurements,
> young lady. And always take them from the adult male." Sound
> advice. (2)

As "lady travellers," the women displace a number of impacted cultural
norms, especially the powerful one that equates masculinity with travel
and discovery and condemns women to lives of sequestered immobility.
Their breaching of this norm (the inspiration for which, Overmyer notes
in a postscript, came from such accounts of Victorian lady travelers as
Evan S. Connell's *A Long Desire*, Luree Miller's *On Top of the World*,
Alexandra Allen's *Traveling Ladies*, and Dorothy Middleton's *Victorian
Lady Travelers*) does not, however, open into further feminist social
critique in the course of the play. Apart from the ironic avuncular advice
just quoted, the complex issue of gender under patriarchy is evoked only

through a kind of running gag, a debate about which is the more suitable dress for hiking, skirts or trousers. Alexandra, who maintains that trousers are not only more practical for such activities as scaling promontories but that they are, in fact, "the future," is opposed by Mary, who argues that "The civilizing mission of Woman is to reduce the amount of masculinity in the world. Not add to it by wearing trousers" (8). Mary is also able to adduce certain compelling examples of the preferability of "a good stiff petticoat" in certain unforeseen situations. "One evening in Malaya near dusk, I fell ten feet into a man-eating tigertrap. Found myself nestled on a cathedral of punji sticks. If I had been wearing trousers, I would have been pierced to the core, and done for. Instead, I found myself sitting on a dozen razor-sharp spikes, in comparative comfort" (9).

The debate concludes in a way that exemplifies the play's political tendency: Alexandra, who has argued for trousers all along, is vindicated. As the women's trek takes them further and further into the future, Fanny concedes that Alexandra's preference was prophetic: "It seems to me that you were right," says Fanny. "Trousers. Trousers trousers trousers. It seems clear to me that everyone in the future wears 'em" (55). The play pursues a kind of politics of demonstration, a playful, light statement that the past world of anthropologized othernesses will give way, must give way, and in fact *has* given way to something less restrictive, less compartmentalized, less heavily coded. It is a politics that might easily be condemned as naive or utopian, were it not for the liberal dose of irony that accompanies it.

As the women discover their own polytopian tendencies to be the structuring principle of the new world of the future, their celebration of the language of faraway places turns out to have unexpected totalitarian powers: in the new world, language leaves its originary places far behind and becomes, itself, the very landscape: "Why do they call it Burma Shave? What's it got to do with Burma?" The plot of the play, if one can identify any such traditional dramatic element in this essentially performative piece, lays out the transformation of language, in the course of this century, from a record of radical and enigmatic otherness—a matter of seraglios and silurians—to a collection of buzzwords and brand names.

Though Fanny is dismayed to find how much "language takes a beating in the future" (50), the play as a whole clings to Alex and Mary's sense of exhilaration at the proliferation of brave new words. The spectator, who does not, of course, share the characters' blissful ignorance of the nature of the lexicon that thrills them so, is positioned in between the two extremes. Neither able to share their relish for the unaccustomed flavor of such words as "The Domino Theory. The Third World. Boat people. Heavy Water. Enhanced Radiation. . . . Melt down. Ground zero" (80), nor quite able to resist their excitement and optimism about the future: "Billions of new worlds, waiting to be discovered. Explored and illuminated. . . . I stand on the precipice. The air is rare. Bracing. Before me stretch dark distances. Clusters of light. What next? I have no idea. Many mysteries to come. I am on the verge" (82). The spectator of *On the Verge* is seduced by the poetry of travel yet is constantly reminded that the "chronokinesis" he or she is witnessing is really an unfolding, through alien eyes and with unaccustomed pleasure, of the shape of the present. And that present is, in fact, an erasure of the fundamental principle of true travel: the difference between places. As the travelers' journey brings them closer and closer in time to us, we see that they are in fact the "tourists" that they so stoutly deny being. The experience of the new they are having is of the order of tourism, a meaningless encounter with the superficial signs of a culture. The culture in question is the very one we have already identified as the limits of homecoming, the structuring of modern existence that has turned the specificity of place into the abstraction of homogenized and anonymous space. It is the culture whose lexicon is filled with such words as Cool Whip, Mr. Coffee, barbeque, rock and roll, jacuzzi, and congoleum ("What's it got to do with the Congo?"). The women have no difficulty in naming it: "From here the future looks . . . positively—AMERICAN" (46).

The merry wordplay that is the sum and substance of *On the Verge* may seem too slight a thread on which to hang a cultural analysis of any kind, much less one that charts the postmodern path out of geopathology. But the play's combination of the figures of travel and photography is immensely suggestive. Photography's ambiguous promise of meaning ("with a little luck . . . documentation"), its retemporalization of the coded bodies of self and others, defined an entire era—and an entire semiology—of travel. The travel that unfolded in the company of the "Kodak" enacted all the desires of modernity: as Mary summarizes it, "Geography, cartography, ethnology, and the natural sciences" (59). As the future emerges, the figure of discovery is slowly reversed: instead of awaiting discovery, the future discovers *them,* filling their mouths with jingles and brand names. "Locating" them. In America.

The mutual meanings of America and travel—a new perspective that reveals their incompatibility—come into view during the scene I mentioned earlier as containing a striking visual image capable of explicating some part of the logic of realism. It is the first scene of act 2 and is entitled "Fanmail from the Future." By now the lady travelers have realized what is happening to them, that they are "beginning to know the future." Strange words are popping into their mouths, and they are even beginning to "osmose" their meanings. Then suddenly, they encounter "A pathway of light. Objects appear in the air before them: a dazzling array of toys and junk and gadgets and souvenirs and appliances and electronic wonders, everything from an acid-pink hula hoop to a silver laser video disc" (44). Two phrases come to their lips to describe this extraordinary phenomenon, and both are fraught with terrible connotations, though of course the delighted speakers know them only as wonderful verbal novelties: "Fallout from the future," they exclaim, and "A rain forest of fossils from the future." The deathly life of objects in the futuristic world of our present appears here, clothed as miracle and mystery, and reveals what the littered stages of modern drama had always already expressed. The "world of things," as Peter Szondi called it, has haunted the obsessive subjectivity of realist drama, silently threatening the dialectic of self-consciousness. When Chekhov's Gaev addressed his bookcase, the embarrassment of his family hid from us the play's own fractured dialogue with the inanimate world, with samovars and rooms and orchards. Among theorists of theater, Walter Benjamin was the one to recognize that the modern drama came into being as a displacement of the realm of things. As Rainer Nägele writes,

In the Baroque *Trauerspiel,* in Calderon's theater, in the Romantic tragedies of fate, things assert their uncanny power. Benjamin gives them his special attention, which arises out of an affinity of experience. The strange intertwining of things and words in the *Berliner Chronik* and the *Kindheitserinnerungen* cannot be reduced to a critique of reification in the bourgeois world. The world of things is too ambiguous for such a reduction because of both the intensity with which they are experienced and the rigorousness with which they are pursued. Even in its social dimension reification is not a purely negative phenomenon for Benjamin. He sees, for example, the reification of the actor into a pure requisite of the film industry as a welcome critique of the bourgeois notions of the subject. (14)

The modern drama's overvaluation of characterology plunged into
the shadows the inhuman world of objects, until (in the postgeopathological figure of America) the erasure of place releases the objects into the abstract space of commodities and consumer culture. A
significant consequence of this new order of things—the reversal of the
causality linking characters with things—is humorously staged in *On the
Verge*. Early in the play, the women come upon a strange object and
speculate about its nature:

> FANNY: What do you think it could be?
> MARY: A fan. For this glaze of tropical heat.
> FANNY: *(Rotors)* Does not generate the slightest breeze.
> MARY: A talisman.
> FANNY: Totem.
> MARY: Amulet.
> FANNY: Taboo. Alexandra?
> ALEX: Marsupial's unicycle.

The object is in fact an old-fashioned eggbeater. Fanny finally puts it in
her belt, "like a six shooter" (11). A little later, Alex finds another eggbeater, and Mary is given yet another ("We're giving these away with a
full tank"), which they too begin to wear in their belts. Periodically the
women draw their eggbeaters and rotor them, for fun, never divining
their true usage. The eggbeaters, then, are among the few facts of their
journey to survive the explicatory force of the oncoming future. Alone
among an expanding store of readable word- and object-signs, the eggbeaters remain objects of pure play for the women. For us, however,
they are revealed for what they are: talismans indeed, but of the triumph
of consumer culture.

What *On the Verge* allows us to see is that the dialectic of words and
things is played out—like all the major dialectics of twentieth-century
drama—within the semiology of place. The approach to the potency of
the present is made through the figure of travel, combined with attendant figures of modernist discourse (notably anthropology) exemplified
through photography. The perfect emblem for this approach is the campaign button the ladies discover early in the play, bearing the mysterious
inscription "Heckw-hod-ont?" The comic hermeneutic that fails to decode this mystery until the companion button is discovered, bearing the

legend "I like Ike," is not only the play's parody of plot. It is also the clearest rendition of its postmodern thematic, where meaning is lodged, contextually, in objects, and signification arises only from the thick web of cultural discourse that lies over everything. Mary, clinging to her modernist faith in the eventual intelligibility of all things, urges her companions: "We have the artifacts—we must find their historical moment" (44–45). But a different principle is now in play. The exciting, experience-giving natural world of typhoons and jungles and icy cliffs is left far behind; in this "orchard of the future" that is our world, objects circumscribe subjectivity, and history vanishes into the ahistorical and abstract expanse of consumer space. "You are not of this era?" Fanny asks Mr. Coffee, who replies, "No. Not exclusively" (50).

The replacement—of things, of people—in history, as well as the consequent erasure of traditional notions of historicity, is in part the subject of Caryl Churchill's *Mad Forest*, where language, especially language as narrative, is tested as a solution to what the play first (and at great and systematic length) identifies as a new geopathology, the actual and terrible ill placements wrought by totalitarianism. In the dystopia of repressive regimes like Ceauşescu's, people have to carve meaning out of silence, and identities have to be negotiated out of a welter of myths and stereotypes and desires and dreams and daydreams. All these modes of thought and imagination are pressed into service in this extraordinary play, as is the figure of America. Here, as in Pinter and Overmyer (and as we shall later see, in many other plays as well), America stands as a principle of abstraction and uncanniness, transforming things into generic and hyperbolic versions of their former—useful—selves.

Reading Romania

The importance of place is announced in both the title and the subtitle of Caryl Churchill's play, *Mad Forest: A Play from Romania*. The subtitle records more than the subject of the play; it also accurately describes the play's composition, for *Mad Forest* indeed hails from Romania, having been created from work done in Romania by Caryl Churchill, the director Mark Wing-Davey, and a group of student actors from London's Central School. The play emerged from an unusual theatrical engagement with a place: the English group worked with Romanian students of the Caragiale Institute of Theatre and Cinema in Bucharest; they also developed the scripts out of long interviews and talks with many people. The problem of place, that is, of relating to and engaging with an unfamiliar place, is one of its main concerns.

Mad Forest explores the peculiarly postmodern effect that makes certain things—especially places—seem both familiar and unfamiliar. This eerie effect, to which the term *uncanny* can perhaps most accurately be applied, is understood in this play to be caused by various mediations, ranging from myth to mass media. Taken all together, these mediations move us toward an auralization of dramatic meaning. In a sense, *Mad Forest* is a demonstration of why the spatial mode of postmodern representations must give way to a renewed narrativity, of why the painfully emergent history of our times must be not only seen (or "shown," as on TV) but *heard*. In the extreme, *Mad Forest* presents place itself as a function of change, and change, in turn, as an effect of language, especially spoken language.

The subject of *Mad Forest* can easily be invoked by certain catchphrases made familiar by the mass media: the failure of communism, the defeat of Soviet-sponsored totalitarianism, the breakup of the Eastern bloc, even (rather grandly) the end of history. Churchill's play begins by systematically (some might even say schematically) evoking the world these phrases conjure up. The first act of *Mad Forest* consists of sixteen brief scenes that employ an up-to-date cinematic idiom to sketch out the horrors and hardships of life under Ceauşescu. In quick succession we get several slice-of-life renditions of moments and situations that illustrate such material conditions as long breadlines, scarcity of products like eggs and cigarettes, school education as pure propaganda, and, above all, the various forms of state terror. Much of the conditionality of living under a terroristic regime is expressed in terms of various pressures on and distortions of language.

In one of the early scenes of the play, three students sit around a table smoking cigarettes and exchanging stories. They discuss politics, though obliquely, and they tell jokes. One of their jokes could well serve as the motto for the play, for it summarizes the peculiar combination of anticipation and surprise—or inevitability and impossibility—that characterizes both its subject and its theatrical functioning.

The joke tells of a man who has just got a long-awaited new car and takes it out on a drive. The car is hit in the rear by a Securitate (secret police) car. So incensed is the driver that he attacks the official car, starting to bang on the hood. Just then a truck hits the Securitate car from behind. The driver of this truck does the same as the first driver had done—he begins smashing the government car. The Securitate man is amazed. "I can understand him being upset," he says to the second driver, "because I hit his car. But what's the matter with you?" The second driver, hearing this, stops what he is doing and says: "I'm sorry, I thought it had started" (21).

The idea of the Romanian revolution as something inevitable, something just waiting to happen, is part of the play's central proposition: that a hyperpredictability informs the way that history and politics are experienced in the contemporary world. Taking up an idea that has preoccupied cultural analysts for some time, *Mad Forest* suggests that history no longer happens but *is played,* or played out, according to a prewritten scenario, for an audience. But the play is not content simply to present this notion, which, after all, is hardly unfamiliar by now, having already been tagged and labeled in such postmodern theories as Jean Baudrillard's ("simulations") or Umberto Eco's ("hyperreality"). In a move that distinguishes her from postmodernists as much as from Brechtians, Churchill passes beyond the abstract idea of a metahistory by insisting that, in spite of this codifiability of events into predictable patterns and outcomes, the future is radically unknowable. This resistance of actual events, especially events that will produce momentous change and liberation, to the deadening imposition of stereotypical master narratives is what gives the students' joke its theatrical (and political) force: "it" will, inevitably, start; the time of totalitarian oppression must indeed have a stop. Yet when it does happen, it will be a complete shock, a harrowing encounter with that worst of all othernesses: the (self-)repressed.

The structure of *Mad Forest* also suggests the logic of a return of the repressed. The play is divided into three acts, two of which occur before the intermission. This intermission is more than a period of rest for the audience and the very active company, each member of which plays several roles and all of whom are onstage for the extraordinarily intense (and expansive) second act that precedes the intermission. The intermission is more even than a period of relief from the harrowing presentation, in quasi-documentary style, of life in Romania under the Ceauşescu regime. What it is, this intermission, is a final spell of familiarity— political, cultural, and epistemological familiarity—before the complicated apparatus of this play fulfills the function it has been designed for from the outset: to take the audience through the looking glass of contemporary politics and show it the hidden, dark face of the present.[2]

The looking glass in this case is the mass media, or, more precisely, the complicity between the mass media and certain contemporary Western imperialistic habits of representation, especially the addiction to stereotypes and sentimentalities.[3] As for what I have just called the other face of contemporary politics, it is the spectator's face: not only the spectator in the theater but also, and more importantly, that same spectator's full-time spectatorial function in that media's reductionist account of cultural difference. *Mad Forest* lays bare the nature of the West's encounter with the othernesses represented by Romania.

This encounter is evoked, first, in the play's title, which refers to a once-real place in Romania, the forest that covered the area where Bucharest now stands. This now-invisible forest has bequeathed its nature to the city and the country that have replaced it: like it, they are "impenetrable to the foreigner who [does] not know the paths" (5). Refusing to claim immunity to the mystery of this place, the play chooses instead to track the difficulties faced by those—spectators, but equally playwright and performers—who seek to navigate its paths. Romania, its people, its history, and its revolution appear here as elements of a radical otherness, resisting all the protocols of intelligibility (including "documentary drama,"[4] including so-called in-depth media coverage) that seek to vanquish—that is, normalize—difference. Among these Churchill singles out for special use one discourse, that of tourism, which most readily appropriates and reduces difference.

The figure of tourism gives the first act its frame. Every scene of this act is preceded by a brief announcement of the action of the scene. The first scene, for instance, is announced as "Lucia has four eggs," while the second is "Who has a match?" What seems to be a simple Brechtian device—an explicit statement of the "gestus" of each scene—becomes much more by the fact that each brief announcement is doubly articulated, spread out over two languages (the phrase is spoken first in Romanian, then in English, then in Romanian again) as well as two speech modes (the first Romanian utterance, each time, is made haltingly, as when one reads out something transcribed in an unknown language; the second Romanian utterance, spoken after the English version, is enunciated clearly and confidently). The device is thus a kind of encapsulated staging of the tourist experience, that most modern and most uncanny of relations to place. Tourism is a method of experiencing other places in terms one already understands, a method for canceling out unfamiliarity. Through tourism the West "reads" otherness by reading *out* all that makes it strange and different. The first act of *Mad Forest* (the second and third acts do not use this phrase-book device) thus presents Romania as a "tourist text," a place whose politics—and whose actual lived human lives—have been placed at a distance from Western experience by the West's own geoconstructions.

But *Mad Forest* does not simply diagnose the West's alienation; it also participates in the possibilities of breaching this alienation, while always guarding against the lure of sentimentality and stereotype. The play's chief instrument for overcoming the mindlessness of false familiarity is its recognition of the exceptional pressures under which language is put in the context of contemporary politics. Language is staged in this play as a comprehensive system of communication, expression, *and their opposites,* a system that is uncommonly responsive to the most varied of personal and political needs.

Ironically, much of the language in the first act (the "tourist" act) exists in the register of noncommunication. Many of the conversations in this act unfold in the palpable presence of a ubiquitous state terror, a police state capable of such effective surveillance of its citizens that not even the most private of places—homes, doctor's offices, lovers' rooms—can provide a safe context for honest speech. In this oppressive environment, all language, even the most innocent exchanges between ordinary people, is twisted, distorted, attenuated, sometimes even obliterated altogether. Words are still used, but almost never as they are meant to be used, to express meaning. Here, in the sequence of brief and often silent or near-silent scenes that make up the play's first act, words are used more often to cover meaning than to express it. The most literal case of this occurs in a scene set in a doctor's office, in which the doctor loudly proclaims that "There are no abortions in Romania" while simultaneously pocketing a bribe in exchange for which he writes down an address and hands it to the desperate young woman.

The problem of censorship provides the frame for *Mad Forest*'s exploration of both the politics of place and the resulting problematic of representation. The first scene of the play makes an explicit and unexpected connection between politics and representation when it shows a couple's use of the radio to mask their conversation from presumed listening devices. The process of the scene is the same as the process of the play as a whole and has three distinct stages. (1) It begins with an image or action that produces an effect of apparent familiarity: the couple look like a typical unhappily married middle-aged couple; when one of them turns the radio's volume up we "recognize" this as an act of typical marital sullenness and hostility. (2) Our sense of "easy readability" is upset in some way: the woman gets up and starts talking to her husband; their conversation is inaudible to us because of the radio. A period of disorientation ensues. (3) In the final stage we move to a dawning understanding, but this understanding has a precise direction: it is not a clarification of the new state of affairs, not, that is, of the shape and meaning of an emerging future, but rather a recognition of the fact that it was the past and the present—the familiar, that is—that one was misunderstanding. The process thus ends with a revisionist insight. At both the levels the play pursues, the personal and the historical-cultural, this process stages a return *to* the repressed, to the archaic materials of personal and cultural identity.

Among the most striking icons of stereotypical cultural identity staged by the play are a vampire and an angel. The latter first appears in act 1 in a dialogue with a priest whom it assures that Romania is a place of freedom: "Not outer freedom of course but inner freedom" (21). The priest expresses shame and anguish about his position (presumably, his lack of resistance to the dictatorship of Ceauşescu): the angel simply advises him to "keep clear of the political side" of things. The scene itself is simple and, in terms of its analysis of the role of religion, perhaps even simplistic. What gives it its enormous theatrical force is its participation in the revisionary structural process of the play. The angel's appearance is so incongruous with the social and political material that has preceded it in the previous eight scenes that its initial appearance suggests a joke, a fancy dress. Then its serious dialogue with the priest tempts one to read it as some sort of internal colloquy, between the priest and his conscience. The scene as it develops discredits this assumption, showing it to be the psychologistic prejudice that it is (and that we have). Eventually there is no "explanation" for the angel: he is there, onstage, part of the discourse about making sense of a truly foreign politics. Once again, the direction of change, for the spectator's understanding, is not toward a clarification of the unfamiliar; it is recognition of the actual enigma of the supposedly familiar.

The vampire, who first appears in the first scene of act 3, entitled "The dog is hungry" (and featuring a talking dog), derives his theatrical pertinence from another stereotype about Romania, recorded in countless vampire movies. The play's relation to that stereotype is complex, as suggested by the simple statement in the production notes to the play

that, in the original production, "the Vampire was not dressed as a
vampire." This vampire, then, both participates in and displaces the pop-
cultural stereotype. He is a literalization at one and the same time of the
perniciousness of cultural reductions and of the actual terrors that these
images often encode: "I came here for the revolution, I could smell it a
long way off" (44–45). He asks the dog his age—"five, six"—and
boasts: "You look older, but that's starvation. I'm over five hundred but
I look younger, I don't go hungry." The fundamental theme of the scene
is hunger, and how much more complicated it is than most political
systems allow. Hunger here is entwined with other needs: loneliness,
love, kindness, relationship. The dog says he belonged to someone who
threw him out: "I miss him. I hate him." There follows a kind of brief
courtship in which the dog successfully wins over the reluctant vampire
as his master.

   Once again, as with the angel, it is tempting to read this scene
allegorically, especially in the light of a conversation two characters have
later, about the dead Ceauşescu:

   FLORINA: Sometimes I miss him.
   RADU: What? Why?
   FLORINA: I miss him.
   RADU: You miss hating him.

                                                                    (61)

But the theatrical force of the vampire and the dog goes far beyond a
simple allegory. These startling figures signify much more than a mere
speculation that people love their oppressors; their origins in cultural
myth, as well as their constitution of a moment of bold antirealistic
theatrology, signify the complex representational context of politics.[5]
This revolution (and any revolution) is not just an event; it is a painful
turn in a long, ongoing narrative that has a logic of its own. The revolution does not define the cultural narrative; it has to *find* its meaning
within it, locate itself within its established narratological codes.

   In a parallel way, the play itself does not attempt to provide an
exposition of the Romanian revolution; it is not that kind of historical
drama. Its link to historicity is by way of a critique of historiography. It
stages the distance between fact and history and uses an early scene to
comment ironically on the political implications of our faith in history.
The scene shows one of the main characters, Flavia, who teaches history

in a school, delivering a lecture on Romanian history. Her speech is easily recognizable as the piece of blatant propaganda it is: "The new history of the motherland is like a great river with its fundamental starting point in the biography of our general secretary, the president of the republic, Comrade Nicolae Ceauşescu, and it flows through the open spaces of the important dates and problems of contemporary humanity" (16). After the revolution, this same teacher finds herself on the wrong side of history and defends herself in terms that define one perspective constantly staged (and contested) by the play: that the meaning of political events is a function of narrative, of texts and textuality, and that people are merely its conduits: "All I was trying to do was teach correctly. Isn't history what's in the history book? Let them give me a new book, I'll teach that" (65). By the end of the play, her perspective has altered enough for her to say: "I'm going to write a true history so we'll know exactly what happened" (86); however, by this time the events of the play have decisively discredited such an idea; the true history, including and perhaps especially the true history of our very own times, cannot be *written* or read, it can only be told—and heard.

Mad Forest stages several scenes of telling, usually showing communication of various degrees of urgency. The joke telling scene in act 1 is one extreme, where brief stories rehearse the desperation of life under a totalitarian regime. The long scene that makes up all of act 2 is the other extreme, a tour de force of symphonic dramatic writing. The many voices and accents woven together here, and the many personal stories about each speaker's moment-by-moment experience of the revolution, read out history as a discontinuous, contradictory, and multiple skein of narratives. As the stage direction says: "Each behaves as if the others are not there and each is the only one telling what happened" (29). The "true history" staged here speaks with so many voices and includes so many perspectives that it quite defeats the dream of a single, stable, and authoritative master narrative.

More importantly and originally, this vision of history also interrogates and revises the notion of community or group, removing the quality of fixed identity—often fixed in place with stereotypes—and replacing it with a sense of fluid association. This revisioning has a distinctly theatrical or performative flavor, for the sense of community that emerges resembles, more than anything else, an *ensemble*. This identification is most clearly seen in the magnitude of the difference between the play's two weddings, in acts 1 and 3, respectively. In some sense the meaning of the revolution, of change, is exemplified more fully by this difference than by anything else in the play. Thus the remainder of my discussion is an attempt to trace the path of the difference between Lucia's wedding and that of her sister Florina. The path I shall describe leads away from geopathology to topography, away from the problem of place to the place(ings) of language.

"What If I Don't Get My Passport?"

Lucia's wedding is the ritualistic conclusion—staged superritualistically, with a priest intoning and repeating a ritual marriage text—of act 1. The action of this act essentially recodes some of the basic gestures of traditional geopathic drama. The plot deals with Lucia's attempts to marry her American fiancé, Wayne (who appears only once, in the wedding scene itself), and go with him to America. But Lucia's geopathic experience differs significantly from that of earlier protagonists in that it is figured as impersonal, general, shared. Her problem appears only as a tiny fraction of a huge problematic that will in no way be solved or even affected if she manages to effect the displacement she so desires.

Moreover, Lucia's geopathic condition, her wish to go to America, is not presented in the psychological terms of traditional geopathic drama. In fact, her feelings about her situation are minimally the subject of the three scenes of the act in which she appears. In scene 1, entitled "Lucia has four eggs," Lucia and Florina come home with eggs and foreign cigarettes, Bogdan (their father) deliberately breaks an egg by throwing it on the floor, and, while the others look on, "Florina gets a cup and spoon and scrapes up what she can off the floor" (14). This simple yet extraordinary action is performed in silence. It is followed by the first of several scenes in which we get indications of the consequences of Lucia's simple desire. Here Radu, who loves Lucia's sister Florina, tries in vain to get his parents to agree to their wedding. "It's not her fault if her sister—" begins Radu, only to be interrupted by his father, Mihai: "The whole family. No. Out of the question" (15).

Whether "the whole family" is unacceptable because of what Lucia is doing or because they are of a lower class than Radu's family is not clear; nor do the subtle politics between these two families ever become very clear. The short scenes follow each other so fast and are so cryptic that what emerges is not a traditional plot between well-defined, self-revealing characters but instead a sense that such a plot is being made

impossible by outside interference, by a surrounding context that interrupts and distorts the unfolding of the story of a group of interesting
people. Thus even the brief conversation between Radu and his parents
about a subject as vital to him as his marriage is set within a strangely
stilted conversation between his parents about how "He" (presumably
Ceauşescu himself, or one of his deputies) "came today" (to Mihai's
architecture office) and made "a very interesting recommendation. The
arch should be this much higher" (14). Radu's question, "And the columns?" forces Mihai to admit that "we will make an improvement to the
spacing of the columns" (14). At the very end of the scene, after Mihai
has quashed Radu's plea to marry Florina, Radu manages a subtle revenge: "So that's the third time he's made you change it?" he asks (15).
Mihai doesn't reply, and the scene ends.

By placing the plot of Lucia's wedding within a context where
language, relationships—even buildings!—are deformed by pressure
from the State, Churchill transforms its geopathic core into a demonstration of the *limits* of geopathology, beyond which lie the realities of contemporary politics. A particularly chilling example of this version of
geopathology is the scene in which Bogdan, Lucia's father, is re-
cruited/ordered to be an informant. The scene begins with the Securitate
man asking Bogdan a question whose innocence masks a truly horrific
kind of geopathology: "Do you love your country?" (17).

Bogdan is then informed that his daughter's desire to marry an
American and go to America exposes the entire family to the charge of
treason. If Bogdan wants "to show that your family are patriots," he
must turn informer: "When they know your daughter wants to marry an
American, people may confide their own shameful secrets" (18). The
scene, in which Bogdan has remained silent except for one word of
denial early in the encounter, ends with a return to the terms of the new,
political geopathology: "What a beautiful day," says the Securitate man.
"What a beautiful country. You will make a report once a week" (19).

Scene 10 comprises the most powerful statement of the kind of
geopathology that is being produced by the deadly infiltration of State
power into private lives. The scene is entitled "This is our brother" and
introduces Gabriel, who has also been approached by Securitate. Unlike
Bogdan, Gabriel has reacted volubly and continues to be loquacious
about his experience, even though this family at first tries to silence him
(Irina goes to turn on the radio, but it is broken; she then begs him to be
quiet, and when he continues, she covers her ears). Gabriel tells of having

been given the same line about proving his patriotism, but, unlike Bogdan, he finds something to say, something he regards as a miraculous escape to "the other side":

> "We thought you might not understand patriotism because your sister this and this, but if you're a patriot you'll want to help us." And I said, "Of course I'd like to help you," and then I actually remembered, listen to this, "As Comrade Ceauşescu says, 'For each and every citizen work is an honorary fundamental duty. Each of us should demonstrate high professional probity, competence, creativity, devotion and passion in our work.' And because I'm a patriot I work so hard that I can't think about anything else, I wouldn't be able to listen to what my colleagues talk about because I have to concentrate. I work right through the lunch hour." And I stuck to it and they couldn't do anything. And I'm so happy because I've put myself on the other side, I hardly knew there was one. (24)

Gabriel's family does not share his sense of triumph. His belief that he has escaped the grasp of the State's powers of blackmail is belied by the last line in the scene, Lucia's fearful "What if I don't get my passport?" (24).

Voicing the terms of a political geopathology, in which individuals' desires both for place and displacement put them in the power of a ruthless and all-powerful State, Lucia's question summarizes the conditionality—such as it can be dramatized and seen by the outside—of life before the revolution. In this context, her wedding to Wayne, for all its high ritual, seems not to amount to much; it certainly carries none of the sense of triumph and closure that accrued to the heroism of departure in the traditional drama of geopathology.

"Ask Granny about Hungarians."

Lucia's stay in America is short-lived. In act 3 we find that this play is, among other things, a drama of homecoming, though once again it revises the fundamental gestures of that paradigm. Lucia's homecoming is neither failed nor an occasion for the revelation of profound—and profoundly buried—truths.[6] It occurs amid all the confusion that marks the aftermath of the revolution, and it has the effect of positioning America as a locus of misunderstanding:

GABRIEL: My sister's coming from America.
PATIENT: Does she know what happened?
GABRIEL: She'll have read the newspapers.
PATIENT: Then you must tell her.

(51)

Lucia, who has watched the revolution on TV ("but they never showed enough" [51]), returns with a description of America that is the perfect companion to that offered by Ruth in *The Homecoming,* extending that desolate vision of a nonhuman expanse of land by stocking it with strangely artificial forms of food and habitation:

> But America. There are walls of fruit in America, five different kinds of apples, and oranges, grapes, pears, bananas, melons, different kinds of melon, and things I don't know the name—and the vegetables, the aubergines are a purple they look as if they've been varnished, red yellow green peppers, white onions red onions, bright orange carrots somebody has shone every carrot, and the greens, cabbage spinach broad beans courgettes, I still stare every time I go shopping. And the garbage, everyone throws away great bags full of food and paper and tins, every day, huge bags, huge dustbins, people live out of them. (51–52)

The shocking conclusion of this paean clarifies the presence of America in the play. It is not there, as in Pinter's play, to explicate the figure and failure of homecoming—to exemplify the principle of placelessness that undoes the figure of home altogether. This America, like the America of *Ice Cream,* exemplifies a kind of prosperity whose history has already been written and whose residue is trash. This America exists here to inoculate the play against a regressive cold war politics, the very politics that continues to distort the West's view of the former East bloc countries and their changes.

America stands, then, as a prefabricated but undesirable alternative to the difficult but self-developing narrative of the Romanian revolution. That narrative, however, is multiple, fragmented, unreliable. Instead of generating the grounds for a new political order, it has spawned a dizzying series of doubts and questions: "Did we have a revolution or a putsch? Who was shooting on the 21st? and who was shooting on the 22nd? Was the army shooting on the 21st or did some shoot and some not shoot or were the Securitate disguised in army uniforms? . . . Where did the flags come from? Who put loudhailers in the square? How could they publish a newspaper so soon? Why did no one turn off the power at the TV? . . . Who poisoned the water in Bucharest?" (50). The emergent order, it seems, is infected with the terrible deceptiveness of the past. Nothing can be known for certain, no one can be trusted. The old ways seem to persist in new forms ("Ceauşescu Ceauşescu. Iliescu Iliescu"[61]) except they are even more intractable ("Who do we know who can put in a word for you?" asks Mihai, and Flavia answers, "We don't know who we know. Someone who put in a word before may be just the person to keep clear of" (67–68).

Among the old habits that die hardest are valuations of racial and ethnic difference. As the final act develops, it becomes clear that prejudice is the strongest element in the structure of the old ongoing narrative within which the new world must locate itself. The new Romania can only come into being through the mad forest of its own ethnic fissures and racial divisions, coded in countless folk narratives ("I knew a woman who married a Hungarian. His brother killed her and ripped the child out of her stomach"). Even Lucia, who loves Ianos, a Hungarian, shows that one kind of tolerance doesn't necessarily entail another:

> Hungarians were fighting beside us they said on TV. And Ianos wasn't hurt, that's good. I think Americans like Hungarians. . . . It's true in America they even like the idea of gypsies, they think how quaint. But I said to them you don't like blacks here, you don't like hispanics, we're talking about lazy greedy crazy people who drink too much and get rich on the black market. That shut them up. (53)

The ugly face of prejudice begins to be seen when, in the final act, a group of the characters visit their grandparents in the country. This unexpected entrance into another kind of place, governed by different semiological codes, promises to furnish a new and better perspective on the confusion experienced as the revolution.

But this place turns out not to be as different as might have been expected. Politics—and political disagreement, doubt, suspicion—is very much part of the conversation going on in this rural place. No long view of tradition is to be found here that might bring the revolution and its aftermath into clearer light. Yet there is a difference between this place

and the city from which the characters have come: here the forces of
stereotype and prejudice are part of the texture of life, not—like the
angel, vampire, and dog earlier—tears in the signifying fabric of the plot.
In one scene, all the characters talk (their speeches overlapping in the
dialogue style favored by Churchill) and try to make sense of the murder
of a local man. The mystery is insoluble not because the killers have fled
but because of the political affiliations of the dead man—and the meaning
of those affiliations is impossible to determine ("I thought the Peasant's
Party was for peasants" [62]). Added to this is the perspective offered by
the grandfather, who first says that the man was killed by a family of
gypsies who worked for him and whom he mistreated, then adds that "a
lot of people didn't like him because he used to be a big landowner [and]
the Peasant's Party would give him back his land" (62). By the end of the
conversation, all that is clear is that the local political picture, like the
national one, is murky with past allegiances and betrayals. The peasant
grandparents are neither more nor less politically lucid than their city
relatives. There is no occasion to rely for guidance on the more direct
materiality of their experience.

The scene immediately following this conversation, the last of the
scenes in the country, reintroduces the other register in which the play's
resolute refusal of an individualist-humanist geopathology is articulated,
the register of individual—but not individualistic—desire. In this wonderful "daydreaming" scene, which is in fact a companion to the explosion of narrative in act 2 and the explosion of dialogue in the last scene of
act 3, Churchill stages an extraordinary flow of desire, pure and simple
and gently self-ironical. The characters lie on their backs and name, with
long gaps of silence in between each utterance, what they want, everything from a trip to Peru, to Toblerone, to the ability to make someone
(for Radu—Florina, for Ianos—Toma) happy. The beauty of this moment of shared desire is never to return to the play; it is a kind of utopian
moment, a marking of one (im)possible political order based on a community's commitment to the desires, *all* the desires, of *all* its individual
members.

"So Was It Just a Quarrel, Not Politics at All?"

Back in the city, the action moves steadily in the opposite direction from
the one briefly invoked in the daydream scene. The nightmare of recent
political events is played out, first literally, as a group of characters enact

the murder of Nicolae and Elena Ceauşescu. The play gets increasingly ugly, violent, cruel, as the characters scream: "We fucked your wife. Your turn now. Murderer. Bite your throat out," and then repeatedly "shoot" at Radu (playing Ceauşescu). His death is played as prolonged agony and profound humiliation. After he seems to be good and dead, the others "all cheer and jeer." At that moment, "Ceauşescu" sits up and asks, "But am I dead?" to which all respond, "Yes." Radu falls down dead again, and the cheering is resumed, accompanied by happy laughter. Just then, Gabriel notices that Ianos has his arm on Lucia, and bursts out: "Get your filthy Hungarian hands off her" (71). Though he immediately collects himself—"only joking"—his shocking outburst has already rewritten the "play" we have just watched, making it clear that hatred and prejudice, not just political anger, were and remain woven into the fabric of the revolution. The old society infects the new with its divisions and oppressions. The habits of State terror and blackmail have seeped into the dream life and the domestic life of people: Rodica dreams she is Elena Ceauşescu though her mouth is full of revolutionary chants that escape every time her lips part; Mihai tells his rebellious son Radu the devastating lie that he only got into art school because of Mihai's influence and contacts.

The wedding party (not ceremony, this time), which comprises the long final scene of act 3, begins with one character's disingenuous allegorization of what is to follow: "What's so wonderful about a wedding is that everyone laughs and cries and it's like the revolution again. Because everyone's [now] gone back behind their masks" (74). Figuring the revolution as a kind of carnival—a period of unmasking and emotional release, a cathartic ritual—this speech tempts the spectator to take it as a hermeneutic guide to the play as a whole. Indeed, if it were not that we had witnessed the second act, the trope of the wedding might well have seemed an adequate figuration of the revolution, bespeaking joy, future promise, and so on. However, all that has occurred between this scene and the scene of Lucia's marriage has made it impossible to conceive of a political event such as the revolution in abstract terms, apart from the flows of cultural narrative and individual desire.

The wedding functions rather to constitute the revolution as an eerie displacement of the familiar, a kind of major blip on the screen of these ongoing lives. In this regard an important scene earlier is the one where Flavia's dead grandmother urges her to *live* her life, to stop "pretending this isn't your life . . . [to stop] thinking it's going to happen some other

time" (26). The pernicious temporalization of a repressive regime stops
the flow of life, of desire, of meaning. Flavia (significantly, the history
teacher) voices this virulent chronopathology when she asks her husband
"do you ever think . . . if you think of something you'll do . . . do you
ever think you'll be young when you do it? Do you ever think I'll do that
next time I'm twenty?" (26). In the opening moments of the wedding
itself, Irina voices another version of the same phenomenon: "She [a
clairvoyant whom Irina is consulting] says we have no soul. We've suffered for so many years and we don't know how to live. Are people very
different in other countries, Lucia?" (74). Most of the nonrealistic scenes
in the play are in fact vocalizations of the asymmetry between desire and
history, and they frame the play's engagement with the revolution. This
revolution is not a wedding party, it is a conspicuous curve in the time of
living, a watershed in the flow of desire. It redirects desire—and anger,
and hatred, and aspiration—toward a future in which the possibility of
no longer being out of sync with life can at least be imagined, if not quite
realized.

"We Can't Have a Traffic Jam Forever."

The wedding party scene stages the infiltration of the unfamiliar into the
familiar and suggests a view of the present as a crossroads where the
future meets the past. The Romanian past of story and legend is present
in the figure of an old aunt, a peasant who shouts a long passage of ritual
chants at the bride until Bogdan silences her with "Hush, auntie, you're
not in the country now." The revolution filters into the life of the family
first as a generational conflict, with the older men dismissing all the
turmoil and doubts of the aftermath as mere whining:

> BOGDAN: Whinge whinge. Gaby was shot, all right. Everyone
> whinges. Layabout students. Radu and Ianos never stop talking,
> want to smack them in the mouth. "Was it a revolution?" Of course
> it was. / My son was shot for it and we've got
> MIHAI: Certainly.
> BOGDAN: This country needs a strong man.
> MIHAI: And we've got one.
> BOGDAN: We've got one. Iliescu's a strong man. We can't have a
> traffic jam forever. Are they going to clear the square or not?
> (77)

The status of the revolution in the minds of the people hovers between two extremes: it is either experienced as an exercise in futility, a charade, an eyewash ("Look at Gaby, crippled for nothing. They've voted the same lot in"), or as a radical change, altering the basic conditions of living: "It's thanks to Gaby you can talk like this" (78). Thus it is as an oscillation of meaning, an open space or aporia in the political "known," that the revolution exists.

Two sources are clearly identified for this failure of the revolution to take definite shape, to acquire a meaning that can take its place in the ongoing story of Romania and allow time to move forward once again. The first of these is the irresolution of the past, the muddying up of history by State terror: "Where are the tapes they made when they listened to everyone talking?" asks Flavia, the history teacher, adding, with unintentional and poetic irony: "All that history wasted" (80). The irresolution of the past also infects the present, so that the face of contemporary politics is hard to discern: "Why don't the Front tell the truth and admit they're communists?" (82) asks Flavia in the middle of a conversation that is turning into a shouting match, with everyone speaking at once. From the point of view of the spectator (as opposed to the reader), the heated exchange signifies little more than confusion and allows him or her to observe the effect but not really grasp the terms of the political dispute in which the characters are mired.

Much clearer to the spectator is the second source of conflict, ethnic prejudice. As the scene develops and the people get more and more drunk, their attention turns increasingly to the familiar issue of the differences between Romanians and Hungarians. Ianos, the Hungarian among them, is increasingly singled out as a target for attack and debate. The conflict between the two groups is expressed in the same terms as everything else in the play: the problematic shape of history ("Hungarians started the revolution," claims Ianos), the treachery of representation ("In the riots on TV I saw a Hungarian on the ground and Romanians kicking him," says Lucia [83–84], to which Gabriel retorts "that was a Romanian on the ground, and the Hungarians—" [84]), and, finally, the interdictions on desire: "Hungarian bastard," says Bogdan, "don't come near my daughter" (84) and Ianos responds: "I'm already fucking your daughter, you stupid peasant" (84).

Above all, ethnic conflict is figured here as language conflict, with Gabriel screaming, "If they want to live in Romania, they can speak Romanian" (83). Ianos argues that "We can learn two languages, we're not stupid" (84), but stupidity certainly has the final word. The conclusion of the argument is a clumsy, drunken free-for-all, in which each character attacks, hits, pushes, or restrains someone else, until finally Gabriel, swinging his crutch, accidentally knocks his father, Bogdan, to the floor. There is a stunned silence, until Flavia, the groom's mother, recalls them to the decorum of the occasion: "This is a wedding. We're forgetting our programme. It's time for dancing" (84).

The distance between Lucia's formal wedding ceremony at the end of act 1 and this prolonged brawl stages the revolution as a vital intervention, however flawed and problematic, into history and desire, into the history *of desire*. As the characters pick themselves up and pair up to dance, the incongruous music of the lambada fills the stage. The dancing begins, and the contrast between this action of the group and its fight, moments before, enforces a performative identity for the group. The community as acting ensemble: this is the figure developed by the play as the only viable context and outcome for the revolutions of the present.

But Churchill seems aware that the extent to which this kind of community can be imagined is seriously impaired by the logic of otherness that defined and continues to define the way groups operate. As if the ugly prejudices that turn the party into a fight were not enough, the angel and the vampire—assorted emblems of alienation and isolation—materialize at the wedding and join in the dance. Finally, the definitive mode of otherness, a foreign language, gives the play its ambiguous closure. As the characters dance, they begin to talk, their speeches overlapping so "that by the end every one is talking at once" (85). The language they speak, however, is not the English we have been hearing throughout the play: they speak Romanian. For the spectator (though not the reader, who is given both the Romanian lines and their English translations) the play ends with a vision of alterity, of unfamiliarity and unreadability. This foreign language figures the foreignness of language, a foreignness that must be faced before there can be a move from geopathology to topography.

The topography enacted by *Mad Forest* involves the retemporalization of dramatic meaning through a revaluation of the power of narrative. Although much is made of dates in this play, the dates do not organize the plot into a smooth flow of time. Instead, the dates (December 21 to December 28) become the focus of multiple narratives, a kind of "temporal space" of experience that can only be told, not shown. The appearance in the middle of the play of this purely narrative space—this

"December" of stories, as the act is titled—is the play's main device for restructuring the usual logic of historical drama. The group who speaks in act 2 is and is not the same group whose stories we follow in acts 1 and 3. These speakers, who are identified not by their names but by their professions, exemplify one kind of divergence from traditional dramatic expression. Speaking in broken English with more or less heavy Romanian accents, they remind us (as does the tourist-phrase-book title device in the rest of the play) of the specifically cultural limits of historical representation. Yet at the same time the eloquence and urgency of their stories suggest narrative as a challenge to the impacted otherness of history. They carve out—onstage if nowhere else—a new place of language, a topography within which the hierarchies and divisions so necessary to the geopathic vision are temporarily suspended, and history is shared, told, heard. Against such competing representations of politics as the ubiquitous TV, the stories encode an experience and an understanding to which mimetic representation cannot do justice. As the painter says, in the scene's last line: "Painting doesn't mean just describing. It's a state of spirit. I didn't want to paint for a long time then" (43).

The Language of the Future

If *Mad Forest* codes the familiar as the *familial,* Maria Irene Fornes's play *The Danube* codes the familial as the unfamiliar, the bizarre, the nearly extinct. In this play, the discourse of home is at the vanishing point, where its exhaustion is explicated, once again, by the figure of America. And America here, like the America of *The Homecoming,* is not so much a place as a cultural strategy, a way of structuring life that makes certain eventualities inevitable. Among these, at the extreme, is the dissolution of the very kind of subjectivity on which the primary myth of America, individualism, was based. This subjectivity that unravels at the logical extreme of the modernity represented by the figure of America is also, of course, the very one that underwrote the drama of realism.

Like many a traditional realist play, *The Danube* begins with an arrival and ends with a departure. The arrival, in Budapest, of Paul Green, citizen of the United States, decisively alters the lives of the Sandor family, whose daughter Eve falls in love with and marries Paul. But Paul (like a properly developmental protagonist of realist drama) is also changed. His transformation, however, is anything but psychological; in fact it is, shockingly, a mutation, and it is undergone by all the characters. This mutation, which seems to be caused by nuclear radiation, is not reassuringly blamed on any group or any person in particular; its sources, unlike those of the pollution in *An Enemy of the People,* are unknown, although—again unlike Ibsen's earlier pollution—they are *visible,* as streams of smoke that rise periodically from the stage floor. This ubiquitous and anonymous poison infects the world of the play so thoroughly that the characters gradually slip their psychological moorings altogether and enter into a strange characterological mode in which they double and are doubled by puppets. Thus the characterological process of the play is just about the reverse of the one in *Enemy,* where ecological catastrophe becomes the ground for a (reverse) geopathic self-discovery and heroism (it is "reverse" in the sense that the discovery of his spiritual ill placement among his fellow townspeople does not cause Dr. Stockmann to slam the door, Nora-like, on their world, but inspires him to stand his ground, center stage). In *The Danube* ecological catastrophe produces a dissolution of selves so complete as to render questions of heroism and responsibility utterly ridiculous.

By transgressing the psychological code within the kind of dramatic structure and a plot that has always supported that code, the play becomes in part an analysis of the drama it is transgressing. Its analysis reveals an astonishing correlation between the geopathological code of that earlier drama and a specific kind of destruction. It contends that what had been the crux of geopathology was alienation from nature and shows its ultimate result: ecological destruction. The course of the radiation sickness in the play is a direct though grim parody of that version of the self that was coded in and by geopathic drama: as an essentially autochthonous and virtually disembodied "voice" (consciousness as the spoken) that gains self-awareness by recognizing some crucial truth about his or her environment, his place. Here, as the play ends, both the main characters split into puppet and puppeteer, and the drama of disembodied consciousness stages itself truthfully as a puppet show.

These puppets are, however, a mere remainder in the somber calculus of geopathology's *reductio.* Before they can be unleashed, the play must articulate the other vital truth: of the vulnerability of the body and of the abuse and loss that body suffers when nature is denied. And since the claims of the body and of nature are precisely what the traditional theater has silenced, their signification must involve forging a new theatrical language.

Like *Mad Forest,*[7] *The Danube* produces a topography, a special conjuncture of language and place, and tests this topography against traditional theatrical meaning. While *Mad Forest* sets topography to work on the problematic of historical representation, Fornes explores the place of language in the catastrophic formulation of Otherness. As in *Mad Forest,* the foreignness of language is staged in this play through the use of a foreign language, in this case Hungarian. In a device that resembles Churchill's tourist-phrase-book device, Fornes uses a language-learning tape to introduce most of the play's fifteen scenes. Each scene begins with a tape-recorded announcement giving the number and content of a language lesson; thus scene 1 is announced as "Unit One. Basic sentences. Paul Green meets Mr. Sandor and his daughter Eve" (44). These taped introductions remain bland and innocuous even as the events—and the condition of characters—get more and more alarming. Even after Paul has sickened to the point of despair, the tape says: "Unit Ten. Basic sentences. Paul Green visits Mr. Sandor. They discuss the weather," (58) while the next scene is said to be "Unit Eleven. Basic sentences. Paul Green goes to the barbershop," (59) although in the course of this scene the barber grabs Paul's leg and says: "What does one say? I want? I want milk? Please, give me beer? Meat? I'm very hungry? It is the heart of the nation. It is very cold. The earth is cold" (60).

The weather forms a constant point of reference in the play, and the way it functions is diametrically opposite to its symbolic usage in Stephen Poliakoff's *Coming in to Land* (which I shall discuss in the following chapter). Some idea of this functioning can be gained from the fact that the original title of the play was (a line that Eve says): "You can swim in the Danube—but the water is too cold" (49). When Paul and Mr. Sandor first meet, and Paul mentions that he is from the United States, the following exchange ensues (and seems to be, at this point, a typical example of clichéd language use):

MR. SANDOR: What is new in the U.S.?
PAUL: The weather is bad.
MR. SANDOR: Is that so?
PAUL: Yes, we have not had good weather.
MR. SANDOR: I see.
PAUL: And how is the weather in Budapest?
MR. SANDOR: It has been bad we have not had good weather.

(44)

Later, when Eve speaks of the coldness of the Danube, she adduces a similar cause: "The weather is bad. It has changed" (49). This point is repeated one last time late in the play, when the nature of the change has emerged in grim earnest. Unlike in *Coming in to Land,* the weather is not performing a symbolic function; there is no pathetic fallacy here. The weather change is horribly literal, and it is plain that it will not change back to normal when all is well with the characters. In this context, making polite conversation about the weather, as Paul and Mr. Sandor do in scene 10, is a chilling twist on one of the clichés of habitual language use.

"We Are the Foolish Race"

However, the main topographic technique of the play is an extension of the introductory language tape, and its consequences for theatrical meaning are considerable. In addition to the introductory announcement, the play calls for tape-recorded versions of some of the conversations to be interpolated into certain scenes, in such a way that the actors' lines are preceded by two taped versions of the same line, first in English and then in Hungarian (so that each utterance is tripled; in some cases, the tape carries only the Hungarian version, thus only doubling the utterances). The production notes call for a formal style of delivery for these taped utterances, to be contrasted by a naturalistic style for the lines spoken by the actors. However, the dialogue itself is such as to make naturalistic acting rather difficult, since it often adopts the style favored by foreign language textbooks: formal and stilted rather than colloquial and idiomatic.

The first scene, in which Paul first meets the Sandors, opens as a typical language lesson conversation, an exchange of pleasantries and a fixing of identities. The first five speeches contain taped interpolations in both languages (the sign // in the script indicates their position):

> PAUL: //Good afternoon Mr. Sandor.// I believe we met at the Smith's last night.
> MR. SANDOR: //Yes, I remember. Your name is Paul Green.
> PAUL: //Yes.
> MR. SANDOR: *(Standing and shaking Paul's hand.)* //Please take a seat. *(They sit.)*
> PAUL: //Thank you.
> MR. SANDOR: //Are you Hungarian?
> PAUL: Oh no. I'm from the U.S.

(44)

The timing of the tape, or rather of its cessation, just when the United States is mentioned, is a way of having the figure of America make a "big entrance" into the play's discourse. As in both *Mad Forest* and *The Homecoming*, the explicit use of this figure is very limited; it is more or less restricted to one extraordinary speech, by a character, the waiter, who appears only in one scene. For the rest, the figure of America, like the smoke that shoots up periodically from the stage floor, is simply and fundamentally *there*, holding down one end of the play's thematic.

The scene in which the figure of America contributes explicitly to the play's discourse on otherness and destruction is set in a restaurant, where the topic of conversation at first is one of the play's favorite ones: food. Numerous conversations in the play besides this one focus on cooking and on various kinds of food, culminating in the sudden shocking plea by the barber for something to alleviate his hunger. In this restaurant scene, the incessant talk about various food items is suddenly interrupted when the waiter, who has just recited the dessert menu, adds, "May I suggest the fresh fruit?" At these words, both Eve and the waiter himself suddenly "freeze," the music stops, and Paul ("speaking rapidly") blurts out the following bizarre characterization of American culture:

> I came from a country where we hear out suggestions. We invented the suggestion box. The best suggestion may come from the least expected place. We value ideas. We don't hesitate to put ideas into practice. We consider ideas that are given to us. We don't hold back our suggesting of ideas for fear of appearing foolish. We are not afraid to appear foolish, as good ideas disguise themselves in foolishness. We are not afraid to appear foolish. We are the foolish race. (51)

The terms for a truly inspired—and outrageous—cultural comparison have been laid out. "You are foolish," says the waiter, "but oh how fast you move forward" (51). Moments later he launches into the play's longest speech, the America speech, also "speaking rapidly" as Paul had done. This time Paul and Eve freeze into position until the speech ends.

To the stereotypical characterization of America as the land of speed and mobility, the waiter's speech adds the idea of lightness, making the association through the phrase "[to] travel light." Then, pursuing the principle of verbal association, he begins to speak of the American antipathy to burdens (which are "heavy," instead of "light"), to obstacles, to delays, to lengthy processes of all kinds: "Your forms are shorter, so is your period of obligation" (52). Though intended by the speaker as compliment and celebration of American ways, the style (of the language, of the composition by verbal association, and of the delivery) is so peculiar—even comical—as to totally ironize this figuration of America. The lightness of America, contrasted to the heaviness of Hungary ("We wish for things that last but we tire of them. . . . Pots that are too heavy to use. Shoes that delay our walk. Sheets that make our sleep a slumber" [52]), appears not as achievement but as a ludicrous, even cartoonish, one-sidedness. The waiter's speech evokes both the truth and the lie of cultural stereotypes. The rest of the play inscribes another truth on the bodies of the characters, who, light or heavy though they may be, sicken and suffer equally; as Paul later says: "She coughs, I throw up and you have diarrhea" (61).

Yet the issue of cultural difference is certainly not of minor consequence to the play's staging of universal destruction. On the contrary, the need to reconfigure the present relative positioning of cultural identity and place emerges as vital to the play's explication of that urgent thematic. In addition, the language lessons that introduce and color most of the scenes are ambiguous statements on the issue of cultural difference, combining both a sense of the radical otherness of other cultures as well as the prospect of translation. The "heavy" Hungarians and the "light" Americans do manage to communicate, even if it is only at such a basic level as discussion of food and weather (both of which topics, of course, prove to be far from simple as the play goes on).

What is at issue in the play is not cultural difference itself but a *view* of cultural difference that underestimates the poetic and personal demands of a truly nourishing relationship to a place. The difference between being in a place and *belonging to a place* is suggested through the figure of tourism, which is first evoked when Eve gives Paul a sightseeing tour of Budapest. The figure of tourism is also suggested by a prominent feature of the otherwise simple set: the "painted backdrops, in a style resembling postcards, depict the various locations" (43). As always, the figure of tourism is negative, suggesting a fraudulent mode of engaging otherness by reinscribing its terms of sameness. Eve's description of Budapest exemplifies the banal and inelegant factuality of the tourist text:

Budapest lies on two sides of the Danube. Buda is on the right side. Pest is on the left. Between the two towns there are six bridges. From the mountains of Buda you can see Pest. On the Pest side is Parliament. The cathedral is not far. Budapest is full of baths. For example the one on Margaret Island. That bath is very beautiful. There's hot and cold water. The island lies in the middle of the Danube. (49)

It is at the conclusion of this dull speech that Eve delivers the line about the Danube being too cold to swim in, and it is difficult not to make a connection, however unlogical, between this melancholy fact and the alienation from place that is signified by the drab rhetoric of her description. The connection becomes clear at the end of the play, where the power of Eve's final speech obviously derives from an altogether different relation to place:

My Danube, you are my wisdom. My river that comes to me, to my city, my Budapest . . . I say good bye. As I die, my last thought is of you, my sick friend. Here is your end. Here is my hand. *I don't know myself apart from you. I don't know you apart from myself.* This is the hour. We die at last, my Danube. Good bye. (64; emphasis added)

The play's last line, Mr. Sandor vainly calling out the name of his daughter—"Eve!"—reminds us ironically of another Eve and another departure; and Paul's last name, Green, proves equally ironic. The world this Adam and Eve are going to is a dead world. Their departure signifies none of the painful but creative possibilities of other final displacements. The family they are leaving will not be any more cohesive because of their "sacrifice." This departure simply "doesn't matter . . . [because] there's no place to go" (65). With the destruction of the earth, all the sustaining logics of geopathology are exhausted.

Chapter Five

Travel Agencies

They think they are coming to a land of opportunity, a multi-racial society!
A home!
—Andrew, in *Coming in to Land*, by Stephen Poliakoff

After midcentury, the figure of exile is decisively qualified by the actual
and widespread experiences of immigration and refugeehood. The huge
movements of populations that characterize the latter part of the twentieth century dictate a different relation to the category of place—to the
relation of self and location—than the geopathological one that has
served the modern period for so long. The reality of immigration literalizes the experiences of dislocation and ill placement that had given geopathic discourse its metaphoric fodder. In the drama, one of the main
reflections of this change from a metaphoric to a literal understanding of
displacement is in an altered model of subjectivity. Whereas the drama of
heroic home-leaving had constituted stable identities by putting people
into transit within and out of stable societies, the new drama, taking
social instability as its basic norm, traces the difficulty of constituting
identities on the slippery ground of immigrant experience.

As Eduardo Machado's play *Broken Eggs* suggests, it is the very
literalness of dispossession that interferes with the construction of "new
world identities." Speaking of the abandoned family home back in Cuba,
in a world that seems like another lifetime or another planet, an immigrant marvels: "The house is still standing, . . . it's still there." The true
meaning of this uncanny fact is immediately voiced by another family
member: "But we are not" (173). This extreme *precision* of ill-placement
("I miss the floor, the windows, the air, the roof") affects every part of
immigrant experience, coloring everything seen and felt, producing a
sort of split self, even a schizophrenia:

My . . . our house. I sometimes think that I live at the same time there as here. That I left a dual spirit there. When I go to a funeral I look through the windows as I drive and the landscapes I see are the streets outside the cemetery in Guanabacoa, not Miami. A while ago I looked out at the dance floor and I thought I was in the ballroom back home. (173)

The schizophrenia of immigrant experience begins, as does exile, with a violent and painful rupture. As Guillermo Gómez-Peña writes: "A child of the Mexican crisis, I crossed the border in '78 and something broke inside of me, forever" (*Warrior for Gringostroika,* 20). After the break comes a lesson in loneliness, in the numerous forms and qualities of loneliness, and of course the slow, dawning sense of loss. Being an immigrant, unlike being an exile, is an evolutionary alienation, occurring over years, sometimes even over a lifetime. It is a process that inevitably raises the specter of return, of the need to recover somehow the true meaning of that very real—increasingly real—place one has left behind. In a sense, then, the discourse of immigration comes into being on the far side of traditional geopathology, beyond the heroism of departure and the poetics of exile.

The literalism of immigration helps to unravel that core concept of traditional geopathology, the figure of home. The mystique of this figure is such that it extends its associations far beyond the single family dwelling: as David Sopher points out, the English word "can refer with equal ease to house, land, village, city, district, country, or, indeed, the world, . . . transmit[ting] the sentimental associations of one scale to all the others" (130). It is this symbolic power that enacts and sanctions what Sopher calls the "domicentric" view of human nature, according to which all wandering, rootlessness, and displacement are stigmatized as lawless and even pathological. This "geopiety," which makes home the figure of order and stability, stands against another discourse, the "domifuge questing myths" found in many cultures, "urging a transcendence of both society and geography" (135).[1]

The tension between these two geomythologies—home and the journey—is nowhere better exemplified than in America, where, while "one American in five changes residences within a year, one of the most widely treasured household icons is a plaque or sampler carrying the words 'Home Sweet Home'" (Sopher, 136). The American desire for both place and mobility (Thoreau, from his carefully cultivated place by

Walden Pond: "Thank Fortune, we are not rooted to the soil, and here is not all the world" [130]) reveals its tensions in the context of immigration. The three plays I shall discuss in this chapter respond variously to that spectrum of immigrant experiences which Gómez-Peña lists under the motifs of abrupt encounter and of sudden lack: "Crossing the border meant much more than to learn English. For the first time I had to confront Protestant ethics, pragmatism, hyper-individualism and racism on a daily basis. For the first time in my life I was truly alone and scared, without a family, a community, or a language" (*Warrior for Gringostroika*, 20). At the same time, the three plays recapitulate the overall narrative of this book: the first, Stephen Poliakoff's *Coming in to Land,* exemplifies the impact of immigration on the dramaturgy of traditional realism, appropriating and ironizing some of its central discourses. The second, Janusz Glowacki's *Hunting Cockroaches,* relates immigration to the figure of America, amplifying the crisis of homecoming by associating it explicitly with an all-too-literal homelessness. Finally, Jose Rivera's *The House of Ramon Iglesia* looks forward to the drama of multiculturalism that is the subject of the next chapter, exploring the relationship between immigration and the figures of the home as house and home as family.

Writing Home: Narrative and the Search for a Place

Judging from its plot alone, Stephen Poliakoff's *Coming in to Land* could have been the exemplary drama of contemporary dislocation. Instead it is the exemplary drama of a new geopathology that appropriates the figure of dislocation for its own purposes. In this new geopathology the exhausted poetics of exile and the defunct heroism of departure are replaced, more somberly but no less successfully, by the anxiety of immigration. And this anxiety is figured as a search for a new and compelling narrative of self-definition. The narrative that actually emerges, however, is an ancient one, compelling the self toward an extremely regressive model of identity.

   Coming in to Land is the story of two people's extraordinary—yet all too ordinary, too typical—encounter with the profound ambiguities involved in the simple bid to immigrate to the West. The two people experience immigration from opposite sides: Halina is a Polish woman, one of fifteen "*mature* students on an exchange course, interior design at the College of Art" (2) in London. She wants to remain in England after the course ends, to remain and settle there permanently. Her cause has been taken up by Andrew, a midthirties English businessman who in his free time helps people seeking to immigrate to the United Kingdom. Andrew's friend Neville, a lawyer, is Halina's coprotagonist in the play, which begins with a curious meeting of the three early one morning in Neville's flat.

The flat itself, because of its appearance and its implied location, will become a kind of protagonist as the play develops, but at present it serves as an unobtrusive setting for the hatching of a rather unusual plot between the three characters. Andrew, it seems, has asked Neville if he would be willing to marry Halina in order to get her her immigration papers. They are now meeting for the first time so that both—but presumably Neville more than Halina—can ask any questions and resolve any doubts before proceeding with the planned fraudulent (and illegal, hence highly dangerous) marriage.

It is dawn, a fact Neville mentions in his very first line: "I didn't realize you meant a *dawn* meeting" (1). He then smiles (the sign of his effort to master his anxieties, to appear ever the self-confident Englishman) and adds: "I'm not really at my best this early" (1). Neville's conviction that he is in fact the best is the cornerstone not only of his personality but also, of course, of that edifice from which he derives it: the modern West, European civilization at the end of the twentieth century. When Neville's firm self-construction begins to crack and crumble, as it soon will under the impact of Halina's silent judgment, it will be because the civilization it reflects is crumbling too, coming apart at the seams.

At present, however, none of the fault lines are visible. Neville is a strikingly well situated person, in every sense of the phrase: his place in the world and in society, as well as his literal place, his flat, are not only secure but apparently so stable that he can afford to risk a little charitable illegality to help a fellow human being.

The one question Neville asks about Halina before she is called in by Andrew is "She does speak English?" But Halina has not waited to be called in; she is already in the room when he asks the question, and from behind him, she answers, "Yes, I think so." Halina's English, so important to Neville, is not only fluent but on occasion (as now) quite devastatingly idiomatic. The conjunction of language and place (which has allowed for that extension into a full-fledged topography that we saw in the previous chapter) is a major thematic of the anxiety of immigration. Among Neville's first remarks to Halina is a repronunciation of her last name, which Andrew, in introducing her, has pronounced incorrectly. Neville's correction, and Halina's reaction to it, is part of an exchange revealing much about the *contingency* of Halina's position. Andrew has said her name "Halina Sonya Rodziewizowna" and added, "That's right, isn't it?" Halina has said, "Yes." When Neville then says, "Shouldn't it be Rodziewizowna?" pronouncing it differently, Halina's response has the mixture of irony and helplessness that will characterize much of her dealings with these self-assured, well-situated men: "Yes, I think so," she says. "That's even better" (3).

The ensuing conversation, in which Andrew and Neville talk at and about Halina, rather than to her, makes it clear that, for the present at least, her "better" and her "best" are entirely in their hands. The topic of conversation is whether there is any "other possible way of getting Halina in—other than marriage." Andrew begins to list, at length, the "cons" or "negative factors" in the prospect of "landing Halina." Landing her, he explains, is the official terminology used by immigration officers (an explanation that does little to alter the absurd and disturbing association with fishing). Strangely, Neville positions himself at an electric typewriter and, after Andrew's lengthy exposition of each negative factor, Neville types and calls out an absurdly brief summary of it: "Too late," is the first, and then: "Bad timing," and "Professional status—absent." Taken together, Andrew's full-blown accounts of Halina's problems and Neville's reductive summaries suggest a level of alienation on their part that fully explains her decision, later in the play, not to accept Neville's offer.

Halina's dawning awareness of her situation vis-à-vis Neville—not Neville the potential helper but Neville the person, and what he really is—is clear in the following passage:

> ANDREW: Halina is not unfortunately a famous dissident, or even a member of Solidarity, no fashionable reason here, nor obviously is she something nationally desirable, like a ballerina, olympic athlete, boxer, squash player, or even a film director!
>
> HALINA: *(sitting with her bags, staring ahead).* No, I think that's probably right. *(Slight pause.)* I'm not.
>
> (5)

The two men then proceed to dissect what they call "her story," looking for "any possible angle." After Halina tells them a chilling story of childhood trauma followed by three decades of quiet desperation, they

declare that "this is very mild." Andrew goes so far as to pronounce
Halina "a victim of a tiny spec [sic] of history, no more than a pimple, so
small the story wouldn't even show up on their screens, so to speak. . . .
She is too small to register" (6–7). Halina listens to this devastating
verdict, so casually delivered, and utters just one word that to the discerning listener should reveal her profound—even poetic—command of
the English language. She says: "Absolutely" (7).

The scene concludes with Neville deciding to do it, and even inviting Halina to stay on in his flat, where, he says, "there's a lot of space"
(10). The now fully lighted room has revealed this to be the case, and we
have by now taken in the pastel and pristine room, whose "almost invisible cupboards, the doors and windows which blend imperceptibly into
the pastel walls" give an "effect of pale and effortless spaciousness" (1).

Halina has, from the start, appeared out of place in Neville's sleek
surroundings, walking heavily around them with her load of dirty and
crammed plastic bags. When Neville invites her to stay, she points out
that she's "already made a mess" (10) (one of her plastic bags has burst
open and its contents have spilled onto the floor). Needless to say, the
mess is to get larger, and the alterations this sophisticated space is to
undergo in the course of the play simply literalize the play's presentation
of a new dialectical or dialogical geopathology, one in which the settled
hero who might once have savored a poetics of exile (Neville, we learn,
is well traveled and proficient in languages; he is also alienated, lonely,
and in need of an adventure to break up the monotony of his successful
middle-class existence) is confronted by a person whose need of a home
far exceeds that of any nostalgic and doomed homecomer.

However, the dialogic that is to develop between Halina and Neville
is not self-contained. Its energy and logic are supplied by the society of
which Neville has so far been a fairly comfortable member. The most
undisguised agent of this society's powers and mechanisms is the immigration office, and, as the first set change makes quite literal and explicit,
the immigration office is simply an unadorned version of Neville's flat:
"one of the pastel squares in the main wall has been removed, revealing a
peeling, flaking wall behind them" (10). At present, the immigration
office is small, poky, and seedy. A few scenes later, it will appear much
larger and will use up more of Neville's luxurious flat. Finally, in act 2, it
will occupy the whole stage and gain all sorts of new depths and definitions.

Poliakoff's symbolic use of stage space is a part of a measured
return—which he makes in the company of other contemporary

playwrights—to some of the structures as well as some of the central concerns of traditional realism. In its new incarnation, realism is heavily laced with irony. The stable correlations of the theatrology of classical realism—correlations between person and role, stage space and fictional place, speech and subjectivity, utterance and meaning—are gently prized apart by ironic realism.

A rich example of how ironic realism functions at the level of stage space is in the specific transformations the set of *Coming in to Land* sustains in act 2. No longer recognizable as Neville's flat, the stage now represents the reception area of the immigration office (the same immigration office, belonging to Immigration Officer Peirce, that had appeared earlier as an undisguised and run-down variant of Neville's posh habitation). The reception area of this office is backed by an extraordinary mural, which "shows people arriving on a shore with blue and white water behind them, shadowy travellers facing an idealized glowing city on a hill, across an expanse of green" (54). Long before the ensuing events ironize this sentimental image, it reeks of falseness. Moreover, it appears to us already ironized, for, as the stage direction notes, "Somebody has drawn one major piece of graffiti on the mural, a monster emerging out of the blue water with its teeth bared" (54). Of course it is not until we see Peirce and his colleague Booth in operation, in the next scene—which consists of Halina's all-important interview—that we have our own sense of who the monster is. This scene (act 2, scene 1) is set up in an interesting way: Peirce's office is formed by having its walls roll in, in front of the back wall with the mural. The mural, however, can still be seen, though "smudged and diffused, through the glass" that surrounds the "oddly large" office door in the wall. But the touch of distinctly ironic realism is the following: "There is a small picture on the wall of people on a golden beach mirroring the mural outside, it is the only ornament on the wall" (60). This replica of the mural ironizes the entire discourse of foreground-background that was one of the constitutive codes of realist theatrology.[2] The picture of the mural introduces the familiar figure of two-dimensional representation, usually figured by/as photography, so common in realist drama. The figure of photography becomes, as here, *the picture of a picture;* it is a sign that the threat of technological pictorialism, which haunted realism even up to its midcentury self-analysis, is over. The drama can now get down to negotiating its place among the ubiquitous electronic media of the present.

In *Coming in to Land,* these media are fully drawn into the play's inquiry into the nature of location—and self-location—in the present day. All the scenes set in Neville's flat open to the sound of radio channels being switched. As the play progresses, the items of world news and cold war politics are increasingly interlaced with reports on Halina's case. Through this device and others, the play alludes to the way the electronic media turn lives into "stories."

Two orders of narrative swirl around Halina's efforts to "land" herself, to find a new place for her to transplant her hitherto drab life. Halina first asks Neville to help her get a job, ostensibly because she wants to pay back all the many kindnesses she has received from people. Though it is illegal, and with regard to her application for immigration, dangerous, Neville gets her a job taking inventory in a shop that sells hi-fi equipment. This shop makes its own complex contribution to the play's analysis of Halina's struggle with geopathology (the geopathology, that is, of Neville and of the society he unwittingly represents).

Halina's coworker in the hi-fi shop is a Black English woman named Waveney, who seems to be Halina's opposite in every way: stylishly dressed, drily knowledgeable about the true state of the promised land to which Halina aspires. Among the items sold in the shop are television monitors and video recorders. On one of these Waveney has taped Halina's surprise—and surprising—television appearance. She plays the tape for Halina, using a giant video screen on the back wall. The way Waveney manipulates—by remote control—the giant image on the screen foregrounds the ambiguous power of the electronic media. The stage image, consisting of the two women and the giant video image of Halina's face, dwarfing them, encapsulates the play's ironic-realist account of subjectivity. Halina appears to us split between the "real" vulnerable self and her self-created media identity, full of power and authority. Halina's reaction to the latter is horror and panic: "Oh my God! *(Looking up at herself)* stop it, please stop the machine. . . . How could anybody believe a thing that looks like that—I look monstrous, like a creation from another planet" (25).

Waveney, however, is quick to instruct Halina in an altogether different approach to the media. "Pointing at the frozen image of [Halina] with a broom handle like a lecturer," she analyzes the tape: "But the stare is good, fastening the audience with that gaze, trapping them in their seats, makes them think 'We have to listen to this woman'—it shows a natural instinct. . . . You look foreign, yes. A little odd—but that's no bad thing" (25–26). The transformation—the trans*narration*—of Halina has begun.

When, a few minutes later, Neville comes in, waving a newspaper, we find out exactly how Halina has decided to thicken her own plot, as it were, and to become something more than what Andrew had proclaimed her, "a victim of a . . . pimple [of history]." Her decision to give them "a story" rather than go through with the original plan of marrying Neville is the central fact both of the play and of Halina's character. It will also be revealed as having been the central fact of Neville's life, though he is far from realizing this as yet. Now he is simply bewildered by what he has seen in "the evening paper, your face staring out of page 5, above an escaped python from Chessington zoo" (27). He reads out the report, himself editing the already sensational account ("the language is a little lurid in your newspapers," Halina comments): "Polish housewife tells dramatic story, breaks ranks with visiting party . . . her story throws disturbing light on what's still going on there, innocent citizens plucked out of their cars . . . arrested on New Year's Eve with friends . . . subjected to a startling and terrifying ordeal . . . prison guards" (27).

Though Neville doesn't know it, he is witnessing the opening passages of a long redefinition of his world. Even at a literal level, he finds out that he is ignorant of many things: for example, what Waveney tells him, that the hi-fi shop, owned by a "client and friend" of Neville, is teetering on the brink of bankruptcy. Neville refuses to believe that this is the case; the lack of customers, he says, is a "momentary lull, that's all, the stampede will start any moment." Waveney's answer is an excellent example of the slightly grotesque language by which ironic realism makes its points: "I ought to know oughtn't I! I'm alone with these machines—I lock them up at nights . . . And dust them down in the morning. *(Defiant smile.)* I'm the one that has to talk to them! *(She moves.)* And I tell you this place is finished" (30).

The unobtrusive allegorical flavor of Waveney's final line links it to one of the play's important rhetorical registers, an allegorical register that, in typical ironic-realist fashion, locates Halina and Neville's story within a barely articulated sociocritique, an indictment of England's faltering self-definition. Why this critique is so muted, why it is never raised to the level of analysis but remains as a hinted background, is a crucial critical issue, going beyond this particular play. One easy answer is that Poliakoff suffers from an unresolved nostalgia for the mythic

England (this would make him a British counterpart to Shepard, who has often been accused of a similar yearning for the America of myth). Certainly this seems to be the case in one instance of more obvious allegory, the opening of scene 6. The scene is Neville's flat again, and the cyclorama shows snow, "heavy incessant snow, for a moment back lit, forming a white Dickensian Christmas scene outside" (38). The Dickensian mood heightened by "the angelic sound of high voices singing the carol, 'Good King Wenceslas.'" However, as the carolers "get nearer and pass right below the window we hear the lyrics to the familiar tune are darker, obscene, unsettling, still sung by high voices. A hooligan version" (38). Andrew comments on the "X certificate carol singers moving down below: They look a fairly terrifying collection to me," and Neville adds, "I've never heard that sound in the square before" (39).

The opening of Neville's ears and eyes to new sounds and sights is (it turns out) the main business of the play, as well as (as I shall argue below) its ironic-realist version of the oedipal plot. In this scene, however, Neville's expression of bewilderment at the new element in his familiar world is supported rather than ironized by the Dickensian set. And the "hooligan" element alluded to in the stage direction (rather than, say, Margaret Thatcher) seems to get the blame for all that is wrong with England. In fact, Poliakoff never fully links Halina's geopathic struggle with any specific ideological or political analysis of England. Instead he evokes a kind of underlying cultural malaise and an absurdly petty cold war politics as the frame for her bid to "land" herself.

In Poliakoff's ironical realist vision, Halina's geopathic predicament has its real meaning within the problematics of representation rather than those (as in Churchill) of actual contemporary politics. It is the different valences of the term *story* engaged by Halina's situation that are most important to the play. *Coming in to Land,* in short, rethinks place—the bid for a place—as narrative *strategy.*

In deciding to supply the dramatic story whose previous absence Andrew has lamented, Halina has inserted herself into the dominant logic of the society she is seeking to join: she has understood, and created for herself, that prime commodity, "media potential." It is clear from everyone's responses to Halina's giant image on the video screen—including her own—that media exposure is a phenomenon of awesome and seemingly autonomous power. But the media's voracious, even cannibalistic devouring of Halina's story is only one of the ways her narrative is processed in the play. The second, surprisingly, is the prosaic immigration office, whose outward air of bureaucratic dullness and plodding routine seem to place it quite out of the reach of the fevered imaginings of the radio and television stations whose frantic bulletins fill the night air in Neville's flat.

When we first see this office it is, as already mentioned, small and seedy. Its denizens, Peirce and his silent subordinate Booth, seem Dickensian themselves, a mixture of the grotesque and the trivial ("I should have *three* sharpened AB pencils ready waiting here" [12]). But Peirce will prove to be as terrifying as he is loathsome. When, later in the play, Waveney says that Peirce wouldn't "bug" his office because "it would take all the skill and art out of his job" (71), she is right; and she might have added, "all the fun."

There is another much more sickening reason why Peirce does not bug his office: there is, in fact, a *surplus* of information coming in to him. In the play's most interesting thematic and plot twist, we learn that Peirce's office is regularly telephoned by anonymous callers offering him all kinds of "modifications and corrections" to the stories that applicants for immigration have told him. We learn this chilling fact along with Neville, who has paid Peirce a visit to find out what he can about Halina's prospects. He offers to fill Peirce in on the case, but Peirce interrupts him: "no, no, save it, no facts please. We want it fresh. Absolutely fresh" (36). The "it" is, of course, "the story," but the connotations of "fresh" are hard to miss when we remember the immigration officers' term for successful applications. To make the point even clearer, Peirce's very next line is: "I have one small task to perform before I go. To rewind the tape and see what we've *netted* during the night" (36). And Neville's next line underlines the key word: "What's been netted?" (36).

Peirce's carps of truth—which he refers to as "a constant source of intelligence, a constant and valuable flow" (36)—are baited with falsehood, enmity, hatred. The first message, a "wild soft jabber" that Neville identifies as Iranian Arabic, is incomplete, causing Peirce to extend his fishing metaphor still further: "He slid off the hook" (37). He also declares the tape to be "a very poor catch tonight" (37).

Not surprisingly, the temptation of the tape will prove too strong for Neville. Later in the play he will call it and leave a message betraying Halina. When he does so, we will remember, ironically, Peirce's understated answer to Neville's question about why the informants do it: "It's safe to say," says Peirce, "their motives vary" (37). It is typical of the ironic realist method to raise the issue of motive—so vital to traditional realism, as we saw in the discussion of *Miss Julie* in chapter 1—and then to sidestep it, to hint that it was not so important after all. The effect of this use of motive (and it is particularly clear in *Coming in to Land*) is to reorient the psychological register of the play, to move it away from the characterological level.

According to *Coming in to Land*, the importance of motives is submerged by the ubiquity of stories and by the media-generated imperatives that structure them. The sheer number of stories, of bits of narrative jostling each other in the "constant flow" of information, makes them powerful. They are the aural background and sonic wallpaper of contemporary lives, the *medium* of existence. Lives, it seems, do not make and shape stories: stories make lives. During her interview, Peirce confronts Halina with the fact that the story of police brutality she has told resembles in many particulars another narrative:

> Snow, darkness, a courtyard . . . a mock execution, people up against the wall knowing they are going to die, there is an echo going on in my head, a sense of recognition, the Russian novelist Fyodor Dostoevsky with whom you are no doubt familiar, the same thing happened to him, the mock execution, thinking he was going to die in the snow. (82)

Peirce accuses her of having plagiarized the story. Halina's response is a masterpiece of narrative strategy: she offers an ironic universalism as an explanation for the resemblance, as well as for the truth of her version:

> I have memories of the story—it would be difficult for me to come here and tell you of any example of arbitrary cruelty which did not have some parallel, the banality of the minds of the people who do such acts means they must often imitate each other. . . . There are no exclusive rights, no copyright on any one method. Anyway it happened to me, and possibly to Dostoevsky—I think that is probably the only thing that we have in common. . . . Though you never know. (82)

Peirce accepts the explanation.

Like Peirce's office, Neville's flat is equipped with a telephone answering machine, and running the tape is one of his rituals as well. The voices on it are always women's voices, usually inviting him to go to parties with him. One of them, however, is the voice of an old woman, hoarse and desperate, and Neville reacts to it with some irritation. She is, he says, a former client, still pursuing him about a hopeless matter. In a later scene we find out, with something of a shock, what that matter is: "I have to see you about my house," says the old woman's voice from the answering machine, "they're trying to get me out of my house. I have to stay in all day, I know they are coming" (39).

The possibly mad old woman's desperate calls represent one strain of a complex and terrifying chorus of dislocation that is heard throughout the play. The many news bulletins about the regular mutual expulsions of diplomats in the cold war represent one, absurd, extreme. The other, poignant, extreme is described by Peirce as he gazes out of his window: "The patterns people make in the snow, extraordinary neurotic shapes as they have a last cigarette before they drag themselves away from the building" (35). The deepest poetic chord of this symphony of dislocation is struck by Halina in the one moment when she reveals the terrifying geopathic imagination—and reality—that lies behind all the stories and *motivates* them all:

> I was determined not to feel the usual conventional guilt on leaving one's country, leaving everyone behind, because if I did I was finished, and so far I've done very well. . . . But there is something else. I am a little afraid, I have a slight terror of being passed from country to country if I fail, being made stateless. A rotting package shovelled from one border to another, getting a little smaller each time, a piece coming off with every frontier, have you ever thought what that might be like—I haven't—with absolutely nowhere to go. Like falling into space, into the crack between land and sea. . . . Not just without a home, but with nowhere to *be*. Ending up in the last possible airport, surrounded by plastic bags. (50)

Halina's fear goes beyond a fear of homelessness: it is a fear of total placelessness, radical illocation. The story she has told and that she must make stick seems woefully inadequate as a tool for warding off the dreaded eventuality of being discarded, like a plastic bag full of garbage, by the world. Moreover, it is not her story itself but one very idiosyncratic response to her story that must do the job. As Peirce points out at the start of the interview, they are there simply "to establish the truth. Or to be more accurate what *I* think the truth is." Halina's response, while purporting to agree fully with Peirce, makes a subtle rephrasing that is in fact a penetrating critique of the whole system she is up against: "Good, that could not be clearer. *(Looking at him.)* Your impression of the truth" (61).

One of the most terrifying things about Peirce is that he seems to be fully aware of the absurd, arbitrary, and cruel nature of the business he conducts with so much pride and skill. He is the first to admit (in what is surely, by the way, an exceptionally graphic formulation of the kind of topography with which these plays respond to the discourse of geo-pathology) that "There are as many approaches [i.e., interviewing strategies, techniques for processing narrative] in this building as there are interviewing officers" (61). Peirce's own technique, it quickly becomes apparent, includes conveying a sense to the applicant that her story is one of many similar ones he has heard, and that it will therefore likely follow certain patterns and rules of discourse with which he is familiar (but she, of course, is not). For example, Peirce tells Halina that since people often stay up all night before interviews, "rehearsing," and because "they are nervous, lies can happen, sometimes almost by accident, and then people often seem to get into a spiral of untruths, which is usually disastrous: if I unpick one false link . . ." (61–62).

Halina's story, already coded by the play as sensational news item and media fodder, is now processed first by Peirce (primarily as a tissue of lies to be unraveled) and then by Neville, who gives it a kind of theater review:

> I can tell you, Halina, it's an extraordinary sensation when you know you've been listening to someone telling a story who you *know* is lying. . . . First reaction: nobody, but nobody is going to believe this! Just tell as little as possible. I wanted to go up and gag you, shout keep it simple for Godsake! And you were so outrageously casual, I thought she wants to get into this country so much and this is the best she can do—but then *(Pause.)* it really did begin to sound not at all bad. . . . There were too many details, of course, the goldfish was severely unnecessary, but it was a skillful mixture, aimed accurately at several nerve-ends, traces of Kafka, a touch of cheap cold-war thrillers, from all that reading you've done *(Moves, indicating building)* it should appeal to people here, on the edge of being too much but not quite. (71)

Neville's review of Halina's performance turns out to have an unforeseen logic when, a few moments later, Neville finds himself (quite unexpectedly for him, and for us) drawn into the center of the stage on which he had hitherto believed himself to have a comfortable side seat. In a development that is typical (indeed constitutive) of Poliakoff's ironic-realist method, the play makes a sudden leap into the allegorical register and at the same time shifts its plot focus as well as its characterological system (which had hitherto appeared to be a single-protagonist one). Peirce suddenly asks Halina to leave the room and Neville to remain behind. Halina demands to know why it is "necessary to talk to him," but Neville himself, in a tone of ludicrous self-confidence, walks into what will turn out to be Peirce's baited hook: "No, no," he assures Halina pompously, "it's best if we do this on our own, settle up—OK!" (72).

Neville's phrase "on our own" barely conceals some quite hideous implications about his exclusionary self-conception: as a male, as an Englishman. His expectation seems to be that he and Peirce share a special code (and privilege) on the basis of which they can come to terms (as gentlemen?) about Halina's fate. But this is precisely where the play makes its ironic-realist intervention, placing Neville in the traditional realist protagonist's position on the brink of self-knowledge, but achieving this placement by means of an unexpected, absurd, illogical, *unrealistic* turn of events. In this case, the strangeness of Peirce's sudden attention to Neville and the almost surrealistic quality of the interview that follows are underlined by an ironic stage picture that develops gradually and makes its own sardonic contribution to the play's discourse on media. When Neville's interview begins, he is asked to sit on the wooden chair center stage that Halina had previously occupied. This chair is situated directly in front of the large double door to the office, above which there is a "fan-shaped window." As the scene progresses, this window is unexpectedly filled with watching faces, including those, eventually, of Halina and Waveney. As the interview becomes increasingly infuriating and Kafkaesque—"And is it your belief, Mr. Grigori, that your parents are wholly British?" (76) and "Can you tell us Mr. Grigori as of this moment are you considered *necessary?*" (79)—Neville gets more and more agitated, starts moving about the stage, shouting, pointing, and finally picking up a chair to throw at Peirce. All the while, as several stage directions keep reminding us, there are "faces staring down." Neville's hour of reckoning gets its ironic flavor from this coding as spectacle: "And is that a public gallery now, are you selling tickets!" (77) he demands.

Neither he nor we will understand the full import of those staring faces until the very last scene of the play, when a similar array of watchers turns Halina and Neville's eleventh-hour union into a poignant spectacle, a case of the damned watching the saved from the precincts of hell. All these "trapped people" (101), as Neville calls them, may or may not be recognized by the audience as its stage counterpart; more important than the metatheatrical gesture is the hinted inclusion here of another medium and another genre into the play's fairly encyclopedic roster (video, TV, radio, newspapers, novels, songs, films). The constitutive acts of theater—watching and listening—are staged in this scene in a deliberately technical way, the channels of each being clearly distinguished. The sound channel is preoccupied with a particularly familiar (and in this context particularly apt) noise, "the sound of aircraft taking off and landing" (93). The visual channel is staged through the watching faces who, because of the noise of the airplanes, can probably not hear much of what Halina and Neville are saying.

The location of the final scene once again engages the play's allegorical mode: Halina and Neville come together in the detention center where foreigners are held prior to being deported. The center is located among the warehouses at the airport, and as Waveney remarks, "It's a weird place to put a prison, right at the end of a runway" (93). Waveney, the Black Englishwoman from the hi-fi store who has befriended Halina, serves as the foil for Neville in being an insider who knows she is really an outsider. During the scenes at the immigration office, several people assume Waveney is an applicant and tell her to sit down and wait for her interview. Now, at the deportation center, she reveals the extent of her alienation from her society when she tells Halina that "I told that bastard immigration officer to take me instead . . . I haven't exactly got much to keep me here" (94).

However, at its deepest level, this play is not geared to encompass the account of radical contemporary placelessness that the combination of Halina and Waveney's stories might have produced. Instead, it is Neville's geopathology that the play turns to in its final moments, and for all its ironic interventions at the level of plot and of staging, the play enters its last phase only to reveal its complicity with the old geopathic dramatic paradigm.

"Your Room's a Little Different Too, Neville."

The change of direction that occurred in the interview scene (and that was marked by, among other things, the appearance of onstage watchers, silently witnessing the events of the scene) was in fact an acknowledgment, an unmasking, of the issue that had concerned it all along: Neville's geopathic condition. As I mentioned earlier, Neville's flat is part of an important scenic discourse that develops during the play. The original pristine condition of the flat is gradually sullied as a result of his involvement with Halina. Halina herself is the first to disarrange the place: "I've already made a mess, " she says (10), spilling things on the floor. This continues in the next scene in the flat, which Halina enters wearing a soaking coat and carrying an umbrella out of which pours muddy water. Later on, much more substantial changes occur, though this time Halina is only indirectly responsible. To his horror, Neville's flat is searched. There are telltale signs everywhere:

> He seems to have been bleeding oil *(She smiles.)* His motorcycle must have been leaking and he brought a lot in with him. *(She moves one of the few decorations on the wall, underneath in black oil fingermarks smeared.)* Probably a little bit of it under most things, smeared his little fingers everywhere. Rather an amateur effort by our standards back home. (47)

The final scene in the flat, the penultimate scene of the play, shows Neville's home to have been quite undone, although the "bare stage with just two wooden floorboards leaning against a wall and a roll of wallpaper" (90) is explained by Neville as a matter of choice: "I had a compulsion to redecorate the flat—of course now they have ripped everything up, they are stopping for two weeks over Christmas! Leaving it looking like a war zone. I can't find where anything is" (90). As always when place is the issue in this play, Neville's remarks have a metaphorical ring: the departure of Halina has left his life in the same condition as his home—torn up, denuded, embattled, bewildering.

The spatial literalizing of Neville's consciousness places it, and him, at the core of the play's concerns and reveals these concerns to be closely related to the long tradition of geopathic drama. Halina's story, it finally emerges, is not the point of the play; it is the catalyst, and she the agent, of Neville's "journey" of self-discovery. This logic is revealed in the final scene, when Neville is given an aria-like self-revealing speech (reminiscent of so many others, including Nora's in *A Doll's House* and Edmund's in *Long Day's Journey into Night*):

> Because over the last few weeks I've been propelled out of my normal existence. You know people that almost die, like in a car crash, for a moment they actually stop breathing and find themselves floating out of themselves and staring down from above at their own bodies, and surroundings—for once I forget the medical term for it—I've had that without the crash, finding myself peering at a world full of dying video shops, with graveyards for their machines, black girls full of startling hostility towards me from the first moment they see me! Those disturbed carol singers, outside the window, the old clients pursuing me full of dark city paranoia—even immigration officers that read Dostoevsky! *It's like a map of the city where all the streets have been re-named.* (100; emphasis added)

The remapping accomplished by *Coming in to Land* is restricted to the consciousness of Neville; it is not shared by Halina, Waveney, Andrew, or Peirce, and I think there is a strong possibility that it is not shared by the audience either. The remapping, after all, does not tell us—or, more importantly, challenge us to or invite us to imagine something new in the way of the politics of location. Instead, it invites us to participate ritualistically—as witnesses, as celebrants—in the self-discovery of the Hero.

The critical issue raised by *Coming in to Land* centers upon the value, force, and direction of what appears to be a new or updated version of the old geopathological drama. The basic question is: does this drama do justice to the tremendous dislocations of our times, or does it simply appropriate them and allegorize them in the service of an essentially regressive notion of place? Or, to be specific: when Neville proclaims that he's "been evicted from my normal certainty, Halina, and the person responsible for that is you" (100), is Halina's entire terrible experience of dislocation not reduced to the status of a mere pedagogical device, an object lesson for the complacent Neville?

I should like to pursue an answer to this question by exploring two fairly inconspicuous strands of the play's thematics that, taken together, do much to explain the nature—and limitations—of ironic realism's engagement with the politics of place. The first of these, more obvious than the other, is the seasonal and climatic references sprinkled all over the play. The choice of Christmas as the time of the play's events (it was also Ibsen's choice for his ur-drama of geopathology) is exploited to the fullest. Hardly a scene goes by without the season being mentioned, often in ways that make an ironic comment on its contemporary, debased version. Thus Christmas is mentioned in connection with shopping: "Christmas, the pre-Christmas boom time, locust time, people stripping whole shops bare" (29). It is mentioned in terms of grotesque social rituals: "Can you imagine anything worse than a Christmas party full of immigration officers?" (69). It is mentioned in terms of frightening social upheavals: "And then across this snow-covered scene these weird psychopathic carol singers wander singing sweet murderous songs—unlike anything I've heard before!" (47).

Finally, Christmas is mentioned—more than mentioned: dramatically used—when, at Neville's invitation, Halina discloses her true feelings about what she is going through. As Halina speaks, explaining why, since "only giants are let in, then from the ordinary material of my life I had to make at least one gigantic episode" (49), she moves toward and then around the Christmas tree. Periodically she reaches out to it, removes one of the hanging Christmas balls, and crushes it in her hands. As she concludes her confession, she "suddenly breaks all the decorative balls on the tree, an assault on the Christmas tree, golden balls popping, as her frustration explodes" (49).

This powerful symbolic action (as powerful, surely, as Ibsen's scenic discourse with Nora's tree) continues the play's general ironic discourse on the holy season, extending it into the psychological register where its traditional connotations (peace, goodwill, family gathering) appear as insensitive insults to Halina's trying situation. Halina's assault on the tree functions in a typical ironic-realist fashion: it evokes and connotatively exploits a familiar symbol system (exactly as Ibsen does in *A Doll's House*); at the same time, it also subtly discredits the symbol in question. Thus it is not simply that Christmas is a motif used to illuminate Halina's experience of unbelonging; rather, Halina's dislocation and Christmas are *mutually* defining (or, in the case of Christmas, *redefining*) elements of the play's meaning.

Another function of the Christmas motif seems to be that of providing a special temporalization for the play, a suggestion that the otherwise realistic events are emanating from a somewhat unusual set of objective circumstances. Not only is it Christmas, and not only is it a Christmas that Neville—and we—cannot easily recognize, it is also a most unusual winter: "And outside here—outside this window, odd things keep happening," says Neville, "There's this violent vivid un-English weather" (46). Several times during the play the inclement weather is remarked upon, and certain bizarre things, like the "X certificate carol singers," seem linked to it: "Maybe they only come out when we have a really bad winter" (39). The weather is also explicitly used as a device to underline the shape of the plot. In the play's final moments, when Halina and Neville have come together on new terms, Neville says: "Have you noticed, the snow's gone at last, Halina, the mild weather's returned" (103).

Neville has a characteristic reaction to the unusual weather: it provides one of several opportunities in the play for him to display his English public school education, his encyclopedic knowledge—broad and nominal—of the world: "My God, what violent rain," he exclaims, "It's probably the Fon." When asked to explain, he declaims: "The Fon. A warm wind they often get in Munich, it comes up from Africa, very occasionally it pierces as far as here, causing thunderstorms. *(He taps the thick glass of the window.)* It can't get in" (13–14).

Neville's sense of security, his conviction that he is protected (and not only from the weather) is to be the real target of the play—not Halina's search for a much more literal kind of security. At its deepest level, the logic of this play turns Halina into a kind of unusual atmospheric condition, a source of some heavy—but necessary—weather for the hero. At its deepest level, then, this is a classic oedipal plot, a know-thyself saga in which the hero is dislodged from a social position and a state of consciousness for which he does not yet have sufficient insight. His world is turned (as Neville says of his own experience) upside down, his life becomes a "careering nightmare," and he is "evicted" from his "normal certainty." Then the storm clears, and light shines again.

The oedipal plot of *Coming in to Land* is held in place by a series of references to the Oedipus story, notably to the figure of deliberate blinding. When Neville visits Peirce for the first time, he remarks upon the spike for papers on Peirce's desk: "I see you're allowed one of these," he says, and goes on to explain: "When I was a solicitor in North London, a slightly decaying inner-city practice, *all* spikes were banned from all desks. . . . Because as you sat there facing this succession of odd, often crazy clients, every now and then a particularly frustrated person would leap up and turn one of these *(He moves paper spike.)* into a deadly weapon—a lunge straight for the eye" (33–34). Later in the play, after the interview takes its disastrous turn, Halina picks up the same paper spike and *"with a sharp but controlled movement, drives [it] into the wall."* She tells Peirce: "You shouldn't keep these things on your desk, somebody next time might go between your eyes" (86). Interestingly enough, Peirce himself subscribes to the oedipal paradigm of knowledge, having boasted to Neville that any discrepancies in what they say, in the passenger's version, are usually "blindingly obvious" (35). He also makes a crucial connection between the oedipal theme and the climatic one, noting that "You're suddenly able to see all sorts of things in this weather . . . that weren't visible before" (35).

If the play unfolds in a hyperexpressive temporality that Halina has caused to develop, like a storm system, around the person of Neville, it could still have something to say about the specificities of experiences like Halina's. However, Halina is actually developed much more as a figure in the play's oedipal logic than in any other way. She is, in fact, a Jocasta figure, starting out looking like a frumpy matron, a mother figure, and then slowly transforming into an object of desire. Or, as Neville puts it: "One moment you're this comic character emerging with a heap of scabby plastic bags that you won't let out of your sight. And now you look like this" (46). Halina's transformation from comic matron to stylish, enigmatic young woman is partly responsible for Neville's Oedipus-like obsession with her "case," an obsession that leads him, as it led Oedipus, to questions about his own paternity ("And is it your belief Mr. Grigori that your parents are wholly British?—And is it your belief that your parents were married at the time you were born?" [76]).

The connection between this plot and the ancient one is made even more explicit—and Halina's role is made even more auxiliary—when in the play's last scene, Neville describes Halina as "this Polish spike," and admits, "I suppose I'm impaled on you" (101). By assimilating Halina to all the other spikes mentioned in the play, which were always possible weapons for violent blinding, she is situated at the center of the play's metaphoric logic, as an instrument of blinding insight. Through Halina, Neville will eventually, in the future, realize the fantasy he has had of seeing "a different view" from his window, "a completely changed London" (53).

The price of this renovated vision of his place will not be, as in Oedipus's case, some terrible mutilation of the hero's body. Indeed on the surface there seems to be no price to be paid at all, as far as the play is concerned, unless one considers Neville's "humiliation" at the hands of Peirce and Booth sufficiently painful to qualify as a price. I would suggest that the price paid for Neville's enlightenment is to be found at a structural and thematic level of the play and takes the form of a betrayal of what Halina represents: the actual facts of dislocation, the material conditions of refugeehood as they are experienced daily by millions of people all over the world.

To understand the relationship between the oedipal plot and the semiology of place—to grasp, that is, the ideological consequences of Poliakoff's staging of Halina as a figure of contemporary dislocation—we can turn to the one other character in the play whom I have not yet mentioned. This is the nameless "Turkish Woman" who appears during the first three scenes of the second act, the scenes set in the immigration office. The Turkish woman is on stage when the second act opens, sitting on a chair, "scarf over her head, heavy boots and coat, and two large plastic bags bulging at her feet" (54). The plastic bags link her, of course, to Halina, to the Halina we first met at the beginning of the play, whose entire identity seemed to be circumscribed by the shabby contents spilling from her plastic bags. The plastic bags semiotically gather Halina and the Turkish woman together into a miserable conglomerate of the world's helpless displaced people, those whom Halina so dreads "Ending up [with] in the last possible airport, surrounded by plastic bags" (50).

But it is this use of the Turkish woman, as semiotic marker, that is problematic if we are looking for a different perspective on place than the old geopathological one. The presence and use of this character entail a coding of foreignness that can only be called Eurocentric, if not downright orientalist. To put it very bluntly, the subtextual message seems to be that Neville's enlightenment can only come through an encounter with a certain manageable kind of foreignness, one from which such irritations as a foreign language and an alien style of dress have been carefully excised. Halina's perfect English, as well as her increasingly perfect fashion sense, seems to be a significant feature of her growing attractiveness to Neville. Her semiotic association with the Turkish woman, then, is rather fraudulent, a way of giving her the badge of actual refugeehood's actual suffering while keeping her, as the plot requires, quite free of its material realities. Indeed, Halina's ultimate characterization of herself as "locked up here with all these other caged people, feeling like me, beating on the walls, you should hear all the different languages echoing around here!" (99) describes her as she appears in Neville's eyes, as singularly (rather than typically) out of place in that cruel (and cruelly multilingual: we remember Neville's early question to Andrew, "She does speak English?") place. The play creates and uses such images of radical foreignness as the Turkish woman, always wildly and hopelessly gesticulating, and the caged foreigners, awaiting deportation, with no Neville to marry and carry them off to safety, not in order to explore them as human experiences that can shed light on the way the world is and should be now, but rather as a kind of atmosphere that can infuse the figure of Halina with more relevance than her role in the oedipal plot allows her to develop as a character.

The muted oedipal plot, combined with, or rather set within, the more conspicuous temporalization (through the figure of Christmas and of unusual weather) simply appropriates the thematic of dislocation for an essentially geopathic narrative: the well-situated hero discovers flaws in his situation and corrects them. This hero, however, does not avail himself of the old heroism of departure; here, the poetics of exile are transferred to the person of an outsider, from whom the hero can borrow them for the purpose of experiencing a kind of figurative—and temporary—displacement. Halina's surrogacy, as well as the temporariness of the experience, is crucial to the logic of the play (as Neville says at one point, "The snow won't last, it never does" [35]), and the conclusion of the play stages this logic in miniature. After Neville and Halina have decided to try again (significantly, this will involve going back to the "old plan," the original marriage plot), they find that the doors of the deportation center have been sealed for the weekend. The following exchange ensues, underlining the play's major themes as well as its rewriting of geopathology's device of departure (complete with slamming doors à la Nora) as *renovation:*

> *Sound of doors being locked, slamming shut.*
> HALINA: You're probably locked in now for Christmas.
> NEVILLE: Good, my apartment is a wreck because of you, the oil went everywhere. At least here I can keep an eye on you.
>
> (103)

Neville can relish a night or two of being locked in (while his apartment is fixed up); like the play itself, he seems to spare little thought for those, the "trapped, caged people," who will leave this place only for something worse, for all the terrors of placelessness. Indeed, in the play's final moments these people (who have served its symbolic system so well) are so thoroughly forgotten that they almost disappear entirely from Halina's description of the place—a topographic betrayal of some significant proportion: "What a place to get engaged, among the warehouses, and this low flat prison, and the cages full of quarantining animals, both monkeys and people locked up around here, and the dead planes parked amongst the long grass, and all the other flotsam of the airport" (103).

A signal failure of creative narrativity—of the ability to imagine and tell new stories about people and places—concludes this play about the quest for place through narrative. The ancient story of an (male) individual's quest for self-knowledge overwrites and erases the experience of contemporary dislocation, and the discourse of place, both geographic place and stage space, is appropriated by an essentially (and also literally) utopian dramaturgy.

Amerika, or The Limits of Exile

> Emigration is the best school of dialectics. Refugees are the keenest dialecticians. They are refugees as a result of changes and their sole object of study is change. They are able to deduce the greatest events from the smallest hints—that is, if they have intelligence!
>   —Bertolt Brecht, *Flüchtlingsgespräche*

> You look smart, why do you write? . . . A smart man never writes. A smart man never leaves any trace behind him.
>   —Janusz Glowacki, *Hunting Cockroaches* (100).

Through both its hidden oedipal plot and its scenic discourse, *Coming in to Land* appropriates the figure of immigration to produce a new, updated version of geopathology. Another recent play, Janusz Glowacki's *Hunting Cockroaches,* wryly excavates the buried logic of this regressive move, uncovering the reasons why immigration as it exists today can never be the frame for a closural narrative of self-transformation. The premise of *Hunting Cockroaches* is that all varieties of contemporary geographic displacement—be it exile, refugeehood, immigration—unfold in the context of a terrible and ubiquitous homelessness. *Hunting Cockroaches* is a send-up of the poetics of exile and uses one of the greatest authors of the exilic consciousness of modernism, Kafka, to make its parodic point.

Kafka is present in the play from its title onward. The setting for the play, a seedy apartment on New York's Lower East Side, is infested with cockroaches to the point of being a major topic of the inhabitants' conversation, which includes at one point a direct reference to Kafka's story. But the true Gregor Samsas of the play are not the roaches; the inhabitants themselves, two Polish émigrés (or would-be émigrés, really refugees), increasingly emulate Gregor's inability to leave his room, his bed. Besides discussing the roaches, they discuss what they should do to earn some money to pay the rent, and it soon becomes clear that—like Gregor—they are singularly incapable of putting any of their plans into effect.

The poetics of exile is parodied by the fact that the man of the couple is a writer (the woman an actress); he has even been offered a chance at publication if he will write a suitably exilic book. His wife suggests a plot: "Hey, you should write a play about Zbyszek. He worked in a shipyard in Gdansk, then he got arrested, was beaten up, sent to prison. He managed to escape, when they caught him they said, prison, or leave the country. He came to America and now he's got a job renovating the Statue of Liberty" (94). He demurs: "Who'll be interested in that? Maybe if he were a Russian," to which she gamely agrees: "OK, so make him a Russian. Imagine a vicious snowstorm, full moon, the waves are rolling, and he's standing right in the torch at the top of the Statue of Liberty, singing . . . in Russian!"

The logic of *Coming in to Land,* in which the suffering of the exile becomes the cause of a settled character's self-discovery, is directly parodied in a scene in which an American publisher approaches the writer, Janek, to write a book. He begins by asking Janek if he likes America, to which Janek enthusiastically replies: "Oh, we think it's a great country and wonderful too." The publisher, a bit nonplussed, corrects Janek: "Of course. But you must understand that not everything in America is as wonderful as it looks. I'm connected with a publishing house which is interested in a slightly different view of America. A more complex view, a more probing view . . . a darker view, if you will." "I *will,*" says Janek hastily, reminding us of the absurd contingency of the immigrant writer's position; his dependence on others to tell him what his experience of otherness should be. There follows one of the most devastating spoofs of the poetics of exile:

MR. THOMPSON: . . . a view which would show us what we Americans have lost . . . For I am of the opinion that you émigrés have got something that we don't.

HE [Janek]: We do?

MR. THOMPSON: Yes, you do.

HE: What's that.

MR. THOMPSON: A soul.

HE: A soul?

MR. THOMPSON: A soul. I've mentioned your name to the publisher. Are you interested?

HE: In writing a book about having a soul?

MR. THOMPSON: No, a book about not having a soul.

HE: I'm definitely interested. Do you think they'll give me an advance immediately?

(121)

The material facts of displacement—poverty, unemployment, discomfort, insecurity, worry, sickness, eviction—stand squarely and immovably in this immigrant writer's path, blocking his path toward the luxury of soulful creativity. The émigré's soul is no match for the terrors of contemporary dislocation.

The distance between the sardonic vision of *Hunting Cockroaches* and the sentimentalities of early (and late) geopathology is most clearly figured in its scenic discourse, which can be read as an ingenious parody of one salient aspect of the scenic discourse of classic realism. The realist stage is often a centrifugal or magnetic space, drawing toward itself all the characters and events required to make sense of an action. The action of realist plays often conforms to this tyrannical closure of the stage, a fact that was deconstructed by Chekhov and parodied by Beckett. Like a totalitarian political system, the realistic stage operates on the principle of total visibility, an impossible ideal shorn up (as I showed in my discussion of *Miss Julie* above) by a systematic occlusion of authorship/authority. It suggests that everything that is meaningful can be shown, can happen right here before our eyes, and that what can't be shown— sex, death, and the past—can nevertheless be *understood* by means of what is shown. This is the principle that was exposed in *The Homecoming,* where the stage space suggests a kind of deliberate breaking into the fourth wall of the realist room but fails to clarify the enigmas of the family past and its sexual present.

In *Hunting Cockroaches,* a wonderful parody of the magnetic stage of realism has all the action take place in the couple's bedroom without bothering to make the various arrivals probable or believable. In fact, all the other characters enter the room from under the bed, and include people like the publisher Thompson and his socialite wife, a homeless bum from Tompkins Square Park, an American immigration officer, and two Polish plainclothes policemen. The scenes that involve these visitors are obviously chronologically—and in some cases geographically—disjunct from the main action; the possibility that they are present as part of an expressionist dream structure suggests itself but is rendered parodic by the constant and hilarious references to insomnia, including the following, one of many bizarre formulations the characters offer of America's otherness:

> Insomniacs have fear and contempt for other insomniacs. Only a sleeper can help me. Sound sleepers run New York, the problem is how to get to them. Insomniacs won't let you, they're crafty. They pretend, and look well rested. They dress very carefully, they put makeup under their eyes. Only their movements give them away. . . . And they boast too much about what a good night's sleep they've had. No more than ten percent of all the people in New York sleep. (89)

The play makes its point about stereotypes by cooking up a number of new ones, their unfamiliarity helping to show up the essential misrepresentation of all stereotypes. Thus the preceding preposterous statistic about New Yorkers' sleeping habits is directly contradicted by other generalizations, at other times: "If it gets out he can't sleep, we're finished. In New York everybody knows how to sleep. I'm trying to get him to pretend he's happy. In New York everybody's happy. . . . I told him he'd never make it here because he doesn't have a sincere smile. Everybody here has a sincere smile" (74).

    Hunting Cockroaches playfully shows that it is especially on the increasingly fractured image of America that the poetics of exile founders. If exile is a painful displacement that nevertheless provides a privileged perspective to the writer, America displaces that possibility by being already so heavily coded, so slippery with self-definitions and others' projections as to provide no stable foothold for the newcomer, no unimpeded point of view. It is not only that the American cultural mainstream has "canned" the American scene (when Jan criticizes the graffiti in the subway, the publisher says: "I'm afraid there I have to disagree. Graffiti is a popular form of a true folk art which expresses the soul. . . . In certain places we still have some [soul] left"); the signification of America is a matter of global (mis)representation. Thus Janek tells of going as a boy to see an exhibit entitled "This is America" in Warsaw, which "displayed loud ties, gaudy billboards, burning crosses of the KKK, and even bugs from Colorado that were trained at special camps to be dropped from planes at night to devour socialists' potatoes. All this to a decadent boogie-woogie soundtrack." The exhibit was intended, of course, as propaganda, and was meant

> to evoke horror, disgust, hatred. It had, however, the opposite effect. Thousands of Varsovians, dressed in their holiday best, waited every day in lines as long as those to see Lenin's Tomb and in solemn silence looked at the display, listened respectfully to the boogie-woogie, wanting in this way, at least, to manifest their blind and hopeless love for the United States. (103)

America, that is, is utterly derealized. Like the Moscow of Chekhov's characters, its existence as an actual place is covered over and ignored in favor of its role in the opposition between one's own painful reality and "somewhere else." In *Hunting Cockroaches,* this opposition is often presented in ridiculous terms, as when Janek favorably compares the map of the United States to that of Europe, praising its neat angularities and deriding the European "boundary lines [which] twist, and turn, and twitch like a can of worms" (103). Equally funny, though darkened by the context (and the speakers!), is what the couple are told by two policemen who take over their apartment in Warsaw:

> How can anyone live in a country like this? Ransacking people's apartments, censorship, a total lack of freedom and justice, erosion of one's moral principles. Whereas you'll be sitting pretty in New York, living it up in Manhattan, all the scotch you can drink . . . and the CIA finances the whole thing, lunch with Susan Sontag, then in the evening as it's getting dark the aliens come down on flying saucers. I wouldn't mind going there myself, but somebody has to stay here and maintain order. (97)

The most fundamental rift between the figure of America and the old discourse of exile comes, however, from the grim reality of home—and homelessness—that greets the already unhomed immigrant. Home,

here, is figured largely in terms of a trope we have repeatedly found
connected to the figure of America, the figure of garbage. The cockroaches who seem to be the real inhabitants of the apartment (and the
city) are said to "eat only garbage. Remember Gregor?" and the bum
who visits them recognizes most of the furniture in their apartment as
former trash thrown out on the streets. The couple defend themselves:

> All right, I admit it, I took that TV set off the street. I'm not in the
> least ashamed to have *one* item in my apartment that we picked out
> of the trash on the sidewalk. *(The Bum taps on the chair with his
> finger.)* Well OK, maybe two items. *(The Bum points to the table.)*
> And the table, so what? Most young couples in New York furnish
> their apartments out of the trash found on the sidewalks. Thanks to
> that *(points to the TV set)* we could watch the birthday party for the
> Statue of Liberty. (107)

The other major definition of this American home, besides garbage,
is homelessness. The bum's attitude inverts the usual affective relation of
these terms, making homelessness seem—absurdly—a matter of freedom, choice, normality: "Our park, it's the best park in the city," he says
proudly (speaking of the infamous Tompkins Square Park, actual symbol of New York's social crisis in the 1980s). "The only ideal location, if
you plan to stay in Manhattan, of course" (106). The couple, two months
behind on their rent, have already taken desperate (and, again, absurd)
measures to ward off the terror of homelessness:

> You came home very pleased with yourself that day. You'd met
> Tomek in a wheelchair going off to work. You asked him what was
> wrong with him, and he said there was nothing wrong with him, he
> just bought himself a wheelchair to avoid paying the rent. A land-
> lord has no right to evict an invalid. And the next day you brought
> home that wheelchair. (90)

In the context of such tenuous living, even aspirations get rewritten in
absurdist terms: "Once we get money, we'll move uptown. To Fourth
Street. It's much safer there. The floors are thicker, you can smash cockroaches and they don't hear you downstairs."

Most telling in the play's analysis of contemporary dislocation is the

nightmarish symmetry that is established between the horrors of totalitarian Poland and terrors of urban America:

> HE: You weren't dreaming about anything?
> SHE: No. I wasn't even asleep.
> HE: But why do you start screaming?
> SHE: Because I felt like it.
> HE: Maybe you were dreaming that we were back in Poland.
> SHE: No.
> HE: Or that somebody broke into the apartment through the win-
> dow.
>
> (75–76)

The reality of contemporary immigration is the radical insecurity and
contingency of urban existence. The contemporary immigrant is between Scylla and Charybdis, or as Americans would say, between a rock
and a hard place. The project of relocation is hemmed in by the special
miseries of each side. The penultimate speech of the play, actually a
rehearsal of a stand-up comedy routine that the woman hopes to use for a
TV audition someday, sums it up (and catches the dark comic tone of the
whole play):

> I have this really funny piece. OK . . . A blind man and a man with
> only one eye were crossing the river in a boat. The blind man did the
> rowing and the man with only one eye steered. In the middle of the
> river, the blind man accidentally swung his oar out of the water and
> hit the man with only one eye in his good eye. "This is the end" said
> the man who used to have only one eye. The blind man reached the
> other shore and stepped out of the boat. (130)

It is not merely a matter of cultural disjunction, although that is real
enough ("How can you teach Franz Kafka to students who drive to
school in sports cars?"). The real problem is that the place where one
seeks refuge is riven with the symptoms of its own dissolution. Whereas
this condition was figured in *Coming in to Land* through a vague sense of
menace disrupting the Dickensian old world of England, in *Hunting
Cockroaches* it is a very specific and all too familiar roster of ills, including
unemployment, poverty, sickness, and homelessness. In this context, the

words of the Polish policemen make a crazy kind of sense and quite obliterate the poetics of exile: "A smart man never writes. A smart man never leaves any trace behind him" (100).

Like the limits of homecoming, the limits of exile are announced through a parody of traditional dramaturgy. This time it is not the hidden secret that is shown to be a defunct device, although there is a kind of "buried child" here too: the baby the woman wants and the husband does not, because, as he says, "Where will we put it?" (The woman's wonderful answer—"Over there"—defeats both the buried-child device and the geopathology it underwrites.) The main element of traditional realist drama parodied in *Hunting Cockroaches* is the implicit promise of *representativeness*, the unspoken pledge that what we are shown is somehow *typical* (and therefore meaningful). The play is framed by a narrator, who appears at the outset to assure us that "Our heroes have been chosen from among hundreds and thousands of ordinary people," and to invite us to "follow their first steps on American soil."

The play ends with the same narrator returning to tell us that "we leave our heroes at the threshold of success. Very soon the diligence, perseverance, integrity and modesty so typical of the people of the eastern part of Europe will prevail." We have just watched our heroes congratulate each other because one of them had a nightmare ("That's great! That means you fell asleep"). But the narrator assures us that they will win Pulitzer Prizes and Broadway roles. Their representative status guarantees their success. The story of "ordinary people" is not told unless those ordinary people do something extraordinary and prove that such feats are within the grasp of all. The narrator's cordial farewell could hardly be more ironic, or more telling: "Good night and God bless you. God bless America."

Real Estate: The Recovery of Place

For all its absurdity, the America of *Hunting Cockroaches* is a recognizable place. As such it is a definite change (and, as I shall be arguing from here onward, a decided improvement) over the Americas in Shepard and in Pinter. Those vast expanses of undifferentiated open space bespoke a conquest of the principle of *locality*, overwriting the crucial differentness of place with an all-powerful and ubiquitous sameness coded as myth.

The reconquest of locality, of the specialness and particularity of place, goes hand in hand with a rethinking of those myths that have rendered America as an immense zone of potentiality, without the constraining precincts or the separate sectors with which other countries map—and acknowledge—the differences within themselves.

As both Pinter and Shepard showed, the myths of American spatiality—myths of infinite openness, of endless progress, of unlimited opportunity—are bought at the price of a crushing, numbing homogeneity. This is the weak spot in the omnipotent figure of America, for the reign of sameness eventually fails to conceal its antipathy to the very projects—of individualism and self-determination—that it is supposed to support. The typical American paradox that makes individualism the highest personal value and conformism the pervasive social reality is exposed most clearly in the case of immigrant identity. Immigration (and here I mean both the experience as well as the figuration of immigration, as they exist in twentieth-century America) runs afoul of the two most cherished images of the American mythos: the lone hero and his (decidedly *his*) relation of utter contingency to place. In contrast to the first, immigration foregrounds the family, the group who is displaced as a whole but reacts to that displacement as individuals, thus setting up a dialectic vis-à-vis the figure of America. In contrast to the second, immigration insists on the reality of one's relation to place.

The immigrant's place of origin (unlike the geopathological hero's desired destination) is utterly, even painfully actual, and so is her or his place of arrival. The reality of the latter may be conveyed in the absurdist terms of *Hunting Cockroaches,* or it may be rendered more realistically; either way, it brings the category of *place* back into the figure of America. The America that, in Pinter and Shepard and Wolfe, had so effectively brought the old discourse of home to a halt by erasing the very category of place is gradually being displaced, especially in immigrant drama, by a new place, a place where phrases like "God Bless America" ring rather hollow.

The America of multiculturalism is the subject of the next chapter. But the multicultural project exists in imaginative dialogue with the figuration of immigration, and one of its greatest achievements is a new sense of place, a platiality to replace the old "spatiality" of America. Interestingly enough, this new sense of place is often articulated in terms of images and figures that already have a long history in the dramatic discourse of place.

Somebody Else's House

In José Rivera's play *The House of Ramon Iglesia* the figure of homecoming is turned inside out. The play deals with the efforts of a Puerto Rican family who have lived on Long Island for twenty years to sell their house and return to Puerto Rico. Like the family in *The Homecoming,* this family has three sons, one of whom is a Joey-like jock (and eventually joins the marines) and one of whom is a Teddy-like misfit, in that he is educated and has moved out of the family. Like Teddy too (and like Vince in *Buried Child*), this son is alone among his brothers in having a woman companion, his Anglo girlfriend Caroline. Unlike Teddy, however, Javier is the clear protagonist of the play, and his marginality to the family is the play's deepest issue. By play's end, Javier is the only member of the Iglesia family (besides Julio, who has already gone off to the marines) who doesn't depart for Puerto Rico. In a sense, then, this is Pinter's play from the vantage point of Teddy. It is homecoming from the point of view of the place that had seemed, in Pinter and elsewhere, to erase the very notion of home: America.

A major difference between this play and *The Homecoming*—and one that fully supports the reversal of perspective just mentioned—is that this family is not an all-male preserve. There is a powerful mother here, and one whose relationship to her husband and sons (unlike Halie's in *Buried Child*) is not particularly problematic. She is the force behind the proposed return to Puerto Rico, having spent a lifetime feeling out of place. The main cause of her very literal and specific geopathology (it is not, like the traditional version, a vague longing to be in some unspecified "elsewhere") is, significantly, a dead child.

The buried child of *The House of Ramon Iglesia* is not a hidden secret or an enigma, although she is connected with a sense of magic and superstition that pervades the play and is one of the ways it counters the figure of America. Her presence is felt from the start, and takes the form, interestingly enough, of a photograph. The photograph of the infant Felicia is part of an altar that the mother, Dolores, has arranged and at which, at the start of the play, she prays. The walls of the room are covered with icons, giving the child's photograph a religious context and meaning. This combination of photography and religion recalls the diegetic space of *Buried Child,* the room "upstairs" whose walls were said to be covered with photographs and crosses. The difference lies, of course, in the lack of irony here: if Shepard's drama used the figure of photography—and especially its false promise of certainty—to ironize all belief in all myths, including family and religion, the literal photograph here seems to take its place in the realm of faith without irony or ambiguity. The picture of the infant Felicia and the way it is used by Dolores bespeak a still intact sense of family and of the continuity between family and faith. Dolores does not, like Halie, have to seek religion outside the house, and there is no cartoonish religious figure like Father Dewis in this play.

The dead child does, however, play a major role in the image of home that this play develops and that both uses and alters—revitalizes, enriches—the existing dramatic discourse of home. That discourse had relied heavily on two specifications of home: home as house and home as family. In *The House of Ramon Iglesia,* the dead child functions to revision both. The house here is characterized as a sort of grave or mausoleum for the dead child, and the child herself functions as an emblem of the principle *underlying* the figure of family: generation.

The house in the play is a kind of *reductio* of the literal home of realist drama, having all its materiality and specificity, but presenting that stalwart edifice (with slammable doors, etc.) at the point of collapse. In a way that recalls the entropic abode of Spalding Gray in *Terrors of Pleasure,* this house is falling apart. Like that play, this one features a ruined furnace, making for constant allusion to the coldness of the Long Island winter. The weather that Caroline mimes as freezing to Dolores and pronounces to be "Murder" (198) recalls *Coming in to Land,* in which weather provided a surreptitious symbolic subtext for a disguised drama of oedipal renewal. In *The House of Ramon Iglesia,* the weather, like the house, is part of a doggedly literal—even referential—system of contrasts between America and Puerto Rico.

Besides its broken furnace, the house has a severe water problem (again recalling Spalding Gray). As act 2 opens, members of the Iglesia family are actually bringing water in in buckets from the neighbor's, and Javier, the son who feels most alienated from the family, asks, "Why hasn't Dad called a repairman? Get some guy to fix the pump, we'll have water like civilized people" (222). Again activating the play's extensive contrast between two very specific places, Dolores counters: "In Puerto Rico he'd walk from his house in Miraflores to my house in Arecibo with two barrels of water—one on this shoulder, one on this shoulder. In the sun. Barefoot" (222).

Javier's critical attitude to his family (which they suspect is also a hatred for his people, for all Puerto Ricans) marks the play's movement toward a new discourse on immigration, wherein the schizophrenia of immigrant experience—the splitting of subjectivity that was evoked by Machado in *Broken Eggs*—plays itself out as a conflict of generations. It is a pattern we will see again in the next chapter, for the issue of generational difference and conflict is a crucial part of the developing formulation of multiculturalism. In this play, the conflict of generations is focused on the project of homecoming and characterizes immigration as a schizophrenia not only of the individual self but also of the group.

Although all the Iglesia children were born in America, only Javier has identified with the land of his birth sufficiently to make the project at hand deeply conflictual for him. Several times during the family's efforts to sell the Long Island house and move to Puerto Rico, Javier and his brothers debate the relative merits of America and Puerto Rico. A number of familiar oppositions are invoked: developed versus underdeveloped societies, first world versus third world, civilization versus the primitive:

> CHARLIE: Anyway, I think Puerto Rico will be fun. Jungles and farms—you can't get that in Holbrook. And Mom says we can buy a horse down there—something else you can't get in Holbrook.
> JAVIER: You can't get malaria in Holbrook either . . .
> CHARLIE: and hang out at the beach all day long . . .
> JAVIER: . . . or tarantulas and hurricanes . . .
> CHARLIE: . . . And all those pretty girls to fall in love with.
> JAVIER: Early marriage, lots of brats, and a fat middle age.
>
> (209)

The last items in Javier's list of prejudices against Puerto Rico refer, significantly, to the matter of generation, the principle that divides Javier most decisively from his family. Like some mythic American hero out of the Wild West, Javier is set on a course of singularity, of self-determination defined as solo determination. This impulse in his character, demonstrated most vividly in the scene when he breaks off so cruelly from his girlfriend Caroline ("I'm not giving you my new address. I don't want you to visit me, sleep with me, or even call me up"), is at the heart of his conflict with his family. The still cohesive, still viable family—so different from the perverse family of *The Homecoming* and the oblivious family of *Buried Child*—inscribes its viability in terms of homecoming, that is, of homecoming *defined as a project* rather than as a pre-coded and fully known experience. By contrast, Javier has imbibed enough of the discourse of America that situates the viable self at the far side of homecoming, beyond the possibility of any recovery of identity.

Very significantly, Javier expresses the limits of homecoming in terms that link up crucially with two broad issues central to the emerging discourse of place. The first of these, discussed at length in the previous chapter, is the issue of language. *The House of Ramon Iglesia* employs a presentational technique that dramatizes this issue, and I shall discuss this further below. The second issue invoked by Javier in his account of a posthomecoming subjectivity will be the subject of the next chapter: the problematic of multiculturalism, of the radical displacement of cultural identity within the context of American immigration:

> I don't speak Spanish because . . . I don't know. Got out of the habit. But I've been starting to think. About our people, you know? And I don't even know what those words mean, "our people." Chicanos in California? Dominicans? Cubans in Florida? Puerto Ricans who still go back to the island and never make a commitment here? I don't know. I look around. I know what our people feel and need and want—and I want to help them someday—and I know I will someday—but something pushes me away. (210)

What pushes him away is obvious: it is the myth of success that he has accepted, according to which group identity—hence family, hence the principle of generation—is an impediment to individual fulfillment. In this play's analysis of immigration, it is this myth that breaks asunder the chain of generations. When Javier claims about his father that "His dreams are killing him," his brother fires back: "*Your* dreams are killing him."

The important contribution that *The House of Ramon Iglesia* makes to the dramatic discourse of immigration is that it links this discourse very specifically with the platial issues that have dominated American drama as well as its European forerunners. Specifically, it offers an account of place wherein the figure of the home-as-house is disjunct from the figure of home-as-family. The literal stage-home of realism is present here, as in Gray's play, in a terminal mode. Whereas the well-furnished homes of realist drama had been unable to stanch the wounds of geopathic desire and were solid only as points of door-slamming departure, this house has never functioned as a home: Ramon recalls that "We moved to Holbrook when Grundy Avenue was still a dirt road. We pulled up to this house—it looked like a witch's cap—and your mother started laughing because she thought I was joking." When Javier asks Dolores if "this [has] ever been home?" she answers unequivocally: "Never" (228).

By contrast, the family of this play, unlike the unraveling families of traditional realism, has remained a family throughout. Indeed, they are a family precisely because this house is not a true home. According to Dolores, "This 'home' took away my little girl. . . . This cold house killed her." To Javier's plea—"You've got to bury her"—Dolores responds in a way that shows that the mark of their true familyhood is that they can envision another home together, elsewhere: "I held her against me, keeping her from the cold air in this dying house. For six days, Ramon tried to work on the furnace, trying to start it, but it wouldn't start. One day, as I was making coffee, while Ramon was at work, she died. I stood by that window for a whole day, facing Puerto Rico" (228).

In all this, Javier is the exception. He does not share his family's longing, and his family is bewildered by the distance between themselves and him: "What's wrong with you?" says his mother. "The first sky you saw was a Puerto Rican sky. Your first drink of water was Puerto Rican water. But you don't remember." The plot of the play evolves one solution to the problem embodied by Javier, the problem of making a home in America. Interestingly enough, the solution is a clearly anti-oedipal plot, a plot in which the protagonist saves his life by accepting—not killing—the father. While the first act of the play is a kind of miniature *Long Day's Journey into Night,* with Javier as the hero who registers the terrible *meaning* of entrapment while his family experiences its reality, its second act records an astonishingly literal journey. In each case, that of the entrapment and that of the journey, the house is the cause.

The deed to the house has to be signed by relatives in Puerto Rico, so that the family can dispose of it and move back to the island. When the father, Ramon, fails to get the deed signed properly, Javier is at first pleased and imagines that this will keep the family in America. Gradually, however, the family's project of return gets through to him, and he agrees to go to Puerto Rico himself, to do what his father failed to do. His decision is the mark of a new understanding for his father; it is also the sign of a profound sea change in Javier himself. (When he asks the potential buyer for three days in which to go to Puerto Rico and clear up the mess, the buyer says: "Three days? Okay. But if you fail you may be living in the bottom of Long Island Sound, and believe me, my family will put you there.")

Javier does not fail. He returns from his journey not only successful in the matter of the deed, but with his vision slightly altered. "There were things . . ." he tells Charlie, "Some of the smells . . . the lightning . . . the buzz of the rain forest all night long . . . some beautiful women . . . simple and direct and sweet" (239). The father and mother who had previously been so alienated from Javier now leave him with traditional benedictions and warm embraces. At play's end, Javier is alone onstage in the empty house, but he is transformed. He switches on a tape recorder and smiles at the salsa music that comes on. He begins to sway to it, moving his hips slowly. Then, as the lights begin to fade, he softly speaks—his own name. At this moment, Javier stands as the vestigial sign of a new possibility for making a home in America. His experience of return has not only changed his view of his old home but has perhaps also given him, as Gómez-Peña writes, a new perspective on his new home: "With my new eyes, I saw this country no longer as the mythical all-white mighty power the Mexicans fear so much, but as a multiracial and multilingual complex with myriad points of view. This realization gave me the courage to stay and the desire to participate in the making of a culture that included my/our vision" ("A Binational Performance Pilgrimage," 32).

The transformation of Javier is in some ways the opposite of the transformation of Nora at the end of *A Doll's House*. Whereas Nora understood and acted out the heroism of departure, thereby creating the exemplary self of humanist modernism, Javier uncreates an anguished, alienated, and lonely self by allowing his family to depart. They depart, as it were, *through* him, their project of homecoming moving across and beyond his sense of homelessness. The Javier who remains is not the consummation of a self-creating process but rather—because of his journey to another "home"—the token of a potentially new, more *multiply situated* model of subjectivity. The drama of multiculturalism that is the subject of the next chapter expands on and explores this new model of subjectivity, but *The House of Ramon Iglesia* already contains one salient device for its articulation: bilingualism.

The production note to *The House of Ramon Iglesia* says: "It should be clear that Dolores is speaking Spanish throughout the play, though we hear her words in English. Characters who do not speak Spanish cannot understand her" (197). This association between the mother and the mother tongue has several meanings and effects. To begin with, it supports the specificity of the "other home" to which the Iglesia family is drawn and from which it derives its cohesion. The issue for Dolores is one of literal belonging, of being where you are understood: "I want to hear my language spoken by everyone I meet, even little children" (228). Javier understands this perfectly, but from the opposite side: he has willfully shunned the Spanish language because it identifies him as an outsider.

The actual outsider is Javier's girlfriend Caroline, who in the play's very first scene has some trouble communicating with Dolores but then succeeds rather well (Dolores offers her coffee, she understands and accepts, and Dolores kisses her on the cheek and goes off to make the coffee). The other actual outsider is Calla, the bigoted but essentially kind and fair Italian neighbor who is to buy the house; he also has trouble communicating with the family and at one time decides to buy another house: "I just want to be untangled from you people once and for all. I've spent nineteen years bailing you people out, left and right, rain or shine, no more. *The man at the other house speaks my language*" (238; emphasis added).

Yet neither Caroline nor Calla really fails to understand and to support the family's purpose of homecoming. Calla finally does buy the house and even drives the family to the airport when all is done! As for Caroline, she insists on helping Javier—now broke as a result of his trip to Puerto Rico—with money: "to get you a place to live." She also gives the family a rather inspired housewarming gift for Puerto Rico: a small glass ball containing a house with snow: "They can shake it and make it winter" (229). Thus the family's conflicts are clearly internal to the family itself; the Spanish they speak is like that of the immigrant woman reported by Oliva M. Espin who told her therapist that "My problems are with my family and my family speaks Spanish, so my problems are in Spanish" (109). For all his representative bigotry, Calla is nowhere near as dangerous to the identity of the Iglesias as is Javier himself. For Calla understands (however comically he may express it) that place, generation, and humanity are one: "We're talking *real estate*," he says and goes on to fill in the following wonderful definition: "people uprooting themselves, promises I gotta keep" (211).

The bilingualism of *The House of Ramon Iglesia*, then, is not the mark of an unbreachable difference but rather of an inviting pluralism. It is a demonstration of the possibility of entertaining two or more cultural contexts simultaneously, of inhabiting two or more homes simultaneously. It is an extension of what Gómez-Peña calls "border aesthetics" and it is, as he says, an ongoing project, far from complete: "By coming to *El Norte* I paid a high price for my curiosity. I unknowingly became part of a lost tribe. As citizens of nowhere, or better said, of everywhere, we were condemned to roam around the foggy and unspecific territory known as border culture. Today, a decade later, we still haven't been able to 'return' completely" (*Warrior for Gringostroika*, 21). For the citizens of nowhere and everywhere there is a vision, beyond homecoming, of return: a vision of coming home by/and going home.

Chapter Six

"If Not Here, Where?" The Challenge of Multiculturalism

It's so important to me that we're all engaged in this social experiment, that we don't give up on it, that we keep on criticizing America and trying to change it. I mean, if not here, where?

—David Henry Hwang

The rhetorical question that concludes David Hwang's reflections on the contemporary American theater—if not here, where?—marks out America as a privileged space for the renegotiation of the problematic relationship between identity, culture, and place. Hwang is in fact expressing the latest version of a well-established American myth, of America as the new frontier, the place of both literal and metaphoric openness, where the history of the future can be worked out.[1]

America's self-consciously immigrant aspect gives its cultural discourse a rich ambiguity. This discourse, while exemplifying like none other the ideological principles of one strong strain of European culture (Anglo-Protestant), nevertheless also evinces a constant commitment, however superficial, to difference. It is highly characteristic of what Ping Chong refers to as the "unmelting pot" of America ("Notes," 65), that the themes of religious tolerance, racial harmony, and ethnic diversity are sounded repeatedly in the official self-characterization of the nation, becoming most insistent when that other superprinciple of American culture, homogeneity, is challenged by racial and ethnic conflict.

The severest tests of this benign part of America's self-image come from the profoundly troubled region of Black-white relations. The histories, past and future, of the two groups' interactions are such as to make the ideals of tolerance seem worse than impossible—irresponsible.

The reality of American racism reminds us that all exiles are not, as Jacques Mounier points out, physical exiles. There is also such a thing as cultural exile, exile within one's own culture: "N'exist-t-il pas un exil culturel, un exil dans la culture, dans la langue ou les langages de l'autre et donc non seulement un rejet, un bannissement et un châtiment, mais aussi une incomprehension, une alienation, une perte d'identité? Et cet exil, s'il risque de contraindre au silence, ne peut il pas conduire aussi à la folie, au refuge dans la folie?" (5).[2] It is this eventuality that George Wolfe's play *The Colored Museum* engages, suggesting that the effects of an internal cultural exile are such that the representations—*and self-representations*—of Black Americans are a collection of the most maddening, offensive, and most disempowering stereotypes imaginable.

The imaginatively debilitating discourse of racism engulfs American cultural discourse and threatens the multicultural ideal of America. The cultural and political fate of all the "other" immigrant groups in America is influenced—deformed, warped—by that failure.[3] The voices that speak from outside this core conflict cannot help reproducing its terms; at the same time they evince a desire to break out of those terms, to express and reflect their experience as immigrants and minorities outside the frame of the culture's racism toward Blacks.

The literature on multiculturalism, both academic and journalistic,[4] is already vast, ranging from problems of definition and nomenclature to theoretical and ideological issues.[5] My purpose here is not to join the debates surrounding multiculturalism but rather to see how some of their central issues, such as the "responsibility" of the minority artist, and the dialectic of ethnic identity and stereotyped cultural representation, relate to the ongoing dramatic reformulation of place that is the subject of this book.

The plays I shall be discussing in this chapter all belong to one particular subcategory of multicultural drama, namely Asian-American drama. I have chosen to concentrate on this group so as to avoid in some measure the problem that multicultural drama in general centrally confronts: the problem of eliding differences *within* in the course of charting differences *between*. The fact that all multicultural drama shares the difficult condition of being marginal to mainstream American drama threatens to homogenize the self-construction of this drama, forcing it into a single and undifferentiated "minority" identity. However, as writers of ethnic minorities are vividly aware, the differences between various ethnic minorities—derived from differences in their respective histories of immigration as well as from the vast religious and cultural differences between their countries of origin—are as profound and significant as their differences from the dominant white culture. To the extent that multicultural drama makes the construction of specific ethnic identities one of its goals, it must resist assimilation not only to the dominant culture but also to a generalized marginality.[6]

Indeed, difference prevails even *within* well-recognized minority groups: for example, writers belonging to what is broadly designated as Hispanic-American literature regularly distinguish between Puerto Rican, Mexican-American, Chicano/a, Latino/a, and Cuban. Similarly, the term Asian-American is frequently broken down into Chinese-American, Korean-American, Japanese-American, and so on.[7]

Needless to say, the problem of the correct identification of ethnic literature is not a superficial matter of nomenclature; it goes to the ideological heart of multiculturalism, which is the issue of identity as politics. Recently, artists like Guillermo Gómez-Peña have sought to take this issue beyond its geopathic impasse (the impasse produced by the impaction of personal identity and place) and have proposed the notion of a "border identity" as the correct response to "the borderization of the world" (Barta, 11). In this model, the experience of diaspora (and its attendant nostalgic and sentimental poetics of exile) is exceeded through association with the postmodern, even millennial, experiences of political apocalypse and ideological transgression:

> From the Tiananmen Square massacre to the Baghdad genocide, we all felt the birth pangs of the new millennium. Many borders were erased and many more were instantaneously created. The amount, complexity and intensity of the political changes in the world surpassed our ability to decodify them adequately. Everything seemed to be up for grabs: language, ideology, identity, religious faith, sexuality, aesthetics. And in the middle of this *fin-de-siècle* earthquake, my colleagues and I were looking *for a new place* [emphasis added] to speak from, and a new set of languages and metaphors capable of articulating our present crisis. (*Warrior for Gringostroika,* 30–31)

This new place to speak from, these new languages and metaphors, is the subject of this chapter. Although the plays I shall be discussing here exemplify multicultural representation in a variety of ways, they all have certain things in common: certain accounts of place, certain approaches to language, and certain metaphors that together move the drama of our fin de siècle toward a practice I call *radical multiculturalism*. This practice is most fully exemplified here in a surprisingly early play, Ping Chong's *Nuit Blanche,* indicating (as I hope my discussion of all the plays will show) that the seeds of multiculturalism were sown long ago,[8] as far back as midcentury, when the geopathic discourse of home began to unravel under pressure from the utopian promises lodged in the evolving figure of America. The drama of multiculturalism requires that those promises finally be made good: "If not here, where?"

Among the figures that organize the drama of multiculturalism is one that has a long history and a complex meaning: the figure of pedagogy. The spectacle of one person teaching or trying to teach another some signal truth, usually a technique for survival as a minority in America, is multiculturalism's thematization of its vital social and political function. The ethnic theater had, from its earliest incarnations, served a dual pedagogical function, teaching immigrants about their native cultures while at the same time exposing them to the new one.[9] The pedagogical scenes of this drama betray a self-critical didactic project, one that is aware of and wants to steer clear of the coercion of didacticism, the effortless pedagogical pressure of dominant culture. In these plays, the figure of the instructor is deconstructed by another ubiquitous figure, or, rather, device: doubling. The many doubles and instances of doubling in these plays work to ironize the earnest pedagogical efforts in them. But they do more. They contribute to the construction of a model of the multiplicity of identity that links the projects of multiculturalism and postmodernism. What Guillermo Gómez-Peña says of Latino experience can be said of multiculturalism in general:

> One thing I know for sure: My identity, like that of my contemporaries, is not a monolith but a kaleidoscope; and everything I create, including this text, has a multiplicity of voices, each speaking from a different part of myself. Far from being postmodern theory, this multiplicity is a quintessential feature of the Latino experience in the U.S. ("Binational Performance Pilgrimage," 30)

"We Are Born Traveling"

A creative alternative to the multicultural reinscription of dominant ideology is to be found in an early play of David Hwang's, the short but extremely powerful *As the Crow Flies*. A great measure of this play's power comes from its explicit inclusion into the multicultural matrix of the experience that always implicitly affects it, namely, Black experience. By framing the discourse of home within a contrast between two very specific and very different histories of displacement, the play actually removes the figure of home from its geopathic inscription and turns it, poetically, toward a healthier possibility. The play tells the story of two American women, one Chinese, the other Black. The Chinese woman, Mrs. Chan, is in her seventies and lives in the comfortable upper-middle-class home that is the set of the play. The Black woman, Hannah, is in her late sixties and works as Mrs. Chan's cleaning woman.

When the play opens, Mrs. Chan is seated in a chair in the middle of the room, where she will remain throughout almost the whole play. Her position resembles that of Beckett's Hamm, and indeed this play is very much a kind of *Endgame,* the final moves in a logic of place and identity that these old people have been playing out for years.

In place of the immobilized Nagg and Nell, this Hamm has a wandering old husband—wandering in body and in mind. Walking into the house with golf clubs slung over his shoulder, he informs his wife that he's just returned from a good game of golf and asks for a cold can of beer. Mrs. Chan informs him that he does not drive anymore, that the Eldorado has been sold long ago (shades of Willy Loman), so "How can you go to golf? You cannot go anyplace" (103). This news, along with his comic-pathetic question, "Where did I go?" (103), puts him in a kind of inner circle of madness in the play, in which, Clov-like, he comes and goes, comes and goes. The scene ends with him leaving again—"I must go to golf. [I'll] take the Eldorado" (104)—asking his wife to have a cold can of beer ready for him when he returns.

By the time he returns, in the last moment of the play, his home has been entirely reconfigured. The play concludes on the threshold of his recognition—or nonrecognition—of the transformation; his presence in the play (which is really not about him or his relationship to his wife at all but rather about the two women) allows for an anticlosural strategy that is, as we will see, crucial to this revisioning of the discourse of home.

The play opens with an astonishing speech. Speaking casually as she goes about her cleaning chores around the seated Mrs. Chan, Hannah says, "I guess I never told you this before, Mrs. Chan, but I think the time is right now. See, I'm really two different folks" (99). Far from showing any surprise at this amazing confession, Mrs. Chan just concentrates on getting it all straight: "When you are here you are Hannah

Carter . . . And, then, when you go outside, and you are . . . someone . . . someone . . ."—"Sandra Smith."—"Um. Okay" (99). When Hannah offers to answer any questions about her double, and even fills in some further details about the situation, Mrs. Chan remains perfectly cool. Her reaction works to characterize the splitting of identity in a way that contrasts sharply with the connotation of the puppet doubles in *The Danube*. This double character is not a self plus a shadow self or pseudoself; these are two full-fledged characters, their doubling made necessary by the magnitude and complexity of their humanity. This interpretation is supported by the unexpected views of Mrs. Chan on the matter of split identities: "So what? So you have two different people . . . So what? My uncle had six!" (100). She then proceeds to describe each of her uncle's "people" and their respective achievements, until Hannah gasps, "This is all one guy?" (100).

Mrs. Chan, so calm and unflappable, seems to be rooted, both literally (in her Hamm-like seat center stage) and psychologically. "Whatever you can tell me," she assures Hannah, "man with six persons inside, man with three heads, man who sees a flying ghost, a sitting ghost, a ghost disguised to look like his dead wife—none of these are so unusual" (100). Of course, they are pretty unusual, even though all the ghosts she mentions do occur in the course of this short play. The second half of the play, after the husband's departure for his "golf game," is essentially a ghost play, in which "a flying ghost, a sitting ghost, and a ghost disguised to look like [a] dead wife" (100) are the main players.

Long before Sandra Smith's arrival, Mrs. Chan has decided that Sandra is a ghost, and one she can easily defeat because of her "American stupidity." For her, then, the Black woman's predicament is an opportunity to call up the worldview and magical lore of another world, a world whose true meaning for Mrs. Chan will only be revealed to her (and to us) in the encounter with Sandra Smith. For the moment, Mrs. Chan can only boast: "She comes here, I will fight her. Not like these Americans. So stupid. Never think of these things. Never think of ghost. Never think of death. Never prepare for anything. Always think, life go on and on, forever. And so, always, it ends" (101).

In preparing for her encounter with the "stupid ghost" Sandra Smith, Mrs. Chan proclaims her quite superhuman indifference to the lure of place. She is, she says, and has long been, impervious to the special attachments that most people form to places they inhabit. Her lot, constant displacement, has inured her to the pain of dislocation:

The day I arrive in America, I do not feel sorry. I do not miss the Philippine, I do not look forward live in America. Just like, I do not miss China, when I leave it many years ago—go live in Philippine. Just like, I do not miss Manila, when Japanese take our home during wartime, and we are all have to move to Baguio, and live in haunted house. It is all same to me. Go, one home to the next, one city to another, nation to nation, across ocean big and small.

We are born traveling. We travel—all our lives. I am not looking for a home, I know there is none. (104)

If ever there was a counterstatement to the poetics of exile, surely this is it. In this multiplicity and serialization of exilic experiences, this paradigmatic evocation of refugeehood, what is left for personal, psychological use but a kind of numbness born of forced perpetual motion? The experience of refugeehood erases, at the extreme, all hope, expectation, belief, even longing. Through her speech, Mrs. Chan emerges as the exemplary subject of the myriad displacements and dispossessions of modern history.

The transformation that Mrs. Chan undergoes in the second part of the play is all the more surprising because of this manifesto of committed homelessness she has proclaimed and has seemed to embody. In effect, this part of the play, which begins with the entrance of Hannah's alter ego, Sandra Smith, is an *analysis* of the figure of home, which Mrs. Chan seemed to have dismissed. Sandra Smith tells the defiant Mrs. Chan all about her cleaning lady Hannah, concluding with a summary that is in every way the opposite of Mrs. Chan's vaunted antihome position: "Everyplace is beautiful, 'cept the place where she lives. Home is a dark room, she knows it well, knows its limits. She knows she can't travel nowhere without returnin' to that room once the sun goes down. Home is fixed, it does not move, even as the rest of the world circles 'round and 'round, picking up speed" (106).

That the play should contain both the geopathic figure of home as prison as well as a posthomecoming rejection of home is not remarkable; what is important and different is that these two geopathic figures are distributed among and explicated through a strangely doubled pair of characters. For by the end of the play it is not only Hannah who is doubled in Sarah; she is also the twin of—and the changeling with—Mrs. Chan. Their twinning occurs, significantly, in relation to the figure of home:

CHAN: What is this? All the time, you talk about home, home, home?

SANDRA: Just like you do.

CHAN: I never talk about home. Barely talk at all.

(106)

Sandra utterly rejects this claim, along with, implicitly, the previous one about not looking for home: "You think, you keep your lips buttoned, that means all your secrets are safe inside? If they're strong enough, things make themselves known, one way or another. Hannah knows, she's not stupid" (106–7).

Sandra then launches into the extraordinary vision that turns the play's conclusion into a poem and the characters into voices complementing each other's expressions of fear and longing. The vision that Sandra shows Mrs. Chan lays out the existential meaning of refugeehood, the inner experience of radical displacement. It is a vision of two figures, no doubt representing the two women themselves, although these are children. What they do gives the play its title and at the same time rewrites the meaning of the titular phrase. The crow whose flight they follow is an emblem of disturbance and contortion, not (as the phrase idiomatically signifies) of short and straightforward connection. The children begin to chase the crow; first down a steep ravine,

and then it becomes dark, and the crow throws disasters at their feet. Floods, droughts, wars. The children see nothing, now. They follow the crow only by the catastrophes it leaves in its path. . . . they run on faith, passing through territories uncharted, following the sound of their suffering. And it is in this way that they pass through their lives. Hardly noticing what they've entered. Without stopping to notice its passing. (107)

In the course of this speech, a remarkable transformation occurs on Mrs. Chan: her dress slowly rises, and she is left dressed in a white slip. Even more amazingly, she rises from the chair in which she had seemed to be so firmly planted. She walks over to Sandra, and the two women begin to speak, alternating lines as if jointly delivering a poem of their own composition:

CHAN: Nothing new.

SANDRA: Nothing blue.

CHAN: Only the scent of home.
SANDRA: I don't know why I follow it.
CHAN: I don't care to know.
SANDRA: Not now.
CHAN: Not here.
SANDRA: Not ever. Perhaps someday.
CHAN: Maybe to remember.
SANDRA: Why I run.
CHAN: Why I chase.
SANDRA: Until I am so—
CHAN: So tired.
SANDRA: Another disaster.
CHAN: Another lonely child.
SANDRA: We follow the scent of home.

(108)

The final transformation is still to occur. Sandra removes her clothes and wig and turns into Hannah. Like Mrs. Chan, she is clad only in a white slip. Thus the stage image momentarily presents the two original women, now appearing strangely interchangeable, as if to underline the symmetrical nature of the action to follow: Hannah slowly lowers herself into Mrs. Chan's chair, while Mrs. Chan, her gaze fixed on the garden outside, where Sandra's words have located the flight of the crow, moves toward the door. Before she leaves, the following exchange raises the issue of interchangeability (and, implicitly, of cultural difference) one last time:

HANNAH: *(sitting, beaming)* Ooooh Nice home, Mrs. Chan.
CHAN: I see it.
HANNAH: So do I, so do I.
CHAN: I see all the way past those mountains.
HANNAH: Welcome home, Mrs. Chan.
CHAN: Welcome home, Hannah.

(108)

The symmetry in the language here is in deliberate contradiction to the visual evocation of difference. Far from implying any interchangeability of experience and identity, the play's rhetoric of doubling and its exploration of the manifold figure of home are dedicated to asserting the *non*interchangeability of experience. Through the poetic experience of

these two women, the figure of home escapes the rigid codings of geopathic discourse. In acknowledging both the need for a literal home
"here" (Hannah's need) and the truth of displacement (which destines
Mrs. Chan to a search for a lost home, "there") the play valorizes both
travel and home. This double validation departs from the poetics of exile
as well, by quite specifically (and politically) asserting that the struggle of
Hannah, poor and Black, must be solved right here. The world must not
merely accommodate her but *locate* her, just as the world must see and
hear the truth of a refugeehood like Mrs. Chan's.

   If this seems too weighty and allegorical an interpretation for so
slight a piece of theater, the play's conclusion recalls us to its fragility.
The comical old husband enters, crazily asking for his beer. He cannot
see Hannah, who sits in the chair center stage, her eyes closed, a smile on
her face. He "is walking towards her as the lights fade to black" (108).
The reason for the old man's presence in the play now emerges. He is
there mainly to create this anticlosural moment, this instance of a stage
discourse asserting itself in all its open-ended potentiality against the
deadly closure of allegory. The home has been redefined, reimagined,
reexperienced; but the play persists. There are relationships to negotiate,
perhaps more troubles to face. The crow flies on.

(Dis)Orientations

   They say, "No, no, we need an accent." You know, THE accent.
              —Bradley, in *Yankee Dawg You Die,* by Philip Kan Gotanda

If certain contemporary plays (like those discussed in the previous chapter) explore the possibility of a new placement through and in language,
the other side of the coin—the reactionary and oppressive fixity of
language—is the subject of a great deal of multicultural drama focusing
on the immigrant experience. Often, the problem of language is explored through extensions into what can be termed a problematic of
multicultural representation. This is the same problematic that we have
seen incarnated in *The Colored Museum,* where the possibility of truthful
and empowering representations of Black life and identity seems to be
ruled out (wishful dancing aside) by a history of racist stereotyping.

   Two other recent plays, Laurence Yep's *Pay the Chinaman* (1987)
and Philip Kan Gotanda's *Yankee Dawg You Die* (1988), present the
problematic of multicultural representation as it impinges on and distorts

the process of immigrant self-identification. The two plays have several things in common: both are two-handers in which the two characters are both men, one young and one older. Each play uses its title to signal its engagement with a prejudice so pervasive as to be a cliché: Gotanda's title is the slogan of a paranoically imagined oriental brutality, while Yep's is both the name of a game as well as, idiomatically, a way of saying "Pay up, pay the piper" (177). Although the plays differ considerably in their form, both employ the same trope as *The Colored Museum*, the trope of performance, to probe the psychological formations and the cultural deformations attendant on being a nonwhite immigrant in America. *Pay the Chinaman* is a straightforward realistic play, in which the figure of performance is internalized, thematized. *Yankee Dawg You Die*, on the other hand, frames itself in performative terms, interspersing "scenes" (from movies, plays) and set pieces (dream narratives, reveries, phone conversations) with realistic encounters and conversations between the two protagonists.

These conversations, the first of which takes place at a party where the two men, strangers to each other, happen to be guests, quickly become highly personal, revelatory, emotionally charged. As such they contrast strongly with the brittle artificiality of the show business world that is the play's paradigm for performance. This world is introduced from the very beginning of the play, in a way that marks it as a totalitarian context for the experience not only of the characters but also of the spectators: The play opens with a series of titles, emblazoned in changing colors and set to "filmic music," which introduces the two characters as if they were actors, and the play we are watching as if it were a film: "[Name of Producing Theatre] PRESENTS . . . VINCENT CHANG . . . AND INTRODUCING . . . BRADLEY YAMASHITA . . . IN . . . YANKEE DAWG YOU DIE . . . (*The entire theater—stage as well as audience area—is gradually inundated in an ocean of stars)*" (5).

The seductive totalitarianism of American showbiz is increasingly revealed as a homogenizing machine, which supports difference only if it can package itself in terms of sameness, of the familiar. Thus Vincent's memories of his days as a hoofer on the "Chop Suey Circuit" in San Francisco are full of reverential references to mainstream performers like Fred Astaire and Ginger Rogers, and Bradley asks him, "What kind of dancing did you do? I mean Fred Astaire kind of dancing or Gene Kelly—like, or, or, like the Nicholas Brothers—flying off those risers, landing doing splits—ouch!" (16). Vincent recalls, among others, "The Wongettes—like the Andrews Sisters" and Anna Mae Wong, the "Chinese Flapper," and Toy Yet Mar, "the Chinese Sophie Tucker."

As for Vincent himself, his most famous role, his Oscar nomination for Best Supporting Actor, was in "*Tears of Winter,* opposite Peter O'Toole" (18). In their second meeting, in the audition waiting room of a theater, Vincent enacts the role for Bradley, "dying" in his master's arms, and imploring him, with his last (rather long) breath, not to let "the dream" die, and to "Win one for the . . . Nipper" (19)! Bradley cheers and confesses that Vincent has been his hero growing up. He goes on to explain, and unintentionally lays out the deeply problematic psychology of identification that has plagued American theater for the past several decades: "I mean, I'd be watching TV and suddenly you'd appear in some old film or an old Bonanza or something. And at first something would always jerk inside. Whoo, what's this? This is weird, like watching my own family on TV" (15).

Bradley's remembered experience of recognition lies at the heart of the many arguments made in the past few decades in American theater for multiracial, color-blind, or nontraditional casting (as it is variously called). This movement seeks not only to increase the acting opportunities available to minority actors but also (and this is where Bradley's experience comes in) to increase the number of represented role models for minority people, especially young people. *Yankee Dawg* contains one of the funniest and most persuasive renditions of the role-model argument ever crafted. Bradley is telling of his teenage years in the San Joaquin Valley:

> Windows down, my girl Bess beside me, the radio blasting away . . . But it continued to escape me—this thing, place, that belonged to me . . . And then the DJ came on the radio, "Here's a new record by a hot new artist, 'Carol' by Neil Sedaka!" Neil who? Sedaka? Did you say "Sedaka." Sedaka. Sedaka. Sedaka. Sedaakaa. As in my father's cousin's brother-in-law's name, Hiroshi Sedaka? What's that you say—the first Japanese American rock 'n' roll star! Neil Sedaka. That name. I couldn't believe it. Suddenly everything was alright. I was there. Driving in my car, windows down, girl beside me—with a goddamned Buddhahead singing on the radio . . . Neil Sedaakaa! I knew. I just knew for once, wherever I drove to that night, the road belonged to me. (20)

But there is a twist, an ironical turn that problematizes what otherwise seems to be a commonsensical, irrefutable, self-evident proposition, namely, that young people of minority backgrounds need role models. When Vincent points out that Neil Sedaka is a "very nice fellow, but definitely not Japanese" (20), Bradley casually admits he knows that and adds that what he has just said is in fact *a speech from a play:* "It's by Robinson Kan, the sansei playwright. It shows the need we have for legitimate heroes. And how when you don't have any, just how far you'll go to make them up" (20). The point of the Neil Sedaka speech becomes, then, not the need for role models but rather (much more interestingly and subtly) the textualizing of what might be called the role-model—or identification—discourse. The crucial thing about this discourse is that it is now a cultural cliché, a staple of the public discourse about ethnicity.

The most recent public airing of this issue in America was the *Miss Saigon* affair, when Asian-American theater people, including David Hwang and B. D. Wong, objected to the casting of the British actor Jonathan Pryce in the lead role of an Amerasian. The support they got from Actor's Equity was quickly withdrawn, not because either the opportunity or the role-model argument was rejected (in fact, the inherent racism of the play in question made such an argument rather problematic).[10] It was rejected because the argument most strongly urged, a supposedly more "artistic" one, was that only an actor of Asian origin could do justice to the role. This kind of contention also surfaced in another recent controversy, August Wilson's insistence on a Black director for the film version of his Pulitzer Prize–winning play, *Fences.*

The sense of cultural determinism that underlies these arguments is deeply troubling to the liberal ideology of the American theater establishment. Moreover, the minority practitioners making the arguments share in that ideology themselves (and have long espoused nontraditional casting). Most would have too much ideological resistance to extending the argument to its logical conclusion in cultural materialism, where determinants like class and gender would have to be included, along with race, into theatrical formulations of signifying subjectivities. Thus the issue remains in an uneasy liberal limbo, from which one of the only foreseeable outlets is the writing of more roles, *and more varied roles,* in plays and films, for minority actors.

Although the Neil Sedaka speech, or more precisely, the information that it is scripted, opens the door to a critique of the current terms of the multicultural-representation debate, Gotanda's play, disappointingly, does not pursue that critique but concentrates instead on the terms of the impasse I have just described. Surveying the situation from multiple perspectives, and powerfully voicing the aspirations and frustrations of minority actors, the play's own ideological orientation can perhaps be discerned from the plot structure it employs. Underneath all its performative expressions, *Yankee Dawg* is an old-fashioned pedagogical play.

From the very first scene, the pedagogical mode, as well as the particular twist it will be given here, is evident: the older man, who presumably has a lot to teach the young Bradley, just starting out, is instead instructed by the latter. When Vincent says "movie," Bradley corrects it to "film"; when Vincent says "low-budget," Bradley corrects it to "independent"; and when Vincent says "oriental," Bradley corrects it to "Asian." The latter bit of tutelage comes out of the play's first articulation of the liberal problematic of multicultural representation. Bradley, encountering Vincent standing alone on the balcony of the Hollywood house in which a presumably "white" party is going on, remarks: "Jeez, it's a bit stuffy in there. With all of them. It's nice to be with someone I can feel comfortable around. *(Vincent doesn't understand.)* Well, I mean, like you and me. We're—I mean, we don't exactly look like . . . *(Nods towards the people inside)*" (7–8). Vincent finally catches Bradley's meaning but rebuffs him with "Actually, I had not noticed. I do not really notice, or quite frankly care, if someone is Caucasian or oriental or . . ." (8). In some sense the rest of the play is an extended gloss on the many ways and reasons that this statement is a lie, and what its costs are.

Meanwhile, Bradley's response shows that his ideological difference from Vincent may be little more than name deep. "It's Asian, not oriental," he says, and then goes on to elaborate the terms of a new nomenclature that may or may not be the sign of actual social changes: "Asian, oriental. Black, negro. Woman, girl. Gay, homosexual . . . Asian, oriental" (8). Bradley himself is not unaware of how superficial or trivial these terminological shifts may be in the big picture of identity politics; he smiles "sheepishly" when Vincent says, "Ahhh. Orientals are rugs?" (8).

Having taken the role of teacher of multicultural correctness, Bradley fails to notice that Vincent has much to teach him; that he has in fact already indicated his willingness and readiness to teach Bradley something much more essential than the correct name for various minorities. Before they have even introduced themselves, in the very first lines of the scene, Vincent has pointed at the night sky and spoken of the constellations, and how to navigate by them. The "Stars, stars, stars" that "wow" Bradley punningly become a rather obvious metaphor for the world the young actor is entering. "And, using the two stars that form the front of the lip of the dipper as your guide, it leads to the"— "The North Star," Bradley interrupts. "Very good. You will never be lost," laughs Vincent, and Bradley joins him (7).

If Vincent is to help Bradley "locate" himself in the firmament of showbiz, he can only do so, as it were, negatively. His experience and to some extent the ideas he has developed based on it stand as practical correctives to the idealistic multicultural theory of Bradley and his generation. As such the play's structure is that of a practical lesson, in which theory and idealism are forced to come to terms with "reality." The ideology that underwrites this structure is, of course, classic American pragmatism. From the point of view of somebody whose life is embroiled—as Vincent's is, and Bradley's—in the problematic of multicultural representation, this ideology reads as accommodation, compromise, impasse.

The young Bradley, just starting out, dreams of performing what he calls "real roles," like "Robert De Niro, *Taxi Driver*. 'You talking to me? You talking to me?' . . . Mickey Rourke in *Pope of Greenwich Village*. 'Hit me again—see if I change.'" (He immediately corrects himself, revealing once again the dilemma of multicultural representation: "Forget I said that about Mickey Rourke. He's an ass-hole—he did that *Year of the Dragon*. I hated that film" [30]. In representational politics as in social experience, the hyphen in Asian-American sometimes becomes a yawning chasm.)

Vincent comes back with his own dream roles: one is Spencer Tracy in *Bad Day at Black Rock*. Bradley remembers that the play was about "some Nisei vet" who doesn't appear in the film: "He's dead. Got killed saving Tracy's life in Italy. After the war Tracy goes to the dead soldier's home to return the war medal to his Issei parents . . . I should have played that role." Bradley, confused (his confusion showing how much he has internalized the culturally coded casting system of Hollywood), says: "but [no Nisei] appears" (30). Vincent's answer reminds us that the solution to the impasse of multicultural representation will have to *be written;* these identities need not only new enactments but new *inscriptions:* "But he could have been a Nisei, Tracy's character" (30).[11]

The inscription of new identities, and, beyond that, new *notions* or *formulations of identity,* is the task the play sets itself. It is a task it fails to accomplish, because it gets embroiled in certain well-established and ultimately defeatist ways, borrowed from traditional dramaturgy, of understanding and figuring the problematic of multicultural representation. Chief among these is the drama of the divided self, that staple of realist drama (and modern literature). The divided self gives multicultural discourse the stamp of literary value (that is, of psychological truth and cultural value); at the same time, it deprives it of its links with a creative Otherness.

The tug-of-war in both actors' souls between the desire to be successful and the need to maintain their self-respect runs through the various scenes of pedagogy and self-revelation between them. One form the battle takes (showing once again how the discourse of multiculturalism often borrows its terms ready-made from the mainstream culture) is as an opposition between Hollywood or showbiz on the one hand and theater or independent film on the other. Bradley belongs to (and believes in) something called the Theatre Project of Asian America. Vincent's comment on this endeavor is: "Poppycock, Cockypoop, bullshit. Theatre Project of Asian America—Amateur Hour" (24). Bradley defends the project, insisting that "Asian American theatres are where we do the real work, Mr. Chang." Vincent's response, a seeming non sequitur, puts Bradley's position in an embarrassingly orientalist light: "Stop calling me Mr. Chang. It's Shigeo Nakada. 'Asian American Consciousness.' Hah. You can't even tell the difference between a Chinaman and a Jap. I'm Japanese, didn't you know that? I changed my name after the war. Hell, I wanted to work" (24).

Vincent's magic word, his talismanic commitment is *to work.* It is how he justifies all the "Chop Suey Charlie" roles he has accepted and played. In his own version of a politics of visibility, he contends that those roles have smoothed the path for people like Bradley, given them the baseline of recognition and respect on which they might build something more:

> You seem to assume 'Asian Americans' always existed. That there were always roles for you. You didn't exist back then buster. Back then there was no Asian American consciousness, no Asian American actor, no Asian American theatres. Just a handful of 'orientals' who for some god forsaken reason wanted to perform. *Act.* And we

did. . . . You, you with that holier than thou look, trying to make me feel ashamed. You wouldn't be here if it weren't for all the crap we had to put up with. We built something. We built the mountain, as small as it may be, that you stand on so proudly looking down at me. (26)

Against this powerful argument, Bradley brings not his experience as an actor (in which role he *has* been helped, or at least inspired, by the likes of Vincent, as he admitted earlier) but as a young Asian-American. In that role, the demeaning representations that actors like Vincent have consented to have hurt him deeply:

See, you think every time you do one of those demeaning roles, the only thing lost is *your* dignity. That the only person who has to pay is you. Don't you see that every time you do that millions of people in movie theatres will see it. Believe it. Every time you do any old stereotypic role just to pay the bills, someone has to pay for it—and it ain't you. *No.* It's some Asian kid innocently walking home. "Hey, it's a Chinaman gook!" "Rambo, Rambo, Rambo!" (26)

The role-model theory cuts both ways: it is important to have representations of minority characters; but it is equally important that these representations not be stereotypic, damaging, insulting.

Of course the play itself thematizes the role-model issue by focusing on two Asian-Americans of different generations, one a potential role model for the other. However, its own response to the problematic of how to create valid minority role models from within a racist entertainment industry (and society) is curiously circular. In fact, the play ends by circling back to its beginning, with Vincent delivering the same demeaning Sergeant Moto speech with which he began the play. This time, however, his delivery is increasingly on his own terms. He gradually drops the heavy accent that had justified the ridiculous lines "I graduate UCLA, Class of '34. . . . No, no, no, not 'dirty floor.' Floor clean. Class of '34." With "THE accent" gone, the lines lose their "comic" sense altogether and are transformed into a cry of frustration and rage: "Listen carefully and watch my lips. 34. 34! 34!! What is wrong with you? I graduated from the University of California right here in the San Joaquin Valley and spent my entire life growing up in California. Why can't you hear what I'm saying? Why can't you see me as I really am?" (50).

The play's own immediate answer to this urgent question is made by way of a return to the image of representation as a seductive totalitarian system: as Vincent and Bradley fade to black, the theater is again filled with a vast array of stars. Reinforcing the totalitarian idea is the fate of the pedagogical plot: the play ends with the two characters having learnt so well from each other that they have exchanged ideological positions. We learn that both have been offered demeaning stereotypical roles in the same science-fiction film; surprisingly, Vincent has turned down the role and has decided instead to go and work on an independent film by a Japanese-American director about "a Japanese family living in Sacramento before the war. Just like my childhood. . . . And my role, it's wonderful. I get to play my father" (49).

Bradley, on the other hand, has accepted the movie role, "Yang's number one son. He's half Chinese and half rock" (49). His reasons (justifications?) for doing so are similar to those voiced earlier by Vincent in articulating his evolutionary theory of minority gains: "I figure once I get there I can change it," says Bradley. "I'll sit down and convince them to change it. I will. Even if it's a bit. Just a small change, it's still something. And even if they don't change it, they'll at least know how we feel and maybe next time . . ." (49–50).

But the play's structure, the defeat by circularity of a double pedagogical effort, emphatically denies that things will be different next time. The only thing to learn, then, is the abject reality of racism and the intractability of cultural stereotyping.[12] And *Yankee Dawg* is indeed an abject play, for all its performative brilliance. Its vision is locked tight within the images, narratives, and structures of mainstream American culture. It can do little more than offer a *demonstration* of the problematic of multicultural representation. As lively and inventive and accurate as this demonstration may be, the terms with which it figures performance, mainly Hollywood categories, cannot furnish any imaginative alternatives to the impasse of assimilation or alienation that they themselves have created.

The problem is not only, as James Moy has argued, that *Yankee Dawg* (along with *M. Butterfly*) presents Asian-American characters who are "laughable and grossly disfigured" (55); the real problem is that the problematic of multicultural representation is understood here only in terms furnished by the mainstream discourse on representation, namely, in terms of identification (the role-model argument) and of realistic representation (see me as I really am). Thus not only do the characters remain inscribed within the economy of what James Moy calls "Anglo-American desire," they do so because they are conceived on a model of desire (the desire of be seen as one "really" is) that is intimately tied up with traditional Western representation (even Moy bemoans the play's failure to present real Asian-American characters [55], as if such a thing were possible.) The Western master narrative that has these characters (and these plays, and critics like Moy as well) in its thrall is not the narrative of success in the marketplace (as Moy argues) but rather the narrative of individualism—the same one that has underwritten a century of geopathic drama—which, while proclaiming the unique reality of each individual, actually fixes identity within cultural categories and pins culture to place.

Double or Nothing

In Laurence Yep's play *Pay the Chinaman,* the paradigm for performance is not show business, at least not in its current form. An earlier and typically American version of showbiz—the snake oil salesman and the con man—provides the terms of this exploration of what is entailed in the representation of that peculiar kind of displacement that is immigration. Yep's historicization of the issue, along with his revisioning of pedagogy within a frame of social dislocation, makes for a more successful inscription of Asian-American identity than was accomplished in Gotanda's attempt.

Pay the Chinaman takes place in the California of the Gold Rush, in 1893. The set itself inaugurates the thematic of doubling that will move this account of immigrant experience away from the dead end of individualistic geopathology. The play is set in the town of Fidele in the Sacramento delta. The river on whose banks the town stands is described intertextually; it "could be straight out of *Huckleberry Finn.*" The classic novel of American individualism and freedom proves an ironic reference for the drama of constraint and group identity that is about to unfold. Moreover, the actual set doubles the world that is to prove so cruelly resistant to new arrivals. Its "two-story, whitewashed clapboard houses crowd one another on the narrow street as in any American town" (181). However, this is not any American town, and its difference is proclaimed through the usual primary signifier of cultural difference, language: "the store signs are bilingual and the English is cheerfully pompous: Fortunate Orchards."

The set's simple and direct evocation of a world of sameness and difference is part of the play's basic representational strategy: all the identities, accounts, and events of the play are filtered through what eventually emerges as the definitional phenomenon of multiculturalism, namely, the paradox of simultaneous sameness and difference. The device of doubling, both at the level of plot and of theme (and, as we have just seen, even set), renders this paradox dramaturgically, making for a quite specifically multicultural dramatic functioning, in which things are systematically *un*fixed from their original moorings in plot, narrative, meaning. The effect of this loosening of dramatic elements is to move the multicultural project away from the impasse of assimilation or alienation that defeated the characters (and the playwright) of *Yankee Dawg You Die*. By rewriting identity itself as a shifting and changeable process, the doubling device intimates that the concepts of place and culture upon which the old model of identity was based may also be in need of revision.

The double is the first topic of conversation between the play's two characters, a young Chinese man and an older one, the con man. The con man enters first, carrying the tools of his trade in two baskets suspended from the two ends of bamboo pole that he carries on his shoulder. He proceeds to set up his stall in the street and begins to beat a gong to attract attention, simultaneously launching into a paean to his "magic elixir." The young man enters, and his appearance echoes the older man's: he also has a bamboo pole on his shoulder, from the two ends of which are suspended the tools of *his* trade. This literalization of the similarity between the two men in effect starts this play at the point where *Yankee Dawg* ended; it is not going to be a demonstration of the deterministic circularities of the multicultural situation. The commonality of experience is here not the *fate* of but the *source* of multicultural identity and is folded into it as a kind of ingrained antidote to the poison of alienated individualism.

The young man's first remarks to the older man once again evoke the double: "Fellow came through last week with a gong just like that" (182). When the con man pretends not to get the message, the young man fills in more details: "Sold a tonic. Said it'd pep people right up . . . Folks got real excited when it took the enamel off their teeth." The con man persists in feigning ignorance and complains that "Fellow like that makes it hard on someone with a tonic that's—" only to be interrupted knowingly by the young man: "A real boon to humanity." The young man's final verdict, "You and that other fellow had a lot in common," amicably seals the matter as a case of sameness and difference (instead of the fraud it obviously was).

The rest of the relationship between the two men is focused on the issue of confidence, of faith and distrust, truth and lies. It is played out on two levels; first quite literally as *play,* as the two men bet against each other in a series of card games, and then as narrative, as each man constructs an ever-changing life story. At both these levels, the activity of the two men is framed within a context of stark and terrifying racism. "Hate's boiling on the stove," says the older man, and later tells of various atrocities perpetrated on Chinese immigrants by "the demons." In an exchange that recalls the first pedagogical scene between Bradley and Vincent in *Yankee Dawg,* the young man protests against the term the other man uses for whites, correcting him: "Americans." Like Bradley, the young man believes that "Names are power. Call them demons and they are demons" (188).

The gambling develops into an apt metaphor for the construction of identity under these circumstances, although the play guards against too facile and "poetic" a conclusion on the matter by putting the metaphor—in a particularly exaggerated and extended form—into the con man's mouth: "I lay out twenty-eight cards like so. They come in waves. Seven at a time. But it's getting harder to come over. So it's only six the next time. Then five. Four. Three. Two. Then just one. And there they are. Guests of the land of the Golden Mountain" (183). The figures of gambling and conning contribute a special version of performance to the encounter of the two men. Unlike *Yankee Dawg,* this is not performance as creativity, nor performance as self-actualization (nor, for that matter, as self-betrayal). This is performance as deception, as subterfuge, as survival. The old man's second performance, after his opening snake oil speech, thematizes the mode of performance as deception. When the young man asks him to "trust me" (that they'll stop playing after the next jar of whiskey), the old man says he "don't put much stock in that word." The young man responds ironically that "all us Chinese got to stick together," and the old man launches into his performance. Playing the role of "an agent" and using a "thick wad of bills" for a prop, he says:

Oh, no, I wouldn't steer you wrong. You'll get rich if you go. Why do you think they call it the land of the Golden Mountain? Nuggets big as your fists right there in the dirt, just scoop them up. Hell,

here's a tip just 'cause I like you. You find yourself a nice hill and lay
down and the nuggets roll right into your palms. . . . You boys
remind me of my brothers. Tell you what I'll do. Got a friend who
owns a boat. I'll put the word in. Treat you and your little brother
like kings. Good vittles and plenty of it. Real beds. Nice sea breeze.
Hell, it'll be like a vacation. (186)

The subtle doubling in this speech ("you boys remind me of my
brothers," and even, possibly, "you and your little brother") once again
links the figure of the double to that of deception and of performance.
The account of identity being developed out of this chain of
associations—identity as shifting, unfixed, unreliable, performative, and
shared—is the play's main contribution to the problematic of multicultural representation. This identity is also shaped through the play's
treatment of pedagogy, which is also present from the start, and which is
related to both the doubling device and to the theme of trust in a particularly intricate and interesting way.

In the context of utter skepticism that has been established early on
by the young man's allusions to the con man's "double," the relationship
between the two has great difficulty taking on the pedagogical form that
their respective ages and experiences otherwise dictate. The young man
is wary of his senior's intentions and cannot respond to him without
irony and derision. The old man, meanwhile, seems to be experiencing a
growing need to counsel and warn his younger countryman: "Listen to
me. This could mean your life. . . . Most guests wouldn't give you the
time of day. Just let you get yourself killed. But I try and help you. And
all you do is bullyrag me" (188).

The young man's recalcitrance is soon assimilated into a particularly
powerful instance of the play's model of the double: "You've got a
temper just like my son," says the older man. The mention of a son,
along with the cryptic information that he is "where he ought to be,"
immediately brings up a reference to a *father*. "What am I going to say to
Papa now?" says the young man, referring to the fact that he has lost all
the money with which he was supposed to start a small barber shop
business. The older man reminds him, however, that it was not a father
but a cousin who had been his partner in his original account. The young
man explains: "Cousin was smoke. Don't like to tell folks how my father
got sharped" (189).

The son and father of the two men's respective narratives double the two men themselves; their sudden diegetic "presence" seems to stabilize the pedagogical plot, to rescue it from the disturbances of gambling, deception, distrust. The old man tries to instruct the younger one again, telling him of the dangers to come: "Soon as the harvest is over, the demons will come." The young man asks the crucial question, the one that is at the heart of the multicultural problematic (and whose other, more benign version, articulated by David Hwang, is the title of this chapter): "Why us? Why here?" Then he adds a sentence that is, in fact, the answer to his question, multiculturalism's defining paradox of simultaneous sameness and difference: "Take down the signs and the ducks and it'd look like any American town" (189).

The "signs and the ducks" interfere in the (re)production of sameness, America's ideological imperative. Interestingly enough, the Chinese-American struggle with this imperative is figured in terms of a horrific inversion of the buried-child motif that is so central to American drama (see chap. 2). The buried child of this play is, characteristically enough, doubled, perhaps even tripled. When he is first mentioned, he doubles the young man: he was, says the con man, a "Young man. 'Bout your age"; later, he is doubled by the old man's son, who is said to have died while looking for driftwood on a beach.

This play's version of the buried child exposes the savagery of the image, which its usual form often conceals. This buried child tried hard to dig itself out of its fate, and, failing to do so, literally goes down in flames, a horrifyingly unmetaphoric victim of race hatred:

> The demons . . . set fire to [the shack]. Foreman says not to panic. Just lie down in the dirt. Wait for the farmer and the sheriff. But the fire's going up the walls. So I go to the back and get on my hands and knees and I start digging. Digging. Digging. Like a dog. And the next moment, the pup's [the boy's] there too. . . . We don't stop. We just dig faster and harder. I go headfirst into the hole. I scoop. I claw. And then my hands break into the air. The blessed, cool air. And then I see the night sky. [The boy] follows. He's got his head and shoulders out of the hole when he jerks to a stop. "Hey!" he says. And the next thing he's sliding right back through the hole like an oiled pig. They were yanking him back inside . . . I try to grab his hands, but they slip right out of mine. And the next

thing I know, we both hear a demon howl. I twist around and see him—head and hair red as blood. And I just spin around and hightail it out of there. (190)

The many terrible associations evoked by this account of appalling cruelty—associations of traumatic birth, of abortion, of death-in-life, of hell—all also inhabit the traditional motif of the buried child and the drama it organizes. In Shepard, the image was literalized to expose its traditional use as dramatic device. Here, however, it is given a cultural and historical specificity that completely overruns and overwrites that usage. Just as Shepard's tiny corpse was in violent excess of all the traditional meanings of the device, so also Yep's burning boy joins with all the other doubles in the play—the fathers, the sons, the ambiguous group of "all of us Chinese"—to define immigrant subjectivity in terms of a cruelly determined *group* identity. While the buried child of traditional drama functioned to guarantee the discovery of a powerful, renewed individuality for the protagonists, this *un*buried child bespeaks the interchangeability of group identity within a racist society, the impossibility of escaping into an autonomous, self-referring identity: the answer to the young man's "why us, why here?" is the simple and terrible truth: "Can't change your skin" (189).

The need to acknowledge and accept the pluralism of identity is this play's contribution to the problematic of multicultural representation. Furthermore, it is not a haphazard or disorganized pluralism that is indicated, but one specifically structured as a ceaseless doubling and tripling of the phenomenal self. The model of identity thus produced is not only shifting, fictional, illusory—"smoke," as the young man says of his cousin—but also endlessly repeated. This is a new understanding of group identity; not just the self as part of a group but the self *as a group,* a self that must perforce realize and express itself as and through a series of doubles. In an image that recalls (but also differs significantly from) the cheerful acceptance of schizophrenia by the old woman in *As the Crow Flies,* the old man here shows the young man a carving that could well stand as the model for this notion of identity as group: "It's a carving of a monkey. And there's a little man inside the monkey. . . . There's an even smaller one inside the little one. Just how many men are inside there?—As far and as deep as you can see" (185). As if to emphasize the personal application of this "signifying monkey," a few lines later the old man tempts the young man to drink in the following way: "You're going to die of thirst if you keep this up. I can just hear your innards. They are like little old men whispering from inside you. Leathery old voices, dried and cracked: whiskey, whiskey, whiskey" (185).

This reference to liquor can allow us to recognize here the presence of that figure which, as we have seen before, often accompanies the discourse of home: addiction. Here, as usual, the figure of addiction occurs in close proximity to that of performance. As the play draws to its close, these two figures are used to make an explicit link between the issue of multicultural experience and the figure of the double. The principle of doubling struggles stubbornly against the vicious realities of racism: "This is the third Chinatown. First one used to be over there in the demon town. But a mob of demons burnt it down. So the Chinese built a new one on this side of the river. And the mob torched that one down. So the Chinese put up a third. Stubborn" (188). The context of deception, however, undermines this powerful pedagogy, and the figure of addiction comes in to support the young man's skepticism: "Is that you or the whiskey talking?" he asks.

Thus in the context of multicultural discourse the double is, as it were, double-edged. While it repeatedly teaches that identity is shared, its participation in a logic of performance as deception makes it suspect. "You or the whiskey" is another formulation of "you or the lies of racism's abjection?" The young man, it turns out, is no more what he appears to be than the con man is what he pretends to be. All the stories are lies (although "every now and then I slip in the truth. Spices things up"); all the others—fathers and sons—are dead. Against the model of identity as group and as shared, there is identity as a blank slate, an inscrutable mask. In a final, ironic instance of doubling, the two adversaries mirror each other's philosophies: "So don't ever let anyone know what you're thinking"—"Or who you are, or what you are. Give people a blank page and they draw their own picture" (195).

In a final and structural doubling, the play ends by folding the thematic of deception onto itself: the identities we have had "performed" for us are revealed to be pure (or rather, *impure*, if we remember the "spice" of truth) fictions. This removes the traditional dramatic possibility of meaning as revelation of true identity, of meaning as self-knowledge. The characters never gain more of an identity than their generic names promised in the first place; they remain typological figures, their oblique and unreliable account being all that is available of the system of meaning that encompasses them. In this system, multicultural

representation derives from and defines the uncanny experience of doubling, and multicultural experience is forged from the paradox of sameness and difference.

In this system, personal identity is only a tiny part of the tradition
that is dislodged. Much larger, and more momentous, is the dismantling
here of the geopathological trope of difference *as place*. The multicultural
imagination can express this dis-placement either optimistically, or otherwise. In the preface to *Pay the Chinaman,* Laurence Yep articulates the
former possibility, a new kind of u-topianism that differs utterly from
Ibsen's erasure of place in being a layering of many places, an experience
of a kind of "superplaceness." Recalling the experience he had on a visit
to Hawaii, Yep writes: "In Hawaii, no one can assume anything by your
appearance. I knew a violinist, half Hungarian and half Japanese, who
had pale skin but Japanese features. On the mainland he is always asked
what ethnicity he is; in Hawaii he's never asked, because everyone there
is more than one thing" (178).[13]

But the other side of the coin of this version of multiculturalism—
multiculturalism as a lavish "place-fulness"—is expressed in the play as
well; it is another sort of u-topianism, in which platial difference is
rendered irrelevant by an abundance of disappointment. If the double
means being "more than one thing," it also means that place is no (longer
a) guarantee of meaning: "Expect the worst from the folks back home.
Expect the worst here too."

Through a Kaleidoscope, Distantly

> The selections were most often made to emphasize the peculiarities
> of earth life.
>
> —Ping Chong, *Nuit Blanche*

In spite of its relatively early date, Ping Chong's play *Nuit Blanche* embodies a radical multiculturalism that makes it an ideal exemplar of what
I am trying to explore here: multiculturalism as a way out of the impasse
of the postgeopathic tradition of failed homecoming. Its early date also
contributes a sensibility that is the ground against which this new discourse can best be seen (much as 1960s environmental theater with its
"politics of ecstasy" is the ground for grasping the stage terms required
by the new "politics of identity" [see my discussion of *Road* in chap. 1]).
Because of its context in the 1960s theatrical avant-garde, *Nuit Blanche*
encompasses the paradoxes and the power of contemporary platiality and

translates that platiality into a theatrology that is a systematic revisioning of realism, especially of its principle of causality.

The structure and functioning of *Nuit Blanche,* like that of much other avant-garde performance theater, is fragmented, elliptical, sub-discursive. That is to say, the story it tells, if it tells a story at all, is told in slices and segments rather than in slabs of action, and the meaning of that story is not lodged subtextually and left for the hermeneutic pleasure of the spectator: it is tied to a powerful, determining, and clearly articulated contextual discourse. In what is, in fact, a version of the pedagogical impulse of multicultural theater in general, this theater announces its interest and meaning as being in the collective and the *cultural* (as opposed to the individual and the psychological). It presents actions that matter only because they are representative actions, typical not only of exceptional individuals (like the protagonists of classical realism) but of so-called ordinary ones. They offer not the hermeneutic pleasures of a dramatic psychoanalysis nor even the ritualistic pleasures of a geoanalysis, but instead the pedagogical *un*pleasure of urgent ideological instruction. Thus Ping Chong's *Nuit Blanche* seeks to show and tell its audience—or, perhaps more precisely, it tries to *find* the means to show and tell its audience—that beneath all cultural difference lies a universal and fantastical reality in which we are all, humans and beasts, terribly vulnerable.

The play's subtitle, *A Select View of Earthlings,* announces the play's difficult and highly experimental perspectival project. The play tries to stage a certain kind of solution to the problematic of multicultural representation. The problem is stated succinctly and personally by Chong in the preface to the play: "In spirit I'm close to my Chinese roots, but in practice I'm very far from them" (4). Out of this all-too-common contradiction comes the conviction—or rather the effort—to globalize culture, to reach for a new electronic utopia. Chong writes: "As another way of trying to feel positive about what I had lost when I left Chinatown, I began to think of the entire world as my culture. I've developed a commitment to the sense that we are all together on this one little planet. It's more and more important for us not to feel so foreign with one another" (4–5).

The defeat of "foreignness" by means of a new global culture is a McLuhanesque idea that dates back to the late 1960s and early 1970s, the period when Chong began working in the New York avant-garde theater. The messianic view of history underlying McLuhan's analysis of the relationship between culture and technology—which retains little credence in serious contemporary sociopolitical thought today—remains a strong part of Chong's (and others', including his sometime collaborator, Meredith Monk's) cultural outlook. According to Chong, "the electronic age is tying us all in, and the inclination is to conglomerate into larger and larger republics. If we don't ruin the planet first, it's likely we will someday belong to one enormous republic" (5). While it is unlikely that Chong would still feel this way now, after the breakdown of the Soviet empire, his theater will probably continue to register the contradictory pulls of cultural difference and what he calls global "harmony."

In *Nuit Blanche,* the sense of a global electronic economy "tying us all in" is presented with all the ambiguity it deserves, that is, as a phenomenon that both afflicts us and liberates us. The opening speech of the play, by a "respectable looking gentleman" of indeterminate profession, nationality, and historical period, is a masterly evocation of contemporary political discourse. Without ever clarifying the exact context, a chilling sense of familiarity is produced by the man's use of phrases like "critical stage," "massive, undisguised brutality," "Our dear leader," "emergency powers," "use every method to crush each dissident voice," "certain political adjustments," "great opportunity," "a more humane society," "a golden beacon in a sad world" (8). The ominous connotations of these words, so contaminated by cynical use in the modern world, recall the word maps of *On the Verge,* where the future emerged as a discourse that, supported by a world of things, quite overwhelmed subjectivity. Here, however, the *verbal* closure of contemporary discursive reality is breached: the world as seen in *Nuit Blanche* is not just an artificial fabric of depleted words and catchphrases; it is also a world of images, of sounds, and of powerfully aleatory human encounters.

The first set of images that appears suggests the link between this play (and its fairly representative mixed-media theatrology) and a figure that has been haunting the dramatic discourse of this entire century: the figure of photography. The first set of images shown in *Nuit Blanche* is part of a slide sequence entitled "Murmurs of Earth," inspired by Carl Sagan's book of the same name, "a chronicle of sounds and images sent, as a record of life on earth, into outer space on the Voyager II spacecraft headed for Jupiter" (8). The documentary power of photography, which, as we have seen, has been confronted and deconstructed in various ways by twentieth-century drama, reaches its logical conclusion in NASA's use of images. The photographs, which are intended to represent Earth and human life to nonhumans, are the modern version of the old antisemiotic fantasy of a universal language. But, as the description of the sequence makes clear, this is an articulated language like any other. It is diacritical (signifying through difference): "[the images] were interspersed with black-and-white grid slides and images in both closeup and long shot of the moon's surface and its topography" (9). And it is ideological: "The selections were most often made to emphasize the peculiarities of earth life" (9).

The photographs in this slide sequence, moreover, are ironized by those in the second slide sequence, some scenes later. This group of images "is similar to the first but without the grid slides and the moon-landing shots." The earth without the moon, and especially without the familiar images of the moon landing, that one and only positive gesture by which humankind has tried to identify itself as a race, conveys a frightening message, "a latent feeling of war, destruction and death" (17). Taken together, the two "Murmurs of Earth" slide sequences give *Nuit Blanche* a platial context of powerful ambiguity. They draw the perpetual vacillations of the figure of photography—between language and reality, sign and referent, fact and fiction—into the scope of the play's analysis of life on earth, producing an account that (like the elderly gentleman's opening speech) rings both true and false, strangely, uncannily familiar.

The perspective supplied by the slide sequences is not quite a god's eye view of human life; it is more ironic than that—a human fantasy of an alien eye view. Or: "us," as we imagine we are seen, by "them." It is this perspective that intervenes most destructively in the causalist discourse of traditional realism, where causality was constructed from the point of view of a rational onlooker (the implied spectator of realism), someone who knew exactly what the world was "like." From the perspective of the imagery of the slide sequences, the world is not like anything else, and everything in it is peculiar (we recall that "The selections were most often made to emphasize the peculiarities of earth life"). From the alien-ated perspective of "Murmurs of Earth," the world is neither rational nor irrational, neither familiar nor strange, neither ours nor quite, yet, not ours.

The principle upon which *Nuit Blanche* is constructed is the factor of *distance*. In its thematics, its characterology, and its dramatic logic, specifications of distance—gaps and intervals and spans—comprise the means whereby the play achieves that postmodern sensibility that Gómez-Peña had alluded to in saying that "My identity, like that of my contemporaries, is not a monolith but a kaleidoscope; and everything I create, including this text, has a multiplicity of voices" ("A Binational Performance Pilgrimage," 30). The first scene of the play, after the opening monologue by the elderly gentleman, is a case in point. The scene, set on a ranch called Estancia La Mariposa in some unspecified Latin American country in the 1800s, is "played entirely in Spanish to distance the viewer both historically and metaphysically." We recall the bilingual experiments of *The House of Ramon Iglesia, The Danube,* and *Mad Forest:* in each of those cases, the fact of linguistic difference underlined and resisted the threat (usually from the homogenizing discourses of the mass media and of America) to cultural difference. Here, however, the time to "save" cultural difference seems long past, and language merely marks the abyss of time and space separating the spectator from the events onstage.

Those events are remarkably simple, even archetypal: a father comes home to his motherless daughter and gives her presents. A young servant girl waits on them. This servant girl, Berenice, is to grow up and give the play what little narrative continuity it has, for the actress who plays Berenice in the first part of the play (set on a ranch in Latin America) plays the role of Miss B. in the second part (set in a dusty North Carolina town.) Besides the actress, the two parts also share a general subject: loss, betrayal. Both the Latin American part of the play and the North American one record actions of simple—and geopathic—loss. The first part, set in the 1800s, sketches out, in a few brief scenes, the efforts of a young North American man to win the hand of the Spanish lady, Gloria Ortega, in marriage. In the final scene of this sequence, an intriguing instance of doubling ushers in the simple announcements, projected as text slides, of the "story's" end. The doubling involves the maid, Berenice, who appears alone onstage and, after making sure she is not being watched, "wildly mimics her mistress in conversation with a person in the opposite chair. Then she jumps up and plays the guest," concluding by "tempt[ing] the audience in a wild, improbable gibberish" (12). The text slide reads as follows:

1853 Slavery is abolished
       Berenice Huarpes makes her way to North Carolina
1854 Gloria Ortega dies in childbirth
1863 La Mariposa is lost at the gambling tables.

The collapse of the dramatic action into wild performance, followed by bloodless chronology, alienates the spectator once again. We are left to find the significance of this chunk of narrative in the overall structure of the piece, to look for the logic that links it to the other narratives and the image sequences that surround it.

One of the logics of the piece involves a certain specific experience of time. The second major chunk of narrative is introduced by time slides of a different sort from the first: instead of years, the scenes now are coded in terms of months and days. In the third and final sequence of action we will find the time scheme to be speeded up still further, the time slides now giving only hours and minutes. The suggestion of a developing action unfolding against a ticking clock imparts a sense of urgency to the implied quest for meaning, for relation and relevance. It is as if the piece were enacting the fact that the alienating effects of distance must be overcome before it is too late. Or, to put it from the perspective of the alien onlooker evoked by "Murmurs of the Earth," we must see ourselves before the "peculiar" way we are seen by "them" defines us.

The second sequence of action, set in North America ("the feeling is rural and southern, perhaps somewhere in the Carolinas"), chronicles a classic geopathic action, with Berenice, now "Miss B.," leaving in search of a man: "At first I thought he'd gone to Nashville, to visit his uncle. Or Tuscaloosa, Mobile, or Orangeville, Louisiana, Fayetteville, or even down to New Orleans. . . . I had a couple items I had to pick up, I had to go all the way downtown Jackson to get the ticket, 'cuz I'd always . . . wanted to travel" (16–17). When Miss B. exits, the stage direction notes: "She has left her world behind" (17). That world, as far as the few glimpses we've had of it allow us to say, was one of tedious hard work and endless waiting.

During the scenes of Miss B. working in her laundry, the rear projection screen carries a long black-and-white slide sequence "of a handsome mulatto man walking through a poor part of town. . . . He moves along, smiling, putting his fingers through his hair, looking off, tilting his head and then finally moving out of frame, leaving only a desolate, burnt-out road and the hungry bark of a stray dog to close the scene" (13–14). Whether this man is the one Miss B. eventually goes in search of, or whether he is the "Franklin" whose offstage voice tries to call her away from her tasks, we never find out. What he clearly is, however, is someone who belongs—but in a disjunct, distanced way— in "her world." The enigma of his connection to her is merely the first of a series of mysterious encounters that will increasingly dominate the dramatic action that follows.

The final part of the play is set in the Haven of Peace—"a resort hotel in a Third World country on the verge of revolution." It is enormously revealing that the radical form of multiculturalism proposed by *Nuit Blanche* situates its conclusion in that archetypal space of modernism, the hotel. The hotel in this play reminds one of Conrad's comparison, in the first pages of his novel *Victory:* "The age in which we are encamped like bewildered travelers in a garish, unrestful hotel" (quoted by Clifford, 97). But the hotel that has functioned as a "chronotope of the modern, . . . a place of inauthenticity, exile, transience, rootlessness" but equally of "collection, juxtaposition, passionate encounter" (Clifford, 97), is not—or rather, *no longer*—the hotel of radical multiculturalism. This hotel is no "home away from home," no haven for expatriate artists and writers.

What has happened to the hotel of modernism—the hotel that Miss Julie's Jean had dreamed of inhabiting—is, in a sense, the whole story of this book. The complex semiology that enshrined the hotel as emblem of an age was what I have called geopathology, by which the figure of home is contradictorily coded as both the cause and the goal of exile, the locus of two incommensurate desires: the desire to find a stable container for identity and the desire to deterritorialize the self. The figure of the hotel embraced that contradiction, functioning as a surrogate home, a stable container for the identity of the deterritorialized self. When this semiology finally exhausts itself—a process that begins at midcentury, in the drama of failed homecoming—the hotel becomes a nightmarish experience of spatial abstraction.

The hotel of *Nuit Blanche* is a space of phenomenal alienation, its inhabitants bearing no relation to each other, no possibility of relationship. Among the guests is an American woman, "dressed like a suburban housewife on a tropical holiday in a country she doesn't like and doesn't understand." She is first seen making a long-distance call to her mother back home, "locating" herself in terms that resonate powerfully for the multicultural stage of the discourse of home:

> No—no, no, Mom, we're not in the States yet. No, we're not home yet, Mother, we're still over here. . . . No, no, we're not there anymore either, we had to leave there, it was getting . . . I can't hear you mother, can you hear me? Yes, yes, that is better . . . Oh,

oh, is that what it was? Well, we're in a hotel . . . oh, its alright, you know, it's the same all over. (18)

The hotel that is "the same all over" recalls the motel, chronotope of an antiplatial postmodernism[14] but unlike that space, this motel is irreducibly unfamiliar, radically *strange*—"the hotel itself seems eternally vague and indifferent." Its other inhabitants are an "American beachcomber type," and a man with dark glasses and a South African accent, "coldly efficient, like a hired killer or a mercenary." The hotel is run by Papa Willie, a European "who has long since forgotten Europe," and a waiter, Ruis, who is heard reciting nationalist slogans throughout the scenes. In the scenes set in the Haven of Peace, this small group goes through a series of abortive attempts at communication, brief, trivial encounters that gain their sense of significance only from the increasingly rapid time slides that punctuate them and are later complemented by the sound of a ticking bomb. The small talk of the guests rings hollow and desperate, and the terror of their situation is ultimately literalized as mysterious figures in black move through the hotel rooms, killing the guests.

Through all this, Papa Willie is seen in shadowplay on the back screen, conversing with an unnamed Asian man, "the only one at the Haven of Peace who is not in any danger. It is possible that he is the cause of the danger." As the guests meet, separate, and die, the shadow of Papa Willie chats amiably with the shadow of this man, offering him English cigarettes ("a friend . . . brings them to me weekly from Belgium" [22]) and cold drinks ("Do you like it? I'm so glad. It's called Tang, T-A-N-G, Tang—it's from America" [25]) and telling him of his shell collection:

I offered them to the museum at Daba. After my death, of course. Oh, no. For myself I don't care, but I don't want my life's work to be broken up and scattered. You understand. Do you know—they refused them. They did not understand what I was offering them. They were not interested. Thank you very much. Shells, shells, shells: we have nothing but shells in this country. Why is he making such a fuss? . . . Well, I look on it as a blessing in disguise. They could have been broken, scattered, dispersed—like the scarabs in Cairo. (26)

Papa Willie's language suggests a kind of haphazard cosmopolitanism, an aleatory and temporary series of engagements with other places and cultures. He seems to be the very embodiment, but in a decidedly negative mode, of James Clifford's formulation of "traveling" identity: "Not 'where are you from?' but 'where are you between?'" He is the encapsulated reason why the emblematic hotel of modernism is no longer viable, for he exemplifies the impossibility of finding a stable container for the deterritorialized self.

The conclusion of the hotel section of the play is "a quiet, elegaic moment" as Papa Willie and the waiter, Ruis, gaze out to sea. Ruis asks: "Papa Willie—you think some day I have a hotel of my own?" Papa Willie shrugs, "and the sound of gunshots rises" (26). On the verge of something—revolution, a coup, national disaster—Ruis's words express the lingering modernist desire for "a home away from home"; the gunshots in the soundtrack, as well as the scenes of death and a deathlike alienation that have gone before, deny that desire any validity at all.

Nuit Blanche has a kind of epilogue: two scenes of such striking contrast as to suggest that the play's principle of distance—of gaps and differences—has called forth a creative counterprinciple: juxtaposition. The first of the two scenes, like the last scene of Churchill's *Ice Cream,* stages an encounter of strangers at an airport. The meeting is brief, their conversation superficial, even mindless. The scene gets its resonance from the device of doubling, for the two characters involved are Miss B. (who is associated with the maid of part 1, Berenice Huarpes) and Papa Willie, who (according to a stage direction) is played by the same actor who played the Spanish ranch owner, the father of Gloria Ortega, in part 1. The meaning of this doubling is never spelled out, but a hint of connection is articulated when Papa Willie, on being told that Miss B.'s name is "Berenice Winfred" says: "It's a name from my co . . . what used to be my country" (27). This, then, in a context of loss and transience, is the play's only narrative closure. The three vestigial dramatic actions we have witnessed—and that "they," the onlookers who take this "Select View of Earthlings," have witnessed—come together at this airport. They serve a construction of experience (which I have called radical multiculturalism) according to which the question of identity is, to use James Clifford's formulation again, not "Where are you from?" but "Where are you between?" The last words spoken by the characters, and the last words spoken in the play, are a pair of mutual "Bon Voyages."

Throughout the scene, as if explicating these bon voyages, are Landsart satellite slides of various parts of the earth scene from space.

The final scene of *Nuit Blanche* returns us to the meaning of the "Murmurs of Earth" slide sequences and insists that there may be other contexts, besides loss and transience, in which the liminal identity formation of radical multiculturalism may flourish. We are returning, in fact, to Gómez-Peña's image of the kaleidoscope, in which the principle of difference does indeed collaborate creatively with that of juxtaposition. As the airport scene ends, the soundtrack presents a mixture of gunshots, airplane engines, and "an eerie moan, as if some kind of indefinable animal were dying. It is a loud cosmic moan that wavers and rises, over and over again" (27).

The last scene takes place in "a Tropical Sacrificial Place" with the stage bathed in blood-red light. There is no dialogue, only a simple ritual action involving the entire cast, who line up around the scene's central figure,

a huge beast [that] lies heaving on its side, dying. Its eyes, lit from within, glow like embers. The entire cast comes forward, and lays out candles, fruit, incense and paper money. Also laid on the beast are strands of blinking Christmas lights. The last figure to arrive, the Oriental, takes out a wad of money and throws it in the air. The money flutters about, to land on the dying beast. The noises dissolve into a collage of night sounds: crickets, wind, water. A film of the moon, seen through branches of a tree, is projected onto the screen. The calm is broken by the members of the cast lining up downstage. They bow. The film continues, as do the night sounds, and the dead Reahou lies still. (28)

The beast was inspired, Chong says in the introduction, by a news item that is printed as an epigraph to the play and tells of the efforts of Cambodian soldiers to drive away Reahou, a mythical monster who was believed to be devouring the moon. "According to tradition, only by making great noise could they prevent Reahou from gobbling up the moon during the eclipse, darkening their nights forever" (6). Chong's own comment on the image is as follows: "It was, for me, a mirror of human beings and our superstitions. By presenting human beings as very primitive creatures I was saying how vulnerable we really are, how small our universe is" (4). Juxtaposed with the airport scene of loss and transience, the scene of the dying animal takes on a very specific meaning. It suggests that the loss of place and connection that is the negative side of radical multiculturalism is intimately related to the death of nature. Unlike the high-tech moon shots of the "Murmurs of Earth" sequence, the moon that is seen here, through the trees, is "our" moon, viewed from the perspectives of earthbound human beings. Sublunary existence binds us together and shows us exactly what we are in danger of losing; the "other" view, the abstracted view from "outside," produces only distance, disconnection, destruction.

Nuit Blanche, then, completes its inquiry into the spiritual-political meaning of multiculturalism by developing a discourse of options, of choice. The erasure of platiality in the modern world seems to be rushing us, to the sounds of a ticking time bomb, to our doom. Yet the figure of the double and the device of juxtaposition suggest possibilities for survival. Identities survive the ruin of their cultural environments. They move on. But they will not (in spite of technological fantasies of "life" on other planets) survive the destruction of their natural environment. The animal, like the loft in *The Wild Duck,* is the nonhuman context for a truer, richer humanity than that afforded by all the technologies of reproduction—from Hjalmar's photographs to the images from the Landsart satellite. The kaleidoscope will glow with beauty and meaning only when—and if—it includes "our" moon, our nature.

America at the End

This is how one pictures the angel of history. His face is turned toward the past. Where we perceive a chain of events, he sees one single catastrophe which keeps piling wreckage upon wreckage and hurls it in front of his feet. The angel would like to stay, awaken the dead, and make whole what has been smashed. But a storm is blowing from Paradise; it has got caught in his wings with such violence that the angel can no longer close them. This storm irresistibly propels him into the future to which his back is turned, while the pile of debris before him grows skyward. This storm is what we call progress.

— Walter Benjamin, "Theses on the Philosophy of History"

The angel of American history confronts something both less poetic and more deadly than the human debris that accumulated at the feet of Benjamin's "Angelus Novus": it is a mountain of garbage. The ongoing and unchecked trashing of America (and the world) and its direct effects on America (and the world) is, quite literally, the overarching reality of Tony Kushner's masterpiece, *Angels in America,* a play whose action could be said to take place (at least from one important character's point of view) directly under the hole in the ozone. Kushner's angel constellates many American fantasies and mythologies, but the single most significant thing about it is the chilling implication that its path to earth is *through* the ozone hole. All of the play's stagings of the logic and problematics of American identity are *set within* this penetrating vision and visitation: finally, it seems, America's self-reckoning must trace the trajectory of its habitual destructions.

Angels in America engages the question of place from its title onward. What America is, what modes of placement and displacement it enjoins—in short, what it means to be here, to be here physically, spiritually, psychologically, and ideologically—is the range of questions that the play's expansive structure is designed to accommodate. The answers come in various rhetorical modes, from argumentation to ranting to incantation—their plurality always qualifying their dogmaticism, their situatedness always deflating their potential sentimentality. Among the most magnificent—and seductive—of these "answers" is the one articulated by Harper, an important female character, who moves in the course of the play toward a vision of mystical healing, in which she sees the souls of the dead flying upward, linking arms to repair the disastrous tears in the earth's atmospheric cloak:

> Souls were rising, from the earth far below, souls of the dead, of people who had perished, from famine, from war, from the plague, and they floated up, like skydivers in reverse, limbs all akimbo, wheeling and spinning. And the souls of these departed joined hands, clasped ankles, and formed a web, a great net of souls, and the souls were three-atom oxygen molecules, of the stuff of ozone, and the outer rim absorbed them, and was repaired. (2:144)

As resplendent as her vision is, it is—in spite of its ostentatiously omniscient point of view—pointedly partial ("At least I think that's so," Harper concludes), participating willy-nilly in the ethic of site-specificity that lies at the core of the play. For Harper's vision comes to her as she looks out of the window of an airplane that is taking her to a new life across America. It is a view of the earth from one who has (temporarily) left it, a view of life from the shifting standpoint of the journey. And the journey is, in this play as in American mythology, a profoundly ambiguous mechanism, a way of life that makes living in a place—whether it be New York City or the earth itself—a near impossibility.

The history of geopathology I have traced in this book began with the paradox of the claustrophobic journey. O'Neill's classic of unhomeliness, *Long Day's Journey into Night,* which explored avenues of escape from the twin sicknesses of performance and addiction (the sicknesses, respectively, of the father and the mother), led the questing hero-son to geopathology's favorite conclusion: death as liberation. In the last years of the century and the millennium, the resurrection of that son is ongoing, his unburial initiated by the midcentury drama of failed homecoming. By this time, however, the root causes of ill-location are no longer mysterious or fog enshrouded. The underlying cause of geopathology, the dispossession of nature, now names itself clearly: it is ecological catastrophe, the recognition that no heroism of departure can redeem the wasteland to which the world has been reduced by the forces of modernity.

Two recent and important plays (one of which I discuss at length below) play out this late, clear-eyed version of geopathology. Kushner's *Angels in America* and José Rivera's *Marisol* both explore the tropes of home, homelessness, burial, ecological disaster, addiction, and performance, adding to these one element that points a way out of the closure represented in the drama of failed homecoming. That element is both surprising and specific: it is an angel. Embodying an alter identity that manages to recognize an overdetermined history (of various religious and hence ethnic narratives and iconographies) while at the same time eluding those stubborn determinisms—racial, genderal, and national— of contemporary identity, the angel points to a new terra incognita, beyond the postgeopathic present.

A crucial element in this vision is its insistent particularity. Both these plays, as well as a third I shall discuss here, Suzan-Lori Parks's *The America Play*, come heavily coded as *specific* views of general conditions. Rivera's play is a meditation on the intersections between urban and immigrant experience, and as such extends the analysis initiated in such plays as Poliakoff's *Coming in to Land* and Glowacki's *Hunting Cockroaches*. Kushner's, subtitled *A Gay Fantasia on National Themes*, loudly announces its project of reversing the usual representation of gay life and gay characters, concerning itself not with how the world sees them (the traditional perspective of gay drama) but how they see the world. Finally, Parks proposes a new historiography based on what Henry Louis Gates calls "signifyin(g)" and associates with African-American modes of meaning production.

There is thus something of a paradox in concluding this study of the discourse of place in modern drama by focusing on works that programmatically reject the idea of general representation and insist instead on the situatedness of all experience, including the experience of place. To look for a "last word" in these works is to risk distorting their fundamental impulse, which is to deny that *any* word can be the first or last word for all of us. All three plays perform the need to open history to question, to dialogue, and above all to a recognition of situatedness. And this is, finally, what gives them their validity as codas to a history of geopathology: the politics of location, they conclude, leads to the principle (not just the practice, now increasingly seen in contemporary theater) of the site-specific. The last word on place will be plural, and it—they—will come from particular places.

Famous Last Words

The paradox of the claustrophobic journey is recognized, at the start of *Angels in America,* as a fundamental principle of American identity. It is opposed, from the outset, to another such principle, that of burial, though it is some time before the play connects itself up with the discourse of buried *children.*[1] To begin with, the burial is that of an old woman, an embodiment of the "Old World" that appears to mumble on in perpetual contention with the New World of America. The rabbi who delivers the opening speech—a *graveside* eulogy—takes these familiar oppositions as his theme: Old World versus New, journeying versus staying, and home versus America. Caught up in these extreme options, the America he sketches out is strikingly similar to the one we saw in Pinter's *The Homecoming:* a derealized *idea* of place lacking all those qualities of rootedness and continuity that constituted the old idea of belonging. The America constructed by the rabbi is a nonplace, a meaningless surface overwritten by other, more potent places: "Descendants of this immigrant woman, you do not grow up in America, you and your children and their children with the goyische names, *you do not live in America, no such place exists,* your clay is the clay of some Litvak shtetel, your air the air of the steppes" (1:10; emphasis added).

This master trope of American cultural history, like the many others in the play, is embodied—and here also *dis*embodied—in a person (as we shall see, the play casts its allegorical net wide, locating ideologies in people, only to set them all spinning, unpredictably, beyond their "demographic profile[s]" (2:104), moving subjectivity decisively out of the comforting fictions of ethnography and ideology). In the prologue, this movement beyond stereotype is centered on the dead woman, of whom the rabbi says:

In her was—*not a person but a whole kind of person*—the ones who crossed the ocean, who brought with us to America the villages of Russia and Lithuania—and how we struggled, and how we fought, for the family, for the Jewish home, so that you would not grow up *here,* in the melting pot where nothing melted. . . . she carried the old world on her back across the ocean, in a boat, and she put it down on Grand Concourse Avenue, or in Flatbush, and she worked that earth into your bones, and you pass it on to your children, this ancient, ancient culture and home. (1:10; emphasis added)

The move beyond fixed stereotypes occurs in the final lines of the prologue, when the rabbi bestows one final and hilariously incongruous epithet on this departed denizen of the Bronx Home for Aged Hebrews. Looking, no doubt, for some stirring finale to his less-than-comforting eulogy, he proclaims: "She was the last of the Mohicans, this one was" (1:11). Thus, into the familiar story of Jewish immigration Kushner drops another myth, apparently wholly incommensurate with the first— its seeming opposite in geography, ideology, religion, worldview, gender roles, everything. At the very moment it is most thoroughly denied, it seems, the figure of America rises up, clothed in one of its most resonant images, and claims old Sarah Ironson for its own.

It is a kind of answer—or perhaps a hint of an answer to come—to the fundamental political question posed by the rabbi's prologue: If the rabbi is right, and America is "the melting pot where nothing melted," and every American is defined by the perilous journey of the ancestors, and every American grows up elsewhere, breathing the imaginative air of far off, foreign places—if no such place as America really exists—how can this ever become what it aspires to be, the most advanced (most tolerant? most caring?) society in the world? What political and social system can embrace so much difference?

The rabbi's startling rewriting of one stereotypically fixed identity into another limns an uncharted direction for an answer: as sedimented ideological systems and their fixed versions of American identities come crashing down under their own weight—which is, in a nutshell, the action of part 1, *Millennium Approaches*—a new discursive space opens up, in which history is confronted afresh by what it has always tried to contain: difference, imagination, and the body. As the corpse of Sarah Abramson, perennial wanderer, joins with the myth of the America's original inhabitants, two versions of America—as principle of displacement but equally as claim of habitation—enter the drama. And just as Sarah is being thus buried/apotheosized, one of the play's main characters, an AIDS sufferer, discovers the new map of America on his body: "K.S. [Kaposi's sarcoma], baby," Prior tells his lover Louis (grandson of Sarah), "The American Lesion" (1:21).

Prior's gallows humor sustains the play's coding of performance as an increasingly heroic strategy of survival. It is a mode that he—in dialogue with other characters, especially Belize—deploys in response to the new history being written on his body. His use of performance is in sharp contrast to another, older strategy of survival, another response to the same condition, that of being homosexual in a homophobic culture: performance as passing. The chief players in this latter performance are the young lawyer Joe Pitt and his diabolic mentor, Roy Cohn. For the latter, passing also extends to the new history of the body, which he strenuously refuses: "AIDS is what homosexuals have," he declares. "I have liver cancer" (1:46). (Significantly, the same denial, in the same terms, comes from a very different source much later in the play: when Hannah Pitt tells a desperate Prior that his lesions are "cancer" [2:105], she marks the distance that persists even after so much ground has been covered between seemingly antipodal subjectivities: love does much in *Angels in America,* but it does not make all things clear to everyone.)

Whereas Cohn performs a terrifying, soul-destroying form of passing by acting out a horror-cartoon version of American self-determination, Joe passes passively, barely aware of what he is doing and what it is costing him. By contrast, Prior performs an exuberant version of gay identity, his repertoire including the famous lines of old movie stars—Tallulah, Greta Garbo, Judy Garland—and culminating in a dream of high-camp drag. It is the same dream he comes to share, miraculously, with Joe's wife Harper, who is not dreaming but wandering in a valium-induced hallucination. The scene ironically brings together modern drama's long-standing tropes of performance and addiction in a way that transvalues both. The commingling of Prior's valiant performances and Harper's addiction produces the new space for a new history of the body. The characters readily name this space; they call it (in a suitable updating of Huxley's "doors of perception") the "threshold of revelation" (1:33). This is, it soon turns out, not a purely subjective characterization, for the scene ends with the first appearance of the angel—at this point only a voice and a dramatic lighting effect—who will be so crucial to forcing Prior's potential new historiography.

Prior—as his name suggests—is the historical principle of the play, and the task he eventually undertakes is to redefine that principle, specifically to free it from its death-dealing tradition. Prior must transform history so that the past is no longer, as Nietzsche put it, "the grave-digger of the present." He must not merely write a new history—the

history of the future cannot be written—but invent a new historiography, a new mode of relating past to present and future. A crucial insight
of the "threshold of revelation" is that imagination is constrained by
history. Harper articulates the insight as follows: "Imagination can't create anything new, can it? It only recycles bits and pieces from the world
and reassembles them into visions" (1:32). Prior's comic agreement—
"It's something you learn after your second theme party: It's All Been
Done Before" (1:33)—sets the stage for his task, which is to discover a
new strategy for facing the future. He will complete this project, at long
last, at the end of the play, when he chooses dialogue and blessing over
theory and despair.

The play's own delicate historicity underwrites Prior's emerging
historiography. Set in the Reagan era of the 1980s, the play's own sensibility is unmistakably of the 1990s, the decade defined equally by the
approach of the millennium and the lack of clear direction in both the
political and the cultural spheres. In the final scene, Louis will speak of all
the political changes of the late 1980s—"It's the end of the Cold War!
The whole world is changing! Overnight!" (2:145)—only to have
Hannah invoke the muddled future that we are already mired in: "I
wonder what'll happen in places like Czechoslovakia and Yugoslavia"
(2:146). This combination of hyperclosure (the millennium) and hyper-
dispersal (history has splintered into a hundred narratives, all equally
impotent in the face of the scourges of the present: AIDS, homelessness,
ecological catastrophe) leaves Prior suspended between two tempo-
ralities, both of which seem marked with death.[2]

The play's positioning of Prior, a person with AIDS, at the fulcrum
of history is Kushner's boldest move, and the key to both the play's epic
structure and its political agenda. The angel who stalks Prior throughout
part 1 comes preconstructed as (in Prior's own words, to which we
acquiesce, oppressed as we are with the statistics of the epidemic) an
"angel of death" (1:21). The graphic deterioration of Prior's body during
the course of part 1 conspires with the geopathic history of modern
drama (and its trope of heroic departures, including death) to interpret
the ultimate appearance of the angel as Prior's death, and to classify the
play as tragedy.

But Kushner is writing—and shows himself to be writing—long
after the dream of a "modern tragedy" has ceased to attract us.[3] The
"common man" who had posed such a stubborn obstacle to the tragic
grandeur sought after by his fellows is noticeably absent from this play,

having been atomized into the varieties of ethnic, religious, and gender types that he had repressed in order to exist (had existed in order to repress?). Instead of a universal American "low-man" or even a pair of generic tramps, we find here six unforgettably specified individuals, each so freighted with social identity as to make their very presence in the same dramatic action something of a miracle.

The "magic of theater" that *Angels in America* employs is only superficially, then, a matter of supernatural visitations and special effects. The real magic is its performance of what Edward Casey (borrowing from Thoreau) calls "cohabitancy," the "coexistence between humans and the land, between the natural and the cultural, and between one's contemporaries and one's ancestors" (290). Kushner's version of this principle locates its source in contemporary society, especially in the possibility of creative interactions between socially "othered" individuals. In a way that recalls a very different contemporary theater practice, that of Anna Deavere Smith's solo re-creations of cities in crisis, Kushner's performance of the possibility of cohabitancy is based on speech. Cohabitancy here is a matter of turning speech (and speeches, including many bombastic, "over-the-top," grandstanding ones) into *dialogue,* and visibility into *vision.* For both transformations, the key is the play's counter-stereotypical characterology, its challenging of current demographic profiles from the perspective of the future.

The invitation to the audience to falsely code part 1 as a tragedy is supported by the action of part 1, which is a series of uncouplings. As the new body-centered history prepares to be written, relationships fall apart, leaving bodies stranded on park benches or wandering in arctic wastes of loneliness. The pillars of society seem to be crumbling (like the columns that frame the stage of the Broadway production), casting its members adrift in an anguish that seems swollen with a whole history of alienated, modernist affect. Just this is the play everyone expected: a scream of rage against the failed promise of America. Just this is the play that Kushner writes *over,* from the clamor of despair discerning a multi-voiced set of dialogues urgently charting a new direction for that promise.

The deconstructive force of the dialogic principle underlying *Angels in America* is first demonstrated in the rabbi's speech, in which the familiar old opposition between past and present, Old World and New, is suddenly disrupted when the so-called New World shows itself to be pregnant with *another* past, *another* old world. The Mohicans who redefine old Sarah Ironson in terms of a uniquely American mythology are the first of the many revenants who haunt the new world, challenging its monolithic self-fiction. The spokesman for the monolith is Prior's lover, Louis, who clings to his definition of America as tenaciously as the rabbi does to his: "there are no gods here, no ghosts and spirits in America, there are no angels in America, no spiritual past, no racial past, there's only the political, and the decoys and the ploys to maneuver around the inescapable battle of politics" (1:92).

By making several of his main characters Mormons, Kushner mobilizes one kind of counterfiction against Louis's. America is not quite so devoid of religious imagination as is sometimes assumed. There has been at least one angel in America, the one who appeared to Joseph Smith, the founder of Mormonism, in (of all places!) upstate New York. Like Harold Bloom, Kushner regards Mormonism as the quintessential American religion:

> Mormonism is a theology that could only really have come from America. The Book of Mormon . . . is fairly clearly a work of 19th-century American literature . . . of a tradition that also produced *Moby Dick* and *Huckleberry Finn*. The theology is an American reworking of a western tradition that is uniquely American; the notion of an uninhabited world in which it's possible to re-invent. (Interview, 11)

So Louis's idea of America as a place unhaunted by the past is not altogether accurate; there is a past here, and it can be reactivated, though not repeated; if the need is great enough, not only will angels come to America again, but ghosts as well, as Prior finds out. If the need is great enough. A large part of *Angels in America* is devoted to explaining why today, as we approach the end of a century and of a millennium, the need for some imaginative visitation, some reinventing, is very urgent indeed. Among the dire prevailing conditions that the play enumerates are many that are well recognized and deplored, such as greed, selfishness, political corruption, homophobia, and ecological catastrophe; but there are also several items in Kushner's diagnosis, lurking under the more familiar ills, that will prove more challenging to some of us: under homophobia, for example, the play finds the traditional nuclear family, about to explode from its inherent pressures and unhealthy containments.

The angel who disrupts the opposition between an Old World and

New World also disrupts the other oppositions—of race, gender, and religion—that the nuclear family rests on. As a creature of ambiguous gender and scriptural tradition (evoking Joseph Smith as well as the angel with whom Jacob wrestled), the angel's interest in the thoroughly skeptical and secular Prior seems to suggest a conversion narrative, a story of the presence of the past and the need to acknowledge that presence. But the play develops a whole three acts beyond that narrative, and Prior lives on not to learn *from* the angel but rather to teach, *against it,* a new lesson of survival to his fellow men and women.

In refusing the expected and indicated tragic closure of part 1—in refusing to make the angel an angel of death, and leaving Prior alive to take his strategy of performance through (and beyond) a whole second play, part 2, Kushner makes Prior's new historiography a matter not only of faith and perseverance but of envisioning new structures of representation. The epic mastery suggested by the play's expansive structure (*Angels in America* is routinely likened to such monumental dramas as Goethe's *Faust* and Ibsen's *Peer Gynt*) is seriously and deliberately put into question by the inversion at the heart of the play. By *not* ending the play (and Prior's life) when all the stage machinery and psychological material of a spectacular conclusion are firmly in place, Kushner discards—while simultaneously marking—a whole tradition of dramatic meaning production. As the ceiling splits open and the angel, "in a shower of unearthly white light," descends upon the cowering, AIDS-ravaged body of Prior, the theater's capacity for grand finales is exploited to the utmost. Speaking, the angel evokes a long history of deus ex machinae, the mechanical sublimation of human experience into some god-ordered realm of capitalized Mysterious Meaning: "Greetings, Prophet. The Great Work begins. The Messenger has arrived" (1:119). This is ending with a vengeance.

Part 2 plays out the terms of that revenge: the vicissitudes of living at and beyond the end. Having squandered the wealth of dramatic climax earned through the hard work of part 1, the task of part 2, *Perestroika,* is nothing short of impossible: it is to remake a world of meaning that has been systematically unmade. Like America itself, a world of squandered wealth and possibility, part 2 (its title borrowed, with delicious irony, from its old adversary, now equally exhausted) stands on the unstructured verge of the future. The challenge it faces is not (in spite of the demand made in the prologue by the Last Living Bolshevik: "show me the Theory" [2:14]) to find a new structure, but rather to demonstrate how life can—*must*—proceed without the consolation of fixed orders, "beautiful theories."

Perestroika is, above all, a going beyond, a trying out, an experiment with the politics of possibility. The latter involves not only a deconstruction of the opposition between Old World and New, but also, more importantly and originally, a contest between the principles of stasis and movement. Although it is not until *Perestroika* that the thematic of stasis versus movement is made explicit (memorably so, in the angel's injunction to "STOP MOVING!" [2:52]), it is there from the beginning, in the rabbi's association of American identity with the idea of the journey. The children and grandchildren of the dead woman, he maintains, are forever marked by her voyage: "every day of your lives the miles that voyage between that place and this one you cross," he says, and then concludes, still ungrammatically but memorably: "In you that journey is" (1:10–11).

However, the idea of an identity formed around the principle of travel (which was, after all, the underlying idea of the old poetics of exile) receives a much-needed ironic twist in Kushner's play, the main thrust of which is to deconstruct American mythologies, including the great myth of the endless frontier. Here, voyaging is associated with (among others) a hallucinated travel agent pointedly named Mr. Lies. Appearing in the valium-soaked vision of the play's main female character, Harper, Mr. Lies is ready with an analysis of her anguish, which is also, he maintains, America's: "It's the price of rootlessness. Motion sickness. The only cure is to keep on moving" (1:18). How ubiquitous the "disease" is in modern culture is suggested in part 2, when the angel tells Prior that God himself has caught the bug: "In mortifying imitation of you, his least creation, / He would sail off on voyages, not knowing where" (2:50).

The play's suggested new theology of constant motion—the lesson Prior learns and teaches, rejecting the angel's pleas for cessation—is tested against the terms of geopathology, the experience of place as an unresolvable conflict between home and exile, belonging and alienation. The greatest achievement of *Angels in America*, it seems to me, is that it decisively overthrows this oppositional structure on which geopathology was based and sketches out an alternative, heterotopic ideal, a vision of place as combining the local and the global, habitation and deviation, roots and routes. It is a vision of the kind Edward Casey calls for in the conclusion to his study of the phenomenology of place:

Alienated we are in many ways—so lost in space and time as to be displaced from place itself—but the existence of pictorial and narrational journeys to and between places reminds us that we are not altogether without resources in our placelessness. When the resources of re-implacement and co-habitancy are drawn upon as well, we find ourselves back on the road to a resolute return to place. The road itself is a route of renewed sensitivity to place, affording a refreshed sense of its continuing importance in our lives and those of others. The sense and the sensitivity offer a viable alternative to being and feeling out-of-place. By taking up the pathway of place anew, we can discover the riches of the place-world again. At the end of this journey, we shall know once more, perhaps for the first time, what it means to get back into place. (310)

Against the grim idea of the journey (and life as a liminal passage: a being *between* places but never *in* them) Kushner first places an alternative vision, its sweetness and beauty enhanced by its surprising source: a Mormon real-estate agent. Sister Ella Chapter shares a lyrical scene with Hannah Pitt, Joe's mother, who has decided to sell her house and move to New York City. Hannah's characteristically acerbic view of things ("It's a hard place, Salt Lake: baked dry. Abundant energy, not much intelligence. It's a combination that can wear a body out" [1:82]) prompts a heart-stoppingly beautiful vision of things from Sister Ella (as cartoonish as the rabbi, and as resonant):

This is the home of saints, the godliest place on earth, they say, and I think they're right. That mean there's no evil here? No. Evil's everywhere. Sin's everywhere. But this . . . is the spring of sweet water in the desert, the desert flower. Every step a Believer takes away from here is a step fraught with peril. I fear for you, Hannah Pitt, because you are my friend. Stay put. This is the right home of saints. (1:83)

It is not only the angel who retrospectively dignifies Sister Ella's vision (her injunction is the same: Stay put); ultimately, Prior also partakes of this vision, though with a crucial difference: the "right home of saints" he comes to pledge himself to is not Salt Lake City but the world itself, life itself, the only place that is a *place* and not an idea, not a hope of heaven. Though it takes a journey to heaven to return Prior to this sense of place (as it takes Harper an aerial vision of Earth's wholeness) the play gives us this sense of place in another way as well, one that transplants the geopathic roots of realism.

The place of *Angels in America* is a New York made up of equal parts of reality and imagination. Just as many scenes are (like the play itself) doubled, two actions occurring simultaneously, the many specific New York locations—the Bronx Home for Aged Hebrews, Central Park, the Mormon Visitor's Center, the Brooklyn Botanical Gardens, fancy restaurants, hospital rooms, coffee shops, doctors' offices, apartments—are doubled by a supernatural world of ghosts and angels and dreams and hallucinations. The characters who wander through this double world, increasingly lost, confused, shedding their "demographic profiles" along with their old loves, fears, and prejudices, finally find themselves (in both senses of that phrase) in Central Park, at the fountain that Prior calls "his favorite place in New York City. No, in the whole universe." (The very locution is quintessentially Prior: its hyperbole typical of his performance style, its familiarity the mark of his lack of pretense, his self-reliance; most important of all is the sentiment it valorizes: the need to have personal relationships to places.)

Crowned with the angel Bethesda ("I like [angels] best when they're statuary," remarks Prior [2:147]), the fountain marks the miracle of place by evoking another place of miracles. The characters gathered together—a miraculous social grouping in themselves—continue their dialogues with each other and with the audience. The new historiography that flows from this place is dialogic and site-specific—a matter of different voices, with no single or dominating voice, no source of a master narrative—not even Prior, who speaks from a specific place.[4] Not only do Prior's "last words" explicitly deny closure ("the world only spins forward," he says [2:148]) but they are set against Harper's famous last words (unlike Prior's, dis-placed, un-earthed, "up in the air") as well as against the ongoing (unstoppable!) dialogues of the other characters.

Moreover, the whole insidious logic of last words is deliciously sent up in the last—and, this time, dying—words of Roy Cohn, whose command to an absent someone to "Hold" (2:115) echoes his first manic telephone speech, peppered with screamed-out orders to invisible others to "Hold" the line (1:11). As anyone who has seen the play in performance can attest, the darkly comic circularity of Cohn's self-hating existence is accommodated within the play's multivoiced program, not silenced by it. In the "America" that is glimpsed around the angel of Central Park, it is quite enough that Roy Cohn doesn't have the last word.

History Repeals Itself

The deadly spell of last things haunts Suzan-Lori Parks's *The America Play*, as much as it does Kushner's. Like *Angels in America,* this play also uses the simple structural device of doubling to undo the logic of last words, but the device is more muted here, contained within a traditional two-act form instead of extended into two full-length plays. In their relationship to each other, however, Parks's two acts are as untraditional as the two acts of *Godot,* a play with which this one also shares a landscape. The second act of *The America Play,* like the second part of *Angels in America,* is a bold extension beyond the various geopathologies located in the first act.

The America Play locates America where the theatrical imagination has long looked for it: in a grave. The play takes place, according to the stage direction, in "A Great Hole. In the middle of nowhere." That this is the dark heart of America (a place whose landscape presents what Howard Kunstler has called, precisely, "The Geography of Nowhere") is soon made clear, for the great hole, we are told, "is an exact replica of the Great Hole of History." The latter, a theme park populated by the dead heroes of America, produces the desire to move on, to travel west, and to reproduce the same stilted images of past greatness:

> Ever-y day you could look down that hole and see—ooooo you name it. Amerigo Vespucci hisself made regular appearances. Marcus Garvey. Ferdinand and Isabella. Mary Queen of thuh Scots! Tarzan King of thuh Apes! Washington Jefferson Harding and Millard Fillmore. Mistufer Columbus even. Oh they saw all thuh greats. Parading daily in thuh Great Hole of History. (32)

The indiscriminate spatializing of history—the leveling of difference by myth—emerges as the special distortion of America, whose endless frontier holds out the promise of countless replications of the original spectacle of greatness. As a mechanism for producing identity, it ensures inauthenticity: "You could look into that hole and see your entire life pass before you. Not your own life but someone's life from history. . . . *Like* you, but *not* you. You know: *known*" (38).

By figuring this spatialization as a theme park, Parks extends the insight of Black playwrights like Adrienne Kennedy and George Wolfe (America as funnyhouse and museum, respectively), suggesting that the simulacral logic of America's self-representation has now burst its confines and moved out from the enclosure of specific discourses to take over the culture at large.[5] As we saw in chapter 2, the principle of the theme park enacts the dispossession of nature that lies at the roots of geopathology; in *The America Play* we are shown the consequences for individual lives of this dispossession.

The play's protagonist, a man who has had greatness thrust upon him in the fact of his resemblance to the long-dead Abraham Lincoln, succumbs to the lure of the all-American journey: "The Lesser Known went out West finally. . . . A monumentous journey. Enduring all the elements. Without a friend in the world. . . . He got there and he got his plot he staked his claim he tried his hand at his own Big Hole" (28). In making the mythical journey West, the Lesser Known was reenacting the core principle of American History. But a feature of his identity—that he was a digger (and nigger)[6]—puts him in absolute conflict with the expected benefits of following that principle. Irrevocably separated as he is (by virtue of his class and his race) from the enabling narratives of the (white) past, the Lesser Known's efforts to connect his identity to the Great Man's prove futile: "The Great Man lived in the past that is was an inhabitant of time immemorial and the Lesser Known out West alive a resident of the present . . . trying to follow in the Great Man's footsteps that were of course *behind* him. The Lesser Man trying somehow to *catch up* to the Great Man all this while and maybe running too fast in the wrong direction" (30). Though he dismisses as "ridiculous" the implication of this historical disjunction—"Maybe the Great Man had to catch him" (30)—this is precisely the main insight and challenge of the play: how and when, asks *The America Play,* will American history make room for its victims? When and how will the story of America take the reflexive turn to glimpse its old blind spots? When will America finally emerge from the black hole of racism?

The Lesser Known's way of countering the nightmare of American history is to reenact it, not only by himself but for others too. Doomed as he is to reproduce the model of greatness established by the long-dead Founding Father, this child of the present, this "Found*ling* Father," as he comes to be called, constructs a performance in which other belated Americans can participate in the deadly funnyhouse of American history. He starts a sideshow in which he plays Lincoln himself at the moment of his hypertheatrical death. Seated in a replicated balcony of Ford's Theatre, watching a performance of *Our American Cousin,* he is murdered over and over again by patrons who first deposit a penny in the head of a bust of Lincoln, then select a gun from a collection provided, wait for their cue, and fire. As person after person goes through the murderous motions, the ludicrous script they follow is gradually transformed through repetition into a ritual, in which what is being celebrated, we realize, is the violence at the heart of American history.

This violence is directed not only at leaders but at fathers, and a rebellion against patriarchy emerges as the animating principle of national history. As the patricidal fantasy is repeated again and again, as the father-son dyad of Founding/Foundling Father returns from the repression of myth into the symptomology of the present, history is rewritten as a collection of desperate death cries. Each patron, after "killing" "Lincoln," leaps from the balcony and shouts one or other of the phrases identified in the play's endnotes as the "famous last words" of various icons of American history: "Thus to the Tyrants" (John Wilkes Booth), "The South is avenged!" (Booth again), "Strike the tent" (General Robert E. Lee), "Now he belongs to the ages" (Secretary of War Edwin Stanton), and "They've killed the president!" (Mary Todd Lincoln). Thus the ritual of American violence is stitched into history by means of textual fragments that then textualize its citizens as Americans. That the fragments consist, one and all, of famous last words—carefully historicized in the play's *end*notes—bespeaks a recognition of the apocalyptic strain in American ideology. But in this play as in her previous *The Death of the Last Black Man in the Whole Entire World,* Parks brings enormous irony to bear on the discourse of endings.

Her anticlosural technique is, however, quite different from Kushner's (with whom she shares a suspicion of teleological master narratives). While Kushner uses the potency of site-specificity to counter the desire for grand finales, Parks uses repetition. While Kushner envisions a history of the future, emanating from the body and fueled by performance and desire, Parks rejects the principle of historiography altogether, exploding it from within by means of her technique of "Rep and Rev": "a text based on the concept of repetition and revision is one which breaks from the text which we are told to write—the text which cleanly ARCS" (quoted by Solomon, 79).

Parks's denial of history occurs at the level of language, or rather of the recognition that history, because it exists as language, is always subject to revision. Like Lucy, the protagonist of act 2, the meanings of history "circulate." Every fresh repetition of one of history's privileged textual fragments rewrites the meaning, the substance and affect, of that fragment. This is the performative principle that undermines the Lesser Known's historical project (and makes the second act, with its different intervention into the past, necessary): instead of recuperating the greatness of the past, the performance of history unravels that greatness, textualizing its performers as inauthentic and belated "bit-players" in the drama of American greatness. Only one "assassin" rejects being thus textualized and instead screams two words of devastating refusal: "LIIIIIIIIIIIIES!" and "LIIIIIIIIIIARRRRRRRRRRRS!" However, powerful as it is, this indictment of American history as performance comes from within that performance itself and seems to leave it unscathed. The nightmare of American history cannot be exorcised from within its own performative frames. A new place must be found, another journey undertaken.

The epigraph of *The America Play,* taken from John Locke, claims that "In the beginning, all the world was *America*" (27). The second act of the play shows precisely where and what America is at the end. It is a postapocalyptic no-place, a Beckettian void where meaning stubbornly refuses to arrive or arise. In search of the Foundling Father's legacy, his wife, Lucy, and son Brazil roam the blighted black hole in which he had sought to emulate American greatness. As a pair they embody the two principles of intelligibility available to those faced with a murky past: they are historian and archaeologist, the one listening for echoes from the past, the other digging for its remains. Lucy urges her son to keep "diggin till you dig up somethin" (31), accompanying his "Spadework" (36) with a geography game in which the states of America are paired with their capital cities. The game concludes with "Nebraska," and its capital, "Lincoln" (36).

This particular instance of the characteristic spatialization of American history dovetails with this particular family's history to reveal the violent patricidal principle underlying both: the name reminds Lucy of the burden of history that has crushed her husband, as she repeats words he has said earlier, constructing a new text of mourning to replace the old one of murderous exaltation:

Nebraska. Lincoln.
(Rest)
Thus year was way back when. Thuh place: Our nation's capital.
(Rest)

Your father couldnt get that story out of his head: Mr. Lincoln's
great head. And the hole the fatal bullet bored. How that great head
was bleeding. The body stretched crossways across thuh bed. Thuh
last words. Thuh last breaths. And how the nation mourned. (36)

A partially hidden part of the patricidal myth now comes fully into view:
the role it enforces on future generations. The nation's histrionic mourning in the past has become, over time, a professional duty. We learn that
Brazil, as a child, had been instructed in the art of mourning by his
gravedigger father, because, as he says, "There's money init" (33). The
son has long rehearsed the actions that make up "what we in the business
call 'The Mourning Moment'" (33), including "the Weep," "the Sob,"
"the Moan," and "the Wail." This transmutation of mourning into a
skillful performance is one symptom of the racism that has made Black
history (as Parks's previously mentioned and extravagantly titled earlier
play shows) an extended obituary. Unlike the sentimental "madness"
with which, in the conclusion of *The Colored Museum,* George C. Wolfe
sought to heal the wounds of racism, Parks's trope of "mourning" allows
her to resist utopian solutions. Rejecting history's traditional strategy of
meaning production—the search for origins—Parks also rejects its opposite: an optimistic futurology of the kind celebrated in Wolfe's final
image. Instead, Lucy and Brazil inhabit a continuous present, a rig-
orously theatrical here and now that is created moment by moment out
of its difference from the past. The past—be it fragments of the performance Lincoln was watching when he was shot, or random objects from
the Lesser Known's re-creation of that event—appears in the problematic
present but does not *solve* it. The meaning of the present cannot be dug
up out of the past; it must emerge in the space between the famous words
and their later repetitions.

   The America Play concludes with a repetition, a final (but unconvinc-
ingly so, after so many repetitions) reference to "thuh last words" (39).
Seeming to "circulate" out of our sight rather than to end, the play leaves
us ("He takes his leave," says the stage direction, rather than "exit")
where it has located us: in the great hole of the present. The "LIIIIEEES"
of the forefathers (the faux fathers) have been exorcised, their utopian
stories exposed as the deadly falsehood of placelessness. The great hole of
the present presents itself as a new whole. The journeys that might begin
here—or the modes of habitation that might make them unnecessary—
are left to the imagination.

   The geography of modern drama declines a grand finale.

Notes

Introduction

1. For a recent and representative sampling of this fast-developing discourse, see Keith and Pile. The two introductions to this volume, as well as the article by Doreen Massey, present historical and theoretical discussions of space-based studies.

2. By virtue of its very medium, the theater, drama is anchored in space; or, to put it another way (paraphrasing and contradicting Julia Kristeva): drama takes (a) place. Its necessary and literal relationship to space enjoins upon it a consideration of place (a consideration that, in the modern period, has taken the form of a discourse of home *and* homelessness). Following Lukács, Walter Benjamin, in his classic essay on Nikolai Leskov, "The Storyteller," contrasted the rootedness of the story to the placelessness of the novel. What Benjamin says of the storyteller, that he is fixed in place by his oral ties to the community, can be equally argued of the playwright, whose creative production is directed in the first place toward a specific audience in a specific theater. But the potential for subsequent production—the afterlife of the dramatic text—makes it share in what Benjamin sees as the geographical freedom of the novel, derived from textuality, from "its essential dependence on the book (87), and its independence from the conversations of a community. The dramatic text, then, can be said to combine the two impulses that Benjamin frames as opposites and that in the course of this study I shall designate broadly by the terms *spatiality* and *platiality*.

3. Philip Fisher writes: "Every history has, in addition to its actual sites, a small list of privileged settings. These are not at all the places where key events have taken place. Instead, they are ideal and simplified vanishing points toward which lines of sight and projects of every kind converge. From these vanishing points, the many approximate or bungled actual states of affairs draw order and position. Whatever actually appears within a society can be interpreted as some variant, some anticipation or displacement or ruin, of one of these privileged settings" (9).

4. The long-term influence of this environmentalism is further suggested by Fisher: "The naturalist form that took its starting point in environment quickly became the essential popular form. Modern best-sellers set in airports and hospi-

tals, communes or political campaigns with their appropriate character types and events, vocabularies and ethos, remain so common precisely because Zola's form contained the matching features for a society that had turned into an economy that could be subdivided into worlds, with free and mobile individuals as the main social actors" (17).

5. An early and influential article by Biddy Martin and Chandra Mohanty, exploring "the configuration of home, identity, community" (191), argued the extent to which "home was an illusion of coherence and safety based on the exclusion of specific histories of oppression and resistance, the repression of differences even within oneself" (196). Although Martin and Mohanty use the figure of home to discuss the politics of racial difference, feminist cultural geographers have been documenting the politics of domesticity with reference to social codings of home and to the spatial divisions within the home in a variety of cultures and periods: Nancy Pollock has discussed gender coding of the middle- and upper-class dwelling in imperial China, in which the women's quarters were situated in the very back of the house along a windowless wall and difficult to access. Similar practices of seclusion and segregation in Iranian households are documented by Khatib-Chahidi and in India by Maria Mies. Janice Monk has shown "how ideas about gender roles permeate the design of domestic space" in the United States and Britain (128), where, from the latter half of the nineteenth century, the polarization of gender between the public and private spheres was enforced through a growing journalistic discourse on good housekeeping. Monk cites Catherine Beecher and Harriet Beecher Stowe's book *The American Woman's Home* as being exemplary of the attitude that "idealised a woman's duty as the spiritual center and efficient manager of the home, which was portrayed as a retreat from the world for the working husband and the center of domestic harmony" (128). This is the image, of course, that is variously reinforced and challenged by the realist drama of ideas (see chap. 2).

6. The peculiarly American version of this conflict is, in Ima Herron's words, "a tendency towards introspection, and a longing for community" (xvii).

7. For a fascinating discussion of the contemporary status—and triumph— of this attempted erasure of the boundary between public and private experience, see Elinor Fuchs's recent article "Theatre as Shopping."

8. Disneyland (or, for that matter, and as Francis Ford Coppola pointed out in *Apocalypse Now*, its political double Vietnam) stands in the American cultural imagination for the *defeat of place*—that is, of platiality, the specific identity of place—and hence for the quasi-supernatural power of displacement. That America is especially prone to imagining itself through this figure is a central recognition of Suzan-Lori Parks's recent *The America Play* (see epilogue), where the logic of the theme park is seen to totally reconfigure American history, transforming its narrative linearity into a homogenizing spatialization. In Parks's vision, the significant figures and events of American history are not (or are no longer) organized as a chronological and differentiated series but rather simultaneously contained within a vast sameness—"the Great Hole of History"—a theme park located, precisely, "in the middle of nowhere."

9. This work is not paginated.

Chapter One

1. The literature on this history is already vast. Some of the key texts that go beyond reporting to theorizing the issue include Michael Kirby's *Happenings,* Richard Schechner's *Performance Theory* and *Between Theatre and Anthropology,* Arnold Aronson's *The History and Theory of Environmental Scenography,* and Marvin Carlson's *Places of Performance.*

2. For a history of this fantasy (though not understood as such) see Arnold Aronson's exhaustive survey of environmental staging practices from the late nineteenth century to the present. Among the models that this fantasy of infinite meaning has produced are such suggestively named projects as "the Endless Theatre" (58–60), the "universal theatre" (60), the "kaleidoscopic theatre" (64), the "Theatre of Total Movement" (65), "Totaltheater" (110), "the Theatre of the Future" (126), the "mobile theatre" (127), and (perhaps most accurately naming the principle underlying and animating all these efforts) the "Theatre of Space" (127).

3. However, Aronson does show how the environmentalist impulse goes all the way back to the nineteenth century, when the first experiments with outdoor staging began (30ff.). Of course Chekhov's *The Seagull* includes an instance of such a performance: Treplev's play, staged on the grounds of the estate and in front of the lake (see chap. 2).

4. Steve Nelson glances at this continuity (though again without considering its ideological implications) in an article on contemporary examples of environmental theater; discussing *Tamara,* the "environmental mystery/melodrama" that was staged in New York and Los Angeles in the 1980s, he remarks: "In many respects the show is a logical extension of the hyperrealism advocated by Belasco and Antoine. But rather than hanging the meat before an audience, *Tamara* serves it to them" (77).

5. With an ambivalence that is typical of all his pronouncements on *Miss Julie,* Strindberg made contradictory claims about the play's position between the poles of tradition and innovation. In the preface to the play Strindberg insists: "In the play that follows I have not tried to accomplish anything new—that is impossible. I have only tried to modernize the form to satisfy what I believe up-to-date people expect and demand of this art" (205). On the other hand, and in keeping with modernism's privileging of originality, Strindberg was at pains to assert the novelty of his play. In a letter to the publisher K. O. Bonnier on August 10, 1888, Strindberg made the famous claim that *Miss Julie* was "the first Naturalistic Tragedy in Swedish Drama" (quoted by Lamm, 212).

6. According to Martin Lamm, "The preface was written after the play, and Edvard Brandes was probably correct in his suspicion that Miss Julie was not the result of the application of conscious theory" (216). In *Strindberg as Dramatist,* Evert Sprinchorn says that the "preface was written to sell the play rather than to explain it" (28). In *The Social and Religious Plays of August Strindberg,* John Ward hypothesizes that the preface was developed as a frame for the play that would counter Zola's criticism of Strindberg's earlier attempt at naturalist drama, *The Father* (58). As is well known, Zola found the characters of *The Father* to be too

abstractly drawn (see Meyer, "Introduction"). A good summary of this issue is presented by Tornqvist and Jacobs, who show how extremely complex the relationship between the play and the preface really is, concluding that it should "teach us that we ought to be on our guard not only against the 'intentional' fallacy but also the 'post-intentional' fallacy" (60). Finally, an important new perspective on the matter is suggested by Alice Templeton, who says, "In adding the preface to the play, Strindberg may have been more interested in positioning himself as an artist *and as a male* than in precisely representing the complexity of the play itself" (9; emphasis added).

7. According to Evert Sprinchorn, Strindberg's preface to *Miss Julie* "is undoubtedly the most important manifesto of naturalistic theatre" (Introduction, 200). Tornqvist and Jacobs assert that "far from being merely a commentary on the 'naturalistic tragedy,' the preface is in fact the most pregnant exposure of the ideas underlying naturalistic drama—even compared to the statements by Strindberg's precursor Zola" (39).

8. Tornqvist and Jacobs remark: "There is an important generic difference between the play and the preface; while the former is an 'open,' strongly connotative text, the latter is a fairly 'closed,' mainly denotative one" (39). Their ensuing analysis of the preface, however, seems to me to contradict this idea.

9. In Julie's dream, she is "sitting on top of a pillar. I've climbed up it somehow and I don't know how to get back down. When I look down I get dizzy. I have to get down, but I don't have the courage to jump. I can't hold on much longer and I want to fall; but I don't fall. I know I won't have any peace until I get down; no rest until I get down, down on the ground! And if I did get down on the ground, I'd want to go farther down, right down into the earth" (230–31). Jean's dream is the diametric opposite to Julie's: "I used to dream that I'm lying under a tall tree in a dark woods. I want to get up, up to the very top, to look out over the bright landscape with the sun shining on it, to rob the bird's nest up there with the golden eggs in it. And I climb and I climb, but the trunk is so thick, and so smooth, and it's such a long way to that first branch. But I know that if I could just reach that first branch, I'd go right to the top as if on a ladder. I've never reached it yet, but someday I will—even if only in my dreams" (231).

10. That Strindberg's postnaturalistic work emerged from an extension rather than a repudiation of his naturalistic interests is persuasively argued by Evert Sprinchorn in "The Zola of the Occult." In "Rereading *Froken Julie*: Undercurrents in Strindberg's Naturalist Intent," John Eric Bellquist traces Strindberg's interest in mythopoesis to his naturalistic plays, "at least a decade earlier than his celebrated Inferno crisis and his recognized turn to occultism and religious myth" (1).

11. Alice Templeton reads the play as "an indictment of the naturalistic vision the preface claims the play celebrates" (471) but acknowledges that "the preface is more complicated than its overt naturalistic claims would make it appear" and that it is "possible and perhaps desirable to read the preface *against* Strindberg's naturalistic claims, just as it is possible to read the play itself against those claims" (480). I believe that it is *the naturalistic claims themselves*—both as

articulated in the preface and as realized in the play—that are fraught with contradictions and are based *upon* (not in opposition to) certain processes (including irrationalism) that are traditionally excluded from the construction of naturalism.

12. Philip Dodd notes the preface's "ambivalence of tone . . . towards the reasoning faculties," attributing it to Strindberg's "fear of the consequences for the theatre of the supremacy of 'judgement'" (148). Strindberg's own sense of his creative process was always diametrically opposed to Zola's ideal of the playwright as dispassionate observer of a laboratory-like empirical reality. His commitment to an essentially nonrationalist worldview predates by many years the so-called mystical or expressionistic plays with which it is usually associated. Even before *Miss Julie,* Strindberg was describing his practice in terms antithetical to the emerging dramatic ideal: in a letter to Jonas Lie on May 24, 1884, Strindberg admits: "I have discovered that I am not a realist. I write best when I hallucinate" (quoted by Meyer, *File on Strindberg,* 51).

13. Besides two references to the "author-hypnotist," the preface also contains the following extended reference to hypnosis: "I have even supplied a little source history into the bargain by letting the weaker steal and repeat words of the stronger, letting them get ideas (suggestions as they are called) from one another, from the environment (the songbird's blood), and from objects (the razor). I have also arranged for *Gedankenubertragung* [thought transference] through an inanimate medium to take place (the count's boots, the servant's bell). And I have even made use of 'waking suggestions' (a variation of hypnotic suggestion), which have by now been so popularized that they cannot arouse ridicule or skepticism as they would have done in Mesmer's time" (208).

14. According to Greenway, "A physician familiar with Bernheim's radically new work [Hyppolyte Bernheim, author of *De la suggestion et de ses applications à la therapeutique* (1886), which was in Strindberg's library] . . . would understand the dialogue and stage directions almost from the beginning as a series of suggestions and responses between the two characters that subtly underscore the play's more easily recognized actions and symbols" (25). Greenway then goes on to discuss these references in detail (26–28).

15. As Bert O. States notes, "We know that human dramas do not unfold in one or two rooms. But when a play seduces us into believing that they do . . . we have the spatial counterpart of the radical improbability that Fate performs in the temporal action. Space is destiny, the visual proof that order lurks in human affairs" (*Great Reckonings,* 69).

16. Freddie Rokem discusses the manipulation of point of view in Strindberg's drama, comparing his practice to cinematography, which allows for the presence of multiple and changing focal points (52–56). This is indeed what happens in the later plays (such as *A Dream Play*), but not in the naturalistic dramas (especially not in *Miss Julie*), where only one plane of the cubistic space of cinema is presented. My point is precisely that the multiple space of cinema, which is the actualization of the contract of total visibility established by naturalism, is only *evoked,* not realized, in *Miss Julie*. The space of this play is, we might say, only potentially cubistic, striving for (but necessarily missing) a representation of total visibility.

17. Greenway notes that "while it is technically necessary for Strindberg to take the cook Kristin off-stage, he does so in a peculiar manner. Both characters notice that she stumbles off in a quasi-somnambulistic state. While Kristin has not been subject to suggestion, Bernheim would observe that both characters now have the idea in their minds" (25). It should also be noted that Kristin is included in the general topic of hypnotism through the reference to her sleep talking. For much of the nineteenth century, artificial somnambulism was regarded as a necessary precondition to hypnosis. It is also significant, I think, that the one example of Kristin's somnambulism takes the form of a repetition of her menial duties: "Count's boots are brushed . . . put on the coffee . . . right away, right away" (229). Here, as at the end of the play, hypnosis is used to rewrite class difference as fate, uncanny and absolute; in this way a tragic outcome can be managed without sacrificing the rationalistic sociological analyses of naturalism.

18. Harry Carlson writes: "Strindberg's own divided sense of political allegiance—democratic on the one hand, elitist on the other—is present in *Miss Julie,* where his sympathies alternate between Jean, the servant, and Julie, the aristocrat" (5).

19. This idea comes across more clearly in Harry Carlson's translation: "during [intermissions] the spectator has time to reflect and thereby escape the suggestive influence of the author-hypnotist" (57), and "when we see only part of a room . . . imagination goes to work and complements what is seen" (59).

20. Borge Gedso Madsen finds it "debatable to what extent the characters are 'determined' by the milieu of the Count's kitchen" (91) and asserts further that "this location is accidental as far as Julie is concerned and has nothing to do with 'determining' her hysterical split personality" (92). My point here is that the determinism at work is more complex than the literalistic one called for by Zola: in *Miss Julie* the characters as well as the space are "determined" by the ideological program underlying naturalism, which must create an illusion of access and clarity (what I have been calling total visibility) but can only do so by actively repressing its own constitutive processes. In this play, that interplay—between a represented Truth and the truth of representation—is not only engaged (as it is in all naturalistic plays), but also *staged*—through the figure of the count.

21. Elizabeth Sprigge is the only translator who makes this fact explicit, adding a line of her own to the opening stage direction to the effect that the double doors leading into the courtyard represent "the only way to the rest of the house" (75). This inference seems to me to be correct, borne out by the dialogue that precedes Julie's going into Jean's room: Julie says explicitly that the only other exits are into the courtyard and into Christine's room.

22. The need for privacy increased as the positions of domestic servants were filled not by members of families who had worked for the house for generations but by new, unknown people. In *Miss Julie,* the dangerous proximity of servants is evoked in the following exchange: *Jean:* . . . I've also listened to educated people talk. That way I learned the most. *Julie:* You mean to tell me you stand around listening to what we're saying! *Jean:* Certainly! And I've heard an awful lot, I can tell you (235). Earlier in the play, Jean tells Christine about spying on

Miss Julie and her fiancé: *Jean:* I saw the whole thing. Of course, I didn't let on. *Christine:* You were there? I don't believe it. *Jean:* Well I was (220).

23. Actually, the class identity that Strindberg has constructed for Jean is a curious combination of several historical stages: Jean is the son of an estate worker (the *statare* were serfs who belonged to the estate on which they were born and were paid for their labor in kind). He grew up, he tells us, on this very estate; however, his relationship to this estate has been interrupted (he has traveled and worked abroad) and altered (he works as a valet, not a farmhand). We are never told why he returned to this estate, so that his relationship to this family and this place has a somewhat unclear and transgressive quality. I would suggest that the mixture of intimacy and alienation that Jean evinces toward this family reproduces the logic of partial visibility that structures the play.

24. This is "experience of experience," in much the same way that Jameson talks about modernism's mourning for "the memory of deep memory; . . . a nostalgia for nostalgia" (156).

25. Allan Kaprow remarks that "audiences should be eliminated altogether," because "all the elements—people, space, the particular materials and character of the environment, time—can . . . be integrated" (188).

26. An important interim stage of this development was regional drama, which married the realist drama's celebrated sense of place to a recognition of cultural diversity. As Brenda Murphy argues, this movement began as little more than an attempt to clothe the melodramatic simplicities of the formulaic realist plays with local color, then developed, in the early 1920s, in the works of writers like Hatcher Hughes, Paul Green, and Lula Vollmer, into "an intellectual recognition of a way of life alien to one's own." Eventually, however, regionalism reconnected with the fundamental project of traditional realism—the desire to give the audience a sense of total access to and total involvement with the dramatic world onstage: Dubose and Dorothy Heyward's *Porgy* (1927), for example, "sought a subliminal identification with [a] way of life, its mores and values. To draw the audience into Catfish Row, they developed an opening that provided first the distancing shock of alienation and then the gradual displacement of that alienation through engagement" (141). Murphy's conclusion is precisely the wishful formulation that *Road* critiques: "Because the audience is with Catfish Row the entire time, it sees the white men as alien and ridiculous, outsiders to the culture to which it feels it belongs. By removing the mediating presence of the dominant culture from between the audience and the stage, the playwrights took a step towards a fuller illusion of reality in representing regional culture. In terms of the nineteenth-century realists, Porgy is a 'truer,' because more immediate, representation of reality than the typical local-color play" (141–43). Cartwright's play, as I shall argue, is constructed to ask precisely how an audience belonging to the dominant culture can be made to feel that it does not belong to that culture, and what the ideological stakes of this illusion are.

27. Ruby Cohn does not detect the irony, only the archetypicality, when she notes that "The road is an old metaphor for human life" (45).

28. In the same way, Cartwright's two-actor play *Two* exploits the tension in realism between typicality and uniqueness. The many couples played by the

two actors raise the question of whether all marriages are the same or each utterly different from all others.

29. Or even its contemporary debased (nonconfrontational) version, in which, as Steve Nelson writes, "The need to change, provoke, alter, or transform spectators no longer seems central to the aims of many practitioners" (92).

Chapter Two

1. The point I am making is easily confused with an established critical formulation that I am in fact attempting to *overwrite* (that is, to preserve and extend): namely, the distinction between early and high realism. Raymond Williams distinguishes between "illustrative" naturalism ("properly described in terms of 'setting' and 'background'" [216]) and the "symptomatic and causal environment in high naturalism," in which "the lives of the characters have soaked into their environment [and] . . . the environment has soaked into the lives." The sort of rupture between character and environment I am after occurs not before or after but *within* this hyperenvironmentalist moment of naturalism. Because, as Williams makes clear, this hyperenvironmentalism is in the service of a *social* drama (in which the stage represents a space "shaped and shaping social history" [217]), it ignores—or even actively obscures—the nonsocial parts of the environment.

2. In her excellent chapter "Place and Personality," Brenda Murphy furnishes several examples of the ambivalence underlying the well-known realist sense of place. For example, Owen Davis's 1921 play *The Detour,* she writes, is set on a farm that "has become the center of conflict between the play's men and its women. It has produced the farmer's sense of rootedness and the desire to escape that the farmer's wife has nurtured in her daughter" (139).

3. David Scanlan writes with reference to American drama, "The struggle to leave and the longing to stay are not only motives of individual plays. They inform the careers of playwrights and shape our drama as a whole" (181).

4. As Jean Sgard notes, although the experiences of exile and imprisonment share the quality of imposed solitude, exile enjoys a dynamism that prison signally lacks: "Even though prison appears as a radical form of exile, it is not lived as such. For exile, there must be displacement, transfer to another social group, and confrontation. Exile remains dynamic; it repeats the image of the voyage; it implies, however little, the hope of change, a return to utopia. As opposed to prison, exotic evasion fixes another frontier. . . . The experience of exile is dynamic and contradictory: it entertains a coming and going between here and elsewhere, the past and the future, nostalgia and hope, exclusion and inclusion, self and others" (293; my translation).

5. For an excellent survey of O'Neill's spatial images, see John H. Raleigh's introductory chapter, entitled "Cosmology and Geography."

6. This equation, I must emphasize, is made in literature and culture, and is seriously at odds with current medical thinking about addiction, which defines addiction as a physiological and genetic *disease,* not a psychological or moral affliction. Interestingly, Alcoholics Anonymous recognizes the futility of what it

terms "geographic cures," the idea that one can conquer addiction simply by a change in one's location. An alcoholic friend reports: "I would decide that the reason things weren't going well for me was due to my location. So, I moved. By the time I quit . . . I had lived in thirty-five places. None of those places 'cured' my problem. It wasn't a problem of place—and places didn't cause my drinking. . . . I drank because I was (and am) an alcoholic." This medical reality notwithstanding, the cultural definition of addiction offers itself to literature as a trope for psychological experience, and links it (as in O'Neill's play) to compulsion and obsession.

7. For a recent treatment of this theme, see Anthony Abbott.

8. This metatheatricality takes many forms, including the most literal one, in which theater or performance are explicitly evoked. More figurative versions include such thematics as illusion and reality, deception and self-deception, and (perhaps the most common conduit for metatheatrical concerns) the figure of the artist. Critical treatments of this aspect of realism are numerous and include Daniel Haakonsen's "The Play-within-the-Play in Ibsen's Realistic Drama" and James L. Calderwood's, "*The Master Builder* and the Failure of Symbolic Success."

9. In a recent production of the play by the Swedish Royal Theatre, directed by Ingmar Bergman (and presented at the Brooklyn Academy of Music's Majestic Theatre in June 1991), this aspect of the play was underlined by the nonnaturalistic set design, which turned the Tyrone's living room into a bare platform that seemed to float in the dark void of the enormous stage space. On this platform the actors appeared as both the expressionistic renditions of profound emotional suffering *and* as actors carefully constructing roles by stringing together behavioral and dialogic signs designed to project themselves to each other and to themselves in certain predetermined ways.

10. William Worthen discusses this aspect of the play at some length, linking the fact that "the family of Tyrones is a family of actors, each performing for others and indeed performing for the internal audience of an evanescent 'self'" (68) to "the anxiety of psychological realism . . . that the self may be only an act" (70).

11. This addiction-produced stage-within-the-realist-stage finally takes over the whole stage—or fills the realist frame—in *The Iceman Cometh*, which O'Neill wrote after he'd stopped drinking. Here, Harry Hope's bar is, in its entirety, a hallucinatory site of radical homelessness.

12. To review these interpretations would simply be to repeat a great deal of the existing criticism on the play (which often becomes mere paraphrases of what the characters themselves say) and is not particularly pertinent to my interest here. The important thing is, as John Orr phrases it, that "O'Neill's quadrangulated vertigo constantly undercuts the 'truth' of confession and countertruths themselves turn into vulnerable confessions as the play spirals into an infinite regress of performance and counterperformance" (13).

13. As William Worthen shows in his fine discussion of realist drama, the figure of the woman with a past was constructed as one for whom *there is no place* in society (36). Worthen's analysis also clarifies the role of the trope of perfor-

mance in early realism, although he does not explicitly link this trope to the figure of (an impossible) home.

14. As Michael Meyer notes: "The terrible offstage slamming of that front door which brings down the curtain resounded through more apartments than Torvald Helmer's" (*Ibsen*, 454). This passage is quoted by Quigley, as is F. L. Lucas's remark that the "door slammed by Nora shook Europe," as part of his important discussion of the role played in the play by "these ubiquitous doors" and the related "insistent focus on exits and entrances" (91–93).

15. Austin Quigley quotes a report that "certain Scandinavian families even went so far as to add to their cards of invitation of evening parties the request: 'Please do not discuss the *Doll's House*'" (91). As for the fascination with Nora's post-door-slamming fate, it continues into the present. June Schlueter writes that "the door Nora slams . . . ends the play, though not for students: the temptation to speculate about what happens to Nora after she slams the door is simply too appealing." She goes on to tell of "'To Norway—Land of the Giants,' the delightful Monty Python scenarios, each only several seconds long, of what happens to Nora." In one of these, moreover, "Nora does not really intend to leave after all but is simply playacting again: she hides behind the door as Torvald charges after her, pushing against the door and flattening her against the wall" ("How to Get Into," 63).

16. William Worthen quotes Hamilton Fyfe's disapproval of Pinero's choice of suicide for his heroine on the grounds that she was undeserving of the heroism this act bestows; for Fyfe, suicide is too good for "weak characters" like Paula (and presumably other fallen women), "merely a way of escape" (40).

17. Quigley himself is an instance of the denial of the possibility of a truly open future. His entire reading of the play hinges on the idea that Nora's final act is not the liberation it appears to be: "The dilemma is apparent. There is nowhere to go. There is no place to be free from the constraining influence of others" (105). Rejecting the common view of Nora as a heroic rebel in the humanist cause and seeing her instead as a partial demonstration of the complexity of actual progressive social change, Quigley's reading brings the play more into line with the sober, even pessimistic tenor of Ibsen's later drama, a fact that complements the reading's internal cogency. While not wishing to contest Quigley's reading, I do want to note that it is part of a critical tradition of resistance to the literal meaning of play's ending. As such it is the latest in a series of contestations—begun by Ibsen himself—of the heroism of departure.

18. Ibsen left his native Norway in 1864 to begin a self-imposed exile that, with the exception of one short break, was to last twenty-seven years. Naomi Lebowitz argues that the tension between two definitions of home, as "the Great World of liberated spirit, desire and art" and the "small world of bourgeois duty," is fundamental in Ibsen. In Lebowitz's reading, place is the primary metaphor for Ibsen's philosophical themes: "The dwindling of our natural habitat to dollhouses constricts divine and elemental powers and passions, and we are cut off from the heights and depths we once experienced as home" (6).

19. Lebowitz reads the entire Ibsen canon as a conflict between "the Great World of liberated spirit, desire and art" and the small world of bourgeois duty,

calling the former "the true protagonist of Ibsen's drama . . . [the] home that beckons us" (13). By contrast, she says, "the small world" literalizes this expansive moral sense of place, effecting a "divorce of house from home and homeland."

20. Lebowitz writes illuminatingly of Ibsen's "power to make spirit of landscape" (5) and of "the dovetailing of physical and psychic maps" on Ibsen's stage (6). Other critics who have discussed Ibsen's "psychic scenery" include Rolf Fjelde and Aage Henriksen.

21. The absurdist version of this mock-mythic moment is the exchange between Didi and Gogo on the subject of Christ's bare-footedness: "But where he lived it was warm, it was dry!—Yes. And they crucified quick" (34a).

22. As Brian Downs observes: "Like his creator, Brand is appalled by the muddy lethargy he finds in 'the sequestered creek' where he was born" (vi).

23. The one time that Nora speaks of her act as desertion is when she is quoting the law, and her response to it, significantly, stresses freedom: "Listen, Torvald—I've heard that when a wife deserts her husband's house just as I'm doing, then the law frees him from all responsibility. In any case, I'm freeing you from being responsible. Don't feel yourself bound, any more than I will. There has to be absolute freedom for us both" (113).

24. We should not forget that Nora too proposes to spend her first night away from her home in the home of her friend Christine, a fact that at least one critic has interpreted ironically: "One of the major ironies of the play is Nora's somewhat inconsistent choice of staying her first night 'alone' with Mrs. Linde" (Quigley, 105). In both Nora's case and Gregers's what is revealed, I think, is the ubiquity of the conventional home and the impossibility of escape.

25. William Worthen's reading of the loft also rejects this simple dualism, but in seeing it as a staging of the problematics of realism (an apparently objective reality that is nevertheless subject to multiple interpretations) he comes to a conclusion that is in effect another reduction: "The tragedy, or irony, of *The Wild Duck* is that the garret theatre seems not to refer to the world but only to the characters themselves" (26). To read the indoor wilderness in this way is to ignore its special power, a power deriving, I suggest, from old Ekdal's transgressive *use* (not merely interpretation) of it.

26. Brian Johnston notes: "Almost the first visual image presented to us in the play is of the elegant, inner room through which, shockingly and incongruously, the figure of old Ekdal, shabbily dressed, wearing a dirty wig, and carrying a brown paper parcel, emerges; we immediately learn, from the servants, of his fall from grace. This startling visual metaphor is *reversed* in the Ekdal home when old Ekdal, against the shabby background, equally as incongruously appears in his lieutenant's uniform. Both images suggest deprivation from a higher life" (88).

27. For an elaborate application of Christian symbolism to the play see Brian Johnston.

28. Dean MacCannell writes: "The great parks, even great urban parks, Golden Gate in San Francisco or Central in New York, but especially the National Parks, are symptomatic of guilt which accompanies the impulse to destroy

nature. We destroy on an unprecedented scale, then in response to our wrongs, we create parks which re-stage the nature/society opposition now entirely framed by society. The great parks are not nature in any original sense. They are marked off, interpreted, museumized nature. The park is supposed to be a reminder of what nature would be like if nature still existed. As a celebration of nature, the park is the 'good deed' of industrial civilization. It also quietly affirms the power of industrial civilization to stage, situate, limit, and control nature" (115).

29. Significantly, the author of this transgressive space is (like Strindberg's author-count) himself absent, or rather his presence is mediated through narrative and photography.

Chapter Three

1. Austin Quigley has noted "Pinter's early concern for the relationship between physical and psychological terrain" (173). For Lucina Gabbard, the "house as psyche" metaphor suffuses many of the plays: "In *The Homecoming* the old family house is psychic memory revisited. In *The Room*, the house/psyche was divided into a conscious mind upstairs and a subconscious mind in the basement. In *The Caretaker* the house is old, and whole areas of it are locked up, unused. Someday it is to be renovated, redecorated; but at present it is piled with junk; it is leaking upstairs. In *The Dwarfs*, Mark, the successful self, has moved to a fancy new apartment. And, in *The Homecoming* the old family home is to be revisited. . . . It is no longer divided. . . . All is open, visible, known. All phases of the self live here and can be observed here" (203).

2. Once again, it is William Worthen who grasps the crucial dislocation of traditional spatial intelligibility in Pinter: "Pinter's rooms seem to have become unmoored, no longer to disclose upon a readable offstage social environment" (83).

3. As Austin Quigley puts it so well in his discussion of *The Room*, the play's tension derives from "the desire to be left alone and the desire to know more about what one wants to be left alone by" (77).

4. The critical evaluation of this limitation has been, by and large, positive and unquestioning. The only critic who actually analyzes it is Austin Quigley, who finds a conflict between private and public worlds at the heart of *The Homecoming*. His analysis of the play shows how the power play that underlies the action is often funneled through professional identities, especially those of pimp and prostitute, which the family finally brings "home" into itself (211). Even Quigley, however, does not entertain the possibility that the play's focus on selves—albeit selves with public and professional dimensions—is anything other than a strong and masterful *choice* on Pinter's part. I shall suggest below that it is something different: not a refusal to include the "outside"—the public, the political—but perhaps an *inability*, within the chosen dramaturgical framework, to present it directly.

5. I disagree with Austin Quigley's idea that Teddy is struggling to balance two incommensurate identities, that of son to this London family and that of an

intellectual professional living in America. That struggle, I believe, is over before the play begins, and the "American philosopher" has won. As I shall argue below, the figures of America and of philosophy delineate a new dramaturgy and a new characterology, of which Teddy is the exemplar. He is, one might say, a refugee from the future, and swirling around him are questions about the what, if anything, lies beyond the failure of home.

6. For a discussion of this issue in relation to Pinter criticism, see the discussion of "sub-text" in Susan Merritt's work of metacriticism *Pinter in Play* (142–48). For a discussion of surface in the plays of Sam Shepard, see Zinman.

7. Perhaps the definitive statement of this critical-hermeneutic refusal in modern drama is Beckett's eloquent self-limitation, in which exegesis is resisted in the name of simplicity: "[When] it comes to journalists I feel the only line is to refuse to be involved in exegesis of any kind. And to insist on the extreme simplicity of dramatic situation and issue. If that's not enough for them, and it obviously isn't, it's plenty for us, and we have no elucidations to offer of mysteries that are of their making. My work is a matter of fundamental sounds (no joke intended) made as fully as possible, and I accept responsibility for nothing else. If people want to have headaches among the overtones, let them. And provide their own aspirin. Hamm as stated, Clov as stated, together as stated, nec tecum nec sinsete, in such a place, in such a world, that's all I could manage, more than I could" (*Disjecta,* 109).

8. As usual, Beckett's response to critics and the practice of criticism is more complex than that of his fellow anticritical modern dramatists, combining both sympathy for and revulsion against the exegete's project of uncovering truth and making sense. For a discussion of this see H. Porter Abbott, who argues that "Mockery is inextricably linked with sympathy for the scholarly attitude, sympathy that also comes from the inside. Beckett, like many of the great modernists, was a scholar who *(despite his protestations of ignorance and bafflement)* continued to wear his learning in almost everything he wrote. In his mature work, scholarship is important not for the erudite display it makes but as a signifier for the effort of scrutiny—the constant seeking of truths in texts" (11).

9. The question of just how obvious the hole in the wall should be is an interesting one, directly linked to the problem of the semiotics of minimalism. According to John Bury, who designed the first production, the original design—"a big victorian room in which someone has built two brick piers and put in a RSG [rigid steel girder]—bothered Pinter. "This Harold felt was too crude, too strong, and turned it into a play about a room with an RSG and brick piers. But I said that this was obviously the right thing, let's just soften it" (28).

10. Contradicting all the critical attention that has been paid to this element of the set is John Bury's revelation (which may, however, be merely speculation) that Pinter put in the famous lines about the missing wall only to avoid having a "composite set," the kind of set that the play otherwise "demanded, . . . because he wanted to see the hall, the front door, and the staircase" (27–28).

11. Lucina Gabbard exemplifies an extreme of psychological interpretation in reading the play as "a multiple wish-fulfillment dream. This family of men," she writes, "needs a woman" (191). Along the same lines (that is, psycho-

structural lines), Hugh Nelson remarks that "The first act is crucial in allowing us to see the motherless, wifeless, sexless family in operation" (148). Gabbard goes on to cite Freud in establishing an explicit link between sexual need and the play's space: "The stage setting itself concretizes this womanless house. The back wall has been removed, making the hall one with the living room. Freud comments on the dream symbolism of such renovations: 'We find an interesting link with the sexual researches of childhood when a dreamer dreams of two rooms which were originally one, or when he sees a familiar room divided into two in the dream or vice versa. In childhood the female genitals and the anus are regarded as a single area—the 'bottom' (in accordance with the infantile 'cloaca theory'); and it is not until later that the discovery is made that this region of the body comprises two separate cavities and orifices' (*The Interpretation of Dreams* 5:354)" (191). Later in her chapter, Gabbard goes even further in reading stage space as emblematic of psychological processes: "When the play opens, father and sons are set in old anal patterns. Here again the symbolism of the removed wall is applicable: it represents the living room as an anus. The house is scrupulously clean, but the family lives with verbal dirt and bestiality. Their sexual activities, real and fantasied, show their fixation on their anal wish to revel and play in dirt" (196).

12. For a sophisticated contemporary revisioning of this idea of the family and its functioning in the play, see Marc Silverstein's Lacanian reading in his chapter entitled " 'The Structure Wasn't Affected': *The Homecoming* and the Crisis of Family Structure" (76–107).

13. More prosaically, the presence of the corn in the living room harks back to the domesticated wilderness in the Ekdal house in *The Wild Duck*. An image of internalized nature, it evokes that profound contradiction within the bourgeois discourse of home, pitting the need for shelter against the desire for participation in the natural life of the earth (a contradiction that was contained temporarily, as we have seen, by the nineteenth-century glass house). A recent news item shows how resilient this contradiction is, and how rooted it is, as Kohlmaeier and von Sartory have argued, in the effort to negotiate the rigors of city living. The news item tells the story of the discovery of the identity of the man who had planted a mysterious stand of corn in "the center divider of Broadway north of 153rd street." The city "farmer," an immigrant from the Dominican Republic, claimed that he had planted the corn to "beautify the streets." He continued, in terms that suggest the very real continuation of geopathic experience in today's world, to say that he planted the corn in "the small park [which is] used by motorists for dumping garbage and by the homeless for sleeping" because the corn is "a recollection, a memory of how things are back home" (Myers, B5). If the connection to *Buried Child* is not clear enough already, consider the article's title: "Farmer Unearthed: He Planted the Corn."

14. The trope of the buried child far exceeds the drama of America: it is a feature of American culture itself, whose significance is illuminated by Harold Bloom's discussion of the importance of the abortion issue in American politics (see introduction, above). A recent article by Linda Ben-Zvi entitled "Murder She Wrote": The Genesis of Susan Glaspell's *Trifles*" also suggests the connection

between the cultural and dramatic versions of the buried child. According to Ben-Zvi, the "bombshell" at the trial of Margaret Hossack, the real Minnie Wright, was that she had been pregnant and given birth to a child before the marriage. "This, McNeal [the prosecutor] claimed, was the dark secret often referred to in the trial, the story Hossack said he would take to his grave, and the reason for the unhappiness in the Hossack home. Just how a pregnancy thirty-three years earlier could have been the sole cause of trouble in the marriage and how it proved Mrs. Hossack's guilt in the murder of her husband was not clear; but, as Glaspell reports, it provided the jury with the impression that she was a woman who could not be trusted. It was with this revelation that the trial ended" (151). The buried child underwrites a drama of secrecy and revelation, of deeply hidden meaning and inevitable disclosure. This is the drama that Shepard's literalization holds up to view.

15. For a discussion of the interpretive struggles of critics of *Buried Child,* see Demastes, *Beyond Naturalism,* 105–7.

16. Thus I cannot concur with the many readings of Shepard's drama as a nostalgic project of return to the myths of America, of which Herbert Blau gives the most memorable formulation, saying that Shepard shares with Ronald Reagan "a sort of frontier nostalgia and—if not a vision of a house on the hill, borrowed from our earliest fantasies—then a bird's-eye view of the American dream from the aerie of Los Angeles, 'city of the future,' as the Europeans say, if there is a future" (522). As always, Blau's reading packs many more layers of insight and is vastly more suggestive than at first appears. Though I disagree about the nostalgia, I am fascinated by the implication that Shepard's vision is "aerial"—surveying the territory of the American imagination as a vast surface or text. Even more powerful is the link Blau makes (so casually) to a potentially nonexistent future: as we shall see by the end of this book, particularly with regard to *Angels in America,* the specter of ecological catastrophe is the hidden driving force behind the rejection of geopathic drama and all its investments, including the figures of roots, of depth, of buried children and meaning.

17. It is worth noting, in this regard, Shepard's use of various actual "frames" in the stage space of the play: throughout the play, Dodge is located on a sofa that is sandwiched by two screens: that of the television, emitting a "flickering blue light," and that of the "screened-in porch" (63). Later in the play, Vince's epiphany of familial identity is mediated by the windscreen of his car.

18. A psychoanalytically oriented version of this same paradigm (of home as originary place) is also present in the play, in the ugly request by Lenny that his father Max tell him "the true facts about that particular night" (36), that is, the night he was conceived.

19. For a full discussion of Genet's systematic "code-analysis," see Chaudhuri, *No Man's Stage.*

20. Howard Kunstler argues that the impact of media imagery extends to the physical life of dwellings, where a vocabulary of surfaces prevails: "buildings cease to use the basic vocabulary of architecture—extrusions and recesses—and instead resort to tacked on symbols and signs" (168), giving the example of a building he saw on a rural highway that had a gigantic sign on it, reading

"Country Store." He links this "habit of resorting to signs and symbols" to Americans' growing incapacity—encouraged by advertising—to distinguish truth from lies, saying (in terms that resonate strongly for Shepard's play): "You could label a house 'traditional' and someone would accept it, even if all the traditional relationships between the house and its surroundings were obliterated. You could name a housing development Forest Knoll Acres even if there was no forest and no knoll, and the customers would line up with their checkbooks open. They had more meaningful relationships with movie stars and characters on daytime television shows than they did with members of their own families. They didn't care if things were real or not, if ideas were truthful. In fact, they preferred fantasy. They preferred lies. *And the biggest lie of all was that the place they lived was home*" (169; emphasis added).

21. Harry Elam Jr. provides a detailed discussion of the play's relationship to African-American literary tradition, analyzing this relationship in terms of Henry Louis Gates's theory of the "double-voiced" nature of African-American texts. Following Gates, Elam argues that *The Colored Museum* is a text "talking to other texts offering critique and revision. . . . [A] process of repetition and revision with a signal difference [that] Gates terms 'signifyin(g)' "(292).

22. Harry Elam Jr. reveals one level of this incoherence in his discussion of the play's gender politics, saying that Wolfe's "negative refiguring parody of black female playwrights does not foreground their place within the matrix of African-American cultural diversity but instead affirms the dominant and conventional patriarchal hegemony." Elam concludes bluntly: "while he praises the contradictions of black experience, he is himself contradictory" (302). While Elam's judgment is based mainly on Wolfe's treatment of Black women writers, mine (in agreement with his) is related to his conceptualization of such basic concepts as home, travel, and America.

23. For a useful survey of recent work on displacement, see Caren Kaplan.

24. Dean MacCannell argues persuasively that America's automobile mythology successfully occludes the excessive control exercised on private lives in America: "We get to work even with our minds on something else entirely, unable to recall having made the necessary stops and turns. We have stayed within the lines, while controlling a device we know is capable of violating boundaries, racing down sidewalks, crashing through the glass front of any office, shop or restaurant. As a constant reminder of the control we ordinarily exercise, fictional cars and drivers in popular entertainments are always driven beyond hope and beyond real physical exigency" (189).

25. The screenplay that Lee dictates to Austin (and that Austin, the professional screenwriter, finds so absurd) is the archetypal American travel story, including all the ingredients that made that story mythical: violence, male rivalry and male bonding, fear. In the story, two men chase each other across a prairie, first in pickup trucks and then on horses: "So they take off after each other straight into an endless black prairie. The sun is just comin' down and they feel the night on their backs. What they don't know is that each one of 'em is afraid, see. Each one separately thinks that he's the only one that's afraid. And they keep ridin' like that straight into the night. Not knowing. And the one who's chasing

doesn't know where the other one is taking him. And the one who's being chased doesn't know where he's going" (27). In this typically American formulation of travel, the experience of infinite ("endless") space constructs a similarly unbounded, unlocated—utopian—self.

26. Another recent play exemplifying this recoding of travel was Meredith Monk's *Atlantis* (1992), in which a group of travelers visited far-flung and idealized places in the world until they emerged into a realm of pure spirit.

27. For an excellent discussion of that critique, see Cody, *"Ice Cream."*

Chapter Four

1. And further: for example, Dion Boucicault's highly successful nineteenth-century melodrama *The Octoroon* (1859) literalizes the idea mentioned in Overmyer's play, of photography's ability to "capture," by having its plot turn on the photographic "capture" of a murder (and, consequently, a murderer).

2. Tony Mitchell cites a metaphor used by the poet Ana Blandiana that captures the structure of the play as it moves from its first and second acts to its final one, in which what is revealed is not something new and different but rather the hidden meaning of what was always known: "The political situation before seemed as fixed and immovable as an iceberg and the evil was solid. Now that things are changing rapidly and the iceberg is melting, we can see just how dark and dirty the water that constituted it was" (507).

3. One stereotype that sorely tried the sentimentalism of the American audience toward the oppressed people of Romania was the latter's addiction to cigarettes. More than a few spectators were heard to remark (during intermission) on all the smoking going on onstage and on all the unhealthy "secondary smoke" they were having to inhale. Given the huge offensive against smoking that has been one of the few successful public health projects in America recently, this issue was not as trivial as it sounds. Or rather, it is the very triviality of the subject of cigarettes and smoking that makes it so apt a theatrical-material metaphor for the play's central problematic (or challenge): to what extent does political support—not to mention human sympathy—depend upon a presumption of sameness? Where is the line between the differences that pluralistic democracy will allow and protect and those it will not tolerate?

4. Churchill's collaborator for *Mad Forest*, Mark Wing-Davey, is explicit about his rejection of this dramatic mode: "This isn't a documentary. . . . And I wasn't interested in the actors trying to *be* foreigners. Much of the play is about being a Westerner in a strange place: the phrase-book passages that open the scenes, for instance, are there as a reminder that this is simply a partial view; it is not *the* truth" (quoted in Robinson, 127).

5. Tony Mitchell links the vampire and other nonrealistic characters to both the play's politics and its theatrology: "In a dramatic extension of its ethnography of the Other, the play's final act incorporates a number of parodic, surrealistic, and supernatural scenes, in which a Vampire, an Angel, a Dog, Ghosts and a Sore Throat make appearances, as well as a highly expressionistic scene based on one of the cast members' dream about a cornered Elena Ceauşescu trying to bribe

soldiers. These serve to disrupt and undermine logical paradigms, and establish shifts from objective to subjective viewpoints which inscribe the presence of author and cast into the world of the play, offsetting the traces of the documentary realism of the second act" (506).

6. It is interesting to note that the "buried child" of this play occurs very early, and in terms that remove the usual disguise from its identity as aborted fetus.

7. For further discussion of the similarities and differences between *Mad Forest* and *The Danube,* see Mitchell, 502–3.

Chapter Five

1. The figures of the journey and of travel themselves register widely divergent attitudes. In *The Mind of the Traveler,* Eric Leed writes: "Ancient and modern conceptions of the 'meaning' of travel are very different, as are their emphases on the transformations effected by the journey. The ancients valued travel as an explication of human fate and necessity; for moderns, it is an expression of freedom and an escape from necessity and purpose. Ancients saw travel as a suffering, even a penance; for moderns, it is a pleasure and a means to pleasure. . . . In general, the ancients most valued the journey as an explication of fate and necessity, as a revelation of those forces that sustain and shape, alter and govern human destinies" (7).

2. For an excellent discussion of this aspect of realist scenic discourse, see Freddie Rokem, 15 ff.

Chapter Six

1. In the same foreword from which the opening quotation is taken, Hwang also says: "Our country's in a transitional phase right now. Over the next twenty years we're really going to see the emergence of minorities, with Caucasians becoming the plurality rather than the majority. That realignment is going to be scary and hard, but *this place is such a great laboratory.* You have people from all these different cultures who interact intimately: some hold on to their cultures, some don't, some hate other ethnic groups, some couldn't care less—it's such an interesting scheme of things. And within all the attitudes we find here there's so much to discover about how people of different nationalities and cultures have always looked at each other, throughout history" (Foreword, 94; emphasis added).

2. "Does there not exist a cultural exile, an exile within culture, within the language or languages of the other, and therefore not only a rejection, a banishment, and a punishment but also an incomprehension, an alienation, a loss of identity? And this exile, if it threatens to lead to silence, can it not also lead to madness, to refuge in madness?" (my translation).

3. In the "Rethinking Multiculturalism" issue of *American Theatre,* Migdalia Cruz remarks: "Growing up Hispanic in America is weird, because you are

trapped between a black and white world. When I was younger I was bused from my local elementary school to a school in Riverdale. There was an article about this event which called us '50 black children from the Bronx.' So, I said to myself, *that's* what I am. I'm black. Since then, I've always been confused about whether I'm black or white. People look at me and think that I'm white, but often I feel that I'm something else" (quoted in Madison, 140).

4. For a sampling of the latter, see the October 1991 issue of *American Theatre*, which has a special section entitled "Rethinking Multiculturalism," and includes articles by many of the major voices associated with this movement.

5. In addition to the many books and articles focusing on the drama and theater of specific ethnic groups, a number of books approach the issue theoretically: Bharucha, *Theatre and the World*; Pavis, *Theatre at the Crossroads of Culture*; Marranca and Dasgupta, *Interculturalism and Performance*; Fischer-Lichte, Riley, and Gissenwehrer, *Dramatic Touch of Difference*.

6. Dean MacCannell warns against what he calls the "colorization" of the philosophical concept of difference: "The concept of *difference* is supposed to be critical theory's 'affirmative action' program. But so far, it has only increased the distance between the controlling cogito and the new class, ethnic and gendered thinking, even as it admits the latter to its club. If the result is human difference without essentialism we can perhaps believe that some gains have been made. But if it is difference without class, gender of ethnic *specificity*, the gains have been taken back. The result is a kind of 'United Colors of Benneton' philosophy" (193).

7. In their introduction to *AIIIEEEEEE! An Anthology of Asian-American Writers*, for example, Jeffrey Chan et al. sharply exclude writers who were "born and raised in China," characterizing them as "Chinese who have merely adapted to American ways and write about Chinese America as foreigners" (xxxviii).

8. Ping Chong remarks: "I've been dealing with the 'other' and differences among cultures for 20 years, so I find it amusing that all of a sudden multiculturalism is such a hot topic. I think there's a positive side to this interest, but the issues are complex and difficult and there are pros and cons to it" (quoted by Madison, 40).

9. Maxine Schwartz Seller notes that "large numbers [of immigrants] were illiterate, not only in English but also in their native languages. Deprived of opportunities to learn about their own culture through poverty, isolation, or political oppression, many arrived in the United States hungry for exposure to their native languages, histories, and literature. Ethnic theater provided this exposure. . . . [It] was also an important agent of Americanization. Plays adapted and translated from the American stage introduced immigrants to many aspects of mainstream culture" (6).

10. James Moy notes: "The producers themselves had advertised *Miss Saigon* as an updated adaptation of *Madama Butterfly*, the very piece which Hwang's play attacks as racist. Accordingly, it seems ironic to say the least that the Asian American community should be lobbying for greater complicity in such a racist production" (*Marginal Sights*, 128).

11. In her introduction to a recent anthology of plays by Asian-American

women playwrights, Velina Hasu Houston shares an anecdote that exemplifies both the difficulty and the urgency of this project. Houston tells of the reaction of her playwriting teacher to a play she had written: "[He] told me that the play had no place in the American theatre because American theater audiences had no desire to see a play set in postwar Japan that focused on the fall of a Japanese patriarch. He said that I would never become a 'real playwright' unless I began writing for a 'wider' audience. I cannot be certain if the professor had said 'wider' or 'whiter,' because the fan in his office diminished the sound quality, but there was no need to ask. In this case, the words were synonymous" (2).

12. This reality is, of course (and unfortunately) by no means outdated in contemporary theater culture. As James Moy notes, "After failing to convince the producer to alter any of the casting choices [of *Miss Saigon*], [B. D.] Wong moved on to his next project, a film role in the recently released *Mystery Date* (1991) in which he plays a Mr. Loo, a stereotypical, squawking Chinese mobster. Given validation by such outspoken critics, these anthropologically achieved stereotypes appear entrenched" (*Marginal Sights*, 128).

13. This heterotopic ideal seems to derive in large part from the genealogical realities of today's "ethnics," exemplified in Velina Houston's self-presentation: "My life defies placement in any singular or traditional category. I am Amerasian, which means I am neither Asian nor American (and yet both) and that I am neither native Japanese, Blackfoot Pikuni, nor African American (and yet all three)—truly multiracial and multicultural. . . . I am an amalgam of three cultures, two countries and three races; I am also an amalgam of the artist and the academic" (3).

14. Unlike the grand hotel, which functioned as a land*mark*, reminding its inhabitants not only where they were but also that they were *away from home* (precisely by trying to duplicate the "comforts" of home), the motel is an undistinguished interchangeable adjunct to the highway. As Meaghan Morris writes, "Motels, unlike hotels, demolish sense regimes of place, locale, history. They memorialize movement, speed, perpetual circulation" (3). James Clifford adds that "the motel has no real lobby, it's tied into a highway network, a relay or node rather than a site of encounter between coherent cultural subjects" (106). The motel is organized to support travel only and makes no reference to home. Its lack of distinction is not only an economic fact but a semiological one, signifying through its anonymity and interchangeability both the homogeneity of American culture and the vastness of the American landscape.

Epilogue

1. It is significant that the buried child of this play is explicitly a fantasy child ("You're not really pregnant," Mr. Lies tells Harper, "You made that up" [102]). This make-believe child is Harper's will-to-health, a being with whom she can *exchange* love and protection and get the nurture she lacked as a child: "Maybe I'll give birth to a child who'll be covered with thick white fur, and that way she won't be cold. My breasts will be full of hot cocoa so she won't get chilly. And if it gets really cold, *she'll have a pouch I can crawl into*. Like a marsupial. *We'll mend*

together. That's what we'll do; we'll mend" (103; emphasis added). By contrast, another epic drama contemporaneous with *Angels in America*, Robert Schenkkann's *The Kentucky Cycle*, reproduces the old logic of the buried child without any self-consciousness or irony. Early in the play, the patriarch Michael Rowen kills and buries the baby girl he has with the Indian woman he had raped and married. At the end of the play, several hundred years later, one of his descendants digs up the tiny body, unleashing a parade of ghosts whose suffering seems to be causally related to—that is, explained by—this hidden secret. This buried child, though as literalistic as Shepard's, is a long way from the latter's deconstructive functioning: digging up this buried child proves to be exactly the exercise in hermeneutic certainty that Shepard's use of the same device had thoroughly discredited. As for Harper's fantasy child, she marks fragile Harper's link to a self-construction that makes her, eventually, the play's greatest visionary.

2. Prior's narrative about his ancestor makes the isomorphism of past and future explicit: "One of my ancestors was a ship's captain who made money bringing whale oil to Europe and returning with immigrants—Irish mostly, packed in tight, so many dollars per head. The last ship he captained foundered off the coast of Nova Scotia in a winter tempest and sank to the bottom. He went down with the ship—la Grand Geste—but his crew took seventy women and kids in the ship's only longboat, this big, open rowboat, and when the weather got too rough, and they thought the boat was overcrowded, the crew started lifting people and hurling them into the sea. Until they got the ballast right. They walked up and down the longboat, eyes to the waterline, and when the boat rode low in the water they'd grab the nearest passenger and throw them into the sea. The boat was leaky, see; seventy people; they arrived in Halifax with nine people on board. . . . I think about that story a lot now. People in a boat, waiting, terrified, while implacable, unsmiling men, irresistably strong, seize . . . maybe the person next to you, maybe you, and with no warning at all, with time only for a quick intake of air you are pitched into the freezing, turbulent water and salt and darkness to drown" (41–42).

3. The inevitable questions of genre are already swirling around *Angels in America* (in spite of—or perhaps because of?—Kushner's playful allusion to genre in his subtitle, *A Gay Fantasia on National Themes*). John Clum discusses the play in terms of Shakesperean romance; Gordon Rogoff makes an extended comparison between the play and *Hamlet*.

4. This aspect of the finale was unfortunately disfigured in the Broadway production, which (in keeping with its generally portentous style) robbed Prior's speech of its playful singularity, turning it into the kind of climactic conclusion that had been so thoroughly discredited by the ending of part 1. A production that lets Prior's voice take its place *among* those of the other characters onstage with him seems much the better choice.

5. That this is not a mere poetic conceit of Parks's devising is indicated in the recent announcement by the Disney Company that they would build a gigantic history theme park in Virginia.

6. "[It's] the kind of joke that really hurts; the digger/nigger joke is so funny that it's painful and you go ouch" (Parks, quoted by Stevens, C10).

Bibliography

Abbott, Anthony. *The Vital Lie: Reality and Illusion in Modern Drama.* Tuscaloosa: University of Alabama Press, 1989.

Abbott, H. Porter. "Reading as Theatre: Defamiliarization in Beckett's Art." *Modern Drama* 34 (1991): 5–22.

Anderson, Kay, and Fay Gale, eds. *Inventing Places: Studies in Cultural Geography.* Melbourne: Longman Cheshire, 1992.

Anderson, Laurie. *United States.* New York: Harper and Row, 1984.

Antoine, André. *Memories of the Théâtre-Libre.* Trans. Marvin A. Carlson. Coral Gables, Fla.: University of Miami Press, 1964.

Aronson, Arnold. *The History and Theory of Environmental Scenography.* Ann Arbor, Mich.: UMI Research Press, 1981.

Artaud, Antonin. *The Theatre and Its Double.* Trans. Mary Caroline Richards. New York: Grove Press, 1958.

Bablet, D., and J. Jacquot. *Le Lieu théâtrale dans la société moderne.* Paris: Éditions du Centre national de la recherche scientifique, 1962.

Baring, Maurice. "On Chekhov and the Russian Theatre." In Emeljanow, *Chekhov,* 78–83.

Barta, Roger. Introduction to Gómez-Peña, *Warrior for Gringostroika,* 11–12.

Barth, John. "The Literature of Exhaustion." In *The Novel Today: Contemporary Writers on Modern Fiction,* ed. Malcolm Bradbury, 70–83. Manchester: Manchester University Press, 1977.

Baudrillard, Jean. *America.* Trans. Chris Turner. New York: Verso, 1989.

———. *Selected Writings.* Edited with an introduction by Mark Poster. Stanford, Calif.: Stanford University Press, 1988.

———. *Simulations.* Trans. Paul Foss, Paul Patton, and Philip Beitchman. New York: Semiotext(e), 1983.

Beckett, Samuel. *Disjecta: Miscellaneous Writings and a Dramatic Fragment.* London: J. Calder, 1983.

———. *Waiting for Godot.* New York: Grove Press, 1954.

Bellquist, John Eric. "Rereading *Fröken Julie:* Undercurrents in Strindberg's Naturalist Intent." *Scandinavian Studies* 60 (1988): 1–11.

Benjamin, Walter. *Illuminations*. Trans. Harry Zohn. New York: Schocken Books, 1968.

Ben-Zvi, Linda. "'Home Sweet Home': Deconstructing the Masculine Myth of the Frontier in Modern American Drama." In *The Frontier Experience and the American Dream,* ed. David Mogen, Mark Busby, and Paul Bryant, 217–25. College Station: Texas A&M University Press, 1989.

———. "Murder She Wrote": The Genesis of Susan Glaspell's *Trifles.*" *Theatre Journal* 44 (1992): 141–62.

Berson, Misha, ed. *Between Worlds: Contemporary Asian-American Plays*. New York: Theatre Communications Group, 1990.

———. "Cabin Fever." *American Theatre* 8, no. 2 (May 1991): 16–23, 71–73.

Bharucha, Rustom. *Theatre and the World: Performance and the Politics of Culture*. London: Routledge, 1990.

Bigsby, C. W. E. *A Critical Introduction to Twentieth-Century Drama*. Cambridge: Cambridge University Press, 1984.

Blau, Herbert. "The American Dream in American Gothic: The Plays of Sam Shepard and Adrienne Kennedy." *Modern Drama* 27 (1984): 520–39.

Bloom, Harold. *The American Religion: The Emergence of the Post-Christian Nation*. New York: Simon and Schuster, 1992.

Bond, Edward. "Us, Our Drama and the National Theatre." *Plays and Players* (October 1978): 8–9.

Brecht, Bertolt. *The Caucasian Chalk Circle*. Trans. Eric Bentley. Revised English version. New York: Grove Press, 1966.

Brook, Peter. *The Empty Space*. New York: Avon, 1968.

Brustein, Robert. *The Theatre of Revolt*. Boston: Little, Brown, 1964.

Bury, John. "A Designer's Approach: An Interview with John Bury." In Lahr, *A Casebook on Harold Pinter's "The Homecoming,"* 27–35.

Calderwood, James L. *"The Master Builder* and the Failure of Symbolic Success." *Modern Drama* 27 (1984): 616–36.

Carlson, Harry C. Introduction to *Strindberg: Five Plays*. Trans. Harry C. Carlson. Berkeley and Los Angeles: University of California Press, 1983.

Carlson, Marvin. *Places of Performance*. Ithaca: Cornell University Press, 1989.

Cartwright, Jim. *Road*. London: Methuen, 1986.

Casey, Edward. *Getting Back into Place: Toward a Renewed Understanding of the Place-World*. Bloomington: Indiana University Press, 1993.

Chan, Jeffrey Paul, Frank Chin, Lawson Irada, and Shawn Wong, eds. *The Big AIIIEEEEE! An Anthology of Chinese American and Japanese American Literature*. New York: Meridian, 1991.

Chaudhuri, Una. *No Man's Stage: A Semiotic Study of Jean Genet's Major Plays*. Ann Arbor, Mich.: UMI Research Press, 1986.

———. "'Who is Godot?' A Semiotic Approach to Meaning Production in Beckett's Play." In *Approaches to Teaching Beckett's Waiting for Godot,* ed. Enoch Brater and June Schlueter, 133–40. New York: Modern Language Association, 1991.

Chong, Ping. "Notes for 'Mumblings and Digressions: Some Thoughts on Being an Artist, Being an American, Being a Witness. . . .'" *Melus* 16, no. 3 (fall 1989–90): 62–67.

———. *Nuit Blanche.* In Berson, *Between Worlds,* 1–28.

Churchill, Caryl. *Ice Cream with Hot Fudge.* New York: Samuel French, 1989.

———. *Mad Forest.* London: Nick Hern Books, 1991.

Clifford, James. "Traveling Cultures." In Grossberg, Nelson, and Treichler, *Cultural Studies,* 96–116.

Clum, John. *Acting Gay: Male Homosexuality in Modern Drama.* New York: Columbia University Press, 1992.

Cody, Gabrielle. "David Hwang's *M. Butterfly:* Perpetuating the Misogynist Myth." *Theatre* 20, no. 2 (spring 1989): 24–27.

———. "*Ice Cream:* Caryl Churchill's Meltdown," *Theatre Three* 9 (fall 1990): 58–67.

Cohn, Ruby. *Retreats from Realism in Recent English Drama.* Cambridge: Cambridge University Press, 1991.

Deleuze, Gilles. "Nomad Thought." In *The New Nietzsche: Contemporary Styles of Interpretation,* ed. David B. Allison, 142–49. New York: Delta, 1977.

Demastes, William. *Beyond Naturalism: A New Realism in the American Theatre.* New York: Greenwood Press, 1988.

———. "Spalding Gray's *Swimming to Cambodia* and the Evolution of an Ironic Presence." *Theatre Journal* 41 (1989): 75–94.

Derrida, Jacques. "The Theatre of Cruelty and the Closure of Representation." In *Writing and Difference,* trans. Alan S. Bass. Chicago: University of Chicago Press, 1978.

Dodd, Philip. "Fairy Tales, the Unconscious, and Strindberg's Miss Julie." *Literature and Psychology* 28 (1978): 145–50.

Downs, Brian. Introduction to *Brand,* by Henrik Ibsen. Trans. F. E. Garrett. London: J. P. Dent and Sons, 1961.

Driver, Tom. *Romantic Quest and Modern Query: A History of the Modern Theater.* New York: Delacorte Press, 1970.

Durbach, Errol. *"Ibsen the Romantic": Analogues of Paradise in the Late Plays.* Athens: University of Georgia Press, 1982.

Elam, Harry J. Jr. "Signifyin(g) on African-American Theatre: *The Colored Museum* by George Wolfe." *Theatre Journal* 44 (1992): 291–303.

Ellenwood, James Lee. *There's No Place Like Home: A Family Lives Together.* New York: Charles Scribners and Sons, 1939.

Emeljanow, Victor, ed. *Chekhov: The Critical Heritage.* London: Routledge and Kegan Paul, 1981.

Esslin, Martin. *The Theatre of the Absurd.* New York: Anchor Books, 1961.

Ewen, Frederic. *Bertolt Brecht: His Life, His Art, His Times.* New York: Citadel Press, 1967.

Ewen, Stuart. *All Consuming Images: The Politics of Style in Contemporary Culture.* New York: Basic Books, 1988.

Fischer-Lichte, Erika. *The Semiotics of Theater.* Trans. Jeremy Gaines and Doris L. Jones. Bloomington: Indiana University Press, 1992.

Fischer-Lichte, Erika, Josephine Riley, and Michael Gissenwehrer, eds. *The*

Dramatic Touch of Difference: Theatre, Ours and Foreign. Tübingen: G. Narr, 1990.

Fisher, Philip. *Hard Facts: Setting and Form in the American Novel.* New York: Oxford University Press, 1985.

Fjelde, Rolf. Introduction to *Ibsen: Four Major Plays.* New York: Signet, 1965.

Fornes, Maria Irene. *Plays.* New York: Performing Arts Journals Publications, 1986.

Foucault, Michel. "Of Other Spaces." *Diacritics* 16 (1986): 22–27.

———. "Questions on Geography." In *Power/Knowledge: Selected Interviews and Other Writings 1972–1977,* ed. Colin Gordon, 63–77. New York: Pantheon Books, 1980.

Fuchs, Elinor. "New York International Festival of the Arts." *Atlanta Art Papers,* September–October 1991, 51.

———. "Theatre as Shopping." *Theatre* 24, no. 1 (1993): 19–30.

Gabbard, Lucina Paquet. *The Dream Structure of Pinter's Plays.* Rutherford, N.J.: Fairleigh Dickinson University Press, 1976.

Gale, Stephen, ed. *Critical Essays on Harold Pinter.* Boston: G. K. Hall and Co., 1990.

———, ed. *Harold Pinter: Critical Approaches.* Rutherford, N.J.: Fairleigh Dickinson University Press, 1986.

Ganz, Arthur, ed. *Pinter: A Collection of Critical Essays.* Englewood Cliffs, N.J.: Prentice-Hall, 1972.

Gates, Henry Louis. *The Signifying Monkey.* New York: Oxford University Press, 1988.

Genet, Jean. *The Blacks.* New York: Grove Press, 1960.

Glowacki, Janusz. *Hunting Cockroaches and Other Plays.* Evanston, Ill.: Northwestern University Press, 1990.

Gómez-Peña, Guillermo. "A Binational Performance Pilgrimage." *The Drama Review* 35, no. 3 (fall 1991): 22–45.

———. *Warrior for Gringostroika.* Saint Paul, Minn.: Graywolf Press, 1993.

Gordon, Lois. *Stratagems to Uncover Nakedness: The Dramas of Harold Pinter.* Columbia: University of Missouri Press, 1969.

Gotanda, Philip Kan. *Yankee Dawg You Die.* New York: Dramatists Play Service, 1988.

Graham, Shirley. *I Gotta Home.* In *Black Female Playwrights: An Anthology of Plays before 1950,* ed. K. A. Perkins, 225–79. Bloomington: Indiana University Press, 1989.

Gray, Spalding. *Terrors of Pleasure: The House, and Sex and Death to the Age 14.* New York: Vintage, 1986.

Greenland, Colin. *The Entropy Exhibition.* London: Routledge and Kegan Paul, 1983.

Greenway, John. "Strindberg and Suggestion in *Miss Julie.*" *South Atlantic Review* 51, no. 2 (1986): 21–34.

Grossberg, Lawrence, Cary Nelson, and Paula Treichler, eds. *Cultural Studies.* New York: Routledge, 1992.

Grossvogel, David I. *The Blasphemers: The Theatre of Brecht, Ionesco, Beckett and Genet.* Ithaca, N.Y.: Cornell University Press, 1965.

Haakonsen, Daniel. "The Play-within-the-Play in Ibsen's Realistic Drama." In *Contemporary Approaches to Ibsen*, ed. Haakonsen, 2:101–17. Oslo: Universitetsforlaget, 1971.

Hall, Peter. "A Director's Approach: An Interview with Peter Hall." In Lahr, *A Casebook on Harold Pinter's "The Homecoming,"* 9–24.

Harrison, Robert Pogue. *Forests: The Shadow of Civilization*. Chicago: University of Chicago Press, 1992.

Hebdige, Dick. *Hiding in the Light: On Images and Things*. London: Routledge, 1988.

Henrikson, Aage. "Henrik Ibsen som moralist." *Kritik* 2 (1969): 69–84.

Herron, Ima Honaker. *The Small Town in American Drama*. Dallas: Southern Methodist University Press, 1969.

Heyne, Eric. *Desert, Garden, Margin, Range: Literature on the American Frontier*. New York: Twayne Publishers, 1992.

Hillman, James. *A Blue Fire*. New York: Harper and Row, 1989.

Holmes, Oliver Wendell. "The Stereoscope and the Stereograph." *Atlantic Monthly* June 1859. Reprinted in *Photography: Essays and Images*, ed. Beaumont Newhall, 53–61. New York: Museum of Modern Art, 1980.

hooks, bell. *Black Looks: Race and Representation*. Boston: South End Press, 1992.

Houston, Velina Hasu, ed. *The Politics of Life: Four Plays by Asian American Women*. Philadelphia, Penn.: Temple University Press, 1993.

Howe, Tina. *Approaching Zanzibar*. New York: Theatre Communications Group, 1989.

Hudson, Kenneth. *A Social History of Museums*. Atlantic Highlands, N.J.: Humanities Press, 1975.

Hwang, David Henry. *As the Crow Flies*. In Berson, *Between Worlds*, 97–108.

———. *M. Butterfly*. New York: Plume, 1989.

———. Untitled foreword to plays in Berson, *Between Worlds*, 92–94.

Ibsen, Henrik. *Brand*. Trans. F. E. Garrett. London: J. P. Dent and Sons, 1961.

———. *Four Major Plays*. Trans. Rolf Fjelde. New York: Signet, 1965.

Jacobson, Lynn. "Green Theatre: Confessions of an Eco-Reporter." *American Theatre* 8, no. 11 (February 1992): 16–25, 55.

Jameson, Fredric. *Postmodernism, or The Cultural Logic of Late Capitalism*. London: Verso, 1991.

Jiři, Vera M. "Pinter's Four Dimensional Home: *The Homecoming*," *Modern Drama* 17 (1974): 433–42.

Johnston, Brian. "The Metaphoric Structure of *The Wild Duck*." In *Contemporary Approaches to Ibsen*. ed. Daniel Haakonsen, 72–95. Oslo: Universitetsforlaget, 1966.

Joseph, S. *New Theatre Forms*. New York: Theatre Arts Books, 1968.

Kaiser, Georg. *From Morn to Midnight*. In *Expressionist Texts*, ed. Mel Gordon. New York: PAJ Publications, 1986.

Kaplan, Caren. "Reconfigurations of Geography and Historical Narrative." *Public Culture* 3, no. 1 (fall 1990): 25–32.

Kaprow, Allan. *Assemblages, Environments, and Happenings*. New York: Harry Abrams, 1966.

Keith, Michael, and Steven Pile. *Place and the Politics of Identity.* London: Routledge, 1993.

Kerr, Walter. *God on the Gymnasium Floor.* New York: Simon and Schuster, 1969.

Khatib-Chahidi, J. "Sexual Prohibitions, Shared Space, and Fictive Marriages in Shi'ite Iran." In *Women and Space: Ground Rules and Social Maps,* ed. S. Arderner, 71–95. New York: St. Martin's Press, 1981.

Kirby, Michael. *Happenings.* New York: Dutton, 1965.

Kohlmaier, Georg, and Barna von Sartory. *Houses of Glass: A Nineteenth-Century Building Type.* Trans. John C. Harvey. Cambridge, Mass.: MIT Press, 1986.

Kristeva, Julia. "Modern Theater Does Not Take (A) Place." *Sub-stance* 18–19 (1977): 131–34.

Kunstler, James Howard. *The Geography of Nowhere: The Rise and Decline of America's Man-Made Landscape.* New York: Simon and Schuster, 1993.

Kushner, Tony. *Angels in America: A Gay Fantasia on National Themes.* Part 1, *Millennium Approaches;* Part 2, *Perestroika.* New York: Theatre Communications Group, 1993–94.

———. Interview by Adam Mars Jones. *Platform Papers.* London: Publications Department of the Royal National Theatre, 1992. 5–15.

Lahr, John, ed. *A Casebook on Harold Pinter's "The Homecoming."* New York: Grove Press, 1971.

———. Introduction to Lahr, *A Casebook on Harold Pinter's "The Homecoming,"* xi–xix.

———. "Pinter and Chekhov: The Bond of Naturalism." In Ganz, *Pinter,* 60–71.

Lamm, Martin. *August Strindberg.* New York: Benjamin Blom, 1971.

Lebowitz, Naomi. *Ibsen and the Great World.* Baton Rouge: Louisiana State University Press, 1990.

Leed, Eric. *The Mind of the Traveler: From Gilgamesh to Global Tourism.* New York: Basic Books, 1991.

Lefebvre, Henri. *The Production of Space.* 2d ed. Oxford: Basil Blackwell, 1991.

Lotman, Yuri. *La structure du texte artistique.* Paris: Gallimard, 1973.

MacCannell, Dean. *Empty Meeting Grounds: The Tourist Papers.* London: Routledge, 1992.

Machado, Eduardo. *Broken Eggs.* In Osborn, *On New Ground,* 143–89.

Madison, Cathy. "Writing Home: Interviews with Suzan-Lori Parks, Christopher Durang, Eduardo Machado, Ping Chong, and Migdalia Cruz." *American Theatre* 8, no. 7 (1991): 36–42, 138.

Madsen, Borge Gedso. *Strindberg's Naturalistic Theatre: Its Relation to French Naturalism.* Seattle: University of Washington Press, 1962.

Male, Roy R. *Enter Mysterious Stranger: American Cloistral Fiction.* Norman: University of Oklahoma Press, 1979.

Marc, Olivier. *Psychology of the House.* Trans. Jessie Wood. London: Thames and Hudson, 1977.

Marranca, Bonnie, and Gautam Dasgupta. *Interculturalism and Performance.* New York: PAJ Publications, 1991.

Martin, Biddy, and Chandra Talpade Mohanty. "Feminist Politics: What's Home

Got to Do with It?" In *Feminist Studies/Critical Studies*, ed. Teresa de Lauretis, 191–212. Bloomington: Indiana University Press, 1986.

Meinig, D. W. *The Interpretation of Ordinary Landscapes: Geographical Essays*. New York: Oxford University Press, 1979.

Merritt, Susan. *Pinter in Play: Critical Strategies and the Plays of Harold Pinter*. Durham, N.C.: Duke University Press, 1990.

Meyer, Michael. *File on Strindberg*. London: Methuen, 1986.

———. *Ibsen: A Biography*. Garden City, N.Y.: Doubleday, 1971.

———. Introduction to *Miss Julie*. In *August Strindberg: Plays One*. London: Methuen, 1964.

———. *Strindberg: A Biography*. Oxford: Oxford University Press, 1985.

Mies, Maria. *Indian Women and Patriarchy: Conflicts and Dilemmas of Students and Working Women*. New Delhi: Concept, 1980.

Miller, Arthur. *Death of a Salesman*. New York: Penguin, 1977.

Mitchell, Tony. "Caryl Churchill's *Mad Forest*: Polyphonic Representations of Southeastern Europe." *Modern Drama* 36 (1993): 499–511.

Mitchison, Naomi. *The Home and a Changing Civilization*. London: John Lane, The Bodley Head, 1934.

Mogen, David, Mark Busby, and Paul Bryant, eds. *The Frontier Experience and the American Dream*. College Station: Texas A&M University Press, 1989.

Monk, Janice. "Gender in the Landscape: Expressions of Power and Meaning." In *Inventing Places: Studies in Cultural Geography*, ed. Kay Anderson and Fay Gale, 123–38. Melbourne: Longman Cheshire, 1992.

Morris, Meaghan. "At Henry Parkes Motel." *Cultural Studies* 2, no. 1 (1988): 1–47.

Morrow, Nancy. *Dreadful Games: The Play of Desire in the Nineteenth-Century Novel*. Kent, Ohio: Kent State University Press, 1988.

Mounier, Jacques, ed. *Exil et litterature*. Grenoble: Ellug, 1986.

Moy, James S. "David Henry Hwang's *M. Butterfly* and Philip Kan Gotanda's *Yankee Dawg You Die*: Repositioning Chinese American Marginality on the American Stage." *Theatre Journal* 42 (1990): 48–56.

———. *Marginal Sights: Staging the Chinese in America*. Iowa City: University of Iowa Press, 1993.

Murphy, Brenda. *American Realism and American Drama, 1880–1940*. Cambridge: Cambridge University Press, 1987.

Myers, Stephen Lee. "Farmer Unearthed: He Planted the Corn," *New York Times*, August 15, 1991, B5.

Nabokov, Vladimir. *Speak, Memory: An Autobiography Revisited*. New York: Putnam, 1966.

Nadel, Alan. "God's Law and the Wide Screen: *The Ten Commandments* as Cold War 'Epic.'" *Publications of the Modern Language Association of America* 108, no. 3 (1993): 415–30.

Nägele, Rainer. *Theater, Theory, Speculation: Walter Benjamin and the Scenes of Modernity*. Baltimore, Md.: Johns Hopkins University Press, 1991.

Nash, Suzanne, ed. *Home and Its Dislocations in Nineteenth-Century France*. Albany: State University of New York Press, 1993.

Nash, Thomas. "Sam Shepard's *Buried Child:* The Ironic Use of Folklore." *Modern Drama* 26 (1983): 486–91.

Nelson, Hugh. "*The Homecoming:* Kith and Kin." In *Modern British Dramatists,* ed. John Russell Brown, 26–42. Englewood Cliffs, N.J.: Prentice-Hall, 1968.

Nelson, Steve. "Redecorating the Fourth Wall: Environmental Theatre Today." *Drama Review* 33, no. 3 (1989): 72–94.

Nemirovich-Danchenko, Vladimir. *My Life in the Russian Theatre.* Trans. John Cournos. Boston: Little, Brown, 1936.

Normington, John. "An Actor's Approach: An Interview with John Normington." In Lahr, *A Casebook on Harold Pinter's "The Homecoming,"* 137–50.

Oelschangaeger, Max. *The Idea of Wilderness: From Prehistory to the Age of Ecology.* New Haven, Conn.: Yale University Press, 1991.

O'Neill, Eugene. *A Long Day's Journey into Night.* New Haven, Conn.: Yale University Press, 1956.

Orr, John. *Tragicomedy and Contemporary Culture.* Ann Arbor: University of Michigan Press, 1991.

Osborn, Elizabeth. *On New Ground: Contemporary Hispanic American Plays.* New York: Theatre Communications Group, 1987.

Overmyer, Eric. *On the Verge.* New York: Broadway Play Publishing, 1986.

Parks, Suzan-Lori. *The America Play. American Theatre* 11 (March 1994): 25–39.

———. *The Death of the Last Black Man in the Whole Entire World. Theater* 21, no. 3 (1990): 81–94.

Pavis, Patrice. *Theatre at the Crossroads of Culture.* London: Routledge, 1992.

Peter, John. *Vladimir's Carrot: Modern Drama and the Modern Imagination.* Chicago: University of Chicago Press, 1987.

Pfefferkorn, Kristin. "Searching for Home in O'Neill's America." In *Eugene O'Neill's Century,* ed. Richard F. Moorton Jr., 119–43. New York: Greenwood Press, 1991.

Pinter, Harold. *The Homecoming.* New York: Grove Press, 1965.

———. "Writing for Myself." An interview with Richard Findlater. *Twentieth Century* 169 (February 1961): 172–75.

Poliakoff, Stephen. *Coming in to Land.* London: Methuen, 1986.

Pollock, Nancy L. "Women of the Inside: Divisions of Space in Imperial China." *Heresies* 11, no. 3 (1981): 34–37.

Poster, Mark. "Words without Things: The Mode of Information." *October* 53 (summer 1990): 63–77.

Quigley, Austin. *The Modern Stage and Other Worlds.* New York: Methuen, 1985.

Rabe, David. *Streamers.* In *Coming to Terms: American Plays and the Vietnam War,* ed. James Reston Jr. New York: Theatre Communications Group, 1985, 1–66.

Rabillard, Sheila. "Destabilizing Plot, Displacing the Status of Narrative: Local Order in the Plays of Pinter and Shepard." *Theatre Journal* 43 (1991): 41–58.

Raleigh, John H. *The Plays of Eugene O'Neill.* Carbondale: Southern Illinois University Press, 1965.

Richards, Shaun. "'A Question of Location': Theatrical Space and Political Choice in *The Plough and the Stars.*" *Theatre Research International* 15, no. 1 (spring 1990): 28–41.

Rivera, José. *The House of Ramon Iglesia.* In Osborn, *On New Ground,* 191–242.

———. *Marisol. American Theatre* 10, no. 7/8 (July–August 1993): 29–45.

Robinson, Marc. "Bracing Grace: Wing-Davey's 'Front Foot' Approach to *Mad Forest,*" *Village Voice,* 24 December 1991, 127.

Rogoff, Gordon. "Angels in America, Devils in the Wings." *Theatre* 24, no. 2 (1993): 21–29.

Rokem, Freddie. *Theatrical Space in Ibsen, Chekhov, and Strindberg: Public Forms of Privacy.* Ann Arbor, Mich.: UMI Research Press, 1986.

Rosen, Carol. *Theatre of Impasse: Contemporary Drama Set in Confining Institutions.* Princeton: Princeton University Press, 1983.

Said, Edward. "Reflections on Exile." In *Out There: Marginalization and Contemporary Cultures,* ed. Russell Fergusson, Martha Gever, Trinh T. Minh-ha, and Cornel West, 357–66. Cambridge, Mass.: MIT Press, 1990.

Savran, David. *Communists, Cowboys, and Queers.* Minneapolis: University of Minnesota Press, 1992.

Sayre, Henry B. *The Object of Performance.* Chicago: University of Chicago Press, 1989.

Scanlan, David. *Family, Drama, and American Dreams.* Westport, Conn.: Greenwood Press, 1978.

Schechner, Richard. *Between Theatre and Anthropology.* Philadelphia: University of Pennsylvania Press, 1985.

———. *Environmental Theatre.* New York: Hawthorn Books, 1973.

———. *Performance Theory.* New York: Routledge, 1988.

———. *Public Domain.* New York: Avon Books, 1969.

Schlueter, June. "How to Get into *A Doll's House:* Ibsen's Play as an Introduction to Drama," in *Approaches to Teaching Ibsen's "A Doll's House,"* ed. Yvonne Shafer, 63–68. New York: Modern Language Association of America, 1985.

———. *Metafictional Characters in Modern Drama.* New York: Columbia University Press, 1979.

Seller, Maxine Schwartz. Introduction to *Ethnic Theatre in the United States.* Westport, Conn.: Greenwood Press, 1983.

Sgard, Jean. "Conclusions." In Mounier, *Exil et litterature,* 289–99.

Shepard, Sam. *Seven Plays.* New York: Bantam, 1981.

Short, John Rennie. *Imagined Country: Environment, Culture, and Society.* London: Routledge, 1991.

Silverstein, Marc. *Harold Pinter and the Language of Cultural Power.* Lewisburg, Pa.: Bucknell University Press; London: Associated University Presses, 1993.

Smith, Ronn. "Brain Food: An Interview with Adrianne Lobel." *American Theatre* 7, no. 11 (February 1991): 15–20, 54–55.

Soja, Edward. *Postmodern Geographies: The Reassertion of Space in Critical Social Theory.* London: Verso, 1989.

Sollors, Werner. *Beyond Ethnicity: Consent and Descent in American Literature.* New York: Oxford University Press, 1986.

Solomon, Alisa. "Signifying on the Signifyin': The Plays of Suzan-Lori Parks." *Theater* 21, no. 3 (1990): 81–94.

Sonderstrom, Goran. "Strindberg's Scenographic Ideas." In *Strindberg on Stage,* ed. Donald K. Weaver, 33–52. Stockholm: Tryckeri AB Småland, 1983.

Sopher, David E. "The Landscape of Home: Myth, Experience, Social Meaning." In *The Interpretation of Ordinary Landscapes: Geographical Essays,* ed. D. W. Meinig, 129–49. New York: Oxford University Press, 1979.

Southern, Richard. *The Open Stage and the Modern Theatre in Research and Practice.* London: Faber and Faber, 1953.

Sprinchorn, Evert. Introduction to Strindberg, *Miss Julie,* 199–202.

———. *Strindberg as Dramatist.* New Haven, Conn.: Yale University Press, 1982.

———. "The Zola of the Occult." In *Strindberg and Modern Theatre.* Stockholm: Strindberg Society, 1975.

States, Bert. *Great Reckonings in Little Rooms: An Essay on the Phenomenology of Theatre.* Berkeley and Los Angeles: University of California Press, 1985.

———. "Pinter's *Homecoming:* The Shock of Nonrecognition." In Ganz, *Pinter,* 147–60.

Stern, Carol Simpson, and Bruce Henderson. *Performance: Texts and Contexts.* New York: Longman, 1993.

Stevens, Andrea. "A Playwright Who Likes to Bang Words Together." *New York Times,* March 6, 1994, C10.

Stone, Lawrence. "The English Country Home and the Concept of Privacy 1600–1990." Paper delivered at the conference "Home: A Place in the World." New School for Social Research, New York, October 27, 1990.

Storch, R. F. "Pinter's Happy Families." In Ganz, *Pinter,* 136–46.

Strindberg, August. *Miss Julie.* In *August Strindberg: Selected Plays,* ed. and trans. Evert Sprinchorn. Minneapolis: University of Minnesota Press, 1986.

———. "On Modern Drama and Modern Theatre." In *Playwrights on Playwriting: The Meaning and Making of Modern Drama from Ibsen to Ionesco,* ed. Toby Cole, 15–22. New York: Hill and Wang, 1963.

———. *Six Plays of Strindberg.* Trans. Elizabeth Sprigge. Garden City, N.Y.: Doubleday Anchor, 1955.

Strunk, Volker. *Harold Pinter: Towards a Poetic of His Plays.* New York: Peter Lang, 1989.

Synge, John Millington. *The Playboy of the Western World.* London: Methuen, 1983.

Tagg, John. *The Burden of Representation: Essays on Photographies and Histories.* Amherst: University of Massachusetts Press, 1988.

Tanner, Tony. "Everything Running Down." *City of Words: American Fiction 1950–1970.* London: Jonathan Cape, 1971.

Templeton, Alice. "*Miss Julie* as 'A Naturalistic Tragedy.'" *Theatre Journal* 42 (1990): 469–80.

Thoreau, Henry David. *The Journal of Henry D. Thoreau.* Vol. 1: 1837–1846. Ed. Bradford Torrey and Francis H. Allen. Boston: Houghton Mifflin, 1906.

Tornqvist, Egil, and Barry Jacobs. *Strindberg's "Miss Julie": A Play and Its Transpositions.* Norwich, U.K.: Norvik Press, 1988.

Ubersfeld, Anne. *L'École du spectateur*. Paris: Editions Sociales, 1981.

———. "Le texte dramatique." In *Le Theatre*, ed. Daniel Couty and Alain Rey, 91–106. Paris: Bordas, 1980.

Ward, John. *The Social and Religious Plays of August Strindberg*. London: Athlone Press, 1980.

Wardle, Irving. "The Territorial Struggle." In Lahr, *A Casebook on Harold Pinter's "The Homecoming,"* 37–44.

Watson, J. Wreford. "Image Geography: The Myth of America in the American Scene." *The Advancement of Science* 27 (September 1970): 71–79.

Waxman, Samuel Montefiore. *Antoine and the Théâtre-Libre*. Cambridge, Mass.: Harvard University Press, 1926.

Wellwarth, George. *The Theatre of Protest and Paradox*. New York: New York University Press, 1971.

Wiener, Norbert. *The Human Use of Human Beings: Cybernetics and Society*. 2d ed. London: Eyre and Spottiswoode, 1954.

Williams, Raymond. "Social Environment and Theatrical Environment: The Case of English Naturalism." In *English Drama: Forms and Development*, ed. Marie Axton and Raymond Williams, 203–23. Cambridge: Cambridge University Press, 1977.

Williams, Tennessee. *The Glass Menagerie*. New York: Signet, 1987.

Wolfe, George C. *The Colored Museum*. *American Theatre* 3, no. 11 (February 1977): 1-11 (inserted between pp. 26 and 27).

Worthen, William. *Modern Drama and the Rhetoric of the Theatre*. Berkeley and Los Angeles: University of California Press, 1991.

Wright, Patrick. *On Living in an Old Country: The National Past and Contemporary Britain*. London: Verso, 1985.

Yep, Laurence. *Pay the Chinaman*. In Berson, *Between Worlds*, 175–96.

Zinman, Toby Silverman. "Sam Shepard and Super-Realism." *Modern Drama* 29 (1986): 423–30.

Index